RULE OF LAW AFTER WAR AND CRISIS

SERIES ON TRANSITIONAL JUSTICE

The Series on *Transitional Justice* offers a platform for high-quality research within the rapidly growing field of transitional justice. The research is, of necessity inter-disciplinary in nature, drawing from disciplines such as law, political science, history, sociology, criminology, anthropology and psychology, as well as from various specialised fields of study such as human rights, victimology and peace studies. Furthermore, the research is international in outlook, drawing on the knowledge and experience of academics and other specialists in many different regions of the world.

The series is aimed at a variety of audiences who are either working or interested in fields such as crime and justice; human rights; humanitarian law and human security; conflict resolution and peace building. These audiences include academics, researchers, students, policy makers, practitioners, non-governmental organisations and the media.

All books published within the series are subject to a double-blind peer review by recognised authorities in the field.

Published titles within the series:

1. Stephen Peté & Max Du Plessis, *Repairing the Past? International Perspectives on Reparations for Gross Human Rights Abuses* (2007), 978-90-5095-492-1
2. Laura Stovel, *Long Road Home, Building Reconciliation and Trust in Post-War Sierra Leone* (2010), 978-94-000-0028-5
3. Andy Aitchison, *Making the Transition. International Intervention, State-Building and Criminal Justice Reform in Bosnia and Herzegovina* (2011), 978-94-000-0140-4
4. Stef Vandeginste, *Stones left unturned. Law and Transitional Justice in Burundi* (2010), 978-94-000-0115-2
5. Antoine Buyse (ed.), *Margins of Conflict. The ECHR and Transitions to and from Armed Conflict* (2011), 978-94-000-0157-2
6. Gaby Oré Aguilar and Felipe Gómez Isa (eds.), *Rethinking Transitions. Equality and Social Justice in Societies Emerging from Conflict* (2011), 978-1-78068-003-3

SERIES ON TRANSITIONAL JUSTICE, Volume 7

RULE OF LAW AFTER WAR AND CRISIS

Ideologies, Norms and Methods

Richard Zajac Sannerholm

intersentia
Cambridge – Antwerp – Portland

Intersentia Publishing Ltd.
Trinity House | Cambridge Business Park | Cowley Road
Cambridge | CB4 0WZ | United Kingdom
Tel.: +44 1223 393 755 | Email: mail@intersentia.co.uk

Distribution for the UK:
Hart Publishing Ltd.
16C Worcester Place
Oxford OX1 2JW
UK
Tel.: +44 1865 517 530
Email: mail@hartpub.co.uk

Distribution for the USA and Canada:
International Specialized Book Services
920 NE 58th Ave. Suite 300
Portland, OR 97213
USA
Tel.: +1 800 944 6190 (toll free)
Email: info@isbs.com

Distribution for Austria:
Neuer Wissenschaftlicher Verlag
Argentinierstraße 42/6
1040 Wien
Austria
Tel.: +43 1 535 61 03 24
Email: office@nwv.at

Distribution for other countries:
Intersentia Publishing nv
Groenstraat 31
2640 Mortsel
Belgium
Tel.: +32 3 680 15 50
Email: mail@intersentia.be

Rule of Law after War and Crisis: Ideologies, Norms and Methods
Richard Zajac Sannerholm

GPRC
Guaranteed
Peer Reviewed
Content

ISBN 978-1-78068-008-8
NUR 828

British Library Cataloguing in Publication Data. A catalogue record for this book is available from the British Library.

For Marcella and Levi

ACKNOWLEDGEMENTS

This book draws on work presented in a Ph.D. dissertation at the University of Örebro, Sweden. I was fortunate in having Per Bergling and Joakim Nergelius as supervisors, and wish to extend my gratitude for their advice and encouragement. In writing this book and the dissertation that went before it I have incurred many debts. I would like to give a heartfelt thanks to Antonina Bakardjieva-Engelbrekt, Martin Krygier, Anna Jonsson, Vivienne O'Connor, Mauro Zamboni, Erik Wennerström, Debra Liang-Fenton, Claes Sandgren, Veronica Taylor, Ingrid Österdahl and Michael Bogdan, for help at various stages of this project

I extend the warmest thanks to my family and friends for their unstinting encouragement over the years. Lastly, Marcella – without your untiring support and insightful comments I sincerely doubt whether this book would have come into being.

Notwithstanding the many debts incurred, any remaining errors are my own doing.

Falkenberg, August, 2011
Richard Zajac SANNERHOLM

PREFACE

This work concerns itself with rule of law assistance in the aftermath of war and crisis. Over the past decade, rule of law has emerged as an essential objective in state-building missions. This has led to a host of programmes and projects on law reform, constitutional development, judicial training, and institutional establishment.

The overriding purpose of this book is to describe and analyse the effects of international assistance, norms and standards on post-crisis legal, judicial and administrative systems. Three central areas are examined – how the rule of law is conceptualised by international actors; what the principal methods are for putting the concept into effect; and effectiveness and international accountability in rule of law assistance.

The first part of this work begins with a description of how different 'types' of conflict affect legal and administrative systems, and what forms of intervention have been employed. It then moves on to analyse how the rule of law is conceptualised by specific international actors and the 'ideologies', views and interests underpinning the various definitions. This examination provides common characteristics and a framework upon which successive chapters are constructed. The relevance of rule of law conceptualisations is also discussed, particularly their prime relevance to criminal, constitutional, or administrative law.

The second part of the book concentrates on what the principal methods are that international actors apply within rule of law assistance. Following three broad themes – law reform and constitutional reform, institution-building, and access-creation – the typical approaches of international agencies are discussed. In other words, what types of approach work, the main difficulties involved, and how methods in rule of law assistance can be improved. The emerging lack of accountability and effectiveness is then addressed, particularly ways of enhancing the mutual accountability of international reformers and national authorities.

Part three is forward-looking and makes suggestions for improving rule of law reform after war and crisis.

CONTENTS

LIST OF ABBREVIATIONS

ABA	American Bar Association
BiH	Bosnia and Herzegovina
CEELI	Central and Eastern European Legal Initiative
CPA	Coalition Provisional Authority
CRPC	Commission on Real Property Claims of Refugees and Internally Displaced Persons
CSCE	Conference on Security and Cooperation in Europe
DfID	Department for International Development
DPKO	UN Department of Peacekeeping Operations
DRC	Democratic Republic of the Congo
EC	European Commission
ECOWAS	Economic Community of West African States
EU	European Union
EUJUST LEX	EU Integrated Rule of Law Mission in Iraq
EUJUST THEMIS	EU Rule of Law Mission in Georgia
EULEX	EU Rule of Law Mission in Kosovo
GEMAP	Governance and Economic Management Assistance Program
GooB	Government Out of the Box
HPCC	Housing and Property Claims Commission
HPD	Housing and Property Directorate
IACA	Independent Anti-Corruption Agency
ICC	International Criminal Court
IJC	Independent Judicial Commission
ILA	International Law Association
IMF	International Monetary Fund
INGO	International Non-Governmental Organisation
JSAP	Judicial System Assessment Programme (Bosnia and Herzegovina)
JSMP	Judicial System Monitoring Programme
KFOR	Kosovo Force
KJC	Kosovo Judicial Council
KLA	Kosovo Liberation Army
KPA	Kosovo Property Agency
KTA	Kosovo Trust Agency

LOJC	Law of Organisation and Jurisdiction of Courts of the Islamic Republic of Afghanistan
LSMP	Legal System Monitoring Programme
MINUSTAH	United Nations Stabilization Mission in Haiti
MONUC	United Nations Organization Mission in the Democratic Republic of Congo
NGO	Non-governmental organisation
OECD	Organisation for Economic Cooperation and Development
OHCHR	Office of the High Commissioner for Human Rights
OHR	Office of the High Representative
OIOS	Office of Internal Oversight Services
OSCE	Organization for Security and Cooperation in Europe
PHARE	Poland and Hungary: Assistance for Restructuring their Economies
PIC	Peace Implementation Council
PISG	Provisional Institutions for Self-Government
SIGMA	Support for Improvement in Governance and Management
SRSG	Special Representative of the Secretary-General
SSR	Security Sector Reform
TAL	Transitional Administrative Law
UN	United Nations
UNAMA	United Nations Assistance Mission in Afghanistan
UNAMET	United Nations Administration Mission in East Timor
UNAMI	United Nations Assistance Mission for Iraq
UNBIJ	UN Basic Principles on the Independence of the Judiciary
UNBPRL	UN Basic Principles on the Role of Lawyers
UNBRO	UN Border Relief Operation
UNDP	United Nations Development Program
UNGA	United Nations General Assembly
UNGRP	UN Guidelines on the Role of Prosecutors
UNMIBH	United Nations Mission in Bosnia and Herzegovina
UNMIK	United Nations Administration Mission in Kosovo
UNMIL	United Nations Mission in Liberia
UNOCI	United Nations Mission in Cote d'Ivoire
UNODC	United Nations Office on Drugs and Crime
UNOSOM	United Nations Operation in Somalia
UNSG	United Nations Secretary-General
UNTAC	United Nations Transitional Authority for Cambodia
UNTAES	United Nations Transitional Administration for Eastern Slavonia, Baranja and Western Sirmium
UNTAET	United Nations Transitional Administration in East Timor
US	United States
USAID	United States Agency for International Development

INTRODUCTION

RULE OF LAW AFTER WAR AND CRISIS

This book concerns the norms, ideologies and methods of rule of law reform in war-torn and crisis societies. The main objective is to describe and analyse the effects of international rule of law assistance on legal, judicial and administrative systems. Rule of law reform is the vehicle through which international law and national domestic laws, practices, and institutions variously intersect, collide, interact and harmonise. International interventions play an important part in diffusing norms and institutions and bring to the fore a new object of study namely transitional legal orders in war-torn and crisis societies.

Rule of law has emerged as a constituent part of international crisis management. From Haiti to Egypt, from Afghanistan to Liberia, international actors now speak of the fundamental need to strengthen the rule of law for the realisation of a successful transition from war to peace. In order to achieve the twin objectives of a legal system and a political culture embedded in rule of law principles, international actors often assume a direct political and administrative state-building responsibility.[1] Failure to establish the rule of law in a war-torn or crisis society may constitute a serious threat to both national and international security. Sustained instability contributes to organised crime, corruption, trafficking, environmental degradation and weapons proliferation. *De facto* 'statelessness' and proliferating poverty between them afford safe havens for the propagation of criminal and terrorist networks.

It should be made clear from the start that no assistance provider would expect that laws and legal institutions subscribing to rule of law principles would be capable of solving such problems alone. However, the faith placed in the rule of law, a concept that Aristotle spoke of as "a government of laws, not men", and which Cicero realised bound humans "so that we might be free", is a notion that is sometimes astoundingly devoid of realism. The concept of the rule of law (as presented and applied by international organisations and national donors) renders unto itself an excessively large claim.

1 State-building is generally undertaken in combination with military support in the form of a United Nations peace-keeping force. The concept of state-building will here be employed as that advanced by Caplan 2005, Ghani & Lockhart 2008, and Fukuyama 2004.

Today it is possible to refer to a 'rule of law consensus' among international actors in relation to war-torn and crisis societies.[2] This consensus is based upon the view that the rule of law represents both the ends and the means for a society in transition. The popularity of the rule of law flows from the assumption that confronting poverty, creating security and stability, and consolidating democracy, and good governance, requires laws, legal institutions, and legal professionals who remain faithful to the values enshrined in the rule of law.[3]

It is important to recognise that rule of law reform as a means and an end is not a recently discovered objective, and several of the questions and challenges facing reformers in war-stricken and crisis societies are accordingly not new. Attempts at 'social engineering' through law became part of development cooperation in the 1960s, championed by the so-called law and development movement.[4] The practice of rule of law reform has also prompted a critical legal scholarship and the emergence of a discipline on rule of law assistance.[5]

This dialectic between theory and practice, according to a growing number of scholars, has produced a 'third moment' in rule of law reform, signifying a momentum for prescribing legal reforms that are more aware of, in tune with, and adaptable to social realities in developing countries.[6] It is argued in this book that despite past experience of development assistance, rule of law reform after war and crisis operates in a more or less autonomous field where best practices and lessons learned are rarely or only superficially acknowledged. The barrier between security and development objectives is perhaps becoming more porous, but it is still largely intact, despite several examples of how a lack of sustainable development continues to threaten security.

CONCEPTS, METHODS AND RESPONSIBILITIES

In order to critically examine, analyse and understand the effects of rule of law reform on war-torn and crisis societies, three fundamental and thematic questions emerge as being instrumental: (1) how the rule of law is conceptualised, (2) how it is put into effect, and (3) what responsibilities international actors assume. The object of study, the norms, ideologies and approaches of international agencies in rule of law assistance, calls for a combination of methods from different disciplines – including law, political science,

2 Carothers 2009 p. 51.
3 UNSG S/2008/39 (2008).
4 This includes a focus on, for example, economic and social issues such as eliminating barriers for entry and exit into the market. See e.g. Dam 2007 and Carothers 2006.
5 See e.g., Trubek 1972 and 2006; Krygier 2005; Carothers 2006; Golub 2006; Bergling 2006; and Ginsburg 2008 and Perry-Kessaris 2010.
6 See, for example, Trubek & Santos 2006.

international relations, and peace and conflict studies.[7] The topical focus in this work nevertheless remains on the legal aspects of transitions from war and crisis.

CONCEPTUALISING RULE OF LAW

Part 1 concerns how the rule of law is conceptualised by international actors. If the international community is to continue promoting the rule of law as part of a state-building strategy, some clear intimation should be made as to precisely what is meant by the rule of law. Scholars and practitioners frequently criticise 'rule of law promoters' of lacking a clear definition of what it is they are promoting and point out that this bewilderment often leads to further confusion, contradiction and conflict.[8]

It should be noted that the rule of law concept has national legal and political consequences and necessitates difficult choices. Rule of law reform is often accorded under UN Security Council mandates, adding a layer of conditionality. When the Security Council adopts resolutions mandating rule of law reform under Chapter VII of the UN Charter, it means that the rule of law is not simply promoted, but enforced.

Chapter 1 describes the rule of law concept forming the basis of this work and examines the various forms of international intervention. It is argued in this book that the rule of law is a legal concept with two distinct and central attributes: *safeguarding against the arbitrary exercise of power and to enable human interaction.*[9] From these two attributes a number of principles emanate – such as the supremacy of law, legal certainty, legal equality, and the separation of powers. Moreover, this book asserts that it is of great consequence to preserve the conceptual clarity of the rule of law in order to retain its 'analytical bite' as a legal concept.

Rule of law reform is in this work discussed as a broad strategy encompassing a host of initiatives. This includes transitional justice (e.g. judicial procedures to address crimes committed during conflict and truth and reconciliation commissions and processes).[10] The main focus lies, however, on activities that seek to directly capacity-build and create legal and administrative structures for state-building purposes. Many organisations involved in crisis management see rule of law and transitional justice as related yet separate fields. The UN, for

7 Trubek & Santos 2006 p. 4f.

8 Fallon 1997 p. 1; Kleinfeld 2006 p. 32; and Davis & Trebilcock 2008. Carothers 2009 explains how differences in rule of law definitions, or rather the imperatives behind the concept, are sometimes ideologically divided, in crude terms, between conservative, left, and centrist perspectives.

9 See, for example, Krygier 2006 and Tamanaha 2009 in describing the two functions of the rule of law as restraining government officials and ensuring social ordering.

10 See UNSG 2010.

example, has a division of labour among its entities where DPKO, UNDP and UNODC work on law reform, institution-building and access creation, while OHCHR has a lead on transitional justice. Rule of law reform after war is typically divided in two 'baskets': transitional justice and the strengthening of national justice systems and institutions.[11] This book focuses on primarily on the latter.

On the conceptualisation of the rule of law, chapter 2 pays particular attention to how specific international agencies apply the concept in legal and regulatory instruments and policy documents. This analysis provides common characteristics and the framework upon which the following chapters are built. The study of rule of law conceptualisation is based upon an empirical stocktaking of international conventions, regulations and resolutions, as well as on policy instruments and similar documents of various organisations and agencies involved in rule of law assistance. The agencies selected for analysis are those most active in rule of law reform, such as the UN and the EU, or those making the most significant contribution to the conceptualisation of the rule of law – the Council of Europe and suchlike.

While there is no one specific international 'rule of law treaty', central principles associated with the concept are drawn from international human rights law. International conventions, case law, as well as the growth of standard-setting human rights instruments of a 'soft law' character, together constitute a framework for rule of law conceptualisation. Apart from international legal instruments, other sources comprise policy documents with a declaratory objective, which both provide insights into how the rule of law is defined, as well as the ideologies behind promotion and assistance.

The last, chapter 3 in Part 1, discusses the relevance of rule of law conceptualisations made by international actors, particularly on whether or not the definitions are primarily relevant in criminal, constitutional, or administrative law. Chapter 3 also considers whether or not rule of law conceptualisations are more focused on deterring and preventing arbitrary uses of power on a state institutional level, or encompass 'enabling' aspects as well that allow individuals a space and avails them of instruments with which to exercise so-called vertical accountability and to assume 'watchdog' functions.

IMPLEMENTING RULE OF LAW REFORM

In Part 2, the second central question on how rule of law is put into effect is addressed, concentrating on what the principal methods are that international players apply within rule of law reform. The understanding and definition of the

---

11 UNSG S/2006/980 (2006) p. 13. See also Bassiouni 2002, separating between rule of law and transitional justice as being respectively forward-looking and backward-looking initiatives.

rule of law at the international level determines the methods applied in interventions, projects and programmes. It is contended in this study that supporting the rule of law in a transition from conflict and crisis is subject to unique demands. It is now a commonly-shared perception among scholars and practitioners that rule of law promotion in these societies has exhibited a poor past record of performance or achievement, and that legal, judicial and administrative reforms all display "a string of expensive disappointing experiences".[12] The same could be said of rule of law reform in development cooperation, though it is generally perceived to have enjoyed more 'above par' experiences.[13] This poor past record is problematic because societies rent by war are measured against the standard of the rule of law. How well they fare in that assessment determines aid policies and strategic decisions for future international commitment.

Under three broad reform categories – law reform and constitutional reform, institution-building, and access-creation – the typical approaches of international agencies are analysed in light of questions and concepts such as 'ownership and political will', 'participation', and 'bottom-up and empowerment initiatives'.[14] In other words, a consideration of what types of approach work, the main difficulties involved, and in what ways methods in rule of law assistance can be improved.

Chapter 4 pays particular attention to the methods and approaches undertaken in law reform and in constitution-making. This chapter centres on the methods that are applied in relation to fundamental areas of reform, such as legitimacy and political will, and the function of international law and 'universal' standards and models in the reform process. Studying the function of international law and standards involves formal rule adoption, for example, post-crisis treaty ratification, but this must extend further. The object of study also concerns ways of instilling international norms and standards into transitional legal orders and the employment of international 'model' institutions.[15] Thus an important source is the somewhat extensive legislation where international players have held some form of executive responsibility – that is, in Bosnia and Herzegovina, Kosovo, East Timor and Iraq, as well as those laws and decrees enacted in the initial period of state-building by national interim governments. Such transitional legislation often incorporates or

12 Ehrenreich-Brooks 2003 p. 2280. See, also, Stromseth, *et al.*, 2006; Studdard & Hurwitz 2005; and Carlson 2006.

13 See DeLisle 1999; Davis & Trebilcock 2001; Garth 2002; Upham 2006; Channell 2006; Kleinfeld 2006; Esquirol 2008 and Golub 2009. But cf. some cautiously optimistic reports, Bhansali & Biebesheimer 2006 and Spence 2006. See, also, USAID 2002.

14 This thematic categorisation draws upon the classification of rule of law assistance by (among others) Blair and Hansen, Jensen, and Carothers, as well as how the UNSG categorises rule of law reform in war-torn societies. Blair & Hansen 1994 p. 11; Jensen 2005 p. 349; Carothers 2006, The Rule of Law Revival p. 7; and UNSG S/2004/616 p. 12.

15 Morlino & Magen Methods of Influence 2009 p. 39.

explicitly refers to international law, whether in constitutional documents, statutory laws, or in codes of conduct for public officials.

Chapter 5 discusses institution-building and strategies aimed at enhancing access to justice. This analysis involves questions on the structure and organisation of legal and administrative institutions, the selection and vetting of legal professionals, and so-called interim measures – for example, where international actors substitute for national authorities. This chapter also examines the establishment of institutions for putting right a lack of access to justice, and identifies areas where such access requires specific attention. Specific reform ventures, whether of judicial training, legislative support, or interim internationalisation, are here discussed as examples or representations of how rule of law assistance can be implemented.

Most reform activities are drawn from missions with an explicit rule of law mandate. These enterprises often have a specific rule of law section or even a designated Deputy Special Representative to the Secretary-General responsible for the rule of law. In other cases, undertakings have been selected where the aim is to support systemic and qualitative features of a particular legal and administrative system under the headings, for example, of judicial independence or legal certainty.

The main test when analysing the methods and approaches of rule of law assistance is to ascertain what it is the actors actually do in the field.[16] A primary starting point is that of the mandates – for example, the UN Security Council resolutions in providing a normative and regulatory basis for rule of law assistance. But rule of law reform interventions are too complex and cannot easily be reduced to mere acts of the Security Council or the resolutions of decision-making organs of other international agencies. Though mandates might provide the normative basis, further elaboration is also undertaken within, for example, the Secretariat and in various departments and specialised agencies. This is not a particularly well documented area that has necessitated empirical research into the 'bureaucracy' of international agencies and the projects and programmes implemented in order to reach a rule of law objective – drawing upon pre-mission assessments, project planning documents, evaluations and progress reports from international agencies. So-called 'mission creep' must also be considered. This is when a project expands beyond its original goal, where between the original idea of the mandate and the reality of international action, 'falls the shadow'.

When relying on secondary sources in the analysis of how the rule of law concept is put into effect, a cautious reading must of necessity be undertaken where time, context, and authorship of documents such as evaluation reports, assessments, and even regulations, laws and constitutions enacted are taken into

[16] Differences between what international agencies say and what they actually do are not infrequent. See Verdirame 2005 p. 91.

account and cross-checked against more than one source. Moreover, the absorptive capacity of the 'host' state has to be considered. Rule of law reform is a fast-moving object of study. It is all too easy to misinterpret or exaggerate the significance of certain reforms, since war-torn and crisis societies are fragile and inconstant, fluctuating between war and peace, and then back again.

The third central question in this study concerns the emerging want of accountability and effectiveness that characterise many state-building missions. This is considered in chapter 6. International participants have assumed much responsibility for supporting legal, judicial and administrative reforms, but their corresponding accountability is only vaguely discussed and defined. Chapter 6 therefore examines matters of effectiveness and international accountability, and suggests ways of enhancing mutual accountability of international reformers and national authorities, and of making assistance more in compliance with rule of law principles. International organisations and other assistance providers frequently contradict fundamental rule of law principles when attempting to support it in peace and state-building missions– that is, by taking top-down decisions while being insulated from national accountability mechanisms. This raises questions on the legitimacy of some current forms of rule of law 'promotion'.

A RULE OF LAW FOR WAR-TORN AND CRISIS SOCIETIES

Part 3 of this work looks onwards. Chapter 7 briefly recapitulates the central questions by setting out the rule of law concept in war-torn societies, listing the typical methods applied and delineating the shape and content of transitional legal orders.

This chapter also makes suggestions for the improvement of rule of law assistance to war-torn countries and communities and picks up on the question posed in one UN report on peace-keeping missions, asking of the UN, and other actors: "Should we be in this business at all?"[17] It is argued that international actors should be involved. Supporting the rule of law in a war to peace transition serves an important function on its own merits. The quashing of arbitrary rule is essential where it has not only been rampant but widely accepted with acquiescence. Furthermore, allowing for laws and impartial institutions to guide and safeguard interactions and the legal rights of individuals (functioning as the 'scaffolding' in society) where such things as kinship, custom, tribe or religion – not to mention gender – are applied to determine individual capabilities, is fundamental.

---

17 Report of the Panel on United Nations Peace Operations (hereinafter the Brahimi Report) 2000 p. 13.

PART I

CONCEPTUALISING RULE OF LAW REFORM

1. RULE OF LAW REFORM – THEORETICAL FRAMEWORK

INTRODUCTION

The purpose of this chapter is to examine the modes of influence and forms of interventions by means of which international players seek to promote rule of law reform in war to peace transitions.

In order to understand the modes of influence that these actors employ, and to place them in a broader context, it is necessary to look at the terminology of rule of law reform, involving transplants, transfers and similar concepts that denote externally supported legal reform. The discourse on legal transplants serves to identify theories relating to problems and prospects of the methods used in externally promoted rule of law reform.

This chapter also analyses the role of the rule of law in war-torn societies, and illustrate, through a description of a crisis anatomy, some of the main features that characterise legal and administrative systems in war to peace transitions. It is important to acknowledge the deficits, problems, constraints and power structures that war-torn societies display, and the history and possible path dependencies in the legal and administrative systems.

International organisations involved in rule of law reform in both development cooperation and in war to peace transitions are increasingly criticised for insufficient understanding of the institutional histories and legal and social challenges in 'recipient' societies'.[18] Rule of law reform in these gravely damaged societies faces different problems than rule of law promotion in development cooperation and this must be taken into account for the purpose of understanding the parts played by international actors, the choice of the methods used, and the role of national operators and their initiatives.

(UN)RULE OF LAW IN WAR-TORN AND CRISIS SOCIETIES

The whole question of rule of law promotion in war-torn societies, and its construction by a combination of parts or in accordance with a design or plan, is

18 Taylor 2009 p. 46.

the function of law itself. This plainly varies depending on a number of general factors. History, culture, tradition, and social norms tend to leave a mark on legal and administrative systems. War-damaged societies also typically display a layered complexity of law: 'formal' state law exist together with customary and or religious law.[19] Moreover, the formal legal system is often disputed and disrupted. The deleterious effects of conflict run wide and deep and the legal and administrative systems of these devastated countries often suffer from a lack of the most simple and basic equipment, like typewriters, pens, paper and legal texts, as well as more serious difficulties such as educated personnel.

War-torn societies are often described as lacking rule of law, or failing to uphold certain rule of law principles. The concept of the rule of law has come to be a central marker in foreign policy and international crisis management whereby the severity of war-torn societies is assessed. Applying the rule of law as an important component of conflict assessment might appear arbitrary, since there is no shortage of definitions of the rule of law in legal theory (and the vagueness of the concept has lent itself to a variety of definitions used by international actors, which will be discussed in Chapter 2).

Nevertheless, it is possible to outline some general background principles of legal theory that are common in most discussions on the rule of law. As a point of departure, it is submitted in this study that the rule of law, typically, is seen as having two primary attributes (or functions):

(1) Protection against arbitrary rule by imposing certain limitations, checks and balances, on the exercise of state power and,[20]
(2) The capacity to guide human conduct – that is, by providing a framework of law which facilitates human interaction in terms of protecting against arbitrary interference from the state and predictability of a system of rules in order to calculate the legal consequences of one's actions.[21]

For the purposes of this book, the relevance of the rule of law discourse is that the concept attempts to answer two long-standing questions. The first is what to do about unruly peoples of states (Hobbes's question) and the second, what to do about unruly states (Locke's question). The first attribute establishes restraints with the requirement that public officials must abide by the law, and through legal limits to the law-making power (constitutional or other). The second attribute seeks compliance with established rules. Further, it enables interactions

19 Baker & Scheye 2007 p. 516.
20 See, for example,the case law of the European Court of Human Rights. Early on, the Court explicitly linked the rule of law to a prohibition on arbitrary measures in Winterwerp v. the Netherlands, Judgement on 25 October 1979 A33. See also Malone v. the United Kingdom, Judgement on 2 August 1984 A/82, para. 68.
21 Krygier 2006 p. 133.

between individuals.[22] Both of these attributes are desirable for their enhancement of predictability, certainty and legal security, both between state and individuals (vertical) and between individuals (horizontal).[23]

Both attributes also approach the rule of law as a principle applicable to all state and individual interactions. Rule of law is in this sense a systemic concept that applies to different areas of state-individual interaction as well as to private-legal entities and other forms of association outside a state government structure.[24] The attributes also have a primary concern in relation to the means by which law comes into being, its form, and how it is interpreted and applied. A reason for this preoccupation with formal system characteristics is that abuses and violations of the rule of law through law itself is a particular form of abuse that is necessary to recognise.[25] Within legal theory, a common distinction is often drawn between formal and material rule of law definitions.[26] A rudimentary distinction could be expressed in this way: formal definitions focus on procedural limits on the state whereas the material adds substantive limitations on the exercise of authority by state actors. International agencies (discussed at length in Chapters 2 and 3) have adopted a material reading of the rule of law.

Does the distinction between formal and substantive (or 'thin' and 'thick' as it is sometimes described) rule of law definitions have any practical implications for rule of law promotion in war to peace transitions? On the one hand it may seem like a theoretical distinction that holds little sway in a practical analysis of the idea and all too easy to: "fall in the trap of the formal/substantive dichotomy", because any definition can, carefully scrutinised, be said to contain both formal and substantive elements.[27] This is a valid point and the dichotomy between the formal and the substantive could hinder a fruitful discussion relating to other perspectives of the rule of law – that is, from a user or actor perspective, or the rule of law from a capabilities perspective. Nevertheless, it is useful to apply the dichotomy in the context of war to peace transitions, simply because international actors make a conscious choice of subscribing to a substantive notion of it. The International Council on Human Rights Policy noted in its 1999 report, Local Perspectives: Foreign Aid to the Justice Sector, that beneficiaries of rule of law assistance perceived international agencies to be chasing 'fads' or

22 Tamanaha 2009 p. 6.
23 O'Donnell 1994.
24 See Kircheimer 1969 p. 429: "for all the differences in historical roots and particular legal traditions their common denominator lies in the simple thought that the security of individuals is better served when specific claims can be addressed to institutions counting rules and permanency among their stock-in-trade".
25 Raz 2003 p. 1. See also Waldron 2008–2009 p. 11.
26 Raz 1979 p. 211, argues: "a non-democratic legal system based on denial of human rights, of extensive poverty, on racial segregation, sexual inequalities, and religious persecution may, in principle, conform to the requirements of the rule of law better than any of the legal systems of the more enlightened Western democracies". But cf. Dworkin 2001 pp. 11–12.
27 Wennerström 2007 p. 83.

'trends' – that is, children's rights or women's human rights.[28] These trends, then, dominated rule of law reform for a period, until abandoned for new substantive issues and concerns.[29] Moreover, a substantive rule of law is how many of the influential organisations in the field define the concept. The OSCE states that the rule of law does not mean mere legality "but justice based on the recognition of and full acceptance of the supreme value of the human personality".[30] This raises questions on the potential difficulties attached to the promotion of a value-laden rule of law concept.[31]

The two formal attributes of rule of law have wide support in legal theory irrespective of whether one employs a material or formal concept of the rule of law or Common law or continental European law theories on the rule of law.[32] The traditional distinction between *Rechtsstaat* and rule of law seem to blend in the international discourse. Conceptually, *Rechtsstaat* embodying the continental European perspective takes law to be part of the structure of the state and not as an external limitation to it, whereas the common law tradition places more of an emphasis on judicial power and activism as an umpire and guarantor of citizens rights.[33] While differences in legal traditions might find some expression in practical orientation (discussed in Chapter 3.3) overall reforms seem largely insulated from the historical variations, using a concept that is perhaps best described as 'international' and also 'instrumental' in the sense that the rule of law is discussed in relation to reaching different ends after war and crisis. The rule of law, from the perspective of legal theory, is primarily a concept that seeks to remedy a potential threat of the abuse of power, and most detailed rule of law definitions are based, inversely, upon remedies to specific abuses. The primary form of violation or abuse of the rule of law is often direct – that is, through discrimination or the arbitrary use of power, but it can also be passive by way of a failure or a refusal by public authorities to act.[34]

---

28 The International Council on Human Rights Policy 1999 p. 74.

29 The UNSG repeatedly emphasise substantive law reform. In the twenty-first report on the UN mission to Sierra Leone the states: "concern has also been expressed about the lack of progress on law review and reform. Old laws that include gender and other forms of discrimination are still on the books". UNSG S/2004/228 p. 10.

30 CSCE/OSCE 1990 1 (2).

31 In the development by the World Justice Project of the Rule of Law Index (created to measure the existence of the rule of law worldwide) the challenges of formal and substantive interpretations of the rule of law were discussed. "On the one hand, it was felt that if the Index was to have utility and gain wide acceptance, the definition must be broadly applicable to many kinds of social and political systems, including some which lack many of the features that characterize democratic nations. On the other hand, it was recognized that the rule of law must be more then merely a system of rules – that indeed, a system of positive law that fails to respect core human rights guarantees established under international law is at best 'rule by law' and does not deserve to be called a rule of law system". American Bar Association & World Justice Project 2008 p. 6.

32 See Fallon 1997 pp. 9–19 and Hayek 2001 p. 75.

33 Krygier 2009 p. 57.

34 See Wennerström 2007 pp. 58–59 for a discussion of threats and remedies relating to the rule of law.

In order to realise the two rule of law attributes, the law is required to adhere to certain standards or acquire of itself a certain 'nature'. What precisely these standards are is disputed, but Fuller's enumeration in his seminal work, The Morality of Law, is widely accepted: In short, there must be:

(1) prospective rules;
(2) laws should be publicly promulgated;
(3) they should be of a general character;
(4) they should be sufficiently clear;
(5) they should maintain a reasonable constancy over time;
(6) they should not contradict other laws and must maintain a sensible consistency;
(7) they should not seek or require the impossible from those subject to them;
(8) there should be congruence between the conduct of officials and a declared rule.

According to Fuller, the eight conditions provide law with an inner morality, though they say nothing, or very little, on what the actual content of the law is. Fuller argued that these conditions were valuable in themselves since they created certain moral values. Rule of law, therefore, is in itself a moral good. Besides, Fuller argued, the rule of law has an 'affinity' with the good because if these formal requirements are met and upheld, a state is more likely to have fair and just laws because people can participate in, act and speak on issues of law-making.[35]

A number of procedural principles can be derived from the two basic attributes of the rule of law in such things as procedural fairness, proportionality, equal application of the law to similar cases, the right to be informed about decisions and the right of appeal.[36] Following these known 'rules of the game', an individual is free to plan and pursue personal ends and this, Hayek suggests, is "the legal embodiment of freedom".[37]

The ideal rule of law, as set forth in legal theory, is manifestly lacking in war-torn societies. While segments of a legal and administrative system might be still intact, or superficial procedures adhered to that give an initial impression of legality and legal certainty, the legal and administrative systems of countries undergoing transition from war generally fail in cardinal ways to ensure the two

35 Fuller 2004 p. 46ff. Raz, 1979 p. 225–226. who criticised this, saw these conditions as constituting a necessary functional good of the legal system, not a moral good: "A good knife is, among other things, a sharp knife.

36 Raz 1979 refers to "principles of natural justice" by which he meant procedural principles such as a fair hearing and impartiality, and has a similar and overlapping list to that of Fuller, with the key distinction that Raz's list focuses on those institutions that enforce laws, and not merely on the legal norms.

37 Hayek 2001 p. 75.

fundamental attributes of the rule of law – the restraint of arbitrary power and the enabling of human interaction.

In the following sections, some of the most salient features illustrating the lack of rule of law in war-torn societies will be examined, ranging from weakness in capacity to the vulnerability of individual persons and the lack of constitutional authority and hierarchy of law.

WEAKNESS IN CAPACITY

According to the UNDP Human Development Index[38] and the World Bank Worldwide Governance Indicators[39] countries such as Afghanistan, the Democratic Republic of the Congo, Sierra Leone and Liberia score on average very low (e.g. low literacy rates, large numbers of people living on less than a dollar a day). Complemented with other statistical sources – for example, Transparency Index and ratings from Freedom House, the same group of countries reappear as underachievers. Countries affected by internal conflicts and systemic crises are at the bottom rung of the ladder of development indicators.

Starting with these development indicators, it brings to the fore two important aspects when discussing war-torn societies and externally promoted rule of law reform. First, such societies share with a much larger group a general situation of 'underdevelopment'. Second, and in light of this, it is clear that international interventions need to address a great many structural legal conditions conducive to conflict. These problems range from impunity for crimes committed during the particular conflict, weak service delivery, and disputes over land and water rights, marginalisation of vulnerable groups (women, children and minorities) and dysfunctional legal and economic frameworks, which create massive inflation, illegal markets and unemployment.

Problems associated with the legal and administrative systems in war-torn societies are compounded by the fact that these systems seem to be specific targets during conflict. One commentator described the view in Kosovo as if "a plague of heavily armed locusts had swept through, scouring the grounds for anything valuable and leaving broken windows and ripped-out electrical sockets in their wake".[40] This description is not isolated to events in Kosovo but seem to be endemic in war to peace transitions. Official records, registries, court files and property titles are often destroyed, propelling legal administrative systems into a vacuum. An assessment by the International Legal Assistance Consortium of the

38 UNDP Human Development Report 2008, e.g., countries such as Somalia, Liberia, Afghanistan and Haiti.

39 The governance indicators measure voice and accountability; political stability and absence of violence; government effectiveness; regulatory quality; rule of law, and corruption.

40 O'Neil 2002 p. 75. See also Strohmeyer 2001, Collapse and Reconstruction p. 48.

legal system in Liberia, shortly after the peace accord was signed, is illustrative. Public buildings in Monrovia were looted extensively: "windows were broken, and records destroyed. Computers, office equipment, carpets, furniture, books, doors, and even lavatories have been stolen from public buildings". The assessment report continued: "consequently, while there is a statutory framework within which the Liberian legal system can operate, the infrastructure on which it depends is nothing more than a decaying shell".[41]

Though physical destruction causes immense problems for the functioning of legal and administrative institutions, the human resource component has proved to be the most difficult to remedy. Public officials are targeted in times of conflict and are either murdered or forced to flee the country. This creates a severe capacity problem in post-crisis transition and makes finding and training people to serve in the legal and administrative systems, alongside vetting mechanisms, a first order imperative.

In many war-torn societies the number of educated legal personnel, police and other public servants is often a problem predating the conflict. Owing to constrained resources, leading to inadequate remuneration and financial security, developing countries have a shortage of lawyers, judges, prosecutors, police and civil servants at all levels of state bureaucracy, which in turn constitutes one of the many barriers in access to justice. In cases such as Kosovo, where Kosovo-Albanian judges and lawyers were prohibited from practicing law during much of the Milosevic regime, lack of experience proved to be just one of many difficulties. Amid growing accusations of biased judges and lawyers towards the Serb minority, the UN authorities in Kosovo deemed it necessary to bring in international judges.

Under such circumstances there typically prevails a low level of judicial independence, a lack of a functioning bureaucracy and a general disregard of legal rules. These conditions might also lead to other elements outside the state taking its functions (i.e. criminal gangs that uphold 'security' or religious systems providing essential services). A common source of weak capacity is exhibited in low respect for constitutionally established authority. According to the World Bank's governance indicators, most war-torn societies display a similar set of weaknesses in the critical functions of the state: in governance efficiency; in political stability; voice and accountability; regulatory quality; and control over violence. Weakness in capacity is in this sense systemic and uniformly affects adversely the functions of state agencies.

Corruption further compounds weak capacity. This is a key theme in general development cooperation but it is only recently that it has become a particular priority in war to peace transitions.[42] In many cases legal and administrative systems are geared towards objectives other than service delivery. Keeping the

41 International Legal Assistance Consortium 2003 p. 4.

42 Rose-Ackerman 2008 p. 406.

ruling elite in power, or the possibility of resource rent and corruption, might well have replaced core functions of governance. This form of perversion of the rule of law is at times sustained by a lack of clear delineation between various branches of government, in particular between the legislative and executive, which creates uncertainty in the enforcement of policies. Combined with a poorly documented legal framework on bureaucratic rules, often unavailable to public officials and citizens alike, a rule of law deficit is made prominent.

VULNERABILITY OF INDIVIDUALS

It should be foremost remembered that conflict and a breakdown of legal and administrative institutions have devastating consequences for the lives of ordinary people. It is often said by international agencies that the problems of legal and administrative systems in war-torn societies is one of capacity. From an outside perspective, crisis states seem weak and incapable of carrying out policies, delivering basic services and upholding law and order. To this end, donor agencies often use the terms of capacity and effectiveness to frame the problems in transitions.[43] To the majority of those living in such places, even a weak and disintegrated legal and administrative system can appear to wield enormous power. For the weak and vulnerable – ethnic and religious minorities, women, children and refugees – who depend upon the state for protection and the delivery of basic services, the method and manner of the dispensation of power is crucial.

While capacity and efficiency are fundamental problems, the issue could equally be seen as one of exclusion: from access to existing (albeit weak) institutions and from the ability to exercise full legal rights. Because legal and administrative systems are often diminished and weak in the aftermath of war, how they function and on what legal basis, become pivotal in ensuring the best use of scarce resources. Not only are individuals excluded, they also suffer from the arbitrary use of power, from abuse, intimidation and repression in their interactions with state agencies – "the common people of failing states have no real stake in the success or failure of their countries [...] they hold no title to whatever they possess, no guarantees against expropriation at any time, and no belief that the conditions they face will ever improve [...] there is nothing to motivate them except the imperatives of simple survival".[44]

Taken together, the layered complexities and legal chaos that many war to peace transitions display, create a nearly insurmountable barrier for citizens seeking to enjoy the benefits of a state taken for granted in many other parts of

43 See, Fukuyama 2004 p. 6f, discussing scope and strength of state institutions in crisis environments.

44 Ghani & Lockhart 2008 p. 24.

the world. For most people living and suffering in crisis societies, uncertainty characterises their dealings with state agencies, which are perceived as being unpredictable, even shrouded in mystery, making it difficult to plan one's actions even under established rules and policies. They are excluded from gaining access to basic services such as health, education, communications and other infrastructures. They are also denied exercising their civic rights, from voting and taking part in the political system of the state in question, and from freely expressing opinions.

In situations constrained by a weak constitutional authority, a lack of clear rules defining competencies and responsibilities of state agencies, of centralisation, politicisation and low levels of accountability, ordinary people are directly affected. While a rule of law deficit in the interaction between public officials and individuals can manifest itself in different ways, it is most clearly illustrated through arbitrariness of treatment, unpredictability and inconsistency, discrimination, and a lack of access to justice.

It is important to note here that denial of access to justice might well be compounded under conditions where customary systems of governance are applied. A particular gender bias is also frequently reported from customary systems, causing access to justice to be particularly difficult for women.

LAW IN TRANSITION AND WEAK CONSTITUTIONAL AUTHORITY

Beyond the issues of weak capacity in relation to drafting and enforcing policies, a major challenge looms on another level: this is the question of applicable law and the lack or weakness of constitutional authority. The issue of applicable law is broader than that of a mere technical decision on what law to apply during a transitional period. The very question of applicable law is political by nature and surfaces in times of transition, where a previous legal order is perceived as being 'tainted' by the former regime or in other ways considered to be inappropriate or ill-suited.

Examples of the highly political nature of this question can be drawn from Somalia and Kosovo. In both cases the UN attempted to decide upon applicable law. In Somalia, the Special Representative of the UN Secretary-General (SRSG) declared that the former criminal law of 1962 was now to be the new criminal law. Legal professionals from northern Somalia resisted this decision, since they perceived the law to be affiliated to or associated with the former dictator, Siad Barre. They preferred instead the criminal code the British had imposed while as the colonial power (a law that had gone the route via India before being implemented in British Somalia).[45]

[45] Chesterman 2004 p. 88.

Similarly, the SRSG decided in the early stages of the UN's administration over Kosovo that the applicable laws should be those that were in force prior to the UN presence. This was resisted by many within the legal community of Kosovo, since this law represented the regime of Slobodan Milosevic. Instead, they favoured the laws in force up until the takeover of by Milosevic in 1989. Eventually, after six months, the SRSG amended its initial decision in compliance with the demands made.

Even where decisions on applicable law meet with little political resistance, it has proved to be a method attended by difficulty. For example, in the Bonn Agreement for Afghanistan, the decision was taken that the constitution from 1964 should apply in the transitional period (save for the provisions on the monarchy, executive and legislative) but its compliance with Afghanistan's international obligations was not settled. No decision was taken on who would assume ultimate authority for intercepting the newly-revived constitution in light of laws passed since its inception in 1964. Moreover, Afghanistan has a vast set of articles of applicable legal codes as well as presidential orders and decrees, all with confusing overlaps and irregularities For example, the Afghan legal framework "presents itself in layers, each layer representing particular periods of governance […] laws were enacted under the Constitutions or Interim Constitutions of Afghanistan of 1964, 1977, 1980, 1987, 1990 and 1992".[46]

Compounding the issue further is the fact that to begin with most war-injured societies suffer from obsolete, outdated and irregularly enforced legal frameworks. Therefore, irrespective of whether or not the choice of applicable law might seem to be somewhat easy, the chosen law will often fail in many respects to be enforced.

Judges, lawyers, and other public officials are often poorly trained, and people are generally unaware of their legal rights. The issue of applicable law therefore (though frequently resolved by reviving a previously interrupted legal order) creates confusion, since it has to comply with new norms and standards. As the case of Iraq has shown, the multi-layered system of laws, regulations, resolutions and fiats created difficulties for the Coalition Provisional Authority: "Hussein has ruled by fiat. Since 1991, the Revolutionary Command Council, which he chairs, has issued some 1,500 resolutions annually, ranging from amendments to the constitution to security decrees to changes in the laws concerning trade and taxes. This has created a legal jumble".[47]

The confusion surrounding the issue of applicable law only serves to reinforce its lack of legality, legal certainty and respect for constitutional authority in war to peace transitions. In some cases, violations of legitimate constitutional authority emanate from problems inherent in the constitution – that is, no provisions on power-sharing, excessive powers given to the executive combined

46 Lau 2006 p. 9.
47 Hartman 2003 pp. 6–7.

with features of centralisation, and weak oversight and accountability mechanisms, sustaining a political law. Local governance in Iraq is a case in point. The Iraqi constitution contains several gaps in relation to local governance, in particular on specifying the structure and form of authority for certain institutions, and on defining the roles and responsibilities of local government agencies.[48]

In other cases violations occur through a tradition of neglect and from ruling by executive decree, despite constitutional provisions to the contrary. A lack of respect for constitutional authority has been repeatedly recorded in Kosovo, particularly at local governance level. The actions of municipal agencies has sometimes been undertaken despite a want of competence contrary to legal responsibility and in defiance of decisions of a higher instance, even from the Supreme Court of Kosovo.[49] There is also much variation on how local government authorities interpret and apply the law, with little coordination and streamlining between agencies.

HISTORY OF RULE OF LAW REFORM

OLD WINE IN NEW BOTTLES?

The promotion of laws and legal institutions for the purpose of achieving development outcomes – 'social engineering' through law – is not a new fad. It began in all earnest in the 1960s with US-based the law and development movement.[50] The rule of law promotion enterprise today within societies torn apart by war is therefore a continuation – some would say a revival of law and development. Yet, a sentiment exists among a growing number of scholars and practitioners involved in rule of law reform that important lessons from past experience of endeavours in rule of law assistance have failed to seep through. Though short-lived, and declared 'dead' by the early 1970s, the law and development movement aroused a lively debate on the possibilities and challenges of externally promoted legal reform. But as Pistor, Berkowitz and Richard lamented several years later: "we are taking stock once more and can hardly avoid the conclusion that the same recipe has failed again".[51]

In the burst of new law and development activities, surprisingly little attention has been paid to best practice, to the pitfalls and mistakes of past

---

48 USAID 2007 Republic of Iraq District Field Manual p. 7.

49 OSCE 2007, Report on the Administrative Justice System in Kosovo p. 16.

50 See, generally, Tamanaha 1995 for a short but penetrating description of the life and death of law and development studies.

51 See Pistor, Berkowitz & Richard 2003. The authors express criticism of rule of law reform in development cooperation as being mainly based upon legal transplants that disregard the importance of process.

experience. When acknowledged it is of little more than as lip-service policy statements. The reasons, of course, depend on a number of factors. It might well be that rule of law promotion has become a business where there is a deficit in knowledge and with few incentives for learning from past experience. Another way of observing this gap is to take the view that the dialectical process of theory and practice in rule of law reform has failed to reach common ground.

The critique that has emerged against rule of law promotion often takes the form of broad calls to acknowledge so-called context-specific factors, that legal reform is a politicised area, and that 'non-legal' strategies can play an important part (sometimes a dominant one) in affecting behaviour and changing attitudes more effectively than 'legal' strategies. Taken together, the critique has been forceful, yet also generalised and at times even philosophical.[52] This is particularly impractical for the actors involved in rule of law assistance. Reformers and people within law and development institutions are drawn to generally applicable models and templates. A great deal of the critique that has emerged against rule of law assistance can be perceived as being difficult to put into effect by international actors since it emphasises context, history and non-legal factors as significant determinants for legal reform, yet often without more informed and constructive benchmarks for improvement.[53]

The quintessence of the predecessor to rule of law promotion in war-torn societies, the law and development movement, was that developing countries needed to mimic Western, and particularly US, laws and institutions in order to attain economic growth. This in its turn was adopted from the so-called modernisation theory.[54] Scholars of law and development also drew heavily on the works of Max Weber. In an attempt to explain the rise of capitalism in Europe (but not elsewhere), Weber turned to law and argued three reasons why European law was more conducive to capitalism: (1) the more rational a legal system was, the more conducive it became for complex economic transactions; (2) European systems were more rational than systems found in other 'civilisations' and; (3) this rationalism had existed prior to the full development of industrialism.[55] A legal system exhibiting those characteristics was seen as more rational and predictable and "only such a normative order could generate substantive provisions necessary to the industrialised system".[56]

52 Peerenboom 2006 p. 868. While there are specific and profound analyses from various countries, these are rarely lifted from the context in which they are produced. Peerenboom 2005–2006 p. 868.

53 Ohnesorge 2008 pp. 285.

54 Tamanaha 1995 p. 471. The theoretical underpinnings of the modernisation theory held that development was inevitable, and that an evolutionary process would eventually result in social and political institutions similar to those in the West. Thus when adapted to a law and development perspective, where development was an evolutionary process that would eventually result in legal systems similar to Western legal systems, the movement sprang into action to assist in and hasten the process.

55 Weber 1978 pp. 973f.

56 Trubek 1972 p. 13.

The law and development movement acted on these things as their fundamental, and perhaps most radical, hypotheses. The assumption was that it was possible to initiate specific legal reform programmes that would transform third world 'primitive' legal systems, putting them on the same footing as European 'modern' ones. Law and development programmes specified the elements required for progress, which involved an almost exclusive focus on reforming state institutional capacity. Law and development scholars did not incorporate non-state justice systems to any great extent in their programming but sought, from a Weberian point of view, to create universal formal rules. Following this line of thought, particularistic and local customary forms of rules did not fit.[57]

Law and development programmes attempted to reform the formal structures of the legal system in developing countries. By importing and establishing Western legal concepts in a top-down and deductive formalised approach, there was an assumption that reforms would 'trickle down' to the rest of society.[58] This would change the legal culture in developing countries, which law and development scholars perceived as being highly 'formalistic': rules were developed, interpreted and applied without adherence to social needs or in consideration of their effect on society. Through the selected transplant of 'modern' Western laws, the developing country in question would benefit from an instrumentalist injection.

Three basic theoretical underpinnings can be singled out as the driving forces behind the action of the law and development movement:

(1) lawyers were seen as social engineers;
(2) legal transplant was relatively easy; and
(3) law was seen as highly instrumental.

This meant that reforms started with a small group of the elite and that reform at that level would seep through to the rest of society.

Implicit in the movement's viewpoint was the conviction that there was no apparent obstacle to instigating legal transformation from the outside. Legal reforms did not have to be 'home-grown' or reflect society, chiefly because legal reforms sought to create a different society. Following this assumption, law did not have to 'fit' the old structures, only those that were in the making. The important task was to create an instrumentalist-oriented legal culture, the framework and instruments so to speak, for the would-be social engineers. If these assumptions were implemented properly they would produce an environment conducive to economic growth, and that would advance political liberalism.[59]

---

57 Trubek 1972 p. 9.

58 Trubek 2006 p. 76.

59 Development policy at the time tended to emphasise economic matters over the political, but not because policy makers lacked interest in political development. It was assumed that

This did not happen, at least not in the scale anticipated by reformers and it is often stated that the law and development movement failed to realise its goals. Above all, after just ten years of law and development programmes, with heavy emphasis on law reform and legal education in developing countries, the movement was subjected to criticism by two of its own leading academics, Trubek and Galanter.[60] After this, financial support to the movement dwindled and various institutes and foundations directed their attention elsewhere.[61]

Scholars and practitioners began to accuse the law and development movement of being ethnocentric and naïve.[62] The export of an instrumental view of law lacked a substantive content, without which an authoritarian government could abuse improvements in the legal structure. Based upon an assumed 'superiority', law and development scholars had positioned their own domestic legal systems over those of foreign 'underdeveloped' systems. That is, foreign legal scholars and practitioners brought with them a notion that the only available path was one of modernisation, and that this required imitation. Critics of the law and development movement also pointed to a fundamental source of challenge – a lack of "empirical knowledge of the third world".[63] Put simply, law and development scholars did not possess sufficient understanding of the function of law in developing countries, which resulted in weak assumptions of its role and prescriptions modelled on Western legal systems.

Criticism against law and development programmes was also spurred on by the ascent of dependency theory, which attacked the notion that the problem was internal in developing countries, and held instead that the real problem was the economic, political and cultural dominance of both developed countries and less developed countries.[64] Within law specifically, the Critical Legal Studies movement emerged, protesting at the export of a "liberal legal model".[65]

In hindsight, a certain caution should be exercised in labelling the law and development movement a complete failure, or as Trubek put it: "the rumour of its death was greatly exaggerated".[66] Similarly, Dezalay and Garth observed that the law and development movement failed to transform legal education in, for

political liberalisation would follow in the wake of economic development through a sort of spillover effect.

60 Trubek & Galanter 1974.

61 Salas 2001 p. 18.

62 Trubek & Galanter 1974 p. 1080.

63 Trubek & Galanter 1974 p. 1089.

64 Davis & Trebilcock 2001 p. 22. The view of the dependency theory was that underdevelopment was caused by the system of "world capitalism, which perpetuated extractive and exploitative relations with the developing world".

65 Sarkar 1999 p. 21. The Critical Legal Studies critique did not propose an alternative to the law and development paradigm, but instead contributed by raising critical questions on the centrality of the state in development, and whether legal development assistance really should be based upon a Eurocentric model, and pointed to the fact that law could reinforce underdevelopment within a society, instead of preventing it.

66 Trubek 2006 p. 7.

example, Brazil. But it succeeded in educating a small elite group of lawyers in US business law that would later spearhead legal economic reforms in Latin America.[67] Furthermore, the law and development movement only existed for roughly a decade, which is hardly sufficient time to evaluate its success or failure.[68] It is important to remember that just as law and development was essentially a Western discourse, so was the criticism against it. Even when the critics attacked law and development for being ethnocentric and accused it of having a Western bias, the criticism never really extended beyond the US and Europe, and drew support and inspiration from events that unfolded in the legal system at home, rather than from what happened (or did not happen) abroad in the countries receiving law and development assistance.[69]

With the end of the cold war there came a revival of law and development tenets. Most of the same ideas and principles underpinning the law and development movement were put in practice in Central and Eastern Europe in what could be described as a second segment of rule of law reform. Numerous rule of law projects were initiated, bringing with them countless legal consultants engaged in reforming judicial institutions, as well as commercial, constitutional and administrative law in the countries moving from planned to market economies and from one-party rule to multi-party parliamentary democracy. This wave of rule of law reform set in motion a rather fierce criticism against what many considered to be a continuation without much modification of flawed assumptions on legal and social change, based upon the law and development tenets. In a way by repeating the cycle of law and development, the practice of rule of law assistance has produced a critical discussion on externally promoted law reform.

Following the second segment of rule of law reform is the rule of law promotion in war-torn societies, which emerged as an explicit strategy in the late 1990s, primarily through the attention offered to the rule of law concept by the UN in general and by the UN Security Council in particular. Rule of law reform in this context grew from the practice of supporting legal, judicial and human rights reforms in primarily the UN missions of the early 1990s as a peace-building strategy. This might serve to give rule of law promotion in such societies certain distinctiveness compared with the previous segments. The segmentation is even emulated in policy and operational directives of international organisations and donors such as the UN. In the 2006 report of the Secretary-General on enhancing UN rule of law reform capacities, a system of 'baskets' is introduced consisting of rule of law on the international level, rule of law in post-conflict and conflict situations and rule of law in the context of long-term

67 Dezalay & Garth 2001 p. 249 and Salas 2001 p. 50.
68 Tamanaha 1995 p. 473. Though only in existence for a brief period, the movement produced a substantial doctrine.
69 Tamanaha 1995 p. 482ff.

development.[70] Though this division of labour is an attempt to maximise the impact of UN rule of law reform, there is also a risk that it enhances parallel structures and uses of the rule of law with little chance of cumulative lessons learned and sharing of good practices.

From the trial and error of the 1960s and 1990s, a set of 'best practices' has emerged. Rudimentary as they are, the best practices still serve as a point of entry to further discuss legal, judicial and administrative reform on a more informed basis. The 'failed' policy of law and development with its top-down institutional focus, the keenness on imitation, and the intrinsic hope for a trickle down (if one could only get the right laws and institutions in place) and their exclusion of non-state justice systems should at the very least act as warning signs for donors engaged in rule of law reform today in war-torn and crisis societies.

THEORIES ON EXTERNALLY PROMOTED RULE OF LAW REFORM

An army of terms has emerged with which to describe what international actors actually do when engaging in rule of law assistance, with legal transplants or transfers[71] being the most common. Other concepts (often developed in opposition to the transplant concept) include legal translations,[72] diffusion,[73] irritants,[74] transpositions,[75] and convergence of values.[76] The basis of this description of rule of law reform is the external involvement in legal reform. International participants assist in the drafting of laws and regulations and in the establishment and strengthening of legal institutions as mentors, advisers and technical experts. In an oversimplified description, international actors are the 'transferees' and local actors the 'receptors'. Transplants and transfers are used for many reasons, ranging from cost saving to legitimacy-generating factors.[77]

It is necessary to recognise the theories and discourses on legal transplants. Theories on legal transplants are useful for placing rule of law reform in a broader context. The theories are made use of in order to shed light on and describe the problems and prospects on the choice of method adopted by

70 UNSG, S/2006/980 p. 13.
71 Watson 1978 p. 313.
72 Langer 2004 p. 29f.
73 Friedman 2001 p. 94 finds the word transplant inappropriate: "what we are talking about is the diffusion of rules, codes or practices from one country to another."
74 Teubner 1998 p. 12 contends that legal transplants give the wrong impression, that is, that the transplanted law will remain the same as in its original form.
75 Örucu 2002.
76 Seita 1997.
77 See Miller 2003 p. 845f.

international actors, as well as to describe those relating to external involvement in legal reform. For the purposes of this work, the primary focus on legal transplant concerns the methodology of transplants, the process of reform, typical approaches taken by international actors, and the benchmarks and best practices that the transplant discussion has produced. Discussions on transplants go right to the heart of the major challenges in rule of law reform. When the EU, UN or the World Bank support rule of law reform after war and crisis, what guarantees are there that the reforms will actually 'stick'?

Criticism against the current rule of law paradigm has revived a debate long present but dormant in comparative law and legal sociology – whether laws and legal institutions can 'travel' between two different legal cultures, and what conditions that can be seen to be favourable for externally promoted legal reform. In a rather crude fashion the contours of the discourse can be drawn accordingly: proponents claim that laws and legal institutions can travel, with little difficulty, while opponents largely reject the notion of the transferability of laws.

Scholars like Watson[78] claim on the one hand that there is little or no difficulty in exporting laws and legal institutions, while on the other, those like Legrand[79] and Kahn-Freund[80] reject the proposition or (as with Kahn-Freund) express scepticism. The dividing line between the two approaches is the view on law in relation to society. It should be made clear that these two opposing views often speak of different things. Proponents, in support of their claim, point to the abundance of so-called 'transplanted' laws in the various legal systems of the world as evidence that law travels. Watson, and other academics supporting the thesis on 'transferability of all law', base their arguments upon an assumption that law is not primarily a reflection or an outgrowth of society, but rather a reflection of values and desires of the legal 'elite' itself (judges, lawyers, prosecutors and bureaucrats all steeped in legal work). Law therefore can, and does, spread by way of interaction between legal elites in two or more countries.[81]

A rich historical record from the reception of Roman law in medieval Europe, to the appearance of Swedish Ombudsman institutions in Latin America, German *Begriffsjurisprudenz* in Japan, and American commercial laws in China, are all evidence of these interactions.[82] Law has become a global commodity, like any other aspect of globalisation.

Opponents of the transplant thesis, on the other hand, while finding it difficult to argue against the globalisation of laws and legal institutions, centre on an entirely different matter: do the laws and legal institutions, once transplanted, function as they did in the country of origin? Thus, if it can be

78 See Watson 1978 p. 313.
79 Legrand 2001 p. 57.
80 Kahn-Freund 1974.
81 Watson 1978 p. 313.
82 Markovits 2004 p. 95.

agreed that law has broken out of the Westphalian nation-state confinement, the central question for consideration is if law is consciously 'exported', what then makes it 'take root'?

Opponents of the transferability thesis hold the view that law reflects society and furthermore that the application of law by a judge, for example, "is a function of the interpreter's epistemological assumptions, which are themselves historically and culturally determined".[83] Through this, the conclusion is reached that laws and legal institutions are particularly subject to a form of law of 'non-transferability' Kahn-Freund argued that transfer of laws to communist regimes would encounter structures and political systems that would cause laws to acquire a new and different meaning from that originally intended. Reformers were therefore advised to seek out functionally equivalent structures and processes rather than to engage in a direct transfer of laws and legal institutions.[84] The metaphors used to describe this phenomenon also portray the core problem. The medical term 'transplant' shows that it is not only a matter of observing the existence of similar type of legal rules in two different societies, but also the function that they assume: will the transplant be received or rejected in the body of the new host?

However black and white these approaches might seem, there are perspectives that fall somewhere in between. Friedman, though saying that anyone with an interest in law as a social or historical phenomenon "simply cannot take seriously Watson's notions about how law changes (or fails to change)"[85] ends up in the middle ground. Friedman sees the spreading of modernity as the key to understanding the transfer of laws and legal institutions and accordingly rejects the notion of transplant, since it tends to obscure what has really been happening – which is a process of modernisation. To deal with difficult situations and to solve problems produced by a 'modernisation' process "countries adapt, beg, borrow, or steal law from places that have faced the same problems earlier, or came up with an earlier response".[86]

This position deals primarily with what can be called 'voluntary' import and export of laws and legal institutions. It is undeniably more problematic in war to peace transitions where legal, judicial and administrative reforms become part of an international agenda where the local legal elite, as well as the broader society, has little say. These societies also face a complete overhaul of the legal and administrative systems, as opposed to specific and isolated legal reform initiatives.[87] Teitel has elaborated extensively on the sui generis situation of law in transition, from authoritarian rule or violent conflict.[88] According to Teitel,

83 Legrand 2001 p. 58.
84 Kahn-Freund 1974 p. 6f.
85 Friedman 2001 p. 93.
86 Ibid., p. 94.
87 See Peerenboom 2006 pp. 831–834.
88 Teitel 2005 p. 6.

law here has a different function from 'ordinary' times. Thus the sui generis nature of law suggests certain conditions on the importation of laws, standards and benchmarks from the outside as would normally not come into play. The central challenge facing rule of law reform of any kind is to transform internationally supported laws, institutions and practices into viable, independent and effective national laws, institutions and practices. This is a challenge where there are many sub-par performances. As the UN Secretary-General (UNSG) states in his 2004 report on UN rule of law reform after war and crisis, "countless pre-designed or imported projects, however meticulously well-reasoned and elegantly packaged, have failed the test of justice sector reform".[89] One reason cited is the failure to contextualise and adapt reforms to a local context, and an over-reliance on foreign experts and foreign conceived solutions.[90]

Theories on transplants could be criticised for representing an over simplification of rule of law reform, failing to include the complexities of the political economy in legal, judicial and administrative reform. Transplants do not capture the mix between externally promoted legal rules and domestic legal political economy. The concept of political economy is here applied as means of describing the vested interests different actors might have in relation to rule of law reform. The interest groups encompass formal practitioners – such as judges, prosecutors, legislators, the executive and bureaucrats – as well as informal groups outside the state structure, but with a particular interest in maintaining the status quo or in reforming the legal and administrative system.[91] At the same time, arguments for and against transplants are essential to acknowledge, since they are at the heart of rule of law assistance: the discourse informs on assumptions, aspirations and potential risks and benefits involved. The metaphors of transplant, transfer, and translation are useful to an understanding of the main methodology of rule of law reform, but these metaphors also have clear limitations since they often describe a deductive and horizontal form of rule of law reform and fail to acknowledge bottom-up or inductive initiatives of legal reform – for example, where civil society actors in collaboration with international non-governmental organisations push for legal reform.

FORMS OF RULE OF LAW INTERVENTIONS

The international community promotes the rule of law in different ways and under different mandates. Forms of intervention and modes of influence can be

89 UNSG S/2004/616 p. 7.

90 Ibid. p. 6.

91 Davis & Trebilcock 2004–2005 p. 129–130. The authors argue that rule of law reform is not a technocratic exercise but an "inherently political enterprise that is intended to constrain those wielding public power".

broadly divided into two categories. The first is where international actors substitute for weak national governments, either through a lack of capacity or because they are yet to be constituted.[92]

This form is sometimes called executive missions or international transitional administrations and implies a direct control by international actors over national legal development. An international organisation or body assumes the principal responsibility for carrying out state functions. Recent instances of the UN or other international actors substituting for national governments include Cambodia,[93] Bosnia and Herzegovina,[94] Kosovo,[95] and East Timor.[96] International transitional administrations provide international players, as in the case of Kosovo, with executive, legislative and adjudicative powers.[97]

The second type of intervention and external influence takes the form of direct government assistance. This often occurs in peace operations with assistance and support as their mandate. As a contrast to the substitution of weak national governments the direct government assistance does not formally provide international actors with the authority to make executive decisions concerning rule of law reform. Instead, international personnel advice, train and capacity-build national actors, sometimes in co-location programmes where technical experts work directly with a particular department, agency or function as part of the regular staff. Examples of assistance and support to national governments include recent missions to Sudan,[98] Burundi,[99] the Ivory Coast,[100] Sierra Leone,[101] Liberia[102] and Afghanistan.[103]

---

92 See United Nations Department of Economic and Social Affairs (DESA) & United Nations Development Program (UNDP) 2007.

93 SC Res. 745 (1992).

94 Annex 10 Art. II of The General Framework Agreement for Peace in Bosnia and Herzegovina states that the mandate of the High Representative will be to monitor the implementation of the peace settlement, to promote the parties full compliance with all civilian aspects of the Agreement and to coordinate the activities of the civilian organisations and agencies in Bosnia and Herzegovina.

95 SC Res. 1244 (1999).

96 SC Res. 1272 (1999).

97 There are parallels with reconstruction after the second world war in Germany and Japan, as well as earlier attempts by the League of Nations with its direct administration over the Saar Basin (1920–1935) and The Free City of Danzig (1920–1939). See Berman 1993 p. 1893. The UN and the EU respectively assumed direct control over two territories in the Balkans. United Nations Transitional Administration for Eastern Slavonia, Baranja and Western Sirmium was established in 1996 on the basis of an agreement between the Croat government and local Serb authorities, the so-called Erdut Agreement, SC Res. 1037 (1996). The city of Mostar was administered by the European Union under the Memorandum of Understanding of the European Union Administration of Mostar.

98 SC Res. 1769 (2007).

99 SC Res. 1545 (2004).

100 SC Res. 1528 (2004).

101 SC Res. 1346 (2001). The revised objective was formulated in UNSG S/2001/228.

102 SC Res. 1509 (2003).

103 UNSG S/2002/278 (2002). p. 16.

A middle-ground between executive and assistance missions are interventions involving elements of international decision-making either by default in the absence of national government capacity[104] or by being confined to certain areas as in the economic governance programme in Liberia, called the Governance and Economic Management Assistance Program (GEMAP).[105] A fourth type, although not that common after war and crisis but often used by donors in development cooperation, is budget sector support.

The areas where rule of law is typically promoted within these broad forms of intervention – substitution, direct government assistance and hybrid missions – can be placed in three broad categories:

(i) law reform
(ii) strengthening of law-related institutions, and
(iii) access-creation.[106]

The focus of this model of rule of law reform is primarily on state institutions, with the requirements of the legal profession determining the agenda. The predominant method in law and development, as described above, was the transfer of laws and legal institutions. This is aptly summarised by Gardner through his taxonomy of legal transfer that took place under the law and development movement:

(i) direct transfer of legal institutions and instruments;
(ii) indirect transfer of legal concepts and models;
(iii) invited legal transfer, where the initiative and encouragement for the legal transfer process comes from the recipient legal culture;
(iv) imposed or uninvited legal transfer at the initiative of the 'exporting' legal culture;
(v) infused – 'premeditated' or 'planned' – processes of legal transfer, direct or indirect, wherein the initiative comes from the exporting legal culture; and
(vi) more occasional ad hoc borrowing.[107]

It can be observed that today's developing and transition economies receive substantial amounts of 'foreign' law in the form of Gardner's taxonomy. This may take the form of a direct or invited transfer, as in the EU enlargement process. Involuntary or imposed transfers of laws and institutions can also be observed – for example, through World Bank comprehensive development plans, or to some extent the IMF's trade rules.

---

104 In Sierra Leone, the UN forces acted as unauthorised de facto regional administrators. See Peacekeeping Best Practice Unit, September 2003 p 18.
105 International Contact Group for Liberia 2005.
106 Carothers 2006 The Rule of Law Revival p. 7.
107 Gardner 1980 p. 14.

When adopting the stylised model of transfers to rule of law reform in war to peace transitions, the direct transfer of legal institutions and instruments, as well as the imposed or uninvited transfer can be noted. While occasional borrowing, infused or invited naturally takes place, the role of the outside agent is heightened, particularly in situations where an international organisation or a coalition thereof substitutes for a national government under an executive mandate. The attention accorded international actors in this book and their conceptualisations of the rule of law is, simply put, determined by their influential role. What international actors say, and more to the point do, influences legal, administrative and judicial systems in war-torn societies.

The scope of international influence in national legal and political transformation is a much debated issue. Morlino and Magen, for example, conclude in their analysis of rule of law reform in four European countries (Ukraine, Turkey, Romania and Bulgaria) that the function of international actors is somewhat exaggerated. Rule of law reform, according to those authors, is "an essentially domestic drama in that they fundamentally concern the manner in which a given demos is governed – a demos which properly exists only at the national-state level and sub-national (hence domestic) levels".[108]

While the description of rule of law reform as a 'domestic drama' seems plausible on the premises presented by Morlino and Magen, the particular situation in war-torn societies begs the question: How dominant is the 'demos' in relation to international influence? In other words, it is likely to assume that given the chaotic circumstances in war-torn societies, the internal or domestic factor is less dominating than in Morlino and Magen's argument, and international influence is thus heightened (when compared with other transitions or situations in development cooperation).

An influential role for international actors in war-torn societies also seems more likely when considering on the one hand efforts to create a 'demos' by supporting civil society organisations, human rights activists, and community-based organisations, and on the other, their pains to establish state structures. In the 2004 report from the UN Secretary-General, helping war-torn and crisis societies restoring the rule of law is described as a daunting and often overwhelming task, given the lack of capacity at the national level.[109] Similarly in the EU CSDP Justice Mission Concept document describes situations where EU justice missions operate as requiring or depending on outside support.[110] Thus, while international actors support the principle of national ownership, this does not always come naturally after war and crisis but require certain manufacturing.

In some of the most recent cases of international rule of law interventions, donors have either substituted for national governments as a whole or in part (Kosovo), and in relation to certain sensitive areas of governance (corruption in

108 Morlino & Magen 2009 Conclusions p. 225.
109 UNSG S/2004/616 (2004) p. 3.
110 Council of the European Union 2011.

Liberia) for example. In other cases, international actors play a large role 'behind the scenes'. Where international actors are not mandated to enforce reforms, or to take executive decisions in the national arena, the weak capacity of national bureaucracies in war-torn societies to initiate, manage and implement rule of law reforms is nevertheless conducive to a substantial international involvement and responsibility. This is not to say that national actors – political leaders, legislators, judges, civil servants and civil society groups – are passive and lack influence. On the contrary, national actors do in fact influence rule of law reform on the ground, but they are most often excluded from defining the agenda on the normative conceptual level. For the same reasons that place international actors in influential positions in societies debilitated by war, theories that seek to explain external influence – that is, on socialisation and conditionality – are here employed more as contextual rather than as theoretical frameworks. International actors employ conditionality as punishment or reward.[111] Conditionality may be applied punitively, where aid and assistance is withdrawn unless tangible progress can be measured, or as a form of reward by allowing membership to organisations and access to favourable trade. Conditionality is used in order to reinforce means of socialisation – that is, through transplants of laws or other forms of 'teaching' of norms.

While empirical evidence exist supporting the effectiveness of political conditionality, particularly within EU accession context, the three core conditions explaining this success – "the size of international rewards, the size of domestic adoption cost, and the credibility of political conditionality"[112] – are difficult to identify in short-term multilateral state-building missions. Easterly, for example, suggest that the incentive structures on behalf of international organisations are likely to be ill adapt to the least developed and most poor countries, and that the enforcement mechanisms at their disposal turns into a practice of rewarding better-off countries who are more successful in their reform efforts.[113] Experience indicates that in situations where there is no strong domestic demand that can complement international reform agendas, typical forms of conditionality have been a failure.[114] Interim governments in war-torn and crisis societies are subject to a range of conditions through UN Security Council resolutions, political compacts at donor conferences, and agreements with regional organisations, calling for rule of law, justice sector or security sector reform. But such conditions are ad hoc, sometimes competing, and often lack a clear standard of assessment.

---

111 Schimmelfennig 2007 p. 27 describes political conditionality as a "strategy of reinforcement used by international organizations and other international actors to bring about stable political change at the state level" – for example, in the promotion of human rights, democracy and in the rule of law.

112 Schimmelfennig 2007 p. 128.

113 Easterly 2001.

114 Fukuyama 2004 p. 34.

Within the transfer model described above, international actors employ different strategies in order to influence rule of law development. One prominent one is through 'socialisation'. International actors such as the World Bank, the US Agency for International Development (USAID) or the Department of Peacekeeping Operations (DPKO), function as norm entrepreneurs. They are, in a sense, "teachers of norms – generating and disseminating information about appropriate templates of policy, institutional design and administrative conduct".[115]

Through modes of socialisation, national actors are under pressure to implement norms and adopt new policies, often based upon international standards and benchmarks – described by Schimmelfennig as "the process directed toward a state's adoption of the (constitutive) norms of an international community".[116] Socialisation strategies can thus be used as a concept to describe the influence of international actors, multilateral and bilateral, on domestic rule of law reform. Morlino and Magen, for example, use taxonomy to describe a socialisation that involves formal rule adoption, a form of adjustment to external pressures and norms. This is followed by rule implementation, meaning the degree of institutional adjustment required to implement the rules adopted. Third and last is the rule internalisation, which is the "acceptance of transferred rules, beyond formal adoption among state bureaucracy, political elites, relevant groups and the wide public".[117] This process seems to be slower, with the intention of anchoring rule of law reforms established through formal rule adoption and rule implementation.[118]

Socialisation thus takes on a route of intergovernmental bargaining and dialogue, and is best characterised as a top-down rule of law assistance strategy where assistance is channelled through government agencies and ministries. In many cases, socialisation involves twinning or co-location programmes where international 'experts' advice, support and train national public officials in the justice system and bureaucracy.

More importantly, international actors are not merely norm entrepreneurs, engaged in socialising transitional governments, but also drafters of norms by means of direct executive control in places such as Kosovo and East Timor. They can also undertake this function in direct government assistance missions. The distinction between substituting a national government and assisting a transitional government directly is difficult to uphold in chaotic environments, and international actors have sometimes taken on a more direct responsibility than that which a narrow interpretation of a mandate would allow.[119]

115 Morlino & Magen 2009 Methods of Influence p. 36.
116 Schimmelfennig 2002 p.1.
117 Morlino & Magen 2009 Methods of Influence p. 40ff.
118 See Schimmelfennig 2002 pp. 8–9 who employs a similar taxonomy.
119 Peacekeeping Best Practice Unit September 2003 p. 18.

Following socialisation strategies, international players frequently adopt a technical approach to norm promotion and norm creation – that is, benchmarks, norms and standards are promoted. The technical approach is founded upon an assumption of 'autonomy' and 'logic', where rule of law reform is seen as a rational choice. National actors, it is assumed, will receive and support rule of law reform based upon rational considerations of functionality, efficiency or international legitimacy that is attributed to certain laws and legal institutions and practices.

This assumption that international actors make, regarding the rational choice of rule of law reform, resembles the argument of Watson and other proponents of the transplant thesis. International actors seem to assume a sense of 'community of legal professionals' that reaches beyond geographic, cultural and socio-economic boundaries. Lawyers in Somalia, Liberia or Kosovo will thus understand, support and defend rational choices of rule of law reform promoted by assistance providers.

The reaction of national actors to the objectives and methods of rule of law reform, however, seem to defy the 'logic of appropriateness' assumed by their international counterparts.[120] When one considers how the local legal communities reacted to legal reform imposed from without in Somalia and Kosovo, the response of national actors has not been that of choosing to support legal reform based upon internationally 'shared' values, modernity or cost-efficiency as anticipated by international actors, but seems to have been influenced at local level by ideology, cost and control.

In a reaction to the tendency towards imposition in rule of law reform, and in an effort to enable its local ownership, international actors have established working structures in concert with their national counterparts. In such cases, both international and national actors share responsibility over the administration of justice. This form has been employed in the trusteeship style interventions of Kosovo and East Timor, but also in assistance-type missions as with Liberia.

Finally, a more marginalised strategy in promoting rule of law reform is to be found in the variety of initiatives that could be termed 'bottom-up'. Through such approaches, international actors provide support directly to non-governmental organisations and community-based groups. The overarching aim is often to empower vulnerable groups and to create access to, and transparency of, government agencies with a view to strengthening accountability and justice delivery. Sometimes the support given to NGOs takes place because of a recalcitrant government, and is then extended to create support for reform 'from below' and to circumvent resistance and the influence of vested interests. Though frequently described as an essential part of rule of law reform, initiatives

120 Morlino & Magen 2009 Methods of Influence p. 44.

concerning legal empowerment and access to justice are less prioritised compared with institution-building and domestic norm development.

The different strategies for promoting rule of law often overlap. Socialisation with a technical approach can be combined with conditionality to reach a certain outcome of rule of law reform, just as socialisation forms a natural part of initiatives applied from the foundation upwards where international actors seek to support grass-roots movements and community-based organisations as advocacy groups for rule of law reform by involving them in an international network of advocacy groups. Rule of law assistance to war-torn societies, in sum, may involve several different forms of influence. This ranges from the most intrusive with substitution of national governments to technical assistance, civil society support, together with socialisation and joint structures of international and national ownership and authority.

DISTINCTIVENESS OF RULE OF LAW REFORM AFTER WAR AND CRISIS

Rule of law reform could generally be described as consisting of three distinct yet interrelated segments, where the second and third operate today in parallel. The first segment consists of initial attempts at 'legal engineering' by the US-based law and development movement of the 1960s. This was followed by rule of law assistance in the early 1990s, which was to a large extent founded upon law and development tenets. The overarching focus of the second segment of rule of law promotion was economic and political transition in central and eastern Europe. The second segment of rule of law promotion has also become a standard component in development cooperation. The third is a latecomer – rule of law promotion in war-torn societies. The objectives here for 'legal engineering' are to support, reconstruct and rebuild legal and administrative systems in societies moving from war to peace. Overall, it is here contended that the three basic tenets of the history of rule of law reform – lawyers as social engineers, the potential of transplants and the instrumental view of law – are replicated in rule of law assistance to war-torn and crisis societies.

While one observes that the methods and modes of influence run through all three segments, rule of law promotion in war to peace transitions is distinctly separated because of the crisis anatomy of war-torn societies. A lack of domestic capacity in such communities, and the confusion and contradictions surrounding applicable law and constitutional authority, renders the procedure of legal reform more vulnerable to external influence. The question of, for example, applicable law, common in these damaged societies, affects the use of the method of socialisation and importation of international norms and standards.

Lessons learned from the two earlier segments of rule of law assistance must therefore be understood in the light of crisis characteristics. Theories on legal transplants and transfers point to the need to focus on procedure and to be wary of contextual and ideological differences between international actors and local interlocutors. In particular, these theories on transplants and transfers must be placed in a context where the international dimension is 'stronger', and where the backing of UN Security Council resolutions sometimes enforces the rule of law. This is particularly relevant where international agencies substitute for national governments. This affects much of can be learned from the past and in relation to benchmarks on the two earlier segments of rule of law assistance. Moreover, in the crisis anatomy of war-torn societies, individuals are vulnerable and the so-called civil society is often fragmented.

Other parts regarding methods and modes of influence in rule of law promotion in these broken societies is the same as with the two other segments. Arguments against supporting a formal rule of law reform, launched in relation to the first segment of rule of law assistance, are still present today – perhaps even more so, since the rule of law that international actors use is in most cases material and value-laden.

Moreover, the content approach is also a similarity, despite that the content of the legal transplants has changed between the rule of law reform segments. Whereas central and eastern Europe, and present development assistance, mainly centre on economic law transplants, war to peace transitions have a security law transplant at the centre. This means a focus, for example, on judges from a criminal law perspective, criminal law from a gender perspective, and a general human rights law (chiefly civil and political rights) perspective permeating all parts of reforms.

2. RULE OF LAW IDEOLOGIES AND OBJECTIVES

INTRODUCTION

The previous chapter provided a context to war-torn and crisis societies through the discussion on crisis anatomy and the overall structure of international responses in rule of law reform. This chapter examines the objectives behind rule of law interventions, and how the concept of the rule of law is applied and understood by international actors. The reasons behind a discussion on conceptualisation are straightforward. How the rule of law is interpreted and defined at legal and policy levels has a fundamental influence on the level of implementation – that is, on how the concept is put to practice and on what type of reforms that are given priority. Simply put, precise and clear conceptions provide for an easier understanding and compliance, with breaches more clearly observed.[121] Conversely, a lack of clarity greatly diminishes understanding and compliance.[122] As a concept, however, the rule of law does not lend itself to an effortless description.

Absence of clear guidelines on what the concept means for rule of law officers and related staff on the ground is illustrated in a survey conducted by the Centre for OSCE Research. The survey targeted 18 field missions of the OSCE, asking questions to their personnel such as whether they based their activities on any particular rule of law definition or if they had criteria for distinguishing rule of law tasks from those of human rights and democratization.[123] The results from the survey describes the absence of rule of law guidance in the field and, one can assume, is not isolated to the perceptions of OSCE staff but rather symptomatic for most actors involved in rule of law reform:

> The field operations have no recourse to a standardized, conclusive definition of the rule of law or rule-of-law promotion. A number of field operations (30 per cent) work without any definition whatsoever. The majority, however, define the rule of law or rule-of-law-promotion, some with reference to Kofi Annan's report for UN rule-of-law promotion, the Copenhagen Document (1990), or the Ljubljana decision [...], and

121 See Dobbs *et al.* 2007 p. 4: "the more sweeping an intervening authority's objectives, the more resisted its efforts are likely to be".

122 See Abbot & Snidal 2000 p. 427.

123 Evers, 2010 p. 9.

> others according to their own preferences. In conversations, field mission staff identified the lack of clear definitions and conceptual frameworks as a definite handicap. They indicated a need for material that would provide a survey of the field and give definitions of terminology [...].[124]

What the OSCE survey reveals is that for some rule of law practitioners in the field there is a lack of a comprehensive understanding of what is meant by rule of law or rule of law promotion.

If the conceptual ground is somewhat unclear, the political logic of rule of law interventions is uncomplicated. Since there exist in most of these societies no organised domestic apparatus able to press for and implement reforms, external assistance is necessary. In the absence of local capacity for the administration of justice (and in the face of suffering arising from that deficit in capacity) the international community assists in the provisions and development of a sound judiciary, competent public prosecutors and capable public defenders, and also implements structural changes in the particular society's legal framework. This rationale is supported both by international and domestic operators, though the former tend to steer and control reform objectives to a greater extent. From the perspective of domestic actors it is at the same time important to note that rule of law reform is sometimes viewed as a legitimacy-generating enterprise.[125] Without a minimum level of legitimacy, states face difficulties of proper functioning, and loss of legitimacy could also be seen as one of the components contributing to conflict.

The rule of law is promoted for several reasons and the dominant objectives are discussed in the sections that follow. One of them is the assumed link with good governance and economic development; another the assumed causality with human rights; the third objective is a latecomer: rule of law linkages to international security and state-building.

OBJECTIVES FOR RULE OF LAW ASSISTANCE

To understand how international actors conceive and put into effect the rule of law, it is necessary to consider the underlying objectives that act as driving forces for its promotion. The rule of law agenda in war to peace transitions is influenced by a number of objectives ranging from an increase in governance efficiency and Security Sector Reform (SSR) to the strengthening of women's human rights.

The different objectives create an interesting mix of agendas, but hardly a fruitful environment for the complicated process of reconstructing rule of law in a war-torn community. As Stromseth *et al.*, noted, advocates of each agenda

124 Evers 2010 pp. 9–10.
125 Miller 2003 p. 854.

(economic, human rights, and security) "quarrel over whether commercial law reform should precede criminal law reform, whether the creation of courts to sort out property disputes [...] should take priority over the creation of human rights and war crimes courts, and whether judicial reform ought to come before police and military reform".[126]

In the complex environment of war to peace transitions, international actors often link three broad objectives to the rule of law: good governance and development, human rights, and security. Attempts have been made at establishing a causal link between the rule of law and these objectives, but it cannot be said that the rule of law is anything but an essential but insufficient component.

According to Rajagopal, the new fascination for the rule of law is somewhat misplaced. Underlying the linking of the concept to other objectives represents the desire to escape from politics by making the rule of law technical, legal and apolitical.[127] By this, Rajagopal argues, international actors implicitly suggest that conflict, insecurity, and human rights violations could all have been avoided through recourse to law. While correct in his observation of the high hopes placed in law, the argument of misplacement is perhaps best seen as something of a default rather than a conscious strategy to avoid the political.

While international participants often deal with rule of law from an institutional perspective, as a matter for criminal justice and as an instrument for human rights protection, legal theory is more modest and less prescriptive. Moreover, legal theory describes the rule of law as a concept encompassing all interactions between the state and the individual – that is, it includes criminal law, administrative law and civil law in matters of state intervention. In this way, the rule of law is portrayed as a systemic concept, almost a perspective.[128]

As will be seen below, in linking the rule of law to human rights and democracy, by pressing for a particular form of governance and content of laws, international actors often advocate for a rule of law that is anything but apolitical, formal and value free.

GOOD GOVERNANCE AND ECONOMIC DEVELOPMENT

Good governance has emerged in recent years in the context of development cooperation. Most commentators define good governance in a much broader way and incorporate the rule of law as a constituent principle of good governance.[129]

---

126 Stromseth, *et al.*, 2007 p. 60.

127 Rajagopal 2008 p. 1347.

128 See Kirchheimer 1969 p. 429 and O'Donnell 2004 p. 35f.

129 Commission on Human Rights Resolution 2000/64 (26 April 2000) enumerates five key attributes:

The present concept of good governance should be understood against the background of economic liberalisation, democratisation and the emergence of an international human rights regime. These forces in combination have produced a global governance reform movement where ideas and prescriptions blend into a common model with a specific economic and administrative design.[130] Public management programmes have swept through developing countries for nearly two decades. Starting with the so-called structural adjustment programmes of the World Bank and IMF in the early 1980s, pressure began to be exerted on the public sector urging it to be more market friendly, reliable and efficient. The good governance objective was given impetus with the start of the political and economic transition of central and eastern European countries in the early 1990s.[131]

Typically, international financial institutions and other agencies support governance and rule of law reform because of what it can facilitate: an environment favourable to a market economy.[132] Economic development reforms rest mostly on the support or strengthening of a legal framework where legal rights, in particular property and contractual rights, are well protected.[133] The empirical evidence supporting the claim that rule of law and good governance contributes to economic development is quite consistent.[134]

The 'economic rule of law' that is part of the good governance paradigm is based upon a set of theories referred to as the 'Washington Consensus'. This agenda stipulates the necessary conditions for economic growth and was adopted by the international financial institutions.[135] This is perhaps the most influential, and most debated, development paradigm. The rule of law aspects of the Washington Consensus covers judicial strengthening and contains such things as revision of private law (e.g. contract, competition, bankruptcy etc.), and establishment of alternative dispute resolutions, enhanced protection of property rights and less, but more refined, economic regulation. Rule of law promotion in development cooperation and transition during the 1990s also

---

(1) transparency;
(2) responsibility;
(3) accountability;
(4) participation and;
(5) responsiveness (to the needs of the people).

See also Commission on Human Rights, Resolution 2001/72 (25 April 2001).

130 Brinkerhoff & Brinkerhoff 2002 p. 512.

131 See Bergling 2006 pp. 10–14.

132 See e.g. Messick 1999. See, also, North 2005 on the role of institutions for economic development and the designation of law as a crucial institution with economic implications.

133 Posner 1998 p. 1.

134 Peerenboom 2006 p. 45.

135 For a description of the good governance paradigm, see Kjaer 2004. The International Monetary Fund, as early as 1996, urged good governance in all its aspects by ensuring rule of law, including improving accountability, transparency and efficiency in the public sector and the tackling of corruption, International Monetary Fund April 2003.

focused on constitutional reform (e.g. for enhanced protection of property rights) and administrative law.[136]

A key concern was how to constrain government agencies so as to allow for economic growth. The approach to administrative law includes setting up and strengthening internal and external checks and balances, involving among other things administrative appeal procedures and judicial review. The initial governance paradigm was seen by many to be a failure in terms of promoting economic development, with the emphasis on 'rolling back' the state, deregulation, and opening up developing countries to foreign investment.[137] The experience led to a new emerging paradigm, sometimes referred to as 'post-Washington Consensus'. In this new form, governance and rule of law were utilised differently from before.[138] Linked with the high-level Millennium Development Goals, it tended generally to emphasise the role of the state as a responsible and engaged actor, social responsibility, with a focus on laws and legal institutions for the benefit of poor people.[139]

In recent years a few empirical innovations within the field of rule of law and economic development have occurred where specific questions have been considered and evaluated. Clague, Keefer, Knack and Olson, for example, have attempted to measure the enforceability of contracts.[140] Other studies, such as those conducted by Kaufman, Kraay and Lobatón, have focused on several legal variables and their effect on development, using data from polls of country experts, or surveys of residents on voice and accountability; political stability; government effectiveness; regulatory quality; control of corruption; and the rule of law, which in the study is taken to mean the incidence of both violent and non-violent crime, effectiveness, consistency and predictability of the judiciary, and the enforcement of contracts.[141] Similarly, judicial reform has attracted empirical studies in order to evaluate first the problem, and then the impact of project activities undertaken in relation to econometric or governance indicators.[142]

---

136 Ohnesorge 2008 p. 248.

137 See Kjaer 2004 p. 174.

138 See Rittich 2006 p. 206.

139 Trubek & Santos 2006.

140 Clague, *et al.*, 1997.

141 Kaufmann, Kraay & Lobatón 1999 p. 8. The rule of law indicators used are seen as measuring the "extent to which agents have confidence in and abide by the rules of society". See also Brunetti, Kisunko & Weder 1997.

142 Judicial reform benefits from tangible variables such as caseload, case management, length of time in proceedings, and so on. Hammergren 2002, Diagnosing Judicial Performance, and USAID 1998. However, it is difficult to track and identify more comprehensive changes. Arguably, judicial performance is measurable, though its influence and effect on society depends on many other constraints and possibilities.

HUMAN RIGHTS

The rule of law revival is not only a result of a economic governance agenda, but also a product of the growing force of the human rights movement, where increased demand for legal and judicial reform insist on treating human rights as justifiable claims rather than as mere aspirations. Rule of law promotion, with its emphasis on judicial independence, constitutional rights and other institutional checks and balances on state power, has become an instrument of rights advocacy.

For those advocates of a human rights-driven rule of law agenda, the constitutional protection of judicial independence and human rights, and an increased socialisation through law, are seen as being far more than mere "window dressing".[143] Measures taken by international actors and national governments to ensure due process, formulation of constitutional rights, a review of criminal justice in the light of international human rights law, as well as the establishment of human rights institutions to keep check on executive power, are considered to be important in the promotion of what is understood to be two mutually supporting objectives: the rule of law and human rights.[144] Rule of law as a concept has possessed itself of a useful rhetoric connecting with entities (e.g. religion, gender, economy) that had previously challenged human rights promotion, apart from possessing the ability to discuss its detailed enforcement.[145] The interrelatedness of the rule of law and human rights regimes is clearly expressed in the advocacy and reform efforts on access to justice.[146]

Starting with state-building missions, as with Cambodia in the early 1990s, contributing states and international agencies have invested in legal instruments: constitutions, independent judiciaries, and human rights commissions, all as necessary guarantors of a lasting peace and democratic gains.[147] Rule of law has come to be seen as one of the principle factors, among others, in a liberal democracy and rights-based rule of law conceptualisation is now an essential part of UN state-building missions.[148]

An interrelated strand of a rights-based rule of law promotion is to be found in the recent developments of the Commission on Legal Empowerment of the Poor, which was established in reaction to a perceived deficiency in the rule of law agenda in development cooperation and transition in order to address

143 See Apodaca 2001–2002 for a more critical appraisal of the link between human rights treaties and actual change of legal and administrative policy for countries that have ratified treaties.

144 See Carothers 2001 p. 85f.

145 Peerenboom 2006 pp. 822–826.

146 UNDP 2004 p. 5, stating that access to justice initiatives must depart from international human rights law.

147 Frank 1999 p. 1.

148 Morlino & Magen 2009 Hybrid Regimes p. 7.

questions central to poor and vulnerable groups. The Commission's focal points consist of access to justice and empowerment through property, labour, and business rights.[149]

SECURITY

The contribution of a security focus to the rule of law promotion agenda is clearly discernible and the logic is straightforward. Rule of law reform is frequently used in relation to, or sometimes interchangeably with, SSR. The perception on rule of law from a security perspective is that injustice and repression together constitute the complex roots of terrorism, crisis and conflict, and if in one sweep it is able to promote economic development and enhance human rights protection, then by extension rule of law should be a key instrument for facilitating war to peace transitions.[150]

In particular with an increasing number of so-called 'failed states' involving the concerns of international alliances, the security perspective tends to dominate. In a report by the UN Secretary-General on the conclusions and closure of UN peace operations, the completion of domestic peace becomes sustainable only when conflicts are resolved peacefully through the exercise of state sovereignty and participatory governance.[151] To facilitate such transitions, the UN Secretary-General recommends that Security Council mandates should include elements of institution-building and furthering the rule of law. Moreover, in a report in 2002 on the protection of civilians in armed conflicts, the UN Secretary-General emphasised the role of rule of law as representing one of the most important components in any transition from war to peace. Since the institutions for security and law and order are often the first to collapse, this creates a vacuum in relation to human rights protection and increased criminality.[152]

As a result of the security focus, SSR strategies are rapidly becoming a standard component in UN multidimensional peace operations. In a 2008 report by the UN Secretary-General on the part played by the UN in promoting reform in the security sector, SSR is presented as inherently dependent on rule of law for effective responses to address insecurity.[153] SSR means, in general terms, giving support to those actors retaining the authority to use force in order to protect the state and its citizens. This includes the civil structures responsible for oversight and management. From a rule of law perspective the relationship between SSR and rule of law promotion in war to peace transitions is most clearly seen in

149 Commission on Legal Empowerment of the Poor 2008 p. 2.
150 Stromseth, *et al.*, 2006 p. 60.
151 UNSG S/2001/394 p. 2.
152 UNSG S/2002/1300 p. 10.
153 UNSG S/2008/39.

those measures concerned with strengthening management and oversight bodies – that is, executive, legislative, financial management frameworks, courts, and complaint commissions.[154]

A recent development seeking to broaden the conceptual foundation of the term 'security' is the Human Security Project. In explaining the interrelatedness of threats in crisis and war-torn societies it presents a broader security concept that goes beyond national security to include threats such as economic disruption, hunger, disease, and natural catastrophe.[155]

An observation of the influences from flanking initiatives, such as SSR, is the growing security-dominated focus in rule of law reform in these societies, where the notion of security is slowly acquiring a more encompassing understanding than before. Rule of law reform taking place in UN and EU missions has undergone a 'securitization' in how is conceived and put into practice, compared with rule of law in development aid or past experience of rule of law assistance in post-communist transitions. In some international policy documents, however, SSR is presented as containing rule of law, placing the end below or besides the means. The OECD DAC Security Sector Reform Handbook with the overall objective to distil good practices in SSR holds that: "'security system', 'security system reform' and 'SSR' all refer to that broad range of security and justice institutions. The terms also denote activities sometimes referred to by international actors as 'security sector reform', 'security and justice sector reform' and 'rule of law'"[156]

Somewhere herein lays the problem and current obfuscation. Rule of law is popular as a concept, and people want it for different reasons in different contexts. Moreover, and more importantly, though the labels of rule of law and SSR might overlap, there is a need for taxonomy in order to better guide and inform international crisis management particularly in relation to environments that are not post-conflict settings yet undergoing a political and security crisis.[157] The problem of unclear linkages between rule of law and SSR is not only conceptual but also organizational, methodological and psychological. On the one hand, rule of law and SSR reformers tend to conceive of their work as significantly different from one another. In any case, both approaches are formed by post-conflict experience and focus predominantly on the reform of the judiciary, criminal justice and security institutions.

Thus, SSR and rule of law represent not only concepts to be dissected and discussed academically, but also prioritisation, sequencing plans and mission strategies, budget lines, staff and personnel titles, job descriptions and career paths.

---

154 See OECD 2004 p. 16.
155 Human Security Center 2005 p. viii.
156 OECD 2007, p. 5.
157 OECD, 2010, p. 9, describe the need to improve coordination and speak of a competition over who should play the coordinating role.

ACTORS AND IDEOLOGIES

Critics refer to the current attempt at promoting the rule of law as a 'template', a 'menu', a 'standard package' or an 'orthodoxy'.[158] These terms are used to characterise a set of rationales as to why the rule of law is promoted and the principal methods employed in projects and programmes.

As discussed in chapter 1, legal theory often takes a formal and procedural approach to the rule of law. Internationally, precisely the opposite view is often taken (a material or substantive definition). Rule of law, from a donor perspective, is closely integrated with, in fact depends on, substantive notions of justice. International actors tend to attach the notion of the rule of law to other concepts: democracy, justice, equality and human rights, and to fill the idea with content. This might well serve to render rule of law reform vague and contentious. One example is that of Bosnia and Herzegovina. In mid-1997, the Republika Srpska's President, Biljana Plavsic, dissolved the entity's parliament. The Constitutional Court found this to be in violation of the constitution and ruled against it. The High Representative overruled that decision, claiming that it had been subject to political pressure. At all events, from a formal perspective rule of law had been served by the decision of the Constitutional Court, and greatly undermined by the High Representative.[159] What the international community sought in this case was not the rule of law, but some other ideal, which the concept of the rule of law failed to satisfy.

A further example from Bosnia and Herzegovina shows again the difficulty of linking the rule of law to other essentially 'contested concepts'. With the repatriation of refugees following the Dayton Agreement, many of them found their homes illegally occupied. The UN High Commissioner for Refugees favoured an interpretation of the existing legislation that would consider humanitarian concerns (even though the unlawful occupation provided grounds for eviction), while the Organization for Security and Cooperation in Europe (OSCE) adopted an interpretation that followed the letter of the law that would lead to evictions.[160] Tension becomes obvious between, on the one hand, strict formal interpretations where equality before the law and legal certainty are unyielding, and on the other, where the rule of law is regarded as a means of realising other goals – in this example, the right to adequate housing.

Beyond a material approach to the rule of law, international actors seem to operate on two levels on its promotion. One of them is generality. Rule of law can be virtually anything that complies and accords with certain values and standards. Form is secondary to generalised and politicised notions of good. The rule of law template thus reads rather like a list of anything that one might

158 See Upham 2006 and Heller 2003.

159 Caplan 2005 p. 187.

160 Caplan 2005 p. 81.

conceivably hope for in a legal system – the possibility to seek redress, impartiality and fairness, justice and equality and security from the state and other individuals – without considering that certain matters sometimes depend on political and social and economic factors beyond the reach of possible accomplishment by rule of law reform.

On the second level, rule of law is often understood as constituting a specific set of institutions. These include a constitutional framework, a judiciary, bar association, prosecutors and public defenders, law enforcement agencies and custodial and prison services. The institutional list is complemented with a specific set of laws, often with an overarching objective to secure fundamental human rights and a proper criminal procedure. Moreover, these laws and institutions are often modelled on the legal systems of participating donor countries or on international norms and best practices.

In the sections that follow, the different applications of the rule of law concept by international actors will be examined. Since the war to peace transition arena is crowded with international agencies, it is difficult to present a precise constellation. This does not preclude a list of the 'usual suspects' with a focus on the most active and influential actors.

Naturally, the list includes the UN, but it is misleading to speak of the UN (or any other organisations for that matter) as a monolithic organisation. Within the UN, the Secretariat, the UN Security Council, and the OHCHR can hold independent and sometimes contradicting rule of law conceptions.

Another international actor is the European Union (EU), because of the increased responsibility for state-building that this organisation has assumed over recent years through various rule of law missions (Georgia, Iraq, and Kosovo). The EU also applies the concept of the rule of law in its development cooperation agreements and is thus an influential participant in both segments of rule of law assistance.

The Council of Europe does not have the same active and tangible engagements, and responsibilities, as those of the UN or EU, but through the European Court of the Human Rights and the European Commission for Democracy through Law (the so-called Venice Commission) it actively contributes to the conceptualisation of the rule of law. Thus the Council of Europe brings with it a particular normative weight by way of European Court of the Human Rights case law and through its standard-setting mechanism of resolutions and recommendations to member states. The OSCE has been active in the Balkan region, particularly in Kosovo where the OSCE, together with the EU, assumed a crucial role in the UN interim administration of the territory.

International financial institutions are playing increasingly important parts in rule of law promotion in war-torn societies. Among the international financial institutions the World Bank is of particular interest, exhibiting a growing commitment to primarily economic rule of law reform in war to peace transitions.

Besides these multilateral organisations, bilateral initiatives play a key part in rule of law reform, particularly in the form of direct government support. This chiefly includes bilateral state agencies such as the UK Department for International Development (DfID), and the USAID. Bilateral assistance also takes the form of state bureaucracy support and twinning programmes.[161]

Beyond organisations and international actors, a specific policy-formulating activity is worth noting, namely peace agreements. While international organisations and other agents in their respective policy documents and guidelines provide entry points towards an understanding of how the rule of law is understood and presented war-torn and crisis societies, which also shed light on the methods and approaches adopted for making effectual the rule of law, peace agreements are important as internal accords between former warring factions (though often internationally brokered).

The methods by which donors identify and establish their objectives in rule of law reform, are based on legal and policy documents. Many of these documents are of a nature that might be termed 'soft law'. The exception is the EU development cooperation agreements, which are international treaties and thus subject to customary international law and to the Vienna Convention on the Law of Treaties. Similarly, the mandates of the UN Security Council are different from general declarations and are legally binding on member states when adopted under Chapter VII of the UN Charter. Though the concept of the rule of law is not explained in the mandates on UN state-building missions (this is primarily provided for by the UN Secretary-General and other bodies, they come with an enforcement power, and have a different projection of power than that of the declaratory statements of other organisations.[162]

While the following descriptions of the positions of international actors towards the rule of law take a centralised perspective of the organisations, it is of consequence to maintain the perspective of plurality. This makes questions on authorship to documents on the rule of law, on the anticipated audience, and on the main reasons for publishing rule of law policies and guidelines, somewhat difficult to answer in general. Furthermore, neither the World Bank, the EU nor the UN are monolithic organisations but instead aim at a plurality of goals, and embrace different ambitions, agendas and approaches. The agenda concerned might sometimes vary within organisations, and policies might be laid out in internal strategic turf wars. Generally, it must be assumed that legal and strategic documents on rule of law are written to improve the regulatory capacity over rule of law reform and to enhance the coherence and effectiveness

161 Other important actors are international non-governmental organisations (INGO) and local civil society and community-based organisations. Some of the most significant INGOs are the American Bar Association, the International Commission for Jurists, Human Rights Watch and Amnesty International.

162 UN Security Council resolutions are considered as binding upon Member States when adopted under the framework of Chapter VII. Shaw 2003 p. 1102.

of individual missions, programmes and projects. They are also often written for a broader audience (supporters in countries participating in missions and those receiving rule of law assistance). In other cases documents are produced by international agencies for the sole purpose of guiding its own personnel and field activities – one such example is that of various 'primers' developed by different entities within the UN. However, what cannot be avoided, is that some part of the discourse exists both for self-legitimising reasons and public relations. This might be more revealing, nonetheless, than its other parts in formulating an understanding of how rule of law is promoted by a particular organisation.

What follows is an analysis of the common denominators of the most influential international actors in rule of law assistance. This analysis to some extent is based upon this question: If organisations are diversified, what is the common denominator keeping them together in the field of rule of law promotion? In other words, what are the comparative equivalents within the arrays of projects and programmes of one particular organisation, and what are the strategic and policy developments in rule of law reform? These common denominators are derived from legal documents, case law, policy statements, projects and programme reports, as well as internal memorandums and operational guidelines. Rather than assuming a common approach to the rule of law, one based upon the use of the definition can be created by way of deduction. So instead of assuming a consensus within the World Bank, or any other organisation's treatment of the concept, it becomes more urgent to look at what makes harmony possible between legal, declaratory and operational definitions.[163]

UNITED NATIONS: IN SEARCH OF COMMON GROUND

In the third preambular paragraph of the 1948 Universal Declaration of Human Rights, the link between human rights and the rule of law is expounded thus: "whereas it is essential, if man is not to be compelled to have recourse, as a last resort, to rebellion against tyranny and oppression, that human rights should be protected by the rule of law". That preambular reference is a reflection of the mandate of the organisation, and a reminder of the time, and times, when the UN was established. Since then, the objective of the rule of law within the UN has grown to embrace a vast range of interests.

The legal basis for most rule of law interventions is to be found in the resolutions of the UN Security Council.[164] As such, its mandates not only

163 Santos 2006 p. 255.

164 But the mandate for rule of law reform might also derive from law on occupation, or on law on occupation and UN Security Council mandates in combination. See SC Res. 1483 (2003) for Iraq.

provide the legal framework for rule of law reforms, but they also serve as first acts of foundation and as blueprints for war to peace transitions. The language of the UN Security Council mandates provides the political and operational framework, both at headquarters rank and at field operation level.

Rule of law as a constituent and essential part of UN peace-keeping and peace-building mandates is relatively new. Reference to the rule of law was first included in the mandate for the peace operation in the Congo in the 1960s, but it was not until the late 1990s that the Security Council started referring to the concept more directly. Since then, the concept of the rule of law has been a constitutive part of UN state-building missions. This policy has characterised the work of UN agencies in the promotion of the rule of law, manifestly in the UN's advisory services and in its technical assistance on human rights.[165]

Initial attempts at defining, or at least providing some form of operational guidelines for the promotion of the rule of law, came in the report from the UN General Assembly in 1994 entitled Strengthening the Rule of Law. Enhanced activity in the UN's technical assistance programme to developing countries and transition economies led to a compelling need to attend to the questions of what the rule of law truly meant in the context of technical support.

In the UN General Assembly's report, 11 devices (with correlating sub-devices) are presented as constituting a legal and institutional framework for technical legal assistance:

(1) A strong constitution;
(2) A strong legal framework, under the constitution, which protects human rights and democracy and provides effective redress in all key areas;
(3) Strong national human rights institutions, including independent commissions on human rights and ombudsman offices, with functions and structures consistent with the principles relating to the status of national institutions, as well as strong national human rights research and training institutes;
(4) A strong judiciary, which is independent and adequately empowered to uphold human rights in the administration of justice;
(5) An adequate national training regime for lawyers, judges and prosecutors, police and prison officials, which includes attention to their role in the protection of human rights;
(6) A military that has ultimate allegiance to the constitution and other laws of the land;
(7) Effective and accessible mechanisms for conflict resolution between and among citizens and groups in society and state organs;

165 The UN is also a strong advocate of ensuring the rule of law in international law. The international rule of law perspective, involving i.e., the International Court of Justice and the International Criminal Court, falls outside the scope of this study.

(8) Full incorporation into the international human rights system, including through ratification of or accession to international human rights treaties;
(9) A society that is educated in its rights and responsibilities, including in national human rights curricula;
(10) A strong civil society; and
(11) Free, responsible and flourishing mass media.[166]

Despite this framework, the UN has for a long time lacked a more coherent rule of law definition of all its agencies, particularly in relation to a growing commitment in war to peace transitions. A number of diverse UN agencies, ranging from the United Nations Development Fund for Women to the DPKO, are engaged in supporting war-torn societies with different rule of law interests. UNDP, to take one influential actor, sometimes adopts a different approach to rule of law reform than that of the DPKO, or the UN Office on Drugs and Crime (UNODC). The UNDP often has a more long-term development and capacity-building focus whereas DPKO or UNODC are engaged in short-term, time-bound or sector-specific issues, often involving criminal justice and security.

In accord with the recommendations of the 2000 Brahimi Report[167] on the capacity of the UN to deal with rule of law issues, the UN Secretary-General set up a task force for the development of comprehensive rule of law strategies.[168] The task force conducted a comprehensive inventory of rule of law expertise in each of the relevant UN departments but did not touch upon what the rule of law actually meant for the world organisations. A crude definition can perhaps implicitly be read from the inventory, which centres on expertise and guidelines in relation to criminal justice, judicial reform, corrections, police and human rights.[169]

Defining the Rule of Law

In 2004, as a reflection of the increased commitment and responsibility to rule of law reform in recent years, the UN Secretary-General launched a common UN rule of law definition. Following the UN's responsibility as an international administrator in Kosovo and East Timor, where the UN had executive mandate, the need grew for a more comprehensive definition. In the seminal 2004 report Rule of Law and Transitional Justice in Conflict and Post-conflict Societies, the problem of multiple definitions and understandings of the concept was noted, and the rule of law described as:

166 UNGA, A/49/512 p. 5–8.
167 Brahimi Report 2000 p. 55.
168 ECPS Task Force for Development of Comprehensive Rule of Law Strategies for Peace Operations 2002.
169 Ibid.

> [a] concept at the very heart of the Organization's mission. It refers to a principle of governance in which all persons, institutions and entities, public and private, including the State itself, are accountable to laws that are publicly promulgated, equally enforced and independently adjudicated, and which are consistent with international human rights standards. It requires, as well, measures to ensure adherence to the principle of supremacy of the law, equality before the law, accountability to the law, fairness in the application of the law, separation of powers, participation in decision-making, legal certainty, avoidance of arbitrariness and procedural and legal transparency.[170]

The normative foundation for the UN's rule of law assistance is also set out in the same report by the UN Secretary-General. Apart from the UN Charter, the normative foundation is said to consist of international human rights law; international criminal law; international refugee law; and international humanitarian law. While the legal implications are unclear, it is argued in the report that this framework creates certain normative boundaries. The UN cannot, for example, assist in the establishment of a tribunal with the authority to impose the death penalty or to broker a peace agreement that would include amnesties for war crimes and crimes against humanity.[171] As a follow-up to the 2004 report the Secretary-General issued a guidance note UN's approach to the rule of law, reiterating the definition and outlining important principles underpinning all UN work in the area of rule of law reform.[172]

Efforts to Enhance Coherence and Coordination

In 2006, two important developments took place. One was the establishment of a Rule of Law Coordination and Resource Group (ROLCRG) within the UN Secretariat. The 2006 UN Secretary-General's report, Uniting our Strengths: Enhancing United Nations Support for the Rule of law, notes that many challenges remain with regard to coordination and communication between field and headquarters.[173] ROLCRG was thus given the task to coordinate system-wide attention on the rule of law so as to ensure quality policy coherence. ROLCRG consist of key UN actors, among them the DPKO, UNDP, and UNODC, and represent an effort to streamline UN rule of law reform.[174]

The second strategic policy development in 2006 for the UN was the division of labour in rule of law reform set out by the Secretary-General where different UN entities were given lead in relation to specific themes and contexts (rule of

170 UNSG S/2004/616 p. 4.

171 Ibid., p. 5.

172 UNSG Guidance Note 2008, UN Approach to Rule of Law.

173 UNSG S/2006/980 p. 13.

174 Several Guidance Notes have been developed by the UNSG, e.g. United Nations Approach to Justice for Children (2008); United Nations Assistance to Constitution-Making Processes (2009); and United Nations Approach to Transitional Justice (2010).

law on the international level, post-conflict, and development). The DPKO, for example, is designated as the lead agency: on strengthening national justice systems and institutions; police and law enforcement; prisons; interim law enforcement agencies; and security support to national law enforcement agencies. The UNDP is described as the lead agency on strengthening national justice systems and institutions where DPKO-led mission do not exist; court administration; civil law; customary, traditional and community-based justice; training; and land and property.[175] Through this division of labour a perception of rule of law after war and crisis as being intimately linked with security is clearly manifest, particularly with the complementary role supposed to be played by the UNDP.

Apart from the common UN definition, the rule of law as a concept is also given content through the UN Commission on Human Rights. From a UN perspective, the interconnectedness between the rule of law, human rights and democracy was emphasised in the resolution adopted by the UN Commission on Human Rights in 2005. In that resolution the rule of law is considered to be essential to democracy and human rights protection, and that states should continually seek ways of strengthening it. They are encouraged to:

(1) Guarantee the separation of powers through legislative and judicial measures. States should also ensure unfettered access to information and engage with civil society organisations in order to increase awareness among people of their human rights, and of remedies in cases of infringement;
(2) Ensure the principle of legality. States hold in this regard work towards ending impunity for violations of human rights and international humanitarian law, to guarantee equal protection before the courts and provide sufficient legal certainty and predictability in the application of the law. Comprehensive anti-corruption strategies as a means of upholding judicial independence is also urged.
(3) Ensure under the law the right to liberty and security without discrimination and to improve access to justice for vulnerable groups; guarantee the right of free and fair trial, and to put in place appropriate means of remedy and sanction for any violations of human rights.[176]

The resolution reflects the political mood in which it was conceived. It is less intended for operational planning and more for use in discussions in intergovernmental bodies and relations.

Taken as a whole the three different approaches to the issue of rule of law promotion, the 1994 framework, the 2004 common UN definition (including the

175 UNSG S/2006/980 p. 13.
176 Commission on Human Rights E/C.N.4 RES/2005 32 para 14.

2008 Guidance Note) and the 2005 Commission on Human Rights resolution, all illustrate the flexibility of the concept of the rule of law in relation to differing agendas. The 1994 framework was primarily designed for development cooperation, whereas the 2004 common definition was essentially adopted in response to the complex situations of UN governance of war to peace transitions. Both are operational, though the 1994 framework is more detailed in its institutional 'check-list' focus, while the common definition seeks to establish a normative foundation for UN engagement and activities in war-torn and crisis societies. It is difficult to assess the strength of the various definitions that have proceeded from the UN. Undoubtedly the common definition carries normative weight, though it has no sanctions or conditionality attached to it. What unites all three definitions is the position taken on the rule of law in its being not simply seen as a system of rules for ensuring procedural legality, but also as one that contains substantive values in terms of human rights.

On putting the policy into practical instructions, the Security Council plays an important part in defining and delineating rule of law through its authority to create peace-keeping or state-building missions.

Several of the early UN missions in the first half of the 1990s stated the need to work with judicial reform, police restructuring, penal reform and human rights promotion. In 1994, the UN Security Council established the United Nations Observer Mission in El Salvador with a mandate to monitor the implementation of the Agreement on Human Rights in El Salvador, with special emphasis on human rights protection.[177] UN Security Council resolution 865 in 1993 on Somalia noted that the re-establishment of the Somali police force was essential for the maintenance of peace, stability, law and order. The resolution also stated that the re-establishment of the judicial and penal system was critical for instituting security and stability.[178] A continued focus on reform of the police, judicial and penal systems was further confirmed in UN Security Council resolution 897 (1994).[179] In relation to both Rwanda[180] and Burundi[181] it called upon states to assist in the rehabilitation of the judicial system.

The work of peace-keeping and state-building missions in the early 1990s on legal and judicial reform was undertaken with no explicit reference to a comprehensive rule of law ideal. Instead, judicial reform, human rights protection and constitutional development were all encouraged and mandated in relation to peace-building objectives as defined in peace accords and by the UN Security Council. So in the latter half of the 1990s, when the UN Security Council began to uphold the rule of law as an all-embracing imperative, this objective had to relate to an already established practice in the field.

177 SC Res. 693 (1991).
178 SC Res. 865 (1993).
179 SC Res. 897 (1994).
180 SC Res. 997 (1995).
181 SC Res. 1012 (1995).

Since the late 1990s, practically every mandate from the Security Council refers to rule of law as a crucial peace-keeping and peace-building component. The Security Council's employment of the concept can be categorised in four categories: broad rule of law narratives presenting the rule of law as an important part of peace and reconciliation; its relation to impunity; as a functional criterion for security and law and order; and in relation to judicial, police and penal reform.[182] The following sections examine the four categories, building upon an empirical stock-taking of Security Council resolutions from 1960 to 2009.

Broad Rule of Law Narratives

On a general level, UN Security Council mandates refer to the rule of law as a constituent end. It is often mentioned together with other political objectives such as democracy, good governance and justice. Broad narratives of the rule of law appear more as political encouragement where the Security Council stresses the importance of adherence to the rule of law and welcomes and urges parties to treat is as a as a principle of governance, rather than as an operational directive. A typical example is that of the resolution on Burundi in 1996 which:

> Expresses its fullest support for the efforts of the Secretary-General and others...to facilitate a comprehensive political dialogue with the objective of promoting national reconciliation, democracy, security, and the rule of law in Burundi.[183]

Many similar resolutions emphasises the rule of law in relation to other principal objectives: as a standard setting for the cessation of hostilities;[184] on addressing the causes of armed conflict;[185] in relation to equality of access to justice (Iraq);[186] as a vital component of democracy (Haiti);[187] as the intrinsic element of a stable society (Haiti);[188] or consolidation of state authority by extending the rule of law throughout a given country (Liberia).[189]

The tradition of bundling together the rule of law as a broad narrative with other goals creates something of a hypothetical desire of all the aspects that a crisis-riven should strive towards and ultimately acquire. On Sierra Leone, the Security Council stressed the importance of extending full respect for the human rights of all people under the rule of law, in addition to taking effective action on criminal impunity and accountability, on the voluntary and

182 See Farrall 2009 pp. 144–145 on separation of UN Security Council rule of law definitions on the basis of law and order; ending impunity for crimes; resolving conflict through law; protecting and promoting human rights; and principled governance.

183 SC Res. 1040 (1996) para. 2.

184 SC Res. 1345 (2001) para. 5. See also, SC Res. 1711 (2006) para. 9.

185 SC Res. 1265 (1999) preamble.

186 SC Res. 1483 (2003) preamble.

187 SC Res. 1658 (2006) preamble.

188 SC Res. 1658 (2006) preamble; SC Res. 1702 (2006) preamble.

189 SC Res. 1777 (2007) preamble.

unhindered return of refugees and internally displaced persons, on the holding of free and fair elections and the formulation of a long-term plan for peace.[190] In other cases, the rule of law is made contingent upon the realisations of other political goals. In several UN Security Council mandates concerning the Democratic Republic of the Congo (DRC), elections are presented as the foundation for the long-term restoration of peace and stability and for the establishment of the rule of law.[191] In the Third Special Report of the Secretary-General on the United Nations Organisations Mission in the Democratic Republic of the Congo, it is stated: "The interpretation of UN Security Council resolution 1493 (2003) has been a major challenge for MONUC over the past year."[192] In this resolution, the Security Council gave MONUC the mandate to, *inter alia*, provide assistance for the reform of the security forces, the re-establishment of a state based upon the rule of law and for instituting preparations for the holding of elections.

In some cases the broad narratives are also formulated as directives to the UN mission. The task is then described in general terms, as in the directive to the staff of UNAMA in Angola where the mission was endorsed to "assist the Government of Angola in undertaking the following tasks: (1) Protection and Promotion of Human Rights and in the building of institutions to consolidate peace and enhance the rule of law".[193] Similarly in the DRC, MONUC was encouraged to provide assistance in the transition period in the reform of the security forces and the "re-establishment of a State based on the rule of law".[194] In a later resolution on the DRC the Security Council decided, in equally general terms, that MONUC would also be granted the mandate to "support the strengthening of democratic institutions and the rule of law".[195] Such vague and broad narratives of the rule of law, formulated as directives to UN missions, are also to be found in relation to Haiti,[196] Ivory Coast and Guinea-Bissau[197] and Liberia.[198]

The Security Council can also turn directly to a group of states for support in a particular war to peace transition.[199] This occurred in resolution 1653 (2006)

190 SC Res. 1346/ (2001) preamble; SC Res. 1370 (2001) preamble.
191 SC Res. 1621 (2005) preamble; SC Res. 1635 (2005) preamble; SC Res. 1649 (2005) preamble; SC Res. 1693 (2006) preamble; SC Res. 1711 (2006) preamble; SC Res. 1756 (2007) preamble; SC Res. 1794 (2007) preamble; SC Res. 1797 (2007) preamble; SC Res. 1671 (2006) preamble. See, also, SC Res. 1503 (2003) preamble, where strengthening national judicial systems is seen as being crucially important for the rule of law.
192 UNSG S/2004/650 p. 17.
193 SC Res. 1433 (2002) para 3 B.
194 SC Res. 1493 (2003) para. 5 italics added.
195 SC Res. 1756 (2007) para. 3; SC Res. 1794 (2007) para. 14.
196 SC Res. 1529 (2004) para. 4; SC Res. 1702 (2006) para. 11.
197 SC Res. 1580 (2004) para. 2 a.
198 SC Res. 1836 (2008) preamble.
199 SC Res. 1577 (2004) preamble; and SC Res. 1602 (2005) preamble. Both resolutions concern Burundi.

where the countries of the Great Lakes region were encouraged, individually and collectively, to strengthen and institutionalise respect for human rights and humanitarian law, including respect for women's rights and the protection of children affected by armed conflict, as well as the promotion of good governance and the rule of law.[200]

The use of broad narratives where rule of law is inserted alongside other objectives is in accord with the UN normative base for reform, including international human rights law, international criminal law, international humanitarian law and international refugee law.[201]

Rule of Law and the Notion of Impunity

The Security Council makes use of the rule of law concept in relation to the offence of impunity (the exemption from punishment or from the injurious consequences of an action). In Burundi,[202] and Guinea-Bissau,[203] the rule of law is invoked as a priority for ensuring accountability for violations of international humanitarian law, human rights, and atrocities. In other cases, eradicating impunity is framed as an important objective supporting the establishment of the rule of law.

The Security Council has repeatedly stated the need for reforming national judicial institutions, primarily to ensure judicial independence. In the context of Liberia, it urged the transitional government, once established, "to ensure that the protection of human rights and the establishment of a state based on the rule of law and of an independent judiciary are among its highest priorities".[204] A similar formulation was invoked in Haiti concerning judicial independence[205] and for reform of the Haitian national police force and the justice and correctional systems,[206] as well as calls on the establishment in Afghanistan for a "fair and transparent justice system, strengthen the rule of law throughout the country and eliminate impunity".[207]

Rule of law also forms part of general encouragement and support to hybrid courts (Sierra Leone and Burundi)[208] and international courts[209] for criminal

200 SC Res. 1653 (2006) para. 4.
201 UNSG S/2004/616 p. 5.
202 SC Res. 1545 (2004) preamble.
203 SC Res. 1580 (2004) preamble.
204 SC Res. 1509 (2003) preamble.
205 SC Res. 1542 (2004) preamble.
206 SC Res. 1608 (2005) preamble.
207 SC Res. 1806 (2008) para. 21.
208 SC Res. 1562 (2004) preamble; SC Res. 1610 (2005) preamble; SC Res. 1620 (2005) preamble; SC Res. 1734 (2006) preamble; SC Res. 1793 (2007) preamble. Clark 2007 p. 765 defines hybrid structures as usually involving "some type of international criminal tribunal and a locally-directed truth commission".
209 SC Res. 1593 (2005) preamble (in relation to Darfur).

prosecutions, or for broad calls on the international donor community to assist in ending impunity.[210]

On the one hand, the inclusion of the rule of law in relation to impunity suffers from the same broad generality as with the rule of law categories discussed above. Rule of law is included as if a consensus on its meaning was presupposed. One example is in the Security Council resolution for Sierra Leone, where the Security Council recalled its determination to end impunity, to establish the rule of law, and promote respect for human rights and maintain international peace and security.[211] On the other hand, references to the rule of law in relation to impunity are more clearly delineated to deal chiefly with the process of criminal proceedings whereby perpetrators of war crimes and human rights violations and atrocities are charged and brought to trial. The links here to both domestic and hybrid, or international judicial proceedings, are clear.

Security and Law and Order

Many resolutions include references to the rule of law, security, and law and order. This can be presented in a general way, as with the resolution on Africa in 1998, part of which stated: "Stressing the importance of promoting good governance, the rule of law and sustainable development as the essential factors in the prevention of conflicts in Africa".[212] Resolutions also frame the idea of the rule of law in the context of protection, and align the concept with other objectives such as human rights.

Resolutions on Angola stress the importance of strengthening the rule of law and human rights for the protection of its people.[213] Similarly, several resolutions with regard to Sierra Leone emphasise the importance of an effective extension of state authority throughout the country, including full respect for human rights under the rule of law, with particular attention paid to the protection of women and children.[214]

Linking the rule of law with security and law and order is more often formulated in specific directives, detailing strategies and focal areas, as compared with general formulations, or it is applied in relation to impunity. As such, a number of resolutions under the security and law and order cluster provide instructions, though not always that clear, to local authorities or UN mission staff. For example, in the DRC a Security Council resolution condemned the exploitation of ethnic differences in the carrying out of violence and called

210 SC Res. 1606 (2005) preamble.
211 SC Res. 1689 (2006) preamble.
212 SC Res. 1170 (1998) preamble.
213 SC Res. 1213 (1998) para 6; SC Res. 1149 (1998) para 4; SC Res. 1157 (1998) para 11; SC Res. 1173 (1998) para 8; SC Res. 1180 (1998) preamble; SC Res. 1202 (1998) para 11.
214 SC Res. 1400 (2007) preamble; SC Res. 1436 (2002) preamble; SC Res. 1470 (2003) preamble.

on the de facto authorities in the regions concerned "to ensure the protection of civilians and the rule of law".[215]

Often these missives are directed towards the support of police forces, correctional systems[216] or for the purposes of reforming the security sector so that it can and will protect citizens and respect the rule of law and the constitution.[217] Recent resolutions on Afghanistan exemplify this well. In one, the Security Council "welcomes [...] efforts to increase their capabilities as important steps towards the goal of an Afghan security force providing security and ensuring the rule of law throughout the country."[218] Another set of resolutions on Afghanistan stresses the reformation of the security and prison sectors as being important activities for enhancing respect for the rule of law.[219]

With the rule of law and its security focus, crime and violence is central. This is seen clearly in Afghanistan where the Security Council welcomed the decision of the European Union to establish a mission for policing and police reform "with the linkages to the wider rule of law and counter narcotics".[220] It is also in Afghanistan that extremist violence and terrorism are linked to direct threats to the rule of law.[221] In Haiti, the questions of due process, respect for human rights and the necessity of dealing firmly with rising crime rates are all seen as essential to ensuring the rule of law and security.[222] While on the DRC, the Security Council called upon that country's government in a set of resolutions, to ensure security and protect its citizens according to the rule of law.[223]

Judicial and Other Institutional Reforms

While the three rule of law categories discussed above bind the concept to central political imperatives, either by describing the rule of law in broad narratives – for example on the fight against impunity, or in relation to increased security – the fourth realm is different. In this, the rule of law is described in practical institutional terms. References to it are also more direct, as shown in the resolution where the UN mission in Afghanistan is requested to institute universally fair and open justice, and to reconstruct the prison system, both in order to strengthen the rule of law throughout the country.[224]

Judicial and other institutional reforms is a strategy for rule of law assistance that has been adopted even in the most difficult of situations. The mandate for

215 UNSG S/RES1417/2002 para 5.
216 SC Res. 1542 (2004) preamble; SC Res. 1812 (2008) para. 13; and SC Res. 1870 (2009) para 19.
217 SC Res. 1756 (2007) para. 8.
218 SC Res. 1746 (2007) para 10; SC Res. 1806 (2008) para 15.
219 SC Res. 1776 (2007) preamble; SC Res. 1806 (2008) para 22.
220 SC Res. 1746 (2007) para. 11.
221 SC Res. 1776 (2007) preamble; SC Res. 1806 (2008) preamble; SC Res. 1833 (2008) preamble.
222 SC Res. 1780 (2007) preamble.
223 SC Res. 1756 (2007) preamble; SC Res. 1794 (2007) preamble; SC Res. 1807 (2008) preamble.
224 SC Res. 1589 (2005) para. 9.

the United Nations Mission in Darfur exemplifies how the rule of law rhetoric is employed in the most inhospitable of environments, stating that the Secretary-General was to "assist in the promotion of the rule of law in Darfur, including through support for strengthening an independent judiciary and the prison system, and assist in the development and consolidation of the legal framework".[225]

The main thrust of the institutionalisation of the rule of law in UN Security Council mandates emphasises the judiciary as a key agency. Extending support to judicial reform as a rule of law strategy takes many different forms. One is from Bosnia and Herzegovina, where the Security Council established a court-monitoring programme.[226] Another is the calling for training and specialisation and of national lawyers and judges in East Timor.[227] From such specifics, resolutions also delve into general comments. A set of resolutions directed at assistance to Ivory Coast, the Security Council decides that the UNOCI mandate should be that of law and order and assist in re-establishing both the authority of the judiciary and the rule of law in all parts of the country.[228]

While not mentioning any particular standards relating to reform of the judiciary, a number of resolutions point specifically to the need for judicial independence.[229] On the DRC one of them declares that the establishment of a state based upon the rule of law and an independent judiciary should be of the highest priorities.[230] References to the importance of judicial integrity are also seen on Afghanistan[231] (fair and transparent) Sudan[232] (independent) and Chad,[233] to mention a few.

While promoting standards of fairness and independence, Security Council resolutions also call for a strengthening of institutional capacity within the judiciary, police and correctional systems, together with the executive and legislative branches of government. Resolutions on Guinea-Bissau,[234] Sierra Leone,[235] Haiti,[236] Burundi,[237] and Afghanistan[238] all contain references to strengthening the rule of law by building on the justice sector. In a resolution on Haiti, MINUSTAH was encouraged to explore the possibilities of "modernising

225 SC Res. 1706 (2006) para. 8 (k).
226 SC Res. 1168 (1998) para. 4.
227 SC Res. 1867 (2009) para 9.
228 SC Res. 1528 (2004) para. 6 (q); SC Res. 1609 (2005) para 2; SC Res. 1739 (2007) para. 2 (m).
229 SC Res. 1778 (2007) para 2 (g).
230 SC Res. 1493 (2003) para. 11.
231 SC Res. 1536 (2004) para. 5.
232 SC Res. 1706 (2006) para. 8.
233 SC Res. 1778 (2007) para 2 (g).
234 SC Res. 1580 (2004) para. 2 (h).
235 SC Res. 1620 (2005) para I (v).
236 SC Res. 1542 (2004) para. 8 (b).
237 SC Res. 1719 (2006) para. 2 (d).
238 SC Res. 1662 (2006) para. 11; SC Res. 1746 (2007) para. 13.

and strengthening the judiciary and correctional systems, including through provisions of targeted technical assistance to rule of law institutions".[239]

A number of resolutions also use the ambiguous term 'legal reform' with which to strengthen the rule of law. In both Liberia[240] and Sudan[241] the UN missions were mandated to assist in developing strategies to consolidate the legal framework. In Iraq, UNAMI[242] had the mandate conferred upon it to promote legal reform in order to strengthen the rule of law, while MINUSTAH in Haiti[243] was mandated to assist, through technical expertise, the review of all relevant legislation on the judiciary. This particular mandate for MINUSTAH is one of the few times when the UN Security Council has been specific on designating areas of legal reform.[244]

COUNCIL OF EUROPE

If the UN is characterised by pluralism in respect to how the rule of law concept is used by different agencies of the UN family, the Council of Europe is more focused. This can partly be explained by the fact that the European Court of the Human Rights provides normative guidance and clarification on a number of rule of law questions.

Central to the work of the Council of Europe is the preparation and conclusion of treaties and conventions. The most salient of its conventions is the European Convention for the Protection of Human Rights and Fundamental Freedoms (1950) and the European Social Charter (1961). To this a host of other agreements can be added relating to corruption, patent, extradition and state immunity.

The Council of Europe has since its inception counted on the rule of law as a practised system as one criterion for membership. In Article 3 of the Statute of the Council of Europe it is stated: "Every member of the Council of Europe must accept the principles of the rule of law and of the enjoyment by all persons within its jurisdiction of human rights and fundamental freedoms".[245] The normative force behind this paragraph is difficult to define. Though states must demonstrate that they are functioning democracies and respect the rule of law when applying for membership to the Council of Europe, a policy to lobby new members 'from the inside' rather than to refuse membership seems to be the standard.[246]

239 SC Res. 1658 (2006) preamble.

240 SC Res. 1509 (2003) para. 3 (q).

241 SC Res. 1590 (2005) para 4 (viii).

242 SC Res. 1637 (2005) preamble; SC Res. 1723 (2006) preamble.

243 SC Res. 1702 (2006) para. 14.

244 See, also, SC Res. 1840 (2008) para 17 calling for a reorganisation and standardisation of court registration processes and the management of cases.

245 Statute of the Council of Europe Art. 3.

246 MacMullen 2004 p. 410f.

Following the demise of the Soviet Union in the early 1990s, states have been admitted on the basis that they have committed themselves to practicing and upholding the necessary standards.[247]

The Council of Europe has actively contributed to the promotion of the rule of law through the enactment of resolutions, recommendations and other instruments relating to rule of law standards. This 'soft law' standard-setting maintains a strong persuasive force. The Council of Europe also works actively through the so-called Venice Commission with technical assistance on constitutional matters and reviewing draft laws.[248] A substantive reading of the rule of law principles has been repeatedly confirmed in the case law of the European Court of the Human Rights. The Court has made clear that the rule of law, identified as one of the essential elements in a democratic society, is inherent in all articles of the European Convention.

The Council of Europe has not attempted to establish a common definition comparable to the efforts of the UN secretariat. References to rule of law must therefore be detracted from the 'soft law' generated by the organisation and statements in authoritative policy documents. In the 2006 document, Building Europe Together on the Rule of Law, the Council of Europe identified five prioritised areas of rule of law promotion:

(1) The legal framework and organisation of a democratic state;
(2) The legal relations between individuals and the state;
(3) The independence and operation of justice;
(4) The scientific revolution and legal protection of individuals and
(5) The rule of law and the citizen's security.

In the same document the Council of Europe delineates further the components of the rule of law as consisting of the following: the supremacy of law, especially in the administrative area; an independent judiciary; a legal order guaranteeing the protection of fundamental rights; protection of human values and security and finally, access to justice.[249]

The Council of Europe operates on a more general policy level (compared to the UN), perhaps a reflection of the constituting charter of the organisation. While the UN has come to deal with situations where it acts as a substitute for national governments, which requires some form of operational clarity, the

247 Once a state becomes a member, the Council of Europe has the power to sanction in the case of a violation of the membership criteria as stipulated in Art. 3 and through Art. 8.

248 European Commission for Democracy through Law, established in 1990 as a partial agreement of 18 member states of the Council of Europe. Its mandate was revised through Council of Europe Resolution (00) 3. See also, Venice Commission 2011 Report on the Rule of Law.

249 CoE 2006.

Council of Europe is primarily involved in providing assistance and advice to its member states.

The Council of Europe works with a broader definition than the UN in the sense that it explicitly includes public administrative agencies and administrative law and not just the institutions of the justice sector. In its resolution (31) of 1977, the Council of Europe emphasised the importance of the rule of law in public administration, since more people encounter and are affected by such agencies and by administrative decisions than they are by the courts.[250] A number of resolutions have also been adopted pertaining to rule of law issues in administrative and civil law matters. An illustrative recommendation is the (7) 2007 On Good Administration with the attached Code of Good Administration. The Code specifies a set of procedures and substantive principles that should bind all administrative agencies, including lawfulness, impartiality, proportionality, on decisions made within a reasonable time, as well as the judicial review of administrative acts.[251] Moreover, the European Court of Human Rights has in several cases confirmed the importance of a right to fair trial principles in relation to administrative decisions and tribunals.[252]

EUROPEAN UNION

The European Union (EU) in its Treaty of the European Union inserted the concept of the rule of law, together with liberty, democracy, human rights and fundamental freedoms, as the foundational values upon which the Union is built.

It is not easy to define what the rule of law means to the EU.[253] Before the conception of the EU, the European Community made scant reference to it. The function and status of the rule of law was given significant weight with the start of new membership negotiations during the 1990s. Since then the concept has been repeatedly referred to in political commitments and declarations by Community institutions.[254]

EU Enlargement and the Rule of Law

Respect for the rule of law is a condition of membership of the European Union. The criteria elaborated by the European Council in its Copenhagen Meeting in 1993 asserted that candidate countries should have achieved stability of

250 CoE Resolution (77) 31.
251 CoE Resolution (07) 7.
252 For example, in Serghides and Christotorou v. Cyprus, Judgement on 5 November 2000 A/98.
253 See Wennerström 2007 p. 34.
254 The dimension of the rule of law as an essential component within the EU/EC falls outside the scope of this work. For a thorough description see Wennerström 2007.

institutions guaranteeing democracy, the rule of law as well as the existence of a functioning market economy.[255]

In practical terms the membership requirements contain one political and one economic component. The European Commission, the institution responsible for membership negotiations, established a policy for measuring financial support to rule of law reforms in candidate countries. Under this policy the rule of law is divided into five main components:

(1) The principle that all acts by public authorities are founded in and subject to the law;
(2) A system of separation of powers;
(3) Respect for fundamental rights and freedoms;
(4) Independence of the judiciary;
(5) Measures against corruption.[256]

Besides the enlargement process, a material rule of law became an essential condition following when human rights became the prevailing trend in EU external relations.[257] In the Commission Communication to the Council and Parliament in 1998, the rule of law was placed within the context of democracy and human rights, with a defined list of broad institutional conditions. Among them were:

(i) A legislature that respects and gives full effect to human rights and fundamental freedoms;
(ii) An independent judiciary;
(iii) Effective and accessible means of legal recourse;
(iv) A legal system that guarantees equality before the law;
(v) A prison system that respects the human person;
(vi) A police force at the service of the law;
(vii) An effective executive that enforces the law and capable of establishing the social and economic conditions necessary for life in society.[258]

255 Council of the European Union in Copenhagen 21–22 June 1993 SN 180/1/93 REV 1 Art. 7 (iii).

256 Wennerström 2007 pp. 175ff.

257 See e.g. Partnership Agreement Between the Members of the African, Caribbean and Pacific Group of States of the One Part, and the European Community and Its Members of the Other Part, Cotonou, 2000 (hereinafter Cotonou Agreement), Art. 9 (1). And the legal basis is found in TEU Art. 11 (1): "The Union shall define and implement a common foreign and security policy covering all areas of foreign and security policy, the objectives of which shall be: [...] – to develop and consolidate democracy and the rule of law, and respect for human rights and fundamental freedoms".

258 Commission Communication to the Council and Parliament COM (98) 146 p. 4.

Rule of Law and Conditionally in Development Cooperation

Rule of law is also part of the EU's development agreements. The Cotonou Agreement with African, Caribbean and the Pacific group of states, for example, is based upon the respect for human rights, democratic principles and the rule of law. Any failure to fulfil an obligation arising from these conditions can result in suspension of the Agreement.[259] The rule of law is presented in the Agreement as a sub-component of good governance, constituted by the existence of effective and accessible means of legal redress; an independent legal system guaranteeing equality before the law and: an executive that is wholly subject to the law.

One example where a breach led to the adoption of certain measures is that of Liberia. The European Council decision of 2002 stipulated that the Liberian government had taken certain actions that violated rule of law obligations under the Agreement.[260] Among other things the Council decisions held that numerous human rights abuses had occurred and criminal impunity enjoyed among the security forces. The Council decision also voiced concern over the lack of transparency in the public accounting system, corruption, mismanagement of national resources, and exploitation by monopolies.[261]

Fearing that assessments of rule of law compliance in its development agreements would cause conflicts and arbitrary application, the Commission developed a 'check-list' for an early warning reporting system so that consultations with states at risk might be instigated. In the check-list, four rather crude 'control' questions are included: How strong is the judicial system? Does unlawful state violence exist? Does civilian power control security forces? Does organised crime undermine the country's stability?[262]

Crisis Management and Rule of Law Reform

The EU has begun to take on a rapidly growing responsibility in relation to state-building in war to peace transitions. In June 2004 the first EU rule of law mission was launched in Georgia, the so-called EU Rule of Law Mission in Georgia (EUJUST THEMIS).[263] The EUJUST THEMIS centred on three topics: guidance on criminal justice reform; support to the co-ordinating role of Georgian authorities in the area of judicial reform and anti-corruption; and support planning for new legislation – for example criminal procedure law.[264]

---

259 Cotonou Agreement Art. 96: 2 (a).

260 European Council Decision 274/2002. The decision includes a long list of measures to be taken by the Liberian government.

261 European Council decision 274/2002 Annex.

262 Wennerström 2007 p. 261.

263 Earlier missions in crisis environments have predominantly consisted of a police or military presence. See Wennerström 2007 p. 272ff for an overview.

264 See Council Joint Action 2004/523/CFSP.

This rule of law mission was followed by a mission in Iraq, EU integrated Rule of Law Mission in Iraq (EUJUST LEX), consisting of the training of judges and other middle ranking to high level officials in criminal investigation techniques.[265] Both of these unusual missions made use of the rule of law concept mostly in criminal justice. The latest EU rule of law mission has been the European Union Rule of Law Mission to Kosovo (EULEX).[266] The main responsibility for EULEX is to fight organised crime, strengthen customs services and support the police and judiciary.[267] Arguably, wider instances of rule of law deficiencies exist throughout the state bureaucracy of Kosovo and it is unclear how the lack of access to justice in administrative system will be put right, or which organisation or national agency that will do it. Within the Common Security and Defence Policy, and interesting development is the 2011 EU Concept for CSDP Justice Missions. Through this concept the EU adopts the UN 2004 definition of the rule of law and identifies a set of areas that are of primary importance for EU rule of law work in crisis management.[268]

The rule of law concept of the EU has many aspects and changes form and focus, depending on where it is applied or promoted. In this way the EU conceptualisation of the rule of law resembles UN policy. As with the UN, the EU is not a single normative order but "a set of normative orders or normative sub-orders".[269] In enlargement processes, the concept has come to signify a clear set of necessary marks that candidate countries must achieve, including measures to fight and defeat corruption. In external relations, development co-operation and trade, the rule of law is more of a declaratory norm used in combination with other "contested concepts" such as human rights and democracy. When put to the test, as in the Cotonou Agreement or in the rule of law mission to Kosovo, it is translated to take in the concepts of stability, law and order, criminal justice and security.

ORGANIZATION FOR SECURITY AND COOPERATION IN EUROPE

The OSCE has its origins in the Conference on Security and Cooperation in Europe (CSCE). In 1975 the CSCE established the Helsinki Process aimed at

---

265 Council Joint Action 2005/190/CFSP.

266 Council Joint Action 2008/124/CFSP.

267 Ibid., Art. 3 set out the tasks of the EULEX mission. The list is geared towards criminal justice and includes measures to fight crime, inter-ethnic crime, ensure public order and security, strengthen cooperation and coordination throughout the whole judicial process, and anti-corruption. All activities should respect international standards on human rights and gender mainstreaming.

268 Council Document 1873/10 2011. Some of the areas include, for example, legal framework, transitional justice, human rights law, international humanitarian law, international criminal law.

269 Wennerström 2007 p. 157.

securing peaceful coexistence between western and eastern Europe. In the early stages of the CSCE, the rule of law was more of a political instrument in discussions between parties in the West and East. With the fall of the Berlin wall in 1989 came an incentive for exploring and delving deeper into the concept's point and function.[270] The CSCE stated in the early 1990s that the rule of law should be perceived as a concept resting firmly upon substantive values:

> The rule of law does not mean merely a formal legality, which assumes regularity and consistency in the achievement and enforcement of democratic order, but justice based on the recognition and full acceptance of the supreme value of the human personality and guaranteed by institutions providing a framework for its fullest expression.[271]

The OSCE has also attempted to define the notion on a more operational basis. Similar to the UN and the EU, in the face of a growing responsibility in crisis environments, the OSCE has been seeking a clearer and more practically attuned rule of law framework to guide its missions and field activities. OSCE field activities are wide and include support to bar associations, judicial monitoring, support for legislative initiatives and a strengthening of the system for the protection of minorities. The OSCE is also involved in the observation of elections and electoral assistance by way of its Office for Democratic Institutions and Human Rights.[272] Most notably the OSCE, in addition to its missions in Georgia, Moldavia and other countries has also shouldered a heavy responsibility in the UN transitional administration in Kosovo, where it was given responsibility under the institution-building pillar.[273]

In the document OSCE Human Dimension Commitments, some of the dominant features of a rule of law definition from the OSCE perspective are stipulated. These include, on a rather detailed and operational level:

(i) The supremacy of law and that government, judiciary and the administration comply with the constitution and act in accordance with the law;
(ii) The principle of the separation of powers;
(iii) Civilian control over armed forces;
(iv) Human rights and fundamental freedoms guaranteed by law;
(v) Publicising and making accessible all legislative acts;
(vi) Administrative decisions must be justifiable and indicate legal remedies;
(vii) Equality before the law and active measures against discrimination;

270 The Charter of Paris for a New Europe 1990 p. 3.
271 1990 Copenhagen Meeting of the Conference of the Human Dimensions of the CSE, 1 (2).
272 OSCE 2005 OSCE Human Dimension Commitments p. xxii.
273 SC Res. 1244 (1999) and OSCE Permanent Council Decision No. 305 1999.

(viii) Independence of the legal profession;
(ix) Ensuring fair trial principles in criminal procedures, in particular the right of habeas corpus.[274]

No legal obligations stem from OSCE documents, yet they carry significant weight in war to peace transitions where the declaratory policy is transformed into practical measures (as in Kosovo under a UN Security Council mandate). The OSCE has taken upon itself a growing responsibility for conflict settlement and reconstruction. Similar to the Council of Europe, it also includes civil law, governance and rule of law in the public administration, though a little more tentatively. In the Sixteenth Meeting of the Ministerial Council in Helsinki 2008, the importance of the rule of law in public administration was included among a number of other objectives for rule of law strengthening in the OSCE-wider area.[275]

INTERNATIONAL FINANCIAL INSTITUTIONS

International financial institutions, including the IMF, the International Bank for Reconstruction and Development (IBRD/ the World Bank) and regional development banks (e.g. European Bank for Reconstruction and Development, and Asian Development Bank) are becoming increasingly engaged in rule of law reform in war-torn societies. The focus of international financial institutions on rule of law assistance is different compared with other organisations. While the UN, EU, the Council of Europe and OSCE are primarily focused on political and security matters, international financial institutions emphasise the rule of law in relation to economic growth and development.

Among the international financial institutions, the World Bank is the most influential actor in war to peace transitions.[276] It was established as a specialised agency within the UN system following the Bretton Woods Conference of 1946. The essential purpose was to support post-second world war reconstruction. This mandate has since evolved and now embraces the granting of loans to developing countries for various projects from the energy sector to law and development.[277]

Under the Articles of Agreement, in art. IV (10), certain activities are prohibited. The article states that the World Bank and its officers "shall not interfere in the political affairs of any member [only] economic considerations

[274] The commitments are derived from seminal meetings, i.e. at Copenhagen 1990, Moscow 1991, and Budapest 1994.
[275] OSCE 2008 Ministerial Committee Decision No. 7/08.
[276] Though the IMF is also of importance. Membership of the Bank is not possible without first being a member of the IMF. See art II, para 1 of the IBRD's Articles of Agreement.
[277] The International Finance Corporation and the International Development Association complement the World Bank.

shall be relevant to their decisions". This apparently bars the Bank from engaging in any form of support for projects involving 'social dimensions' of law – that is, the promotion of gender reform and human rights, or to impose conditionality on loan agreements pertaining to 'political' matters. For a long time the World Bank retained a reasonably 'pure' economic stance. However, the experience of structural adjustment programmes and the ensuing critique of the Washington Consensus began to mark a shift towards creative 'lawyering' in reinterpreting the Articles of Agreement. With the introduction of governance reform and in particular the matter of the rule of law in its 1992 report Governance and Development, rule of law is now considered necessary for providing security for economic development.

Though the World Bank has been a dominant player in development co-operation, engagement in war to peace transitions first emerged towards the end of the 1990s.[278] Two events brought about that commitment. The first was when the Bank was approached to administer a host-fund of international assistance for reconstruction in the West Bank and Gaza in 1994. A year later the World Bank was asked to take a lead, in cooperation with the European Commission, to plan and coordinate international support to post-war Bosnia and Herzegovina.[279] Since then the Bank has been an active participant in a number of war to peace transitions, either as a provider of funds or as a more direct partner in supporting specific projects and programmes.

On a more operational level the World Bank works with rule of law reform based upon two categories: judicial reform and legal reform. The former component is where most of the resources are invested. The aim here is to create an effective and efficient judicial system, by supporting standards of integrity within the judiciary, including confidence in court administration procedures, by encouraging openness in court proceedings, and in supporting other means of dispute resolution. On legal reform, most investment finds its way in the drafting and reform of commercial law, but also in training initiatives and the support of law reform councils.[280]

The World Bank defines the rule of law in a more or less formal way. Four criteria make up the rule of law definition in its declaratory statements:

(1) the government is itself bound by the law;
(2) every person in society is treated equally under the law;
(3) the human dignity of each individual is recognised and protected by law;
(4) justice is accessible to all.

278 For a general overview of the commitment of international financial institutions in war-torn societies, see Boon 2007.
279 World Bank 2004, The Role of the World Bank in Conflict and Development, p. 4.
280 See World Bank 2002, Legal and Judicial Reform p. 28f.

Furthermore, the World Bank concludes that the rule of law requires transparent legislation, fair laws, predictable enforcement, and the accountability of governments.[281] The World Bank, it seems, attaches importance not only to the formal and procedural aspects of the rule of law, but also to the contents of laws. It often argues for substantive legal economic reform, for example, and a strict formal interpretation of the rule of law concept would limit its reach of engaging in comprehensive reform under the economic and good governance objective. The concept would lose its function as a facilitator of economic development if the substantively 'right' types of law such as contract, securities, bankruptcy, and company law were not inserted as important prerequisites of the rule of law.[282] As a reflection of its mandate and articles of agreement, the focus on rule of law programmes and projects in development cooperation (for both reimbursable and non-reimbursable credits) is towards reform of the legal and administrative regulatory regime of the economic and public sector.

This perspective is also to be found in the World Bank's engagement after war and crisis under its Low Income Countries under Stress Initiative. As such, the World Bank focus is separated from the rule of law programmes of other international actors, which are more concerned with criminal justice, human rights and security. At the same time, the reference to human dignity in the World Bank conceptualisation, as well as other references to the protection of human rights, muddies the waters of the Bank's image as that of purely an economically centred organisation.

Through a reinterpretation of the Articles of Agreement 'social issues' and human rights are also seen as interlinked with economic performance, since they are considered to be a constitutive goal in development. They are perceived to be vital for a particular political climate with the potential to attract international investment capital, and are assumed to contribute to better economic development outcomes.

BILATERAL AID AGENCIES

Bilateral aid agencies often refer to the rule of law in a declaratory form through the particular agency's policy documents.[283] Operational definitions are sometimes difficult to identify and must instead be sought from a deduction of

281 World Bank 2004, Initiatives in Legal and Judicial Reform p. 3.

282 See Ohnesorge 2007 p. 14.5ff.

283 Excluded from this discussion are non-governmental organisations (NGOs). A rich crop of NGOs has emerged in recent years to work on rule of law reform, but they do not carry the same weight as international organisations, financial institutions and states' bilateral aid agencies. An exception might be some of the more influential NGOs such as the American Bar Association (ABA) and the Ford Foundation. The ABA, through its Central and Eastern European Legal Initiative (CEELI) programme, has been involved in several rule of law reform activities.

various rule of law practices and activities falling under a democracy and governance support, justice and security, or under a rights-based approach.

The most influential actors in the field of rule of law promotion in war-torn societies are the DfID and the USAID. They have made attempts at defining the concept so as to guide their work in legal, judicial and administrative assistance.[284]

USAID considers the rule of law to consist of seven conditions:

(1) Where the social contract is observed by citizens and the state authority alike;
(2) Where the terms of the social contract are enforced either voluntarily or by legal processes;
(3) Where violations of the contract are punished according to the law;
(4) That basic human rights are protected;
(5) Where market-based economic activity is enabled;
(6) Where justice is accessible to all.[285]

In that declaratory policy, the rule of law is integrated with broader social and political frameworks of governance. To promote it, USAID assumes an institutional approach at the operational level that concentrates on ensuring that constitutions and laws in force comply with basic international human rights norms. It is concerned with providing assistance in legislative drafting that conforms to sound economic norms (e.g. the protection of property, sanctity of contracts and laws that promote timely and efficient dispute resolution), strengthening of equal access to justice by increasing the supply of services, information and the elimination of barriers such as informal and formal institutional biases, and supporting effective and fair legal institutions able to solve disputes in a timely, predictable, and reliable manner while upholding principles that ensure equality of access to justice.[286]

DfID, in comparison, pursues a more holistic approach to the rule of law. It is an integrated concept in broader strategies of safety, security and poverty reduction. In Justice and Poverty Reduction, published in 2000, equitable and accessible justice institutions are emphasised as a core strategy. DfID also focuses on non-state justice organisations and on the importance of strengthening those justice delivery institutions that enjoy legitimacy and the trust of the people.[287]

---

284 Other bilateral agencies with a significant function in rule of law assistance in general are the German Gemeinschaft fur Technische Zusammenarbeit (GZT) and the Australian Agency for International Development (AUSAID).

285 USAID 1998 p. 19.

286 See USAID 2008, Guide to Rule of Law Country Analysis p. 7 in describing the essential elements of the rule of law as consisting of order and security; legitimacy; checks and balances; fairness; and effective application.

287 DfID 2000 pp.13–15. See also, DfID 2010.

DfID and USAID are united with other actors described above in that they often assume a justice and security institutional stance. From the perspective of USAID this institutional centring concerns mainly formal state institutions, and for DfID both state and informal non-state agencies play a significant part in rule of law reform. Similarly, as with most of the players discussed above, the rule of law is chiefly seen as being of relevance in relation criminal justice. Even in the DfID 2002 publication Safety, Security and Accessible Justice: Putting Policy into Practice, which purports to provide guidelines for a new strategy to make justice systems work better for poor people, the role of the broader administrative and regulatory framework of the state appears little more than as a correlating device to the justice sector.[288]

PEACE AGREEMENTS

Over the past 15 years the number of peace agreements following intrastate conflicts has grown. It is important for three reasons to include peace agreements in the examination of how the rule of law is conceptualised by international participants in war-torn societies.[289] First, while peace agreements are primarily 'contracts' between national actors, they are often brokered and drafted with international support. This international influence makes peace agreements an additional source that can affect how the rule of law is conceptualised. Second, peace agreements also provide an understanding of so-called root causes to a conflict or crisis, and the methods by which these should be remedied in a transitional period. Peace agreements can also illustrate how national actors perceive rule of law issues. Third, peace agreements often function as interim constitutional frameworks – or sometimes as more permanent frameworks, as in Bosnia and Herzegovina. As such, peace agreements carry a certain normative weight in a war to peace transition.

Bell contends that peace agreements are "clearly defined documents" and that the common features and usage suggest a certain legal practice, a "lex pacificatoria".[290] This has importance for the compliance of agreements and for their status as documents, whether in the internal constitutional context or at international level. Peace agreements are political compromises that seek to reconcile what are often conflicting views between different warring sides. Generally, their objective is:

288 The policies of DfID and USAID cannot be taken to apply to all other bilateral state aid agencies. It is also worth noting that on the rule of law conceptualisation excluding other areas – for example public administration – USAID has recently developed an administrative law guide for its officers in this area. See USAID 2008, Using Administrative Law Tools and Concepts.

289 The term 'peace agreement' is not clearly defined in the legal doctrine. See, Bell 2006 p. 376ff.

290 Bell 2006 p. 407f (italics original).

(i) to sustain a cease-fire;
(ii) provide a framework for governance that attends to the root causes of conflict;
(iii) demilitarisation; and
(iv) to provide for new constitutional structures, including governance, elections, transitional arrangements on power sharing and on legal matters concerning human rights, the structure and composition of the judiciary and the applicable legal framework.[291]

Many peace agreement objectives relate to the rule of law and vary from broad declarations on a par with UN Security Council resolutions, to detailed lists of intentions for specific reforms. The cumulative study of 27 peace agreements by the CMI Chr. Michelsen Institute illustrates how issues relating to reforms in the justice sector are frequently included in different accords. Almost all accords (85 per cent) include at least one provision related to such reform. Public administration and governance is also included in most cases (70 per cent) but is more generally found in 'new' accords, with emphasis on civil service reform, reorganisation of public administration, anti-corruption policies and strategies for revenue collection.[292]

Most peace agreements include third-party signatories. A state or an international organisation signs as 'observer' or 'guarantor'. Another form of international involvement is to link the peace agreement to UN Security Council resolutions. This has been the case in Kosovo, East Timor and Afghanistan, where these respective agreements became part of a UN Security Council mandate. What effect this has on peace agreements is unclear. It may well influence the agreement in its taking a certain form and content that reflects current trends on the international agenda, while third-party signatories can reinforce the parts played by 'outside' states and organisations as 'norm promoters'. In other cases peace agreements might also function as control and assessment markers, allowing for international supervisions and diplomatic pressure. One example is the 2005 UN Security Council resolution, in which the Council called upon the president of the Ivory Coast not to remain in office for longer than 12 months, and stressed that the 'consensus' prime minister should have all the necessary powers of a head of state, in accordance with the Linas Marcoussis agreement, until presidential elections could be held.[293]

Peceny and Stanley use Central America as an example of outside agencies acting as norm-promoters and contend that peace accords concluded with international involvement follow a certain path where norm promotion is visible. First, local actors adopt 'liberal practices' in order to position themselves as legitimate interlocutors on the international plane. Second, mediations involving

291 Bell 2006 p. 377.
292 Suhrke, Wimpelmann & Dawes 2007 pp. 23–24.
293 SC Res. 1633 (2005) para. 8.

international or third-party actors persuade adversaries to abstain from violence and move towards political competition according to the 'rules of the game'. Third, international participants such as the UN become involved in substantive efforts to support the course of peace process.[294] According to this perspective, certain types of concept, such as 'justice', 'democracy', 'gender' or 'rule of law', are at times inserted into agreements because by doing so local actors seek to generate international legitimacy.[295]

The concept of the rule of law appears in a number of peace agreements but typically without any form of definition. Most often it is put together with other aspirational values. In the Arusha Peace and Reconciliation Agreement for Burundi (the Arusha Agreement) of 2000, the following reference is found: "In its functioning, the Government shall respect the separation of powers, the rule of law, and the principles of good governance and transparency in the management of public affairs." Rule of law is here treated as supremacy of law, and a lack of respect for the rule of law is singled out as one factor causing conflict.[296]

Similarly, in the preambular paragraph of the peace agreement for Liberia (the Accra Agreement) the parties reaffirm "the objective of promoting better relations among ourselves by ensuring a stable political environment in which our people can live in freedom under the law".[297] In the Bonn Agreement for Afghanistan, the only explicit reference made is in relation to the establishment of a Judicial Commission, where it is said that the commission will rebuild the Afghan justice system in accordance with Islamic principles, international standards, the rule of law and Afghan legal traditions.[298]

While the rule of law is only referred to as a sub-component, or not explicitly mentioned at all, peace agreements often contain rule of law principles – that is, legality, the separation of powers, legal certainty, legal equality and the protection of fundamental rights and freedoms. As such, the Bonn Agreement attempted to settle the issue surrounding the applicable law by declaring that the Constitution from 1964 would apply (except for the provisions relating to the monarchy, legislative and executive bodies) and that the previous law in force would continue to apply insofar as it did not contradict the agreement, the constitution or those international treaties to which Afghanistan was a party.[299]

---

294 Peceny & Stanley 2001 p. 151.

295 The studies by Dezalay and Garth show that local actors often adopt 'international strategies' in order to build their power at home. Dezalay & Garth 2002 p. 7.

296 Arusha Agreement Protocol II Chapter I Art. 2 (5).

297 Comprehensive Peace Agreement Between the Government of Liberia and the Liberians United for Reconciliation and Democracy (LURD) and the Movement for Democracy in Liberia (MODEL) and Political Parties, Accra, 18 August 2003 (hereinafter the Accra Agreement).

298 Agreement on Provisional Arrangements in Afghanistan Pending the re-establishment of Government Institutions, 2000 (hereinafter the Bonn Agreement) Art. II (2).

299 Bonn Agreement, Art. II.

The Arusha Agreement, one of the most detailed and comprehensive agreements, contains a list of legal, judicial and administrative reform measures such as a charter of fundamental rights; provisions relating to the structure and composition of the judiciary, including appointments, training, and the official language of the court; rules relating to public administration and principles of behaviour for civil servants (efficiency, courtesy, impartiality and equity); setting up an ombudsperson; and rules for the legislative and executive powers.[300]

The Accra Agreement and the Linas-Marcoussis Agreement also contain provisions for certain rule of law reforms to be implemented during a transitional period. The former calls for the establishment of a governance reform commission to promote good governance and to ensure accountability and transparency, which would also act as a form of ombudsman.[301] The latter agreement provides for a review of the administration of citizenship and land tenures that, as noted in the agreement, had failed to abide by the law, were inconsistent, unclear discriminatory.[302]

The absence of attempts at defining the rule of law in peace agreements might be because there is simply no need to define it. The rule of law is included as a broad aspiration, together with justice, democracy, good governance, good economic governance, unity, reconciliation and other such values. The absence of definition can also be explained from a political and security perspective. It might be difficult for former warring parties to agree to a common definition, one that essentially aims at establishing formal and substantive legal constraints on the exercise of government authority. Peace agreements also often include a condition that obliges public officials to observe international human rights standards and UN Security Council resolutions. It is unclear what kind of effect this "institutional enmeshment" with international legal norms has. At the very least it could be argued that by incorporating UN Security Council resolutions, or referring to international human rights law, peace agreements hope and aspire to provide guidance and standards for the transitional phase and for the establishment of interim governments.[303]

In comparing how the rule of law is conceptualised in the legal, policy and operational guidelines of international actors, and how the same concept makes its appearance in peace agreements, there are a few, but interesting, differences.

First, the rule of law and what can be identified as rule of law principles (legality, the separation of powers, formal equality) are in peace agreements given different weights and functions depending on the context and nature of conflict to which the agreement corresponds. The Accra Agreement stresses accountability and rule governance in relation to exploitation of natural

300 Arusha Agreement.
301 Accra Agreement Art. XVI (c).
302 Linas-Marcoussis Agreement Annex (I).
303 See, for a discussion on 'institutional enmeshment', Keohane 1992 p. 179.

resources, while the Arusha Agreement emphasises equality before the law. The Linas-Marcoussis Agreement concerns itself with due process in dealing with citizenship and land tenure. Rule of law appears to be flexible and adaptable to the problems and difficulties of the particular war to peace transition.

Second, judicial reform, the establishment of national human rights commissions and the strengthening of systems for the protection of human rights have generally been standard components in those peace agreements concluded over the past decade. The question of accountability for public officials is often raised as well as measures seeking to strengthen the ways and means of legal redress and the creation of ombudsman institutions to provide proper opportunities for citizens to voice complaints. This is different compared with how most international actors conceptualise the rule of law. Taken together, while a definition of the rule of law is reasonably absent from the text of peace agreements, a reading of the reform agendas reflects a rather broad and systemic approach to the rule of law, with issues that generally go beyond rule of law in the justice sector, in criminal law reform and other salient characteristics of how international actors understand and present the concept.

3. COMMON POINTS OF DEPARTURE AND CONVERGENCE

INTRODUCTION

This chapter summarises and concludes the first part of this work. In particular, it elaborates on matters of how international actors employ the concept of the rule of law as examined in the previous chapter. Three key points are discussed.

The first concerns the tendency to translate the idea of the rule of law into institutional check-lists, and the tension between formalism and instrumentalism. This includes the discourse on material as opposed to formal rule of law definitions, and the problems and constraints that respective definitions bring with them in terms of application to war-torn societies.

The second concerns the tendency to exclude from the conceptualisations of international actors, areas outside the justice sector – for example, customary law and public administration. Third is how the rule of law policies employed by international actors seems to ignore the users of the legal and administrative system undergoing reform.

FORMALISM AND INSTRUMENTALISM

Any comparative analysis of rule of law definitions made by international actors is compounded by the fact that those actors sometimes operate in various ways to achieve different ends.

The UN, for example, has had several rule of law definitions for distinct purposes. One emerged within the UN Secretariat because of increasing assistance in development cooperation. A second definition is the Human Rights Commission whose significance has to be read in light of the political compromises that characterises resolutions from the Commission. A third definition comes from the UN's engagement in war-torn societies in general, and in particular the mode of influence provided through the substitution of national governments. The EU, similar to the UN, also applies the rule of law to different situational responses. The first is the rule of law standard for EU membership. Second, the EU makes use of the rule of law as a criterion for its development assistance, as expressed in the Cotonou agreement. A third end is to be found in relation to the EU's recent rule of law missions to Georgia, Iraq and Kosovo where the EU now has adopted the UN 2004 definition of the rule of law.

The Council of Europe employs the rule of law as a barometer for membership, and the concept is central to the protection of rights enshrined in the European Convention on Human Rights. The OSCE, in its turn, applies the rule of law not only to the means of cooperation and security, but also in a wider context of 'human dimension' where the concept appears side by side with democracy, human rights and minority protection.

International financial institutions, and the World Bank in particular, utilise the concept in rather different ways from other international actors. First of all, the World Bank and other financial institutions promote the rule of law because of the assumption of its direct relevance to economic development. Second, the Articles of Agreements of the World Bank limits the Bank's focus on aspects that are too 'political'. Accordingly, its definitions are less value-laden, with fewer direct references to human rights (applying instead the term of 'human dignity').

A discrepancy is evident between how the rule of law is defined in legal theory (briefly discussed in Chapter 2) and how most international actors interpret and employ the concept. For the most part, they tend to centre on institutions or devices on how to implement the rule of law and define rule of law in institutional terms, whereas legal theory more often concentrates on certain principles, values or ends of rule of law. Moreover, the rule of law concept that emerges in relation to war-torn societies is a notion primarily relevant to the justice sector and not to other areas of state-individual interaction, or other forms where authority is exercised, such as customary law.

Despite this divergence there are some common points of convergence. First of all, theory and practice take the idea of limited government as an all-embracing principle where the basic ideal is for government officials to count rules as their stock-in-trade rather than as personal contacts and matters of discretion. Second, international actors and legal doctrine both require that the law should be clear, accessible and generally prospective, though this is emphasised more in legal theory than in rule of law assistance.

The main divergence between legal theory and the policies of international actors is to be found in the perception of the concept's autonomy in relation to other constituent ends. Legal theory, for the most part, tends to view the rule of law existing as a more or less autonomous concept. This is also part of the rhetoric of donors, but on a closer examination of objectives and operational guidelines there are also significant features of instrumentalism. The essential objectives (good governance, human rights and security) legitimate an instrumental use of law that, at times, may perhaps be in conflict with a more autonomous reading of the concept. The rule of law is stretched and bent to fit certain objectives. If the objective is to confront organised crime and high levels of criminality, rule of law is accorded a basic law and order function. If the objective is increased human rights protection, the rule of law is presented as being mainly an instrument of safeguarding and implementing a protective system.

Most definitions at a policy level of international actors are vague, considering that such policies will be translated into practical activities. While the notion of the rule of law is sufficiently broad enough to satisfy the many demands and entry points of the various actors, as result it is also difficult to put into effect.[304] The difficulty is that international actors solve this problem by assuming a certain institutional model for putting the concept into practice. This is not specific of rule of law reform in crisis management, but is also a feature of rule of law reform within development cooperation.

The institutional slant represents a blend between two competing perspectives on law: formalism and instrumentalism, and despite their contradictory messages these two perspectives remain integrated in rule of law assistance. Formalism assures reformers that they can concentrate on rule of law reform without mixing with politics, because the legal system is seen to be self-contained and autonomous. At the same time, reformers also hold the view that once supported, legal professionals and the institutions in which they reside will spearhead development in certain directions and be able to influence and change policy. Self-contained yet also instrumental concepts such as human rights, judicial independence and judicial review become standardised 'packages' that can be promoted with little effort since they have acquired an aura that detaches them from their historical and political lineages. This approach often results in segmented and narrow operational plans that give weight to the justice sector institutions and the legal profession from the perspective of a judge and other legal professionals.

Difficulties of implementation are reinforced by a general tendency to look at the rule of law as a substantive value-laden concept. Studying the various programmes and activities implemented by donors, the rule of law appears as the rule of 'good' law. From this standpoint rule of law assistance to war-torn societies might be described as being political.

It seems to be the case that those actors with a substantial field presence, and where policy has been largely driven from ad hoc practical and operational activities in development cooperation and in after war and crisis, there is a common denominator. These agencies, including the UN, OSCE, and the World Bank, approach the rule of law concept from the perspective of institutions: courts, police, prosecutors and so on. The Security Council, for example, has been influential in defining focus and rule of law responsibilities in the field. This began as a practice when peace-keeping and peace-building missions in the early 1990s already had experience from working with legal and judicial reforms in the justice sector. This practice was later made into a rule of law policy. The

304 The particularisation between different agencies involved in rule of law reform is noted in a recent UN inventory report. Executive Office of the Secretary-General, Inventory 2006 p. 46–47.

Council of Europe, with a more limited operational responsibility, takes on a more systemic view of the rule of law that seems more influenced by principles than a certain institutional setting and situational response.

Peace agreements reflect the 'root causes' of conflict and contain 'backward-looking' details for rule of law reforms. The ends to which the rule of law notion is applied in peace agreements differ. It is often inserted as an aspirational and general goal, but can then be used in order to reinforce the importance of specific initiatives such as criminal law reform, constitutional reform or governance reform. What unites the approaches of international actors with a direct responsibility for rule of law reform in the field are three broad yet distinct markers:

(1) That the rule of law concept involves both formal and instrumental features;
(2) That it is a concept seen as interrelated with, or more often equal to, substantive notions of justice – that is, democracy, human rights and equality; and
(3) That the rule of law is defined and approached based upon the perspective of the judge and that as a result, other forms of justice-delivering systems are omitted from the rule of law conceptualisation.

Considering the way that the rule of law is conceptualised in relation to war-torn societies, with its focus on criminal law, security, and human rights, perhaps it makes more sense to speak of a *particular* rule of law concept, one that applies to the unique situations of international assistance in war to peace transitions. The rule of law conceptualisation by international actors, found in legal and policy documents, seems to have acquired a certain distinct character applicable to war to peace transitions.

INTERNATIONAL RULE OF LAW AND LOCAL LEGAL CULTURE

A repeated 'lesson learned' from past experience with rule of law reform is that it is not only about law. This translates into a prediction that supporting the rule of law is not only a matter of technical expertise in drafting the right types of law or supporting the right institutions, but that without political will and support, and without some form of adjustment to the local context, legal, judicial and administrative reforms would likely face resistance and remain, at best, law on books.[305]

---

305 Blair & Hansen 1994 p. 6. But c.f. Goodpaster 2003 p. 689 in suggesting that the quest for political will can be misguided, since political leaders will always be more responsive to the forces in their societies than the persuasions of international donors.

If political will and context adjustment are accepted as something essential for the implementation of rule of law programmes, this brings to it certain limits as to what reformers can hope to achieve through law in war to peace transitions. Even based upon the most formal and minimalist conception, the rule of law requires a normative commitment to the project of law itself, and for governments and other powerful forces in society to agree on the non-violent resolution of disputes, to govern through law and to be governed by law.

For example, Blair and Hansen explicitly warn against engaging with countries where government and judicial corruption is rife, with minimal respect for human rights. The authors conclude that constituents and coalitions in such countries are so fragmented and fractious that it could eliminate any effective programmes of activity. The advice to rule of law reformers, unless political support or reform constituents from below can be created, is to steer clear and instead choose other developing countries more conducive to reform. What Blair and Hansen describe as conditions constituting an unlikely environment for legal reform, and their primary group of reference countries are developing countries, is the standard deal for international agencies involved in war-torn societies. Such recommendations impose a certain amount of caution against the promotion of ambitious reform programmes where rule of law is linked with substantive notions of good.

Afghanistan is one example of the dilemma that international actors face in societies where fundamentally different views and opinions exist on notions of rights, duties, justice and law in relation to other normative systems, primarily religion. As explained in a USAID field survey in Afghanistan: "against the international framework of justice as a universal application of rights and obligations, Afghans prize a notion of 'fairness', which is often relative and shaped by local norms".[306]

Afghanistan has an extremely poor past record of performance in upholding rule of law principles.[307] But the question of whether or not customary or Islamic law should be applied and interpreted in light of certain substantive values is not easily resolved by recourse to the rule of law. While certain practices and laws might contradict 'backbone' principles such as legal equality, the supremacy of law, or other conditions on the rule of law, the determining of what specific content laws should have is more difficult through a recourse to the rule of law.

Criticism and condemning rhetoric that fuse human rights and rule of law might not be helpful from a reform perspective, since they run the risk of averting much needed reforms and solutions to problems within the legal system. Instead, international actors could initiate dialogue and capacity-building within the Afghan legal community on Islamic law.[308] International

306 USAID/CHEECCHI 2005 p. 9.

307 See Barfield, Nojumi & Their 2006 for a description of the role of the non-state justice system and contradictions and violations of the formal state system.

308 Afshar 2006 p. 598.

agencies could also assist in measures aimed at clarifying the relationship between the constitution, general laws and Islamic law, and to establish formal procedures for determining when recourse either to Islamic or customary law is legally permitted.[309] While international agencies can assist in rule of law reform by enhancing formal clarity, in light of the difficulties of implementing a rule of good law and the recommendations on political will and context adjustment, they wade into murky waters if they use rule of law rhetoric in order to criticise the legal system in a general and value-laden way.

To recognise that an overloaded agenda imposing a rigorous set of standards and reforms is more difficult to realise does not mean an acceptance of cultural relativism or double standards. On the contrary, it suggests that donors should concentrate on strengthening the means of producing substantive outcomes, rather than providing substantive content.[310] Rule of law assistance should focus on providing the means for desired outcomes, with awareness of the fact that the rule of law concept involves a compromise between various political ends. When rule of law is given a strong moral and value-laden connotation, a risk exists that it will become a blunt instrument meaning little more than a general notion of 'good'. This represents a problem, because the rule of law could devolve into an empty phrase.[311]

For example, in many Asian countries discussions of the rule of law have a tendency of becoming entangled in the highly politicised 'Asian values debate', and in Islamic states the discussion tends to become stranded on the function and status of religion in relation to (predominantly as of late) women's human rights.[312]

An alternative to the risk of becoming stranded on a debate on values, or on what institutions to 'export' or establish in a recipient country, is to start with the attributes of the rule of law: preventing government tyranny and facilitating human interaction – and then decide on how an institutional framework could be designed to effectively limit arbitrary government action and enable people to interact.[313] Such an approach accords with how the concept historically evolved, as Tamanaha explains, and represents a more pragmatic way that can be made to fit the socio-cultural context of the war-torn society, as opposed to simply prescribing a set of institutions and corresponding rights.[314] Starting with the values from a teleological perspective will not avoid conflict with other values –

309 For example, the Afghan Constitution allows for recourse to Hanafi jurisprudence when there are no provisions in the constitution or ordinary laws on a pending case. Courts are then to apply Hanafi jurisprudence, within the limits of the constitution. For an analysis of the Afghan constitution and the relationship to Islamic law, see e.g. Mahmoudi 2004.

310 Ohnesorge 2008 p. 303.

311 Tamanaha 2004 p. 114.

312 Peerenboom 2006 p. 25.

313 As Krygier 2005 p. 272 suggests: "ask what the point is, why bother, what's the fuss?" See also Krygier 2006 for an elaborate discussion on a teleological approach in rule of law reform.

314 Tamanaha 2004 p. 139.

that is, notions of justice, the purpose of religion, and the rest – but at the same time does not demand adherence to a certain institutional form or agenda with a vague content.

LEGALITY AND LEGITIMACY

The main argument advanced by scholars who equate the rule of law with substantive values is that without it the idea would be unthinkable, since it provides no moral limits on state power.[315] This is not a strong argument for asserting that the rule of law requires substantive values to exist.[316] It only asserts that such a definition would be desirable (or that the lack of moral imperatives is less desirable).

Furthermore, it is not a new argument. One of the staunchest critics of the first phase of the law and development movement of the 1960s, Trubek, stated that legal reforms in Brazil were abused by the then authoritarian regime whereby it was given a form of "authoritarian instrumentalism".[317] This is also what other critics warn against, that an effective system of formal rule of law might actually serve to strengthen and enhance the grip of an authoritarian regime by according it a "patina of legitimacy".[318] Carothers point to the recent slide towards authoritarian rule in a number of states that have adopted a 'reductionist' rule of law agenda and how western policy actors, wishing to find signs of positive change: "salute their rule-of-law promises, overlooking the damage that the reductionism may cause to the health of the broader rule-of-law agenda".[319] Supporting a rule of law concept inter-linked with international human rights norms is by donors seen as providing legitimacy on both the project of rule of law assistance in itself, and credibility for the war-torn state as such.

Golub proposes another form of this argument, favouring a reorientation of the rule of law field, subsumed under 'justice' as an organising principle.[320] In Golub's argument, the field has become technical and constricted, and has failed to produce the promised results such as alleviating poverty, enhancing social justice, advancing economic development and standing up for human rights. Subsuming the various rule of law programmes and projects under the

315 Raz 2003 p. 1: "the law can be valuable, but it can also be the source of much evil. Not everyone agrees to these truisms, and there is nothing inappropriate in challenging them, or examining their credentials".
316 Rajagopal 2008 p. 1360.
317 Trubek 1972 p. 47.
318 Tamanaha 2004 p. 103.
319 Carothers 2009 p. 55.
320 Golub 2009 p. 63.

organising principle of justice would then provide a broader "conceptual and analytical framework".[321]

While Golub's observations of a narrow and top-down focus with the failure to deliver on promised ends is shared by many commentators in the rule of law field, the introduction of a comprehensive principle of justice raises several questions. Similar to the argument that a formal rule of law would be less desirable because it fails to introduce certain values, but leaves the question of values open ended, it is unclear how justice is defined. In many ways, justice is an essentially contested concept, as is the rule of law.[322]

If the formal definition of rule of law can be criticised for being empty of values, so too is the material rule of law slated on the basis of overloading the concept with values. Enhancing formal procedural aspects of the rule of law, including issues such as clarity, consistency and transparent legislation, and respect for due process principles in the application of the laws, play an important function in the achievement of other policy objectives. Without effective procedure, any material obligations will be declaratory and depend on the benevolence of the rulers.[323]

Though the arguments for a substantive rule of law, based on the observation of the potential dangers of a formal concept make a valid point, it should be recognised that in the constrained and often chaotic transitions of countries torn-asunder by war, excessive legality is generally not one of the challenges. Quite the contrary, it is the disregard of existing legal limits that have caused harm to begin with. When international agencies attempt to introduce a particular agenda, they also risk undermining their own efforts by possibly clashing with local culture, tradition and custom.[324] Conflating the rule of law with democracy, justice, and equality leads to a conceptual confusion where it is difficult to identify those activities necessary for change.[325]

Summers puts forward three principal reasons as to why the rule of law should continue to be defined according to a formal conceptualisation. The first relates to the fact that formal rule of law principles will, most likely, command general support. If material considerations are brought into the rule of law concept, controversies are more likely to occur because different views exist over substantive issues. Second, and this is perhaps a more useful argument, keeping the rule of law formal enables criticism of a violation of the rule of law to be sharp and more centred. If material norms are included, criticism risks being

---

321 Ibid., p. 64.

322 Golub's argument has a further and more practical dimension. Later in his argument the all-embracing principle of justice is framed more as an approach or method of legal reform where the problem that people face should be the starting point for a discussion on what institutions and laws can be useful to support.

323 Wennerström 2007 p. 55.

324 See Stromseth, *et al.*, 2006 p. 90.

325 Peerenboom 2006 p. 145.

stranded on different interpretations of what type of material goods the rule of law is supposed to realise. Third, separating 'first order' law and 'second order' principles also make the conflict between them easier to ascertain, discuss and criticise.[326] A separation between the formal and the material makes it more plain and easy to detect when a court departs from formal rule of law grounds, for example, if substantive policy or notions of justice are seen as overriding formal rule of law principles.[327]

From a formal or 'minimalist' standpoint, the rule of law has many important virtues of its own.[328] At a minimal level, a superficial rule of law conception provides some degree of predictability and limits on state power, with some protection of human rights. While this may seem like too thin a reading, even the harshest critics of a formal rule of law acknowledge that making a government comply with the law is no small accomplishment. The principle of formal equality before the law is doubly important. Not only does it embody the principle that everyone, state officials and citizens, are subject to their own laws, and can only justifiably act through them, but it can also be interpreted as a manifestation of public commitment to the reasons why citizens are treated equally so long as relevant and acceptable grounds for differentiation can be presented.[329]

'GOOD ENOUGH' RULE OF LAW

A perhaps more realistic view (than the one presented by Summers in the above) is to argue for a compromise that minimises substantive references in the rule of law conceptualisation. The reason is that promoting a material rule of law in a morally diverse society will run the risk of disagreements over not only interpretation of the moral good, but also on what the rule of law includes in the notion of the moral good. Forging too close a link between the rule of law and broader disputes over substantive justice risks depriving the rule of law concept of an "independent analytical bite".[330]

When rule of law reform becomes interlinked with, for example, democracy and human rights promotion, there is a risk that the tools and approaches for ensuring respect for the core values of the rule of law become obscure. Rule of

---

326 Summers 1999 pp. 1692–1695. First order laws are directed at the legal relations between different actors (citizens, public officials, legal enterprises, associations) and the law. Principles of the rule of law are 'second order' principles, concerned with the creation and implementation of first order law. Rule of law principles are in this sense systemic, applicable in all areas and sectors of legal relations.

327 See Hart 1958 p. 621.

328 See Fuller 1958.

329 Gaus 1994 p. 350: "the principle of formal equality before the law thus articulates the liberal state's commitment to rule through public reasons only".

330 Fallon 1997 p. 54.

law reform makes use of and moves in an area that is in many ways different from democracy or human rights promotion, or both. Such things as electoral reform and election observation, assistance to political party formation, or support to accede to international human rights instruments are not necessarily less 'practical' than rule of law reform but are more related to political and diplomatic missions.

This does not mean that the political economy of the rule of law is in any way easier to overcome, but that rule of law assistance takes as its point of departure, for want of better words, technical legal difficulties. Nor does this suggestion mean that the rule of law is completely independent as a system of rules. For example, ensuring accountability through national human rights or ombudsman institutions necessitates at least a minimum of political commitment to accountable democratic governance. But there are also grounds for going beyond the political element and focusing on institutional deficiencies conducive to a lack of rule of law.[331]

Rose-Ackerman argues that much of the discourse centres on political will and moral leadership as being the essential requirements in the establishment of effective governments in war-torn societies, but that this is insufficient since "moralizing risks degenerating into empty rhetoric – or worse, witch hunts against political opponents. Policy must address the underlying conditions that create corrupt incentives, or it will have little lasting effect".[332] Following on from this line of reasoning an argument could be made out for not pursuing rule of law and democracy promotion cumulatively, but instead as separate yet reinforcing objectives.[333]

Maintaining the independent and analytical 'bite' of the rule of law concept appears to have formed an influential part of the deliberations of the Rule of Law Index by the World Justice Project. That index provides a methodology that can be employed in a range of countries and under different circumstances, based upon more than a hundred variables.

In the deliberations on developing the index the concern lay in how to establish a working definition applicable to different forms of governance systems, notions of justice, and legal traditions. The rule of law definition that forms the basis of the index includes four broad principles:

331 Reif 2000 p. 24: "at the foundational level, national human rights institutions usually cannot fulfil their functions effectively in states that do not have some minimum level of democratic governance".

332 Rose-Ackerman 2008 p. 34.

333 This should not be interpreted as an argument of sequencing where other policy objectives must wait for the rule of law, but as a tentative argument for separate yet simultaneously implemented agendas. Carothers 2009 p. 56 argues that the assumption (which in his view has taken root in Western policy towards authoritarian or semi-authoritarian regimes) that democracy promotion must wait for the rule of law is seriously flawed because "the image of the austere, wise autocrat who slowly but systematically builds the rule of law may be attractive, but it is more the exception than the norm".

(1) supremacy of law;
(2) clarity, fairness and stability of laws that also protect fundamental rights;
(3) an accessible, fair and efficient process for law-making; and
(4) enforcement of laws and access to justice by fair and impartial legal and administrative institutions.[334]

Those principles strike a compromise between formal and material rule of law definition and were guided by these considerations:

> The principles address the extent to which a country provides for fair participation in the making of the laws – certainly an essential attribute of self-government. *But the principles do not address the further question of whether the laws are enacted by democratically elected representatives.*
> The principles address the extent to which a country protects fundamental human rights. But given the impossibility of assessing adherence to the full panoply of civil, political, economic, social, cultural and environmental rights, the principles treat a more modest menu of rights, primarily civil and political, that are firmly established under international law and bear the most immediate relationship to rule of law concerns;
> The principles address access to justice, but chiefly in terms of access to counsel and access to tribunals, rather than in the thicker "thicker" sense in which access to justice is sometimes seen as synonymous with the legal empowerment of the poor and disfranchised. Access to justice is a critical cornerstone for the implementation of policies and rights that empower the poor.[335]

The index provides a pragmatic guide to rule of law reform, particularly in war-torn societies. The dilapidated state of most legal and administrative systems in war to peace transitions, in addition to the political sensitivity surrounding many matters of a more substantive character, speaks for a pragmatic conceptualisation. The absorptive capacity of many legal and administrative institutions is low, making complex and resource-intensive reforms difficult to implement and maintain.[336] Absorptive capacity, institutional strength, and political and constituency support do not of themselves necessarily indicate a decreased commitment to rule of law values, but rather denote an ambition to ensure that reforms promoted are viable and effective.

It should be noted and made clear that the considerations expressed in the index above, as well as in other such calls for more modest and calibrated approaches, are not free of political connotations themselves, and even a more

334 American Bar Association & The World Justice Project 2008 p. 8f.
335 Ibid., p. 7 (italics added).
336 Patrick 1998: "states recovering from war often lack both the absorptive capacity needed to manage considerable sums of money emanating from diverse foreign sources for multiple purposes and the administrative structures required to design and implement comprehensive plans for reconstruction".

scaled down interpretation of the rule of law would not be politically neutral. If it is accepted that the institutions of rule of law to some extent embody the state "we must also face the fact that this makes them extremely sensitive areas in which for outsiders to get involved in".[337]

An understanding of the political nature of externally promoted reforms aimed at the organisation and function of the state, as well as the need for pragmatism and a balance that considers the absorptive capacities of the receiving institutions, have been expressed in a discourse centred on reaching 'good enough' governance. The concept of 'good enough' governance was coined by Grindle in response to a complex and expanding good governance agenda.[338]According to Grindle, the good governance agenda, formulated by international actors and often embraced by national authorities, "is unrealistically long and growing longer over time".[339] From the list of 'must do' activities, there is "little guidance about what's essential and what's not, what should come first and what should follow, what can be achieved in the short term and what can only be achieved over the longer term, what is feasible and what is not".[340]

The 'good enough' governance alternative emphasises the need to think realistically about sequencing and is reflected in the policy formulated by DfID. According to that policy, international organisations and other donors should concern themselves with:

(1) selectivity, focusing only on the main causes of instability and the main capacities of the particular state;
(2) achieving visible results in the short term, however modest, to create a momentum for future reform;
(3) avoiding the most politically or socially controversial issues;
(4) avoiding reforms that are too ambitious for the implementing capacity of the country concerned;
(5) ensuring that reform does not erode what capacity already exists and;
(6) strengthening accountability and legitimacy of government whenever possible.[341]

Considering the anatomy of war-torn societies (discussed in Chapter 1) DfID's list of focal points could be submitted as an argument for a more formal rule of law approach – a 'good enough' rule of law assistance.

The idea of 'good enough' governance (or of rule of law) is controversial, primarily because it might be interpreted as opening up the application of double standards to war-torn societies. At the same time, it brings to rule of law

337 Potter 2004 p. 11.
338 Grindle 2004 and 2007.
339 Grindle 2004 p. 526.
340 Ibid.
341 DfID 2005 p. 20.

assistance more emphasis on asking questions on what should take priority, when they should be implemented, and by whom. This is particularly pertinent, since local ownership, consultation and participation are frequently held to be critical to the implementation of rule of law reform. Yet international actors do not seem to have clear standards for determining when to invite local agencies, and when it might be counter-productive to do so. Grindle's suggestion of 'good enough' governance also invites international players to consider carefully reforms in light of the objectives of their missions.[342] This represents an argument for clear and transparent decision-making on the part of international actors on when it becomes functionally necessary to implement certain rule of law reforms, in what way, and in what order, set against a standard of a 'bare bones structure' on rule of law principles.

The formal and material definitions present a particular challenge for international reformers. A reading of policy documents of international actors, including the growing body of UN resolutions, declarations, instruments and guidelines, support a material rule of law. On the one hand, several difficulties are associated with a material approach – for example, that there might exist different notions of good, and the frequent calls for political will and context adjustment. On the other hand, a formal and minimal interpretation is difficult to imagine. The general intertwinement of the international human rights regime in rule of law promotion renders it difficult to separate the formal and the material.

'Good enough' rule of law could provide a middle way. A starting-point and a source of legitimacy could be to acknowledge the growing human rights within the framework of a more scaled-down rule of law approach. Then, arguing for the principle of legality would also mean adherence to and full respect of a country's international legal obligations. Many war-torn societies today have constitutions that accord precedence to international treaties to which the country is a party.

This growth of human rights in terms of treaties and general acceptance means that an increasing number of states are participants to a host of conventions, from the Covenant on Civil and Political Rights to the Convention on the Elimination of All Discrimination Against Women. A 'new' formal approach to rule of law after war could then be that of emphasising the capacity of the legal, judicial and administrative system to safeguard and implement the international legal obligations in an impartial and efficient way. If a country has ratified a human rights treaty, any argument from a formal rule of law standpoint on the necessity to strengthen legality, predictability, and free and fair trials also involves, implicitly, human rights advocacy.

International actors should at least be conscious of the impediments following each route of formal, material or compromises between the definitions.

342 Grindle 2004 p. 535.

There also appears to be a need for clarity and openness when pursuing any one particular rule of law definition, or when emphasis in promotion is placed on certain substantive values, for example, and for international actors to be able to motivate particular decisions and approaches in the light of rule of law values. There is a risk that lacking adequate criteria for determining how to approach the rule of law in its substantive and formal dimensions can cloud reform efforts.

EXCLUSION OF NON-JUSTICE SECTORS

A difference in international rule of law assistance and legal theory is the comprehensiveness of the notion of the rule of law. Legal theory typically takes a systemic approach and view rule of law as a cross-cutting issue that requires a multisector approach. International players, on the other hand, take a narrow sector definition and place rule of law efforts mainly in the realm of criminal justice and human rights.

It is difficult to assess whether the institutional slant on the justice sector, and primarily the judiciary, is inspired by common law or simply because it is a more easily recognisable area of reform activity. A cursory glance might suggest that the common law conception of the rule of law has been the main inspiration. It could also be argued that this depends on the actors concerned. The World Bank, which has an institutionalised tradition of American influence, could perhaps be described as leaning towards common law interpretations. Others, such as the UN family or the EU, are more difficult to categorise.

On a practical and operational level, international actors have taken a keen interest in the justice sector, chiefly the judiciary, emphasising the role of lawyers and with a confidence in litigation. Whether or not this has been determined by the influence of a certain type of legal tradition, is difficult to establish. Through an examination of the rule of law definitions applied by international actors the historical connotations of common or continental European law seem to be of less importance. Through usage and rhetoric in contexts that host a set of unique factors, the rule of law has every appearance of having acquired an original conceptual status – rule of law as ends and means for assisting war-torn societies. Thus it makes more sense to talk of a form of context-bound rule of law, a rule of law concept for promotion in war-torn societies, rather than rule of law as a national or regional historically evolved idea.

Administrative Law and Public Administration

There is nevertheless one particular Anglo-American influence on today's rule of law promotion that draws inspiration first and foremost from Dicey's work, which criticised the emergence of public law and the rise of the 'administrative state' on the continent. His emphasis on the 'ordinary courts' should be read as a rejection of special courts – that is, administrative tribunals of various sorts.[343] Following Dicey's classic description of the rule of law, a lot else is discarded which acts as rule of law, functions as rule of law, and gives the impression of being rule of law, though it is not, according to Dicey, and cannot be.

Krygier argues that following Dicey's reasoning, the welfare state is out because it provides discretion to administrators. France and the rest of continental Europe are also out because they employ a separate system for administrative tribunals: "so just dip your toe in the English Channel, and you're about to drown in a sea of unruliness".[344] Moreover, Krygier says, a Frenchman or an American might merely be amused by this disqualification of their legal systems as rule of law states: "If you were a Pole in 1989, or perhaps an Afghan or Iraqi today, struggling for the rule of law, this is very bad news indeed: it's not just that things are hard, as everyone knows. It's as though you were barred not by mere hard facts but by ontology: your institutions are not English."[345]

Ontological exclusion might not be as onerous as Krygier predicts, but it brings to the fore the limitations and challenges of present day rule of law reform. Non-justice sector institutions, and non-state dispute resolution, are marginalised areas within the rule of law concept in war-torn societies. While there seems to be a clear leaning towards common law lawyers and legal experts involved in rule of law reform, it is difficult to establish a causal relationship that tends towards the exclusion of non-lawyerly aspects such as public administration or non-state justice. If public administration is taken as an example of the 'ontological exclusion' it may be that such exclusion merely follows a narrow understanding of the function of public administration, and that for international actors, reform of the law of administrative procedure might not be as glamorous as constitutional reform or involvement in other more 'symbolically' important areas such as juvenile justice or police reform.[346] Projects such as judicial reform attract funding more readily than reform of the regulatory framework governing wastewater, or attempts to reform land laws and the training of civil servants.

---

343 Dicey 1959 pp. 195–196 asserted three characteristics of the rule of law: "No man is punishable [...] except for a distinct breach of law established in the ordinary legal manner before the ordinary courts of the land. In this sense the rule of law is contrasted with every system of government based on the exercise by persons in authority of wide, arbitrary, or discretionary powers of constraint [...] here every man, whatever be his rank or condition is subject to the ordinary law of the realm and amenable to the jurisdiction of the ordinary tribunals. [...] the general principles of the constitution...are with us the result of judicial decisions determining the right of private persons in particular cases brought before the courts; whereas under many foreign constitutions the security (such as it is) given to the rights of individual results or appears to result, from the general principles of the constitutions".

344 Krygier 2006 p. 131.

345 Ibid.

346 Kritz 2001 p. 808.

Public administration is here used as a catch-all concept to describe the implementation of policy within a state framework outside the justice sector. Public administration relates to the organisation of government at state, federal, and local levels and includes agencies with responsibility to oversee, implement and administer public programmes. Such agencies, which extend from tax collection institutions to land and property registration bureaus, can often also set policy, make sub-laws with regulatory functions and adjudicate on disputes.[347] In that sense, they form the nexus between the state and the individual. Public administration is that part of the state with which most people interact in their daily lives, and the breakdown of governmental machinery in times of conflict creates a devastating ripple effect on the organisation of the state as a whole.[348]

Owing to the way in which most donor agencies conceptualise the rule of law, in policy documents and operational instruments, a great many rule of law issues are discarded. As suggested by one observer, the current heavy emphasis on judges, lawyers, and courts, is analogous to a health service that concerns itself only with centralised hospitals and doctors and ignores rural areas and ancillary services.[349] The rule of law concept in war-torn societies could be described as that of a 'rule of lawyers' – with courts, litigation, criminal law, and criminal procedure law as its central features.

Security and Development Perspectives

In 2000, the Brahimi Report presented a comprehensive review of peace-keeping missions and observed the need for a holistic approach to intervention and reconstruction in war-torn societies. Most peace-keeping operations approved by the UN Security Council since the Brahimi Report have been multidimensional and integrated missions in the sense that they seek to tackle and solve an array of problems.[350] It was shortly after the Brahimi Report that the rule of law made its way into UN Security Council resolutions. Though the ensuing integrated mission approach represents an improvement of rule of law policy, there are several difficulties. Above all activities falling within a development category are funded separately from the rest of the peace-keeping mission, the so-called core mission funding.[351] Attempts to designate 'baskets' of rule of law work, as the UN has, risks merely to accentuate a sectorisation of the rule of law and a false dichotomy where certain issues are seen as more relevant on the basis of how a situation is categorised rather than depending on the actual needs and demands of the context. As a result, rule of law strategies narrowly

347 See Bergling, *et al.* 2008 p. 8.
348 UN Programme in Public Administration and Finance (UNPAN) 1995 pp. 5–6.
349 Golub 2006 p. 106.
350 Brahimi Report 2001 p. 7.
351 UNDP 2006 Evaluation of UNDP Support to Conflict-Affected Countries p. 24.

construed to concentrate on security matters during reconstruction receive financial support through the peace-keeping budget, while other legal reforms involving issues such as assistance to the creation of a commercial law framework or support to administrative law reform are separately funded. These initiatives are thus subject to separate drives for pledges of aid.

A continuing gap between security and development ideologies was confirmed in the UNDP 2006 evaluation report on assistance to conflict-affected countries, which notes that while the UNDP and other international actors have largely succeeded in stabilising conflicts it has failed to address structural conditions conducive to conflicts.[352] The international response, according to the recommendations in the report, should integrate development concerns with the UN strategic considerations of security. Weaknesses in the international presence in war to peace transitions are described as the failure, *inter alia*, to protect civilians, to establish legitimate political authority and to prioritise development objectives from the outset, all coupled with an excessive interest in security.[353]

Despite the observations and recommendations in the two reviews of UN assistance to societies in transition from war, there remain a number of difficulties on the comprehensiveness of rule of law support.[354] While rule of law initiatives in the justice sector form part of an important strategy for the purposes of creating a safe and secure environment, it is insufficient to that end, and international agencies still treat rule of law and public administration as separate projects.[355] The state's legitimacy and capacity to move forward in the transition process also depends on rules and structures with which to organise the fundamental structures of society, politics and the economy. As argued by the UN expert group on public administration, reform in this area should start, if possible, at the beginning of an international intervention or state-building mission.[356]

The neglect of the rule of law in the public administration of Kosovo exemplifies how a narrow justice sector interest creates practical difficulties in state-building missions. At the time of the OSCE's first review of administrative justice in 2007, only two judges (supported by two legal officers) attended to all of its administrative law cases.[357] Since the Supreme Court only retains few judges,

352 Ibid., p. 40.

353 Ibid., p. viii.

354 Rule of law in public administration is also side-stepped in governance and public administration programmes. Noted in the UN Program in Public Administration and Finance report: "writings in public administration usually ignore law, whereas lawyers usually ignore the problems faced in public administration". UNPAN 1995 p. 3.

355 Bergling, *et al.*, 2008 p. 3.

356 UNPAN 1995 p. 13.

357 Before 1989 (according to the President of the Supreme Court), five judges used to handle all administrative law cases. Towards the end of 2006 there were 2,164 administrative cases pending. To make matters worse the Supreme Court as a whole for 2006 accepted a total of

the two assigned to administrative cases were often required to also adjudicate in criminal and civil cases.[358] Though the European Court of Human Rights has established that a temporary delay might be justified, under exceptional circumstances, states should take appropriate measures to remedy any constraints.[359] A backlog in the Kosovo Supreme Court meant that there were no conclusions to contested matters and appeals, with no means of correcting mistakes made at lower levels within the system. Ultimately, a backlog might well sustain and entrench discriminatory practices within administrative agencies.

While the EU rule of law mission, EULEX, is now in place in Kosovo there is little that indicates that this mission is interpreted to apply outside the justice sector.[360] While the EULEX mission is geared towards the issue of the rule of law in custom services, prosecutorial services and in law enforcement, with particular emphasis on organised crime, it does not concern itself with the rule of law beyond these difficult areas.

The World Bank, for example, is one leading participant in this field (together with the UNDP). A number of economic and good governance projects have been launched by the Bank in war to peace transitions. Several of such projects and programmes deal with 'legal' issues in environments typically suffering from a lack in the rule of law, they are often free from any such explicit recognition and commitment. Public administration reform, in contrast with rule of law initiatives in the justice sector, is often oriented towards increasing general efficiency, managerial skills and organisational matters.[361] There might be a contradiction here between the typical rationales of public administrative reform and the 'quality' dimension of the rule of law. In war-ravaged societies the issue is not so much one of rationalising and cost-cutting by improving fiscal discipline, but of rebuilding institutions and ensuring accountability and in attending to past grievances of discrimination and repression in the bureaucracy.

4,856 cases, considerably increasing the size of the backlog. OSCE 2007 Report on the Administrative Justice System in Kosovo pp. 16–17.

358 OSCE 2007 Report on the Administrative Justice System in Kosovo p. 16.

359 *Zimmerman and Steiner v. Switzerland* no. 8737/79, judgement 13 July 1983, para. 29; *Duclos v. France* no. 20940/92, 20941/92, 20942/92, judgement 17 December 1996, para. 55.

360 Council Joint Action 2008/124/CFSP Art. 3 lists the customs service, law enforcement and the judiciary as primary institutions to support with regard to the focal points of war crimes, terrorism, law and order, organised crime and corruption. Despite the narrow mandate, the UNSG notes in a 2009 report on the UN mission to Kosovo that the UNMIK rule of law component is expected to be phased out. UNSG S/2009/149 p. 5.

361 See USAID 2006, Reforming Public Administration in Post-conflict Societies p. 4.

RULE OF LAW CONSTITUENCIES

With the disparate and sometimes contradictory messages contained within international organisations' policies on the rule of law, it is not easy to tell who actually benefits from rule of law reforms. While proclaiming to promote the rule of law to safeguard and protect vulnerable groups, and in order to increase human rights protection generally, much attention seems to be directed towards the needs of a rather limited set of institutions.[362]

Yet, the ultimate beneficiary should be the populace just as much as private enterprises and associations. All should be able to rely on fair, predictable and impartial rules and legal institutions in their interaction with state agencies, or in their dealings with others. The needs formulated by legal professionals might not correspond at all to the requirements of ordinary people who often find themselves at loss as how to formulate the legal challenges that they face. This is one of the key tests in the whole enterprise of state-building – making the law matter for ordinary people and private enterprises.

In all, a reading of the polices of international actors on the rule of law, reveals a lack of an explicit recognition of the need to enable individuals to understand, use and even challenge laws and legal institutions. The demand must be made to embed or internalise rule of law reforms. As Merry argues in relation to human rights promotion: "if human rights ideas are to have an impact, they need to become part of the consciousness of ordinary people ... research on law and everyday social life shows that *law's power to shape society depends not on punishment alone but on becoming embedded in everyday social practices, shaping the rules people carry in their head*".[363] A similar argument, for example, could be made for rule of law principles where the supremacy of law, legal equality and legal redress as enabling constraints become part of social practice and ways of thinking about law.

Just as the consumer of the rule of law concept in war-torn societies is unclear, it is equally elusive as to why national authorities should commit themselves to rule of law principles. The most common answer for a commitment would be that it is necessary in order to attain good governance, human rights protection, and security. This argument is in accord with the three major objectives that drive the rule of law agenda today. While they might be considered to be morally convincing with some empirical support, they do not

362 This can partly be explained by the way in which the issue of quality within the justice sector has been viewed in the US and Europe. For a long time, quality was seen as encompassing the end result, i.e. the judicial decision, rather than how the 'users' of the system – private citizens and businesses – perceived quality. See Albers 2009 pp. 54–56 on discussing quality measurement in Europe and the US, and how there has been a shift towards incorporating end-user perspectives.

363 Merry 2006 p. 3 (italics original).

always carry a persuasive weight in war-torn societies.[364] As noted in a UN Secretary-General report on Liberia, a significant challenge five years after the UN began working on rule of law reform is that no coherent strategic plan has been adopted among the major stakeholders in the justice sector. This has constrained cooperation and co-ordination.[365] To many of the political elite and public officials, the rule of law, good governance and security are in stark contrast to the social order necessary for them to retain a grip on power (or to enjoy a profitable position from the fruits of power). Accordingly, a part of the political elite in these societies will always see rule of law reform as a personal 'win-lose game'.

There is often a public commitment to rule of law reform on the part of national and transitional governments in war to peace transitions, but such support could be just that – a noncommittal public support towards rule of law principles.[366] Sometimes merely lip-service is paid to statements on these principles in peace agreements and at donor conferences. Such rhetorical commitments undermine rule of law assistance where the principal methods rely heavily on modes of socialisation. A parallel might be drawn to human rights promotion, where outside pressure on national governments to show a commitment to human rights often leads to the ratification of human rights treaties.[367]

Lack of real commitment appears to be particularly apparent in measures directed at rule of law reform in public administration and in relation to supervisory and accountability systems, and in civil society participation.[368] It could be contended that rule of law reform in sensitive areas such as public administration and other areas of 'high politics'[369] – that is, reform activities aimed at subjecting the authority and control of the executive branch of government to legal scrutiny, requires the negotiating leverage of tangible benefits. Reforms in this field do not fail simply because they yield unsatisfactory outcomes once implemented, but the real difficulty is instead that they rarely get past the stage of implementation at all. They are blocked outright or only put into effect in a weak and fragmented fashion.[370] The reason is a lack of political commitment and bureaucratic support.

---

364 See Goodpaster 2003 p. 682 in describing the rule of law as a fallback or second best solution that can gain support from power holders when other options are exhausted or of too high a risk.

365 The response from UNMIL was to propose a "national rule of law retreat" for all the principal agents. UNSG S/2008/553 p. 10.

366 Or to initiative reforms for the purpose of indicating to outside observers a commitment in order to attract funding, trade agreement or organisational membership. See Farber 2002.

367 Hathaway 2001–2002 p. 2020.

368 See Peerenboom 2006 p. 841 on administrative law reform in China.

369 Morlino & Magen 2009 p. 234.

370 Palidono 2001 p. 1.

There is a readily perceivable need for a reorientation of the rule of law conceptualisation. This requirement is based primarily upon the fact that there is a lack of clearly defined goals for reform. While it could be argued that a broad consensus and common objectives exist on what the rule of law is good for, and its close links with substantive values, this approach is fraught with difficulty. For one thing, such an approach provides little guidance at field level (as will be discussed in the next chapter on putting the rule of law concept to practice).

What is of great consequences is that the rule of law concept in war-torn societies excludes aspects outside the justice sector. It also fails to identify – individuals and civil society groups – as 'consumers' that can be favourable reform partners when the rule of law message proves to be a 'hard sell' to the political elite, the expected but often elusive reform partner.

PART II

IMPLEMENTING RULE OF LAW REFORM

4. LAW REFORM AND CONSTITUTIONAL REFORM

INTRODUCTION

The previous chapters examined the conceptualisation of the rule of law in war to peace transitions. What has emerged from the investigation of policy documents, UN Security Council mandates and operational directives is a concept that appears to be a situational response. In other words, the rule of law is defined and formed to fit challenges and problems as identified by international actors specifically in war-torn societies. The following chapters will proceed to consider how the rule of law is put into effect by way of tangible actions.

The first topic for consideration is law reform. This is one of the top priorities of rule of law reform in those societies torn apart by war.[371] Countries such as Afghanistan, Liberia and Kosovo underwent an intensive law-making activity at the start of each transitional process. The typical mode of law reform involves providing technical support and legal advisory services to governments, assisting them in ratifying or acceding to international conventions, and helping legislatures in the drafting of new laws in accordance with international standards and benchmarks. Several law reform initiatives are also founded upon laws drafted in other state-building missions.

Numerous parallels, but also substantial differences, exist between the approaches of earlier segments of rule of law reform and those rule of law reforms that are effected in war-torn societies today. One crucial difference is that the primary source for transplants in war to peace transitions does not rely as much as before on individual countries that happen to have an interest in the region in question – that is, through trade relations or historical ties (though this still occurs). The process of law reform and constitution-making in these societies draws more on international law, standards and benchmarks.

International law is emphasised by the UN Secretary-General's listing of the normative sources for rule of law reform. The normative framework is presented as that consisting of various branches of international law – criminal, refugee, human rights, and humanitarian law.[372] As seen in the previous chapter, the intimate link between international human rights law and the rule of law

371 Strohmeyer 2001, Collapse and Reconstruction p. 58.
372 UNSG S2004/616 p. 5.

concept for war-torn societies is held to provide legitimacy and credibility in reforms. Moreover, international law is the source of a general and growing impact on areas previously regulated exclusively by domestic governments – such as criminal law, the environment, and trade.[373]

A second difference between law and development and rule of law reform after war and crisis is to be discovered in topical or thematic articulation. While the reform assistance provided in development cooperation typically involves commercial law, rule of law reform in war-torn societies tends to focus on criminal justice, fundamental rights and freedoms, constitutional law and security legislation.[374] Naturally, the transplanting of commercial law models is also common in these disintegrated societies. Kosovo, Iraq and Afghanistan have all received external support in this area,[375] but the focus is on substantial criminal law, procedural criminal law reform, election laws, and constitutional reform with emphasis on civil and political rights.

This chapter examines in what matter international agencies approach law reform and norm promotion. The part played by external actors in determining applicable law represents one area of analysis, since the issue of deciding on applicability is of central concern in the early phases of transition. This chapter also investigates how international law and the different standards and model laws that exist are employed, and how at the initial stage of a state-building the transfer of foreign laws, or decisions by external actors on the issue of law has been received. The different approaches to constitutional reform will also be examined. Constitutional reform plays a pivotal role in war to peace transitions, since it provides a structure and 'rules of the game' for the transitional phase and for any future political order.

APPLICABLE LAW AND LAW REFORM INITIATIVES

The methods applied and processes initiated in law reform depend ultimately on the mandate of the international presence, and the availability of resources. The form of authority also influences the way that rule of law reform is implemented in terms of participation and consultation with local counterparts.

As discussed in chapter 1, there are four broad categories of mandate. Kosovo and East Timor are examples of state-building missions where the UN substituted for governments that were yet to be constituted. In such cases involvement and responsibility over the legal reform process is more substantial than in the direct government assistance missions in parts of Africa and Asia. In

373 Miller 2003 p. 841.

374 See e.g. Posner 1998. See, also, DeLisle 1999 who describes the frenzied activities of legal reform in the early stages of rule of law support to former communist countries.

375 See Kassinger & Williams 2004–2005.

the latter, international actors, on the surface of things, are more constrained in giving advice and in influencing and promoting rule of law objectives. In other missions, such as the one in Liberia under the Governance and Management Assistance Program, both features of international direct influence and assistance are present. In the fourth form of intervention, donors provide direct sector or budgetary support. In most forms of intervention, international experts act in different advisory capacities through various collocation programmes. In some situations this is more direct and follows the influence of previously already established relations.[376]

Writing Laws for War-torn and Crisis Societies

The influence and methods applied by international actors should also in part be understood in relation to the financial capacity of the 'host' or 'recipient' state. East Timor, for example, was at the start of the UN administration almost completely dependent on international financial support. This allowed for a more direct international influence and "laws on demand" from both multilateral and bilateral donors.[377] Moreover, in the case of East Timor, the law reform position was further complicated by the fact that there were no pre-existing legal structures, save for Indonesian law. Since that law was constantly circumvented by UNTAET legislation and reinterpreted through the medium of international human rights standards, this created an opaque transitory legal order.

Though consultation and participation by the East Timorese was firmly introduced in the UNTAET mandate, this was difficult to implement in practice. On the drafting of an East Timorese electoral law, Morrow and White observes that even though it is conceivable that UNTAET could claim that the National Council of East Timorese Resistance and the East Timorese National Council together created the electoral law "as things transpired this was impossible. The UN was repeatedly called upon to introduce standards from international law into the legal framework of the election, without having any reliable guide [...] as to whether those standards were acceptable to the people of East Timor".[378] UNTAET, it seems, acted on the basis that since from their organisational and constitutional perspective, international law was fundamental to the establishment of the rule of law, it would naturally be acceptable to the people.[379]

In other cases, spheres of influence follow more direct routes based upon reach and authority, such as the US influence in Iraq since the invasion of 2003. In its first year, the CPA in Iraq issued more than 100 orders that included

376 East Timor Judicial System Monitoring Program 2004 p. 8.
377 Morrow & White 2002 p. 29.
378 Morrow & White 2002 p. 34.
379 Greenfell 2009 p. 164.

amendments or additions to Iraqi law. Those orders were drafted by CPA experts, but followed consultation with Iraqi officials.[380] Two wide swaths of economic and criminal law were substantially altered through CPA legislative measures. In accordance with White House policy to restructure and reactivate the Iraqi economy, a host of law reforms were implemented in the initial stages of the occupation. The law reform process included key regulations such as a company law aimed at reducing state oversight of corporations and enable access to loans. In addition, a salary schedule for government employees, oil production, tax law, securities law, bankruptcy law and public contracts law were all subject to various measures. In order to enable Iraq to join the World Trade Organization, intellectual property laws were amended to comply with the Agreement on Trade-Related Aspects of Intellectual Property Rights.[381]

Apart from mandates, established relationships, and the absorptive capacity of the host state, the dominance of one organisation or country also influences methods and processes. Such influence can also be somewhat surprising. The Italian lead on legal and judicial reform in Afghanistan is one example. In order to enhance coordination in the field, Italy was given the task of presiding over criminal law reform in Afghanistan, and Italian legal experts on the whole created the Criminal Procedure Code for Monocratic Courts, enacted by Presidential decree in February 2004.[382] Another form of influence is how East Timorese banking laws have helped shape and remodel those of Iraq.[383] While it is perhaps not initially exactly clear what the two have in common, the journey of East Timorese banking law makes sense when one considers that the same organisations were involved in both reconstructions.

Assisting National Law Reform Processes

Several UN rule of law missions in Africa and Asia have involved substantial investment in law making and law reform. Though these missions have been described in terms of 'assistance' to national governments, they have resulted in a great many new laws drafted under the auspices of international agencies.

This type of international involvement in law reform by way of an assistance mission is rarely recognised, and therefore seldom discussed.[384] The external influence reveals a built-in tension in the work of interested countries, and the

---

380 Kassinger & Williams 2004–2005 p. 220.

381 Boone 2008 pp. 544–545.

382 ICG 2003, Afghanistan: Judicial Reform and Transitional Justice. But cf. the criticism of the ICG on Italy's lead in judicial reform. In particular, the criticism concerned the sub-contracting of judicial reform to the International Development Law Organization (IDLO). While having substantial experience in judicial training in developing countries, IDLO was inexperienced in war-torn societies and statebuilding missions.

383 Boon 2008 fn. 235. See UNTAET/REG/2000/8 and CPA Order No. 94.

384 National law makers might also have an interest in making it appear that new laws are 'homegrown'. See Bergling 2006 pp. 77–78.

UN in particular, between policy decisions that reforms should be based upon local contexts and should take local ownership seriously, while in reality and for all practical purposes this is an unworkable approach owing to the scarcity of national capacity to allow for long-term law reform processes. The missions established in Sierra Leone and Liberia, for example, were not granted executive powers, but the guise of 'assistance' should not detract from the fact that laws are initiated, drafted and promoted by international experts. Accordingly, the distinction is not always clear between executive and assistance missions.

As teachers of norms the UN, for example, assisted the Ministry of Justice in Liberia in reviewing and redrafting laws relating to human trafficking, juries, and the financial autonomy of the judiciary, but the UN did not have the authority in Liberia to enact laws as it did in Kosovo and East Timor.[385] The UN has also assisted in drafting national plans of action for the protection of human rights in Sierra Leone and Liberia.[386] In the DRC, the UN mission was charged with assisting in re-establishing a state based upon the rule of law. This led to the creation of a Joint Commission with the Transitional Government on essential legislation, including post-transitional constitutional drafting.[387] The United Nations military forces also exercised executive responsibility in that country despite the lack of mandate to do so.[388]

There are several other instances where missions have become involved in rule of law reform without having the necessary mandate to do so. One lesser known instance is the United Nations Border Relief Operation (UNBRO), established in 1979. This was an emergency relief mission to the large refugee camp (housing 370,000 persons) on the border between Cambodia and Thailand. At the request of camp leaders, UNBRO officials agreed to draft an interim legal code to be applied in the camp called the Code of Justice and the Court System.[389] Most certainly this was never within the literal meaning of the mandate provided for UNBRO by the General Assembly, but under the circumstances the pressing need for a rudimentary legal order in the management of the camp rendered the action necessary.

It is also possible to identify the influence of international actors on the basis of focal areas of law reform. UN agencies, bilateral aid agencies and international non-governmental organisations, frequently invest in substantive and rights-based legal reform measures, whereas international financial institutions concentrate on legal matters relating to economic reconstruction. As such, the IMF provides advice or takes part in the drafting of laws on central banking,

---

385 UNSG S/2005/391 p. 9.

386 Commission on Human Rights E/CN.4/2006/106 2006 p. 12 and UNSG S/2005/391 p. 11.

387 UNSG S/2004/650 p. 6.

388 See Peacekeeping Best Practice Unit 2004 p. 3.

389 Reprinted in Cambodian Humanitarian Assistance and the United Nations (1979–1991) 1992.

currency and taxation, but will not involve itself with criminal law reform or constitutional reform.

FINDING THE LAW

Given the crisis anatomy of war-torn societies one of the first priorities is often to determine the applicable law before any long-term law reform measures can be undertaken. Determining applicable law is a crucial 'act of foundation' for future rule of law reform. Since transitions signify a break with the past the questions of what law to apply also become pertinent for symbolic and political reasons. The establishment of an early act of foundation is something that international and national actors have approached in different ways. A common method is to tackle the problem of 'finding' the applicable law by way of restatement or 'internal legal transplants'. This simply means that the existing law in force continues to apply, or that an 'old' law is revived. Restatement of existing law was the procedure adopted by the UN in Somalia, Kosovo, and East Timor. A similar path was taken by the Coalition Provisional Authority (CPA) in Iraq.[390] In Afghanistan, those involved in drafting the Bonn Agreement for Afghanistan chose instead to revive the earlier penal code and constitutional framework of the 1960s.[391] Sometimes the whole question of applicable law is directly addressed by the infusion of new legal codes.

A lack of available knowledge frequently makes the whole law reform enterprise difficult. International practitioners have limited access to information on the legal and administrative framework of a war-torn society. When the UN through UNOSOM II became involved in supporting rule of law reform in Somalia, it was deprived of practically all written information on the Somali penal code. The only existing textbook on Somali law was found in the Los Angeles County Law Library. This was a translation of the Somali criminal code of 1968 and had to be despatched to Somalia, photocopied, and distributed.[392] Similarly, when the UN assumed the function of governance in Kosovo and East Timor, access and understanding of the local law proved difficult. Thus when international participants take in the functions of norm-promoters, their positions on access to information and bureaucratic support from different state agencies, as well as opinions from civil society groups, are severely constrained from a knowledge perspective.

The gaining of access to information and material is a structural problem relating to all forms of intervention, but becomes acute in rule of law reform

390 See CPA/REG/16 May 2003/01.

391 Bonn Agreement Art. II (1).

392 Lorenz 2002 p. 830. See, also, Greenfell 2009 p. 161 in noting that it took more than ten months for UNTAET to obtain a full copy of Indonesian law.

where international support should ultimately be based upon existing law. In response to this 'legal lacuna', the Brahimi Report suggested that UN officials should arrive equipped with a 'justice package' that would apply during a transitional period. This suggestion of a universal justice package and the development of model codes will be considered later in this chapter. In addition, the legal frameworks of these societies in transition are often fraught with confusion, contradiction and overlapping layers of laws, decrees and executive orders. That is, even when there is easy access to legislative documents, regulations and jurisprudence, they might well prove to be obsolete or contradictory.

The process of law making in societies torn asunder by war has often been chaotic and confusing, particularly where an authoritarian regime has employed executive orders, decrees and fiats instead of laws. The legal framework might consist of different layers of laws with varying degrees of legality – that is, a mixture of laws, orders and decrees that contradict one another, that are seldom used, but frequently violated by state agencies. The President of Liberia stated in 2006 that "we have had so many interim governments, and they have passed so many laws, that some of them are duplicating each other, while others are contradicting each other".[393] Similarly in Iraq, the multi-layered system of laws, regulations, resolutions and fiats has created problems for the CPA. The Revolutionary Command Council, through which Saddam Hussein ruled, passed some 1,500 resolutions annually from 1991 on matters ranging from security decrees, taxes and amendments to the constitution.[394]

Where decrees and similar executive instruments have before conflict and crisis been promulgated in uncontrolled ways, the question of applicable law and a constitutional framework is difficult to settle. This results in a weak regulatory capacity on the part of the state and undermines the legal accountability of public officials. The complex layer of law severely limits the capacity of the rule of law to function as 'scaffolding' in society creating legal security. The UN Secretary-General observed in the report on the rule of law and transitional justice: "the legislative frameworks often show accumulated signs of neglect and political distortion, contain discriminating elements and rarely reflect the requirements of international human rights and criminal law standards".[395] This is also what the Brahimi Report noted:

> Even if the choice of the local legal code were clear, however, a mission's justice team would face the prospect of learning that code and its associated procedures well enough to prosecute and adjudicate cases in court. Differences in language, culture,

393 UN Office for the Coordination of Humanitarian Affairs Liberia: Interview with President Ellen Johnson Sirleaf, Press Release 29 June 2006.

394 Perito 2005 pp. 6–7.

395 UNSG S/2004/616 p. 10.

> custom and experience mean that the learning process could easily take six months or longer. The United Nations currently has no answer to the question of what such an operation should do while its law and order team inches up a slow learning curve. Powerful local political factions can and have taken advantage of the learning period to set up their own parallel administrations, and crime syndicates gladly exploit whatever legal or enforcement vacuums they can find.[396]

Because of difficulties with existing legal frameworks, international and national actors often insert a mutatis mutandis clause. These clauses emphasise the transitional and interim character of a restated law, or make provisions similar to repugnancy clauses, which state that the applicable law is to be applied to the extent that it does not contradict or breach a new or higher set of norms.[397] The repugnancy clauses also represent a specific form of socialisation or 'enmeshment' of national law with international law. This is particularly illustrated in the UN regulations for Kosovo and East Timor, where a number of international human right treaties were decided to apply directly to the new legal frameworks.[398]

The restatement approach can thus also be adopted when there is no change in a legal framework, but where the intention is to introduce or emphasise values and norms that will guide state-building efforts during the transitional process. According to the Arusha Agreement for Burundi the applicable law remained the same as before the conflict, but on condition that the National Assembly initiated a review of the legal framework for its compatibility with the transitional arrangements, in which a list of fundamental rights was included.[399] Through this form of enmeshment or socialisation, there is no direct change in the legal framework, but a new legal source is added as a standard of assessment and measurement.

Somalia: Deciding Applicable Law from the Outside

In several of the more salient of the recent state-building missions, international players have had authority to decide upon the question of applicable law. They have approached its restatement on the basis of international human rights on the assumption that reception of the restated law will be approved based upon rational and independent considerations of the legal community, academics and practitioners and constituents of the war-torn society. This has proved to be

396 Brahimi Report 2000 p. 14.

397 See, for example, Allott 1976 for a description of repugnancy clauses in many African countries in the years before and after independence.

398 See UNMIK/REG/1999/1 and UNTAET/REG/1999/1.

399 Arusha Peace and Reconciliation Agreement for Burundi, Section II Transitional Arrangements Art. 16 (2): "the transitional National Assembly shall as a priority review all legislation in force with a view to amending or repealing legislation incompatible with the objectives of the transitional arrangements and the provisions of the present Protocol".

problematic, since the issue of applicable law is not a just a legal exercise involving rational choices on what law best meets international standards.

The political sensitivity that surrounds applicable law became clear in Somalia. The UN Operation in Somalia was established in 1992 to provide humanitarian assistance.[400] Because of its humanitarian objective, it did not at first participate in rule of law reform.[401] In a later resolution from the UN Security Council, a determination to restore peace, stability and law and order and to facilitate political reconciliation was inserted. Despite this, international forces did not engage in the support to Somali police forces or in the reconstruction of the judiciary.[402]

It was not until the international presence was mandated with a state-building objective, following UN Security Council resolution 814, that the Council requested the Secretary-General to assume responsibility for maintaining security throughout the country.[403] The mandate also included assistance in the re-establishment of the Somali police force, including investigating and facilitating the prosecution of serious violations of international humanitarian law. By the time state-building responsibilities were included in the operational objectives, it was too little and too late.[404]

The SRSG, in an attempt to fill the 'rule-of-law-vacuum' that had emerged, declared the Somali Penal Code of 1962 to be the applicable criminal law. Apart from the fact that factions in the north-west rejected this, it is unlikely that UN Security Council resolution 814 conferred upon the SRSG legislative powers, though interpretations of a missions mandate sometimes place it at the 'floor' and not the 'ceiling'.[405]

The UN Commission of Inquiry set up to investigate attacks on UNOSOM II, suggested that unilateral action by the SRSG could be one reason that provoked hostilities by Somali warlords in relation to a perceived illegitimate escalation of UN authority there.[406] When the SRSG acted as a legislator, warlords like General Aideed and his faction were capable of interpreting this as an illegitimate escalation of UN authority, and the SRSG as overstepping the mandate issued to UNOSOM II by the Security Council.

---

400 SC Res. 751 (1992).

401 SC Res. 794 (1992).

402 See Kelly 1999 p. 37f. See, also, Lorenz 2002 p. 830 and UNSG S/25354.

403 SC Res. 814 (1993) para. 14.

404 Besides the new and revised mandate, UNOSOM II lacked proper funding and equipment for restoring the police force and engaging in rule of law reforms. Ganzglass 1997 p. 28. An UN evaluation report from the United Nations Peacekeeping Best Practice Unit, observed the difficulties of 'operationalising' the mandate and found it ironic and foreboding that the Task Force (UNITAF) "handed over operational responsibility to UNOSOM II, which was given far less authority but a much broader mandate". United Nations Peacekeeping Best Practice Unit 1995 para. 14.

405 Chesterman 2004 p. 85.

406 Commission of Inquiry S/1994/653 para. 64–69.

Legal Chaos in Kosovo

Legal developments in Kosovo represent a unilateral and top-down approach to law reform and the issue of applicable law, similar to the events in Somalia. The question of applicable law in Kosovo also demonstrates how international players have approached rule of law reform based upon flawed assumptions, and failed to acknowledge the political sensitivity of externally supported reform efforts.

The international presence in Kosovo is founded on UN Security Council resolution 1244. This authorised the UN Secretary-General, through the assistance of relevant regional organisations, to "provide an interim administration for Kosovo [...], and which will provide transitional administration while establishing and overseeing the development of provisional democratic self-governing institutions to ensure conditions for a peaceful and normal life for all inhabitants".[407] In both theory and practice, such broad and sweeping powers made the transitional administrator and UNMIK the governing force in Kosovo. This also added another legal 'source' – the regulations enacted by UNMIK.[408]

The use of a restatement of applicable law was employed in Kosovo. The first regulation by the SRSG decided that the applicable law would be the law in force on 10 April 1999:

> The laws applicable in the territory of Kosovo prior to 24 March 1999 shall continue to apply in Kosovo insofar as they do not conflict with standards referred to in section 2 [referring to international human rights standards] the fulfilment of the mandate given to UNMIK under United Nations Security Council resolution 1244 (1999), or the present or any other regulation issued by UNMIK.

Kosovo-Albanian judges and other legal professionals rejected this restatement. The criminal laws of Yugoslavia were seen as instruments of discrimination against Kosovo-Albanians by the Milosevic regime from the early 1990s.[409] Only after a legal void of six months did the SRSG amend the regulation, to decide that the applicable law was to be the law in force before Milosevic came to power in 1989.

407 SC Res. 1244 (1999) para. 4.

408 UNMIK/REG/1999/1: "all legislative and executive authority with respect to Kosovo, including the administration of the judiciary, is vested in UNMIK and exercised by the Special Representative of the Secretary-General". The Coalition Provisional Authority in Iraq, in the first regulation, stated the same form of authority as UNMIK in Kosovo, CPA Reg. N. 1: "the CPA is vested with an executive, legislative and judicial authority necessary to achieve its objectives, to be exercised under relevant U.N. Security Council resolutions, including resolution 1483 (2003), and the laws and usages of war. This authority shall be executed by the CPA authority".

409 Strohmeyer 2001, Making Multilateral Interventions Work p. 12.

Even though the pre-1989 law had some clear deficits, this was a decision favoured by most Kosovo-Albanian legal professionals. The pre-1989 criminal law did not take in narcotic crimes and the labour law was based upon a concept of "workers self-management" from the socialist Yugoslavia.[410] Furthermore, it was difficult to gain access to copies of laws from the times before 1989. The restatement of applicable law in Kosovo also created and reinforced a built-in problem of interpretation. UNMIK regulation 1999/24 (amending the first regulation on applicable law) established this hierarchy of laws:

> The regulations promulgated by the Special Representative of the Secretary-General and subsidiary instruments issued thereunder,
> The law in force in Kosovo on 22 March 1989. In case of a conflict, the regulations and subsidiary instruments issued thereunder shall take precedence.[411]

On how to interpret this new hierarchy of laws, and the question of how to decide on the inevitable collision between old, new and 'foreign' laws in the form of UNMIK regulation 1999/24 declared:

> 1.2 If a court of competent jurisdiction or a body or person required to implement a provision of the law determines that a subject matter or situation is not covered by the laws set out in section 1.1 of the present regulation but is covered by another law in force in Kosovo after 22 March 1989 which is not discriminatory and which complies with section 1.3 of the present regulation, the court, body or person shall, as an exception, apply that law.
>
> 1.3 In exercising their functions, all persons undertaking public duties or holding public office in Kosovo shall observe internationally recognised human rights standards, as reflected in particular in:
>
> (a) The Universal Declaration on Human Rights of 10 December 1948;
> (b) The European Convention for the Protection of Human Rights and Fundamental Freedoms of 4 November 1950 and the Protocols thereto;
> (c) The International Covenant on Civil and Political Rights of 16 December 1966 and the Protocols thereto;
> (d) The International Covenant on Economic, Social and Cultural Rights of 16 December 1966;
> (e) The Convention on the Elimination of All Forms of Racial Discrimination of 21 December 1965;
> (f) The Convention on Elimination of All Forms of Discrimination Against Women of 17 December 1979;
> (g) The Convention Against Torture and Other Cruel, Inhumane or Degrading Treatment or Punishment of 17 December 1984; and
> (h) The International Convention on the Rights of the Child of 20 December 1989.

410 See Hethy 2002 p. 65.
411 UNMIK/REG/1999/24.

Sections 1.2 and 1.3 illustrate the dangers of approaching the choice of restatement as being a technical legal exercise and as a simple choice between legal regimes where new legal obligations can easily be added to or detracted. The new regulation, set on amending the legal void created by the original regulation on applicable law, made matters worse and was criticised by the Ombudsperson in Kosovo. UNMIK and the decisions of the SRSG, together with the Legal Office at the UN Headquarters in New York (which assisted in reviewing the 'constitutionality' of drafted regulations), were jointly accused of creating 'legal chaos'.[412] The UN Human Rights Committee also criticised the contradictory legal framework and urged:

> UNMIK, in cooperation with PISG, should ensure that any new law or regulation specifies which formerly applicable laws or provisions are being replaced, that laws and regulations are made accessible to the public in all official languages of Kosovo via the Official Gazette and the Internet, and that former Yugoslav laws that continue to be applicable can be consulted easily. UNMIK, in cooperation with PISG, should also designate a competent body to determine which of the former Yugoslav laws and provisions continue to be applicable and address the issue of parallel Serbian court and administrative structures in parts of Kosovo.[413]

More than eight years after the first regulation on applicable law was enacted, there is still considerable confusion within the Kosovo legal framework. The seventh annual report of the Ombudsperson for 2007, noted that the two fundamental problems with the legal system were still a lack of legal certainty and openness.[414] It is still not clear which laws apply from the times of Yugoslavia. To further complicate matters, no competent higher judicial body exists to address the matter in a comprehensive way.

This legal chaos has had unintended consequences. One of them affects the autonomy and discretion that individual courts retain in the interpretation of applicable law, a discretionary power that encroaches upon the authority of the legislative assembly. UNMIK's approach to the question of applicable law turned the law reform process into a judicially-driven process with little overall coordination.

While legal uncertainties persisted the SRSG in 2003 issued a blueprint for state-building called Standards for Kosovo.[415] The UN Security Council later endorsed these standards, which were a set of objectives that had to be met before talks on future political status could begin.[416] The standards were based

---

412 Ombudsperson Institution in Kosovo 2004 p. 8.

413 Human Rights Committee CCPR/C/UNK/CO/1 14 August 2006 p. 2.

414 Ombudsperson Institution in Kosovo 2007 p. 12.

415 The Kosovo Standards Implementation Plan 2004. These standards were agreed between Kosovo Provisional Institutions for Self-government and UNMIK.

416 SC S/PRST/2003/26 and SC S/PRST/2004/13.

upon the precondition that self-governing institutions together with substantial autonomy would depend on Kosovo having a functioning democracy, with institutions adhering to the rule of law and guaranteeing freedom of movement. The various measures and actions required to reach the standard for rule of law provides an extensive catalogue, spanning disparate issues such as a review and amendment of existing witness protection legislation; the implementation of a sustainable system of civil and legal aid compatible with European standards; and gender and human rights education incorporated as core elements in school curricula.[417] In light of the problems surrounding the applicable law, several of these standards have proved difficult to attain.

On deciding cases involving collisions of law, the Constitutional Framework for Kosovo, enacted in 2001, called for the creation of a Special Chamber of the Supreme Court for constitutional matters.[418] The new Kosovo constitution of 2008 also stipulates the establishment of a constitutional court but there are doubts on whether it can deal with the issue of compatibility between the older Yugoslav laws and the Kosovo assembly laws.[419]

Undermining Applicable Law in East Timor

In East Timor, where the UN substituted for a national government, a similar approach of restatement was taken. The question of applicable law was seen as being less politically controversial in East Timor than in Kosovo, and the SRSG decided through regulation 1999/1 that the Indonesian law in force when UNTAET was established should continue to apply.[420]

Exceptions were explicitly made with regard to the Law on Anti-Subversion and the Law on Social Organisations, together with a number of other 'security' laws, and with the abolition of capital punishment. UNTAET also explicitly listed the set of international instruments to be directly applied in this first regulation (as opposed to Kosovo where a list was added later).

UNTAET had no criteria, and neither the time nor the resources for determining further those provisions in Indonesian law that were contradictory and thus invalid. Decisions had to be taken "on the run".[421] Though the choice of Indonesian law did not create and outright rejection and protest from the small legal community in East Timor, as it did in Kosovo, later events would illustrate the political sensitiveness surrounding this important subject of debate.

In 2003 the Timorese Court of Appeal declared that the Indonesian occupation of East Timor between 1975 and 1999 had been illegal, rendering the Indonesian law illegal and illegitimate. In fact, the Court noted in its decision

417 The Kosovo Standards Implementation Plan 2004.
418 UNMIK/REG/2001/9 Chapter 9.4.1.1.
419 Ombudsperson Institution in Kosovo 2008 pp. 12–13.
420 UNTAET/REG/1999/1.
421 Greenfell 2009 p. 164.

that the reference to the applicable law in the UNTAET regulation could only mean Portuguese law, since Portugal had been the only legally recognised power to administer East Timor.[422] The East Timor National Parliament settled the matter of applicable law a few months after the decision of the Court of Appeal, by designating Indonesian law as the law in force. The dispute concerning the act of foundation for East Timor shows that a simple revival or restatement of a particular legal regime is not merely a matter of legal technical expertise, but also involves the considerations of political, social, historical and cultural aspects.

Even though the UN mission seemingly established Indonesian law as the applicable law, several key decisions by UNTAET were based upon other legal sources.[423] The law on registration of political parties, for example, is in large part a copy of the UNMIK regulation for Kosovo.[424] UNTAET also continued to bypass Indonesian law through its own regulations, in particular for areas of law where the continuing application of Indonesian law met with considerable resistance from the Timorese leadership.[425]

UNTAET regulations, a mix of model codes from Kosovo, international law, international non-binding or 'soft law', all created a transitional legal order that in reality meant that the choice of Indonesian law as the applicable law was circumvented. This step-by-step bypassing of Indonesian law seems to have been motivated by pragmatic reasons: the UN, responsible for the administration of justice, did not have the capacity to understand and implement Indonesian law in the short time that the UN administration over East Timor endured. While choosing the path of pragmatism, the fact that Indonesian law was still to be applied alongside UNTAET provisions added a complexity to the transitional legal framework.

This complexity is seen in the development of a new criminal code in East Timor. Instead of applying and at the same time revising the Indonesian Code of Criminal Procedure, in accord with international human rights standards, UNTAET began drafting a new code on criminal procedure. This translated into a protracted "and ultimately sterile debate on the respective merits of inquisitorial versus adversarial procedures", eventually culminating in a long-delayed UNTAET Code with which many East Timorese lawyers obviously felt uncomfortable.[426] Among the few remaining lawyers and judges in East Timor at the start of the UN administration, most had obtained their education and gained their experience under Indonesian law.

---

422 Prosecutor v. Armando dos Santos, East Timor Court of Appeal, 15 July 2003 cited in Judicial System Monitoring Program (JSMP) 2003. See also, Greenfell 2009 p. 161.

423 See Morrow & White 2002 pp. 9f.

424 See, for a comparison, the formulations in UNTAET/REG/2001/2 and UNMIK/REG/2000/16 on the registration and operation of political parties.

425 Morrow & White 2002 p. 11.

426 Morrow & White 2002 pp. 11–12.

Interpreting Restatements of Law

A fundamental problem with the restatement or revival approach is that the method is rarely supported with instructions on how to assess the compatibility of existing national laws with international human rights. In Kosovo it was left to the judges to interpret compatibility. They therefore faced the task of interpreting the criminal code or the criminal procedure code, for example, in light of international human rights law, UNMIK regulations and older Yugoslav laws. This amounted to a *de facto* "re-writing [of] virtually the entire set of previous criminal laws".[427] The courts in Kosovo could, according to regulation 1999/24, request clarifications from the SRSG on matters of implementation, but it remained unclear what the status and binding nature of such clarifications were.[428]

The choice of applicable law by restatements or transplant is of course motivated and influenced by the extensiveness of the legal regime in place, but also by motives of both cost and legitimacy. It is undeniably less expensive to redesignate or revive a previously suspended legal framework than starting a process with the aim of creating new structures, at least if viewed in the short term. It is also considered easier to gain legitimacy in the whole law reform process by utilising something 'old' and familiar.[429]

Familiarity, on the other hand, might carry specific disadvantages. In cases such as Haiti, the UN found the law generally outdated. In other situations the laws went back to the seventeenth century, with few updates, creating contradictions with recent improvements and international obligations.[430]

The ineffectiveness of the existing criminal justice system in Bosnia and Herzegovina in getting to grips with 'modern' crimes became apparent in the war to peace transition. The criminal law in Bosnia and Herzegovina was lacking in clarity and meaning. Definitions of offences such as corruption, money laundering and other economic crimes were either obsolete or absent. The consequences of clinging to the existing criminal law structure were that the police, judges and prosecutors did not possess the adequate means of dealing with contentious cases, resulting in few convictions for economic crimes in the first phase of the transition.[431]

---

427 Strohmeyer 2001, Collapse and Reconstruction p. 59.

428 UNMIK/REG/1999/24 Section 2. A request for clarification to the SRSG was made, for example, in relation to the anti-discrimination law. See Mole 2001 p. 296.

429 UNSG S/2004/616 p. 7.

430 See e.g. Culolo 2001.

431 ICG 2002, Courting Disaster: The Misrule of Law in Bosnia and Herzegovina p. 27. It should be noted that the lack of a criminal law and criminal procedural law review was largely because of recalcitrant political leaders in the particular entities. The Office of the High Representative began the development of a unified criminal code for the whole of Bosnia and Herzegovina in 2000, simultaneously with the establishment of the so-called 'State Court'.

The simple restatement method is clearly not an appropriate solution for all cases, despite its recent popularity as an act of foundation in the early phase of a transition from war and crisis. With deficient legal frameworks requiring long-term law reform measures, a simple basic restatement is likely to cause further confusion and contradiction on the applicable law problems that it was meant to solve, unless such an approach is carefully modified in relation to the capacity of the existing or emerging local legal institutions and to specific problems and constraints within the legal environment.

The very processes by which restatements are made also seem to influence their reception. In both Kosovo and East Timor, there was only minimal consultation with the legal professionals concerned and with others directly responsible for implementing and upholding the rule of law. It seems reasonable to assume that a top-down decision on such a controversial aspect of rule of law development can be counterproductive.

CONSTITUTIONAL REFORM

ACTS OF FOUNDATION

Interrelated with (yet also separate from) the question of applicable law are those decisions taken on constitutional authority. One difficult and crucial aspect in war to peace transitions is to restore constitutionally established authority, because when weak or absent it affects fundamentally the legal and administrative system.[432] Constitutional reform also occupies a special place in rule of law reform because it demonstrates a long-term commitment to reform, since constitutions by their nature are intended to be more enduring than restatements of applicable law or other law reform initiatives.[433] Moreover, the hope is that elaboration of constitutional arrangements will contribute to the long-term non-violent resolution of conflicts.[434]

In recent decades much has been done in support of constitutional reform.[435] It follows from constitutional reform procedures in Iraq, Afghanistan and Somalia that the drafting of constitutions rarely takes place in times of political stability, but rather during great upheavals and political turmoil.[436] The influence of international law is clear in constitutional reform, most often through the creation of a 'Bill of Rights'. A new constitution is in this way interlinked with international law that allows for international conventions,

---

432 DESA & UNDP 2007 39.
433 See, Guidance Note of the Secretary-General, 2009.
434 Jackson 2008 p. 1254.
435 See e.g. Samuels 2006. See also the numerous Venice Commission opinions on draft laws relating to constitutional reform and amendments.
436 Scheppele 2008 p. 1378.

particularly on human rights, to become immediately part of domestic legal systems. International support in constitutional reform thus enables international actors and national rights-based groups and organisations to advocate and press for increased compliance with international obligations.[437]

In addition, constitutions provide the rules of the game by determining how power is exercised (and the consequences of violation) – that is, the defined functions of the executive, the legislative and judicial bodies, the proper allocation of power and the regulation of access to it, and the rights of citizens. Drafting a constitution in times of violent change thus becomes an act of practical and symbolic significance. Societies torn by conflict, with an authoritarian past or internal division, might see the opportunity to progress, to improve living conditions and right past wrongs. Constitutions in this sense look both to the past and future "informed by a conception of constitutional justice that is distinctively transitional".[438]

The newly enacted constitution of Kosovo in 2008 is a good example. The constitution adopted after the declaration of independence from Serbia sets a broad aspirational framework, and includes provisions that give international law direct applicability and higher status than domestic law (save for the constitution). The constitutional court has a composition that allows for six national judges, and three international judges, the latter appointed by the international civilian presence in Kosovo with support from the president of the European Court of Human Rights.[439] The constitution also seeks to institutionalise a framework for a multi-ethnic state in response to past ethnic division and conflict. Chapter 3 stipulates the specific rights of communities and their members (referring to the minority groups). Beyond rights to language, culture, freedom of movement (contacts between communities), this chapter also intends to secure representation and participation of communities. This is achieved through consultative councils at national level, established in Article 60, with the right of communities to comment on legislative or policy initiatives initiated by government. At local level, the Kosovo constitution has introduced a mechanism intended to automatically trigger the representation and participation of minority groups. Article 61 established the office of Vice Presidency of Municipal Assemblies in communities representing at least ten per cent of residents in any municipality.

Despite recent movements in externally supported constitutional reform in war to peace transitions, there is no blueprint. Different situations still require context-specific solutions. In some cases, notably Burundi, constitutional reform has been incremental and focused on adding or linking international standards

437 Fogelklou 2003 p. 17: "it is primarily the constitutions and the public law legislation that protects human rights and contributes to the emergence of the rule of law".

438 Teitel 2000 p. 191.

439 Morina 2010 p. 133.

to the framework. In other constitutional reform processes, as in East Timor and Afghanistan, the approach has been characterised by a grand design that provides wholly, or partially, new constitutions. Furthermore, the forms of constitutional support may be distinguished between a drafting negotiated between elites or a course that includes the population and a broad range of stakeholders, or constitutional reform imposed from the top or from outside in a rather more authoritative way.[440]

POLITICAL COMMITMENT AND OWNERSHIP

A central question in constitutional reform concerns limits on executive power. Establishing limits, and holding governments accountable, depends inherently on the will of the executive to subject its authority to legal rules and independent review. In societies torn asunder by war, the necessity of political will and commitment to the moral significance of the rule of law becomes accentuated in constitutional reform, when one considers that typically the political landscape preceding transitions has been governed by the gun.[441] Constitutional reform also expressly highlights the need for ownership as a central feature for the successful 'anchoring' of constitutional norms to political elites.

The centrality of political commitment towards the creation of a transition blueprint of act of foundation is illustrated in the context of post-war Liberia. Following the cessation of hostilities, and the creation of a transitional government and parliament, the interim government sought to gain revenue and income and "each warring faction was given key public corporations and autonomous agencies, with promises to allow them to continue siphoning off state resources".[442] Comprehensive constitutional reform seeking to strengthen transparency, openness and accountability under such circumstances is naturally difficult to implement.

Accepting Constitutional Restraints

Constitutional reform and political commitment makes plain the 'win or lose' vein inherent in rule of law reform. Indeed, constitutional reform might also further aggravate an already tense situation. From the perspective of the need for political will and commitment in constitutional reform, the rule of law could to a certain extent be described as a pattern of behaviour. The executive accepts being subject to constitutional constraint because of tradition, ethics, integrity, or because of the 'electoral connection' – that is, "rulers develop an interest in

440 See Jackson 2008 p. 1260, describing different models of constitutional processes after war and crisis.
441 See Elkins, Ginsburg & Melton 2007–2008 pp. 1142–1143.
442 ICG 2003, Liberia: Security Challenges p. 2.

binding themselves through institutional mechanisms of accountability if voters punish them at the polls should they fail".[443] Considerable pressure might also be exerted by the civil society to an extent that constitutional reform is unavoidable. In other circumstances they might find economic incentives from playing by the rules – that is, by creating political and legal stability in order to attract foreign investors.[444] In any case, in certain countries and regions, the liberty to act at pleasure and the unfettered exercise of power have become entrenched features, where governance and politics are informed by 'big man' rule or patronage in which personal relationships trump formal rules.[445]

Just as the 'big man' personalisation of political power in many respects describes a form of an entrenched behavioural pattern, it does not mean the predestination of a particular system of governance. There are several cases where personalised power has become institutionalised. For example, since the 1990s most leaders in Africa have left office through institutional means in contrast with previous decades where there tended to be violently deposed by coups, assassinations or other forms of violent force. In those instances where political leaders stayed in power longer than the term of office decreed, a majority did so institutionally by changing the constitution.[446] These and other examples of a shift from personalisation to institutional rule remind us that culture is not static, though it is sometimes relatively easy to hide behind the cultural factor when criticising or dismissing the possibilities of rule of law and constitutional reform in a particular society.

On a cautiously optimistic note, constitutional reform appears to play an important part in support of a culture of 'playing by the rules'. Political commitment to constitutional authority is further affected by levels of national ownership in reform procedures. This is the extent to which national authorities and strong interest groups are able to control and own the reform process in relation to international actors. Thus the idea is that political commitment can be facilitated by allowing national elites to set agendas and reform imperatives.

National Ownership

The sort of catch-all concept of ownership did not emerge specifically within the rule of law, though it has some precise linkages to law and the process of law making. Rather, the concept of ownership emerged as a lesson learned in the general debate on aid and development assistance. More broadly, the concept has

443 Schedler 1999, Conclusion p. 334.

444 Hathaway 2002 pp. 2002f. Similar to human rights treaties, rule of law assistance could also be said to have a dual function: being instrumental in terms of creating new laws and legal institutions while also functioning as an expression or declaration, sometimes with little genuine meaning.

445 Posner & Young 2007 p. 127. See, also, Jackson & Rotberg 1984.

446 Posner & Young 2007 p. 127.

come to mean that donor agencies should consult, listen to, include and provide for ownership for local stakeholders in the course of reform. The Organisation for Economic Cooperation and Development (OECD), for example, included in its 1995 policy document New Global Context a passage on ownership, arguing that for successful advancement the people of developing countries must be 'owners' of their policies and programmes.[447]

The concept of ownership was given a further boost with the launching of the World Bank's Comprehensive Framework for Development.[448] The Comprehensive Development Framework called for increased ownership in development cooperation. According to this framework, developing countries must be in the 'driver's seat' and should determine priorities and the sequencing of reforms. The subsequent Poverty Reduction Strategy Papers, initiated by the World Bank and the IMF in 1999, sought to bring local people and organisations into the strategic planning process.[449] They were intended to work as instruments in the drafting of development strategies in which local actors received assistance in formulating policies.

Ownership matters are sometimes regulated through peace agreements or UN Security Council resolutions, where the establishment of constitutional drafting commissions or interim assemblies under a joint structure with both national and international agencies are detailed. While the text of peace agreements and international mandates emphasises the importance of democratic institutions being accountable to the constituency, the very presence of international actors in effect makes this difficult to uphold. The Dayton Agreement, for example, establishes Bosnia and Herzegovina as a democratic state that should be both responsive and accountable to its citizens. At the same time, the structure of international governance with the Office of the High Representative and the Peace Implementation Council, undermines and compromises such standards.[450]

National and international actors engaged in the drafting of a new constitution in a war to peace transition do not normally enjoy the luxury of unlimited time, and are often under immense political pressure. In such circumstances drafters are prone to apply model constitutional frameworks. This can be attended by difficulty, since turning to the nearest solution to the most pressing of problems means that national and international actors will not always have "sharp understandings that the institutions they are creating have necessary characteristics flowing from the very nature of the institutions".[451] Constitution-making also suffers from 'ad hocism', and reform initiatives

447 OECD/DAC 1995.
448 World Bank 2003, Conflict Affected Countries p. 1.
449 See Craig & Porter 2003 pp. 56f.
450 Dayton Agreement, Annex 4, Arts. I, II. See, also, OHR 1999 Report by the High Representative to the Secretary-General of the UN.
451 Tushnet 1999 p. 1300.

founded on happenstance, with international experts are all too eager to assist by providing best practices and advice based upon constitutions that they know and with which they are familiar.[452]

Feldman argues against the form of imposed constitutionalism in which international participants simply supply a ready-made constitution. Though the actual document might satisfy the establishment of liberal values, such as equality, it is a short term strategy (according to Feldman) so long as such values are imposed from the outside and in opposition to the interests of the political elite. The external influence on substantive values is in this sense only as sustainable commensurate with the amount of international pressure applied to the particular state.[453]

When one considers that constitutionalism means more than just a modern constitution on paper, and that implementation depends on an institutional framework, appropriate behaviour, and a willingness on the part of the authorities concerned to uphold the laws, the temporary international involvement would seem to be limited unless values and principles are 'anchored' to the relevant local circumstances. Samuels found (based upon 12 cases of constitutional reform) that where constitutional processes include politically contentious issues that threatened established power-structures (formal or informal), the power elites tended to react "by undermining the constitutions, amending them, preventing their adoption, or preventing their enforcement".[454]

That conclusion accords with Feldman's main point, that values promoted by international actors will only evolve if they are in the interests of political elites, which means allowing them to negotiate constitutional outcomes without external imposition.[455] In those situations where international actors exert strong pressure or directly draft provisions containing substantive content, for example, in terms of human rights law this could (paradoxically) reduce the odds of constitutional agreements that respect such values.[456]

While caution against imposing values externally might appear to be a pragmatic strategy, it does not account for the affect of the imposition of values from the inside by one or several influential groups, for example, as with the Iraqi constitutional process. Though the external pressure was evident, internal voices also sought to be heard – such as religious and secular factions arguing for and against a more explicit role for religion. Islam is stated to be a foundational source within the constitution. At the same time, no law can be contrary to the rights enumerated in the Iraqi constitution or to principles of democracy. The introduction of democracy and individual rights as interpretive instruments came as a result of an attempt to limit the notion of Islam as a foundational

452 Ibid., p. 1229.
453 Feldman 2005 p. 879.
454 Samuels 2006 p. 5.
455 Feldman 2005 p. 888.
456 Ibid., p. 882.

source of law: "Shia negotiators opposed this language but could not win over the combined Kurdish and secular negotiators."[457] Thus, while an imposition from the outside might lead to an actual undermining of substantive outcomes, it should also be recognised that the consequences of internal negotiations over substantive outcomes can lead to uncertainties, for example, on the hierarchy of norms which might prove to be just as counterproductive.

Public Participation in Constitution-Making Processes

In contrast to the Realpolitik argument of allowing political elites to negotiate constitutional arrangements, is the fact that involvement and participation in much broader senses are not merely catch-phrases thought up by the donor community. Constitutional reform, which in the past was undertaken by way of elite-brokered power maps, is now increasingly regarded by local constituencies as responsive instruments that should include and allow for civil society participation.[458] In contrast with post-second world war experiences, where the US drafted a constitution for Japan, constitution-making after a conflict now takes on rather more subtle and complex features.[459]

The assumption behind inclusion and participation of the public is that it results in different innovative forms of governance.[460] The common people in war-torn societies are also increasingly expected to participate, to be consulted and have their say on the formulation of new constitutional frameworks. There are indications that where such participation and consultation has been lacking, citizens and political leaders "have tended to reject constitutions imposed on them without their involvement".[461] Another aspect of inclusion and participation extending beyond political elites is that such things could lead to a constitutional framework that increasingly respects free and fair elections, political equality, human rights and the means of accountability.[462]

A general international experience in brokering and assisting in the drafting of constitutions in crisis-ridden societies is that often the best practices and principles for consultation, transparency and participation fail to be adopted.[463] One example is the constitutional proceedings in Iraq. A matter of days before the constitutional referendum, a provision on the legislative body was added which had not formed part of the printed constitution circulated for review.[464]

457 Danchin 2009 p. 86.
458 See, for example, the course of constitution-making in Rwanda. Banks 2007–2008 p. 106.
459 See e.g. Elkins, Ginsburg & Melton 2007–2008 discussing the characteristics of 'occupation constitutions'.
460 Banks 2006–2007 p. 112.
461 Samuels 2006 p. 5.
462 Ibid., p. 6.
463 Chesterman 2004 p. 211.
464 The article inserted at the last moment was Art. 142. It stated that the elected legislative body should "at the beginning of its work" form a committee to make recommendations "within a

The constitutional process was characterised by time constraints (though there was a time extension from the date set in the Transitional Administrative Law – TAL) hastily hurried in by the US, and was undermined by a lack of participation by Sunni representatives (owing both to a failure to include them and a conscious decision by their leaders to boycott the drafting process and the referendum). How the constitution was drafted, according to some observers, might even in the long run, "do more to exacerbate inter-group conflicts than to ameliorate it".[465] Moreover, and as mentioned above, there was considerable focus on the part of international actors on the inclusion of a 'modern' Bill of Rights in order to firmly establish a post-Saddam political system of governance. The preoccupation with primarily civil and political rights was evident in the drafting of the TAL, which superseded the development of the Iraqi constitution. But the real problem was not how the Bill of Rights should be formulated, but lay instead in the area of 'high politics' – that is, the structure of the government, the division of power between the centre and districts, what part religion would play, and how to adopt the final constitution.[466] None of these contentious and predominantly procedural issues were satisfactorily settled in the TAL, and many remain controversial in the final Iraqi constitution.[467]

The difficulty of ownership is also present with regard to the whole question of government in a transitional period. In Afghanistan, the Bonn Agreement established an Interim Administration until elections could be held. The question of whom to invite into the new government was to be decided according to "professional competence and personal integrity" and "with due regard to the ethnic, geographic and religious composition of Afghanistan and to the importance of participation of women".[468] The mismatch of former warlords and Western educated diplomats that came to occupy posts in the Interim Administration (and later, also, in the Afghan parliament and government), illustrates the difficulty of ownership from an external actor perspective.[469] The Emergency Loya Jirga that elected the new Afghan government was accused by international human rights groups of failing to live up to its promise of blocking those who had committed human rights violations.[470]

Questions of ownership, in the minimal sense including national elites, and in a broader sense a form of popular ownership, thus present a host of difficulties. While international players assert the necessity of ownership in constitutional

period not to exceed four months" concerning "necessary amendments". It also called for voting rules both within parliament (absolute majority) and by required popular referendum (majority vote). This approach violates good practices on referendums. See, for example, Venice Commission 2007 No. 371/2006 on good practices for referendums.

465 Stromseth, *et al.*, 2007 p. 96.

466 Diamond 2004 p. 51.

467 USAID 2007 pp. 7–8.

468 Chapter III A 3 of the Bonn Agreement.

469 See Human Rights Watch 2002.

470 Ibid.

reform, it is not always clear whose ownership they mean, nor is it clear what standards are to be set for genuine interlocutors to be identified in war-torn societies. In addition, it is not clear what national ownership means if such control were to go against international human rights provisions or the constitutional mandates of international agencies.

TRANSITIONAL CHARTERS AND THE REVIVAL OF CONSTITUTIONAL TRADITION

Another difficult question to address concerns the form and purpose of constitutional reform in transitions. Two distinct approaches can be identified: transitional charters and fully fledged constitutions. The extensive literature on constitution-making in eastern and central Europe after the fall of the Berlin wall and the dissolution of the former Soviet Union tend to emphasise the important part played by transitional charters as means of progress in constitutional reform.[471]

While formal changes to the constitutions of several central and eastern European countries were made immediately, more comprehensive constitutional advance spanned a longer time and its course was incremental.[472] It is particularly noteworthy that these processes took place without bloodshed or significant political violence. The piecemeal fashion of consultations and round-table negotiations, which characterised many of the transitions, allowed for a deliberate democratic bargaining over a longer time. This in turn managed to avoid violence and political turbulence.[473]

The relative stable and incremental processes in central and eastern Europe can be contrasted with situations in war-torn societies. The first step towards constitutional reform typically occurs under an interim government whose composition reflects the outcome of the conflict rather than popular sentiments and actual representation established through democratic elections.[474] It is often the case that before democratic elections can be held, an interim governing body of sorts needs to be formed that will be responsible for formulating the 'rules of the game' for movement towards democratic and rule of law institutions.

The combination of interim governments composed of former warring parties and other non-elected influential actors poses a challenge for

471 See, generally, Örkény & Scheppele 1999; Pribá & Young 1999.

472 See Jackson 2008 p. 1256ff.

473 Ibid., p. 1267. One can also make a comparison with the experience of South Africa. Early on there was an interim constitution, adopted in 1993, with basic principles for the negotiation of a permanent constitution. The interim constitution also set up a Constitutional Court as the final arbiter. The incremental process contained a massive public education and outreach programme with extensive circulation of drafts of the constitution.

474 See Jackson 2008 p. 1249 who argues that the process of drafting a written constitution may actually be contrary to the constitutional values that the document seeks to espouse.

constitutional reform in terms of legitimacy. On the one hand, it could be maintained that the frameworks adopted during an interim government are expected to be changed at a later stage, and that the establishment of constitutional reform commissions and interim assemblies are necessary from political and security perspectives. On the other hand, it must also be acknowledged that interim bodies, and the rules drafted under their stewardship, might prove difficult to depart from at a later stage. While the 'rules of the game' can be rewritten it is difficult to "disempower those who have been given power and authority under interim rules".[475] Furthermore, those granted power during an interim period are also likely to be involved in the writing of more permanent rules. Interim governments and transitional charters may therefore be short in duration but cast a long shadow into the future.[476] The time of change can turn out to be anything but transitory in nature, and even entrench vested interests and informal rules from before or during the period of conflict.[477]

Afghanistan exhibits the difficulties related to transitional charters in a war to peace transition. Constitutional reform in Afghanistan has also involved a variety of unique actions such as the reliance on customary institutions and practices – that is, the emergency *loya jirga* and the constitutional *loya jirga*. The course of events leading up to the 2004 Afghan constitution began with an interim charter. In accordance with the Bonn Agreement, which provided the first ground rules for the transition, the previous constitution of 1964 was determined to apply. The conditions for the 1964 constitution's applicability were that it could not contradict the Bonn Agreement or Afghanistan's international obligations. Moreover, the provisions relating to the monarchy, the executive and legislative bodies of the constitution were explicitly determined to no longer apply. The existing ordinary laws and regulations fell under the same conditions, and the Interim Authority, created through the Bonn Agreement, was vested with the power to repeal or amend laws and regulations that contravened to the conditions of the restatement.[478]

The problem with the revival approach in Afghanistan was that the new provisions, calling for the 1964 constitution to remain in force, were supposed to supersede all previous constitutions, laws, decrees and fiats. This restatement was also to be interpreted with reference to Afghanistan's international legal obligations. As discussed above in relation to Kosovo and East Timor, decisions on applicable law are difficult. Even where it might conform better with

---

475 Manning 2007 p. 54.

476 Ibid.

477 See Davis & Trebilcock 2008 p. 935 who sees informal rules and various non-legal norms as having a substantial influence on commitment to formal constitutional principles. The power structures and previous function of law in terms of authority and autonomy would then seem to have a strong affect on transitional charters, and in the long term on constitutions proper.

478 Bonn Agreement (2001) Section II (1).

international law and modern standards, it might still be resisted locally for political reasons.

With weak capacity in the legal community of Afghanistan, the lack of qualified legal professionals, and the struggle to establish state authority and jurisdiction throughout the territory, the revival of the constitution was fraught with difficulties. The burden involved how the constitution would be assessed, and defining the authority that would issue the mandate to provide a definite statement on compatibility between old laws and regulations and the new legal framework including reconciling these things with Afghanistan's international legal obligations.[479] The embryonic state of Afghanistan was seen to have no less than 22,626 articles of applicable legal codes and some 52, 458 presidential orders and decrees.[480] There were also regulations, decrees and customary norms. This layered complexity in relation creates uncertainties on applicable law, as for example regarding the legal frameworks on property rights and the right to housing where the civil code, Shariah law and customary practices overlap.[481]

Afghanistan provides simultaneously arguments for, and caution towards, constitutional drafting in the immediate time after the conclusion of a peace agreement. The need for a re-establishment of constitutional authority in Afghanistan was clear following the ousting of the Taliban regime and the formation of an interim administration through the Bonn Agreement. At the same time, the initial measures taken in the constitutional reform process also illustrate the risks associated with placing too much faith in weak constitutional traditions.

As with the revived 1964 constitution that provided the executive branch of government with a central and powerful position under the period of democracy in the 1960s,[482] the Bonn Agreement also vested the new executive with great authority. It granted the interim administration vast powers – that is, to establish courts (below the Supreme Court which was set up through the Bonn Agreement); to establish a judicial council for the appointment of judges; to issue decrees; and to establish an independent civil service commission (for the appointment of civil servants).[483] The interim authority was required to abide by a code of conduct in accordance with international standards, and a member of the interim government could only be excluded by other members.[484]

---

479 See Chesterman 2004 p. 175f. The issue was later referred to the Afghan Supreme Court. According to Art. 121 of the 2004 constitution, the Supreme Court holds ultimate authority in determining compliance between the constitution and international obligations or other laws.

480 Report of the Consortium for Response to the Afghanistan Transition 2002 p. 21.

481 Commission on Human Rights E/C.N.4/2004/48/Add.2 p. 11.

482 Grote 2004 p. 905.

483 Bonn Agreement III C (5).

484 Bonn Agreement Articles II (2), III C (1), III C (5), and III C (7–8).

Centralisation and the provisions of extensive powers for the executive in the 1964 constitution and in the Bonn Agreement, were subsequently carried over into the drafting of the 2004 constitution. Thus the turbulent time during which the new constitution was drafted also compounded the notion that what was required was a strong role for the president and executive in the constitutional structure of Afghanistan.[485]

In the 2004 constitution the legislative power of parliament was partially bypassed through the extended rights of the president to issue regulations, together with the presidential veto against legislation that could only be overruled by a two-thirds majority.[486] Moreover, the president has authority to legislate in the place of the parliament in "emergency situations".[487] The meaning of "emergency situations" is not defined in the constitution, as opposed to the more commonly used term "state of emergency" that allows for some derogation from fundamental rights in times of war, threat of war, serious rebellion, or natural disaster. "Emergency situations", according to the Afghan constitution, are to be defined by the government. Considering the current turbulence in Afghanistan, and the rather bleak outlook for security and stability, there is a risk that "emergency situations" will be declared and defined by the executive, providing the president with *de facto* legislative powers similar to those of a legislature.[488]

Moreover, the 2004 constitution allows only for restricted judicial review.[489] The Supreme Court retains the competence, but only the government or lower courts can make a request for review. There is no right of individuals to institute proceedings in the Supreme Court, claiming that fundamental rights have been violated by either action or inaction on the part of the state. The Independent Human Rights Commission is supposed to provide for that type of legal redress, and can refer a case to the "legal authorities", but its relationship to petitions founded on an administrative act is unclear in the constitution and in the decree establishing the commission.[490]

The questions raised in the Afghan constitutional process provide some cause for concern as well as insights into the difficulties attending the drafting of constitutions in war to peace transitions on the basis of interim arrangements. It also calls into question the viability of reviving previous constitutions, where

---

485 See Grote 2004 pp. 897–915.

486 Constitution of the Islamic Republic of Afghanistan Art. 76: "to implement the fundamental lines of the policy of the country and regulate its duties, the government shall devise as well as approve regulations, which shall not be contrary to the body or spirit of any law"; and Art. 94 on presidential veto.

487 Constitution of the Islamic Republic of Afghanistan Art. 79.

488 Grote 2004 p. 909.

489 Ibid., p. 911ff. For a detailed description of the organisation of the judiciary in Afghanistan, see Moschtaghi 2006.

490 See Decree of the President of the Interim Administration of Afghanistan on the Establishment of an Afghan Independent Human Rights Commission 2002 Art. 58.

such revival means more a text on paper than a culture and tradition of constitutionalism involving the values of a separation of powers and accountability before the law.

INTERNATIONAL LAW, NORMS AND THE PURSUIT OF RESPECTABILITY

In the restatement process, as well as in constitutional reform, a commonly applied method of influence is to push and lobby for something 'new', by supporting war-torn societies in acceding to international treaties. Human rights law in particular is frequently employed as a model for review and as an overall assessment of law reform and constitutional drafting.

The reasons for an emphasis on international human rights law depend on the legitimacy that such norms are perceived to confer on rule of law reform itself and on the war-torn state. International human rights law, besides UN norms and standards are by international actors perceived to be "a solid basis for guidance" and for offering a form of orientation and inspiration in rule of law reform generally.[491]

Furthermore, human rights also correspond with many of the root causes of conflict as reflected in many of the recent peace agreements. In particular, for the UN's work in war-damaged states, international human rights law functions as a foundational framework. In a report on rule of law reform in war-torn societies, the UN Secretary-General stated that assistance must be based upon international norms and standards, because such standards are inherently possessed of a certain legitimacy that cannot be said to be true of exported national standards and laws.[492] In the Handbook on UN Multidimensional Peacekeeping Operations, international human rights are seen as the first entry-point to law reform in order to establish the rule of law, requiring the enactment of legislation that demonstrates governmental commitment "to internationally recognized minimum standards of justice and human rights [...] including ratifying appropriate international treaties or covenants and incorporating them into national legislation or through the overhaul of existing legislation to ensure compliance with international norms and minimum standards for criminal justice".[493] Similarly, the World Bank's vice presidency states with regard to the

491 See e.g. United Nations Basic Principles on the Independence of the Judiciary (1985). See, also, UN training and instructions manuals, United Nations Criminal Justice Standards for Peace-keeping Police 1994; Manual on the Effective Prevention and investigation of Extralegal, Arbitrary and Summary Executions (1991); and the Guidelines for the Conduct of United Nations Inquiries into Allegations of Massacres (1995).

492 UNSG S/2004/616 p. 4.

493 Peacekeeping Best Practices Unit 2003 p. 94.

Bank's work on rule of law reform that countries should as a first step "take stock of the international laws and treaties that are binding on them".[494]

International human rights also work as 'levers' by actors involved in rule of law promotion, particularly those who advocate a strong material reading of the rule of law. The provisions in some of the more salient human rights conventions emphasise that all are equal before the law, entitled to legal protection before the law, and have the right to an effective remedy when rights are violated. The International Covenant on Civil and Political Rights provides specifically in relation to arrestable offences for a "fair and public hearing by a competent, independent and impartial tribunal established by law" as well as the right to "be informed, at the time of arrest, of the reasons for his arrest", and to be "brought promptly before a judge or other officer authorised by the law to exercise judicial power [...] entitled to trial within a reasonable time or to release".[495] At regional level a number of human rights treaties can be applied as levers and models in rule of law reform, including the European Convention on Human Rights, the American Declaration on the Rights and Duties of Man, American Convention on Human Rights, and the African Charter on Human and People's Rights.

The Venice Commission represents an example of how international human rights norms, in this case regional human rights through the European Convention on Human Rights, can play a decisive part in law reform efforts. The Commission, established in 1990, has been active in the two most salient state-building missions in the Balkans – Bosnia and Herzegovina, and Kosovo – and provided advice on constitutional reform, law reform and on matters to do with the judiciary. In a direct and practical, the Commission advised the Kosovo and Bosnia and Herzegovina legislative assemblies on draft laws that were submitted to it for review, for example regarding people's advocate in Kosovo and conflict of interests in government institutions in Bosnia and Herzegovina.[496]

Treaty Ratification After War and Crisis

The UN often pushes for war-torn societies to accede to or ratify international treaties.[497] These attempts at 'socialisation' result in the interaction and integration of international standards on human rights with the national legal systems of such societies over a relatively short time. From the perspective of international actors, treaty ratification is seen as having the potential to assist a state to "reassemble domestic legal infrastructure as well as demonstrating

494 World Bank 2000 p. 38.

495 ICCPR Art. 14 (1), Art. 9 (2), Art. 9 (3).

496 See, for example, Venice Commission Opinion No. 434/2007 on the draft law on the people's advocate in Kosovo and the Opinion No. 466/2008 on conflict of interest in government institutions in Bosnia and Herzegovina.

497 See Vienna Convention on the Law of Treaties Art. 11: signature, exchange of instruments constituting a treaty, ratification, acceptance, approval or accession.

public support for important international principles".[498] Liberia sets the example. With the support of the UN, it ratified 14 different treaties in 2004, only a year after the peace agreement was signed.[499] The following year the chairman of Liberia's National Transitional Parliament signed 83 treaties.[500] A further example of the infusion and influence of international law is that of the new criminal code for Kosovo, promulgated in 2003. This includes chapters on crimes under international law – that is, war crimes and crimes against humanity, as defined in the Rome Statute of the International Criminal Court.[501] During the course of the law reform in Kosovo, international and national drafters took stock of international standards in order to create a modern criminal code.

On constitutional reform, the newly drafted constitutions of Afghanistan, East Timor, and Kosovo all contain provisions setting out in the opening paragraphs the key international human rights treaties to be observed, as well as lists of fundamental rights and freedoms. In the recent 2008 constitution of Kosovo, a host of international agreements were accorded direct applicability and to "have priority over provisions of laws and other acts of public institutions".[502]

The infusion of human rights law, either in the form of a Bill of Rights or of provisions stipulating direct applicability, is often the result of international pressure, combined with support from rights advocacy groups within the particular country. In Afghanistan, Article 7 of the constitution requires the state to observe a number of international treaties, including the UN Charter and the Universal Declaration of Human Rights. This constitutional provision was driven by "strong international pressure on the transitional government and key participants at the Loya Jirga".[503]

The inclusion of international treaties in national legal frameworks might provide human rights defenders with an advocacy platform for litigation and 'watchdog' functions, depending on the independence and capacity of the judiciary concerned to accept and deal adequately with human rights claims in domestic law. However, the uncertain status of interpretation of international

---

498 Durham 2009 pp.177–178.

499 See UNSG S/2004/972.

500 See Treaty Event during United Nations Summit Receives Record Number of Treaty Actions (Press Release) 22 September 2005.

501 Human Rights Committee CCPR/C/UNK/CO/1 (2006) para. 5. But as Durham 2009 p. 189 notes: "the technical resources needed for genuine incorporation of the principles found in the 103 treaties into Liberia's domestic law would be considerable. Furthermore, in such a short time frame, it is unlikely that there could have been genuine attempts to foster debate in the broader community about the new obligations and responsibilities to be assumed by the country".

502 Constitution of the Republic of Kosovo Chapter II Art. 22, i.e. Universal Declaration of Human Rights, European Convention on Human Rights, International Covenant for Civil and Political Rights, Convention on the Elimination of all Forms of Racial Discrimination.

503 Schoiswohl 2006 p. 842.

law in Afghanistan today, as in many situations after war and crisis, raises doubts over the possibility of human rights defenders having any substantial impact in this way.

Generally, the ratification of treaties and the technical evaluation in the process of ensuring formal compliance provides an opportunity for review and the identification of reform priorities. It is also possible that new obligations flowing from international law can alleviate national tensions in certain areas – that is, by elevating domestic disputes to be resolved by recourse to international obligations.

Importing International Norms

Furthermore, where the UN has been mandated to perform executive functions, there has been a practice of applying international law in a more direct way, possibly also binding the staff of the UN and other international actors. In Kosovo and East Timor, the transitional administrations respectively decided that public officials should observe international standards of human rights in the administration of justice and in their official functions.[504] What the term 'observe' means is difficult to assert. It might simply mean a form of guidance and a yardstick for public officials. The phrasing 'should observe' does not seem to imply a direct effect of the different international human rights treaties in the respective domestic jurisdictions of Kosovo and East Timor.[505] The UN Committee on Human Rights, however, argues that it does provide a direct applicability and that "the Covenant was [...] binding on all persons undertaking public duties and or holding public office in Kosovo".[506]

It is unclear what influence or effect the importation of international norms and standards has, in particular international human rights law, where the retaliatory costs of non-compliance are "low to nonexistent", as Hathaway argued.[507] While several law reform projects founded on international law incorporation have yielded changes in criminal law, commercial law and even administrative law, it is uncertain to what it is that these changes will 'stick'. While it is possible to observe a change on the surface level of law in the form of new laws and regulations, new institutional structures and mandates, it remains to be seen what substantial changes it will bring.[508]

504 UNMIK/REG/1999/1 and UNTAET/REG/1999/1.

505 Alvarez 2006 p. 179: "no one knows for sure whether the matter is a question of legal duties or an ex gratia assumption of responsibility, whether it applies to all IOs with respect to all operations, or even if all of international human rights law does apply to the UN, how it does so".

506 Human Rights Committee CCPR/C/UNK/CO/1 (2006) para 5.

507 Hathaway 2002 p. 1938.

508 Morlino & Magen 2009 pp. Methods of Influence, 40–43. It is rather easy to observe changes regarding rule adoption, but more difficult to predict rule implementation and rule internalisation.

This method of law reform seems to be applied after war and crisis because it reflects the institutional mandates of international agencies, and that domestic governments comply in hope of engendering some sense of legitimacy and social good will. However, there are many ways of undermining new treaty obligations and it must be considered what different treaties require in terms of compliance – that is, to bring national law into conformity with the treaty obligations, as well as the national constitutional rules in a war-torn society, for such process of legal transfer to be effective.

Implementation or 'internalisation' of international norms and standards is difficult to achieve even in rule of law reform in developing countries, without the constraints of conflict and systemic crises. For national public officials and international personnel in UN administrations, such as Kosovo and East Timor, the introduction of a non-exhaustive list of human rights treaties to be applied in the initial stages of an intervention can be difficult considering the anatomies of societies in crisis, and the logistical and practical demands to which those situations give rise.[509]

It should also be taken into consideration that the direct linking of international law to domestic constitutional and statutory obligations might be of more a noncommittal approach than open support of all aspects of international treaties enmeshed in domestic law.[510] As Hathaway observes: "when a country ratifies a treaty, it may do so for purely disingenuous reasons [...] for aspirational reasons [...] or for self-interested reasons".[511] Feldman even considers that in the recent constitutional reforms in Afghanistan and Iraq, the inclusion of provisions that incorporate international treaty obligations can be partly explained by the fact that "some or even many of those persons who ratified these constitutional documents were unaware of the far-reaching domestic legal consequences of the provisions in question."[512]

Incorporating international human rights treaty obligations provides a constitutional platform for many issues considered controversial in the local context without explicitly saying so. Despite the possibility of international law being used as a 'Trojan horse', once incorporated national actors often find ways of circumventing and undermining its influence.[513] Rule of law reform after war and crisis faces not only regulatory practices that can 'water down' imported

509 Devereux & Anderson 2005 p. 303: "there may also be some residual 'economic relativism' – that is, the belief that a country can be 'too poor' to look at meeting international standards".

510 Durham 2009 p. 179 takes the view that treaty ratification is no panacea for post-war states and "if undertaken for purely symbolic purposes, the process can reduce the legitimacy of not only the ratifying state, but of the international legal system as a whole".

511 Hathaway 2002 p. 2022.

512 Feldman 2005 p. 871.

513 Gillespie 2007 showed in his study of rule of law reform in Vietnam on commercial law, how regulatory practice by national actors was used to 'manage' imported legal rights through subordinate legislation, discretionary licensing and other measures.

norms, but also an extremely weak capacity with which to implement them, should political commitment actually exist.[514] Many war-torn societies also display a plurality or layered complexity of law which means that the infusion of human rights norms, for example, are contested and marginalised because of competing legal systems or because of weak outreach on the part of the formal legal system. Treaty ratification or the direct injection of international law in constitutional arrangements also has to be recognised as resource-intensive, requiring action going far beyond a solitary event. As Durham contends, for treaty ratification to be effective it demands both a clear understanding of any new obligations and a discussion directed towards generating constituency support for new legal regimes.[515]

Apart from this direct instilling of human rights law, for example, to serve as normative guidelines in Kosovo and East Timor, and the pushing to accede to new international treaties as in Liberia, the UN also provides a general treaty-monitoring function of compliance with international human rights law. In state-building missions, human rights monitoring is often a constituent part of the mandate, and is either found within the UN mission structure, or complemented by treaty-monitoring bodies and independent rapporteurs of the UN OHCHR. In certain cases, as with the Balkans, such supervision has been 'contracted out' in part to regional organisations. The OSCE is responsible for monitoring the legal system in Kosovo, primarily overseeing the criminal justice system, though the organisation recently added superintendence of the administrative law system to its work.

The adding of new treaty obligations thus provides an extra monitoring and reporting function for these afflicted societies. While this might function as an extra lever and a credible source of identifying areas for reform, one might also consider whether adding reporting and monitoring might further weaken the capacity of legal and administrative institutions. Devereaux and Anderson, for example, express scepticism on whether new reporting mechanisms under human rights treaties is helpful to weak interim governments, in light of the fact that governments in these cleaved states are already subject to numerous reporting obligations as part of international assistance and humanitarian aid.[516]

---

514 Feldman 2005 p. 872 also considers the option that drafters of a constitution accept international law provisions while having no real intention of observing them, and warns that this undercuts the fundamental normative basis of constitutionalism – "that the constitutional document ought to guide actual realities of government practice".

515 Durham 2009 p. 178.

516 Devereaux & Anderson 2008.

INTERNATIONAL STANDARDS AND MODELS FOR THE JUSTICE SECTOR

Despite their normative authority and frequent invocation, it would appear that international and regional human rights instruments are of limited use as technical 'tools' in rule of law reform. There is no treaty on the rule of law, and the normative content must be sought in different human rights agreements. Rules on habeas corpus, for example, do not explicate what 'promptly' means in terms of time (hours or days) nor do the provisions on competent, impartial and independent tribunals provide guidance on what types of institution that this might mean. These questions have to be dealt with on a more detailed and practical level in order to have any substantial influence or effect on rule of law reform.

Owing to the vagueness of many international human rights treaties, donors have come to rely on non-binding standards and principles that provide more detailed instructions. Many of these axioms have been adopted and developed by influential international actors – that is, the UN, the Council of Europe, and international non-governmental organisations. The field of judicial reform, with the objective of securing independent judiciaries, has in particular seen an almost exponential growth in documents stipulating standards and guidelines.

The most well known and commonly referred to set of standards are those of the UN Basic Principles – that is, the Basic Principles on the Independence of the Judiciary (UNBPIJ);[517] the Basic Principles on the Role of Lawyers (UNBPRL);[518] and the Guidelines on the Role of Prosecutors (UNGRP).[519] These non-binding principles attempt to make concrete international standards central to the rule of law conceptualisation in relation to war-torn societies and development cooperation. The UNBPIJ, for example, contains articles relating to the independence of the judiciary with regard to freedom of information, qualification, selection and training, as well as issues concerning the tenure and service of judges. On a regional level the Council of Europe has developed basic principles enunciated in the Recommendations on the Independence, Efficiency, and Role of Judges and in the European Charter on the Statute for Judges.[520]

---

517 Basic Principles on the Role of Judges 1985.

518 Basic Principles on the Role of Lawyers 1990.

519 Guidelines on the Role of Prosecutors 1990. Other central standard-setting tools include: United Nations Rules for the Treatment of Women Prisoners and Non-Custodial Measures for Women Offenders (2010); Code of Conduct for Law Enforcement Officials (1979); Guidelines for the Effective Implementation of the Code of Conduct for Law Enforcement Officials (1989); Basic Principles on the Use of Firearms by Law Enforcement Officials (1990); United Nations Rules for the Protection of Juveniles Deprived of Liberty (1990); and Guidelines on Justice in Matters involving child victims and witnesses (2009).

520 CoE Recommendation (94) 12 and CoE DAJ/DOC (98) 23.

The UN basic principles in particular, but also the common UN rule of law definition,[521] have influenced a rather recent set of devices designed for rule of law reform in war to peace transitions. The UN High Commissioner for Human Rights in 2006 launched a post-conflict 'tool kit', consisting of five sets of instruments:

(1) Truth Commissions;
(2) Mapping the Justice Sector;
(3) Prosecution Initiatives;
(4) Monitoring Legal Systems; and
(5) Vetting.[522]

In 2008 the UN OHCHR floated two more on
(6) Reparations; and
(7) Hybrid Courts.[523]

They are each considered to respond to some of the supreme tests and demands that international actors face in war to peace transitions, and are intended to be employed as practical guidelines in rule of law missions for UN personnel. The respective devices specify 'best practices' regarding monitoring court proceedings, on lessons learned from prosecuting contraventions of international humanitarian law, and how to best conduct overall assessments of the capacity and function of a legal system in a country in transition from war to peace. The ways and means concentrate directly on matters within the justice sector, though it is acknowledged in one of the guidelines that rule of law reform must, early on in any state-building mission, promote greater transparency and accountability in public administration – that is, on such things as vehicle registration, building permits, rubbish removal, public health inspection, banking regulations, and tax collection.[524]

Though standards and benchmarks are non-binding, they do have a significant influence in rule of law reform in war to peace transitions. One example is from Afghanistan and relates to the establishment of the Judicial Reform Commission through presidential decree in 2002.[525] Besides setting down the duties of the judicial commission in identifying and assisting in the selection of judges, the decree also stipulates a set of guiding principles of which the commission must take note when initiating law reform. These guiding

---

521 UNSG S/2004/616 p. 4.

522 OHCHR 2006 HR/PUB/06/1; 2006 HR/PUB/06/2; 2006 HR/PUB/06/3; 2006 HR/PUB/06/4; HR/PUB/06/5.

523 OHCHR 2008 HR/PUB/08/1 and 2008 HR/PUB/08/2.

524 OHCHR 2006 HR/PUB/06/2 p. 14.

525 Afghanistan Presidential Decree No. 153: Formation of the Judicial Reform Commission and its Duties 2 November 2002.

principles relate to the legal frameworks of the law enforcement agencies and the judiciary, as well as the Ministry of Justice, the Attorney General, and the Bar. The guiding principles annexed to the presidential decree refer explicitly to UNBPIJ, the role of prosecutors and a code of conduct for law enforcement personnel.

The elevation of international standards and principles into a guiding implement in a rule of law reform process demonstrates the immediate part that international standards play, and how direct the forms of socialisation can be when international actors function as both teachers of norms as well as norm entrepreneurs.

'JUSTICE PACKAGES'

Another tool used in fashioning rule of law reform in war to peace transitions has recently emerged – the so-called 'model codes project', which attempts to translate international standards and benchmarks into tangible legal rules. The project draws upon the recommendations in the Brahimi Report, which noted a gap in relation to applicable law in cases where the UN substitutes for national governments. Rule of law objectives could benefit, the report argued, from a common UN 'justice package'. Such a thing would allow UN personnel to apply an interim legal code pending the final answer to the 'applicable law' question.[526]

In Kosovo the potential use of model codes became apparent when in the early phases of the state-building missions the Kosovo Force (KFOR), consisting of NATO troops, assumed responsibility for law and order and became involved in large-scale arrests as a result of mounting insecurity and a rise in serious crimes – including arson, grievous assault, and murder. After only two weeks of its operation, KFOR had made more than two hundred arrests. However, the means of holding judicial hearings was lacking, creating a backlog.[527] So, following the line of reasoning in the Brahimi Report, UN personnel in cases similar to Kosovo, would henceforth rely on an already established model law, without undertaking the difficult task of understanding and applying local law, or deciding on applicable law, so that the mission could discharge its rule of law duties.

The codes project, driven by the United States Institute of Peace and the Irish Centre for Human Rights, has developed a set of modules in cooperation with legal experts and practitioners in worldwide consultation. The codes project falls under four headings:

(a) Criminal Code;
(b) Criminal Procedures Code;

526 Brahimi Report 2000 p. 14.
527 Strohmeyer 2001, Collapse and Reconstruction p. 49.

(c) Detention Act and;
(d) Police Powers Act.

The codes are a hybrid of elements of common and civil law.[528]

The intention behind the recommendations in the Brahimi Report and in the codes project was not for the adoption of interim codes in whole or in part in a war-torn society. Besides, this would be difficult considering the plurality of views reflected among different legal systems on crime and correlating punishment. Instead, the codes are intended to serve as a practical device for both international and national actors when they are responsible for law and order, or when involved in criminal justice law reform.[529] The codes – for example the criminal code with more than 225 provisions, including substantive commentaries – seek to make practical recommendations of international standards and principles, such as the right of a person to appear in a court within 72 hours of apprehension.

A circumstance supporting the codes project is that they come fully sustained and do not rely upon the existing legal framework of a particular war-torn society. Since they would be introduced externally, and apply during an interim period, there is a greater chance of their being received and respected. They would also arrive with legal personnel trained in the interim legal framework, and so would not entirely depend on a domestic structure. Some support for this strategy may be derived from Markovits, who argues that laws and legal institutions that come more or less fully supported – like 'potted plants' – are likely to meet with less resistance than other rule of law reforms simply because they do not require adaption to existing frameworks.[530] As demonstrated in the above examination of applicable law, those cases where international actors introduced new elements of law (by infusing international human rights) and required local legal structures to adapt to them, met with considerable difficulties.

Ironically, the external aspect of the codes has often been used to voice criticism of their potential for applicability. The codes are external, but so too are the restatement approaches alien to the legal environments of Kosovo, East Timor and Somalia. Moreover, international interventions in Liberia, Sierra Leone and Haiti, for example, were largely welcomed by war-weary populations

528 See e.g. O'Connor & Rausch 2006.

529 See O'Connor & Rausch 2006 and the several possibilities of using the codes beyond interim measures, as suggested in the Brahimi Report.

530 See Markovits 2004 p. 110 who argues on the basis of rule of law reform in central and eastern Europe, that law reform that is autonomous to a certain degree makes it easier to transplant those "reforms that carry with them their own surroundings ('potted plants') will do better, the more institutional support and personnel they have and the less dependent they are on local cooperation and approval".

and enjoyed a legitimacy that, it seems reasonable to assume, could also attach to external interim codes.[531]

The common problem in East Timor, Kosovo and Somalia was that the designated law in each had repressive pasts. External model codes would at least avoid this perception. Interim codes, applied by trained UN personnel, would allow a longer period of time for deciding on the issue of applicable law. At the same time such codes would require both strong endorsement from the UN and a high level of preparedness on the part of UN personnel. However, just as it cannot be assumed with regard to decisions on applicable law, or on the infusion of international human rights norms, that local political elites will respond based upon a logic of appropriateness, neither can model codes expect support on the basis of their interim and universal character.

INTERNATIONAL STANDARDS AND MODELS OUTSIDE THE JUSTICE SECTOR

The examination in Chapter 2 and 3 of the rule of law concept adopted by international actors demonstrated that rule of law issues outside the justice sector are often excluded – for example, on public administration. Exclusion at the conceptual level is reflected at operational level. The tools and guidelines, for instance, from the OHCHR are for the most part designed for the justice sector. Despite recent developments in normative standards, and in the tools and guidelines for rule of law reform in the justice sector, there are few comparable guiding documents that deal with reform in public administration and other spheres.

The scarcity of general guidelines and devices for the reform of public administration cannot be explained by a lack of widely agreed norms and standards. The formulation of a framework of rule of law principles applicable to public administration founded on internationally recognised standards was proposed as early as 1995 in the UN report entitled The Legal and Regulatory Framework of Public Administration. It proposed a framework for rule of law reform in public administration consisting of:

(1) constitutional reform in order to institutionalise provisions that support citizens' claims and allow for different venues of appeal;
(2) the promotion of provisions for an administrative procedure of appeal, including in such procedure the right to be heard, the right to be informed of any decision, and a further appeals procedure;

---

531 Stromseth, *et al.*, 2006 p. 145: "the general population, exhausted by years of warfare, crime, and disorder, will often be prepared and eager to cooperate with international forces, promising order and a gradual restoration of normalcy".

(3) establishing laws regulating the civil service in matters of recruitment, careers, discipline and codes of conduct;
(4) regulating and clarifying the relationship between public and private actors, including rules on fair competition and transparency;
(5) addressing the issue of which pattern of governance is most desirable, and for what purposes, and to adapt the law accordingly.[532]

Moreover, the Council of Europe, for example, published in 1995 its report The Administration and You, a handbook on principles of administrative law setting out the relationship between administrative agencies and private persons.[533] The publication was designed in the context of the social and economic transition that countries in the former communist block underwent during the 1990s, and drew upon articles in the European Convention on Human Rights, on case law from the European Court of Human Rights, as well as on other instruments developed by the Council of Europe. In another report from the Council of Europe Directorate General of Legal Affairs, Working Together to Build Europe on the Rule of Law, a number of points were covered, most notably the rule of law in relation to administrative and civil law.[534] The report stated that the Council of Europe attached especial importance to administrative law and the administrative courts.[535]

In addition, the Council of Europe has issued a number of resolutions and recommendations on the administration of justice.[536] Most notably, it has developed a set of principles of good administration in Council of Europe member states that could form the basis for rule of law assistance in the same way as the UN Basic Principles, or with other similar instruments on justice sector standards.[537] The Council of Europe principles includes lawfulness, proportionality, and the requirement to inform of decisions, courtesy and many other rules of conduct considered to form the framework of administrative law necessary for sustaining good governance.[538] These normative standards could be applied as entry-points for the development of assessment tools and indicators in state-building missions.

The EU's Charter of Fundamental Rights of the EU of 2000 also provides a normative base for rule of law reform in public administration. The Charter and the rights enshrined in it are specifically limited to a Community context, but this does not preclude its use as a model and benchmark on rule of law issues in

532 UNPAN 1995 pp. 19–29.
533 Council of Europe 1996.
534 Council of Europe Directorate General of Legal Affairs 2003 pp. 29–30.
535 Ibid., p. 29.
536 CoE (76) 5; Recommendation No (95) 5; Recommendation No R (03) 16; and Recommendation No. (04) 20.
537 Council of Europe Recommendation (07) 7.
538 Ibid. and the appendix Code of Good Administration.

relation to state-building. Article 41, Right to Good Administration, expresses the right of seeing the fair and impartial execution of administrative affairs by the institutions of the Union. It also includes the right to be heard before any individual negative measures are taken, the right of access to the files relating to the case in question, an obligation on the part of the administration concerned to give reasons for its decisions, and the right to "have the Community make good any damage caused by its institutions or by its servants in the performance of their duties, in accordance with the general principles common to the laws of the Member States".[539] Good administration in this context should be understood as focusing directly on the organisation of the state, that is, the administrative agencies directly or indirectly under the executive power of the state.[540]

Some recent developments worth noting seek to provide general guidelines for rule of law in public administration. One of them is a somewhat similar idea to the model criminal codes, but with a broader reach. This is the Government Out Of the Box (GooB) project by the Crisis Management Initiative. It centres chiefly on rebuilding public administration, with modules for regulating governance in areas such as civic registration, local security, basic education, health services and other essential services. The idea is derived from the observation that "there is a tendency to focus on organizing elections and avoid painful administrative reforms".[541] However, the idea of introducing ready-made modules of public administration should perhaps be approached with caution. Compared with the challenges the application of model criminal codes would face it is doubtful whether communities could model their administration on the basis of completely new rules and procedures immediately after a peace settlement has been reached. In the case of pre-established public administrative law modules, the external element would be significant, and the requirement of local adaptability and commitment fundamental to their successful applicability. Other general tools are the UNDP best practices report on civil service reform[542]and the USAID guide on administrative law reform. The USAID guide concentrates mainly on administrative procedure and judicial review in the context of development cooperation and economic transition.[543]

It is instead at the field level where initiatives on the development of guidelines and the apparatus for enhancing rule of law reform in public administration are primarily to be found. These initiatives are context-bound and have emerged in response to problems particular to a specific transition. An

539 Charter of Fundamental Rights of the European Union Art. 41.

540 See the classic description of administration and bureaucracy by Weber, who states that bureaucracy is characterised by impersonality, predictability and formalism.

541 Crisis Management Initiative 2007 p. 31.

542 UNDP 2003 contains best practices from case studies in ten countries ranging over a decade of civil service reforms.

543 USAID 2008, Using Administrative Law Tools and Concepts.

example of such an initiative is that of the OSCE Handbook for Mayors and Municipal Council Members of the Republic of Macedonia.[544] It directs itself to the needs of local decision-makers, mostly mayors and councillors, and is intended to help them better manage their responsibilities. It begins with a basic introduction to the legal framework of local self-government to make sure that the fundamental rules and regulations are correctly understood. References are made to the 1985 European Charter on Local Self-Government and the principles enumerated therein.[545] It then proceeds to explain the mechanism for supervision of the constitutionality and legality of the local administration. Much attention is directed towards defining and explaining competencies so that local administrations can avoid acting inadvertedly ultra vires. It also discusses independence under the law. Moreover, in latest EU accession process, several tools were developed by the Support for Improvement in Governance and Management (SIGMA) on administrative law, civil service and administrative justice and integrity.

In Iraq and Kosovo, similar guideline documents have recently been developed. The USAID guide to district governments focuses on the constitutional authority in Iraq and the legal framework of district governments.[546] The OSCE Guide to Municipal Participatory Governance is directed at increasing levels of inclusion and consultation by strengthening the capacity of local administrators and the legal framework on access to public documents, public consultations and the right to speak, in addition to questions on participatory governance.[547]

While these and other manuals from the field represent a timely development of rule of law in public administration, there is a need for more generic instruments. Technical support for securing the rule of law in public administration could, with some adjustments, be based upon the same sources as the rule of law in the justice sector – that is, the UN OHCHR and its Rule of Law Post-Conflict Tools on mapping, monitoring and vetting.

Ensuring that the rule of law prevails in public administration is pivotal, for a number of reasons. Common to the effects of dysfunctional justice sector institutions, weak administrative structures also affect the rights of people – in particular, vulnerable groups. Strengthening rule of law in this sector is also crucial to the organisation of the state after war and crisis.

Increased attention to public administration, specifically the regulatory capacity of the state, is also essential in light of the fact that many new public-private initiatives are formed during transition. Because interim governments often lack the ability to provide essential services, a recent trend has been to

544 OSCE 2005, Handbook for Mayors and Municipal Council Members in the Republic of Macedonia.

545 Council of Europe ETS No. 122 1985.

546 USAID 2007.

547 OSCE 2007, Report on the Administrative Justice System in Kosovo.

outsource public administrative functions.[548] In many transitions from war and crisis where public management capacity is limited, donors have turned to new forms of service delivery arrangements. In large infrastructure and service provision projects, they often support ministries and state-owned enterprises to build, operate and transfer capacity in telecommunications, water supply, electricity and transport.[549] Under a capacity transfer agreement a private sector actor develops and manages a project until state capacity achieves a level at which it can assume control. Public-private arrangements are useful for getting essential state functions up and running but at the same time requires close attention to the contractual relationship between state and private actors, with a degree of state regulation and monitoring to oversee implementation. Moreover, many of these arrangements involve critical state services such as water, electricity and telecommunications and financial oversight mechanisms, so it is essential that their management is subject to a measure of control, accountability and openness.

SUBSTANCE, FORM AND CAPACITY

Most international support to law reform and constitutionalism focuses on the substance of law, not on the process of drafting and enacting it, nor yet on its implementation.[550] The more 'technical' issues of legal drafting – that is, subsidiary laws and regulations applied in order to implement new laws, are often not a priority among international donors or national stakeholders. The lack of attention paid to issues of form and procedure affects the capacity of the legal system to maintain a consistency of the hierarchy of norms, to ensure that new laws do not contradict old ones, and to disseminate adequately the result of planned or already implemented law reforms. The tendency to place substantive concerns over formal and procedural needs could also be seen as a reflection of the value-laden way that the rule of law is conceptualised in relation to war-torn societies.

Kosovo displays many examples of insufficient attention to formal and procedural aspects of law making. In general, law reform in Kosovo has been marred by a failure to ensure internal legal consistency, to establish a hierarchy of norms, and in a lack of methods in the interpretation and resolution of conflicts between the different normative regimes constituting the transitory legal order. Despite the fact that international experts have managed the process of law making, several problems of a formal and procedural nature have persisted that could have been easily avoided.

548 See DESA & UNDP 2007 p. 87.
549 DESA & UNDP 2007 p. 99.
550 Stromseth, *et al.*, 2006 p. 199.

In the fourth report of the Ombudsperson in Kosovo in 2004, UNMIK was roundly criticised for deficiencies in drafting. According to the Ombudsperson, UNMIK had failed in adequately making new regulations public and in acknowledging the need for a vacatio legis – that is, the time between the enactment of a law and when it's entering into effect. Most UNMIK regulations entered into force as soon as they were signed by the Special Representative of the Secretary-General, which allowed for flexible and rapid law making, but gave local authorities have had limited time to adjust and learn about new regulations.[551] UNMIK responded in part to the criticism – for example, on publishing new regulations in languages other than English. It now provides translations of regulations. However, problems still persist with making the regulations publicly accessible. Regulations were for a long time routinely posted on UNMIK's webpage. Poor dissemination, coupled with the lack of a vacatio legis, has meant that the Kosovar authorities insufficient time to prepare and react to new legal obligations imposed upon them.

The constitution-making process in Afghanistan also illustrates how substance sometimes takes precedence over ensuring form and procedure. As described above, the making of the Afghan constitution was influenced by international actors who, together with local advocacy groups, sought to strengthen human rights protection in its final draft.[552] This led to Article 7 recounting the obligation of the government to respect international agreements, as well as a rather comprehensive enumeration of fundamental rights and freedoms. Complicating this enmeshment of international law is that the constitution does not provide clarification or adequate instruments for the implementation of international obligations. Schoiswohl argues that the "facially ambitious Article 7 [...] merely restates that Afghanistan will abide by its international obligations, without providing for a specific incorporation mechanism".[553] The duty of the Afghan government to respect international treaties exists irrespective of whether or not they are incorporated in the constitution. The situation is further complicated by article 3 in declaring that "no law can be contrary to the beliefs and provisions of the sacred religion of Islam".[554] This provision, in conjunction with the right of the Supreme Court to review compliance "with the Constitution of laws, legislative decrees,

551 Ombudsperson Institution in Kosovo 2004 p. 9.

552 Schoiswohl 2006 p. 842.

553 Schoiswohl 2006 p. 859.

554 See Danchin 2009 pp. 84–86 for an account of constitutional reform in Iraq, similar to the Afghan reform process, and the role of Islam as a legal source. In Iraq, the final wording of Islam as a "founding source" reflects, according to Danchin, a compromise between certain Shia and Kurdish groups. This too leaves open the question of the hierarchy of laws and on how to settle a conflict of apparently equal norms. Art. 2 of the Iraqi constitution also states that "no law may be enacted that contradicts the established provisions of Islam; no law may be enacted that contradicts the principles of democracy; and no law may be enacted that contradicts the right to basic freedoms stipulated in this constitution".

international treaties and international covenants, and interpret them in accordance with the law", creates uncertainty on the role of international law when interpretation goes against Islamic belief. Infusing substantive norms while failing to ensure formal and procedural mechanisms for their implementation, risks diluting advancements that came at great political cost.[555]

Moreover, substantive law reforms often lack an institutional capacity to ensure that laws have a real impact. Miller describes the initial law making in Kosovo by UNMIK as being dominated by laws on demand and a process that disregarded the implementing capacity of local institutions. The different organisations involved in Kosovo besides the UN – that is, the EU and the OSCE, brought with them numerous legal experts: "with an enormous number of proposals for legislation [...] these persons were experts in their fields, such as banking or finance, with a determination to propose the very best legislation as they saw it. An example is the lengthy and highly complex banking law".[556]

Miller also observed that other regulatory initiatives were straining the resources, time and efforts of UNMIK. Among the first 20 regulations was a law prohibiting casino-type gambling, a reform that could hardly be considered a top priority "but was apparently pushed by visiting donors and so it became an UNMIK priority".[557]

Another such example of a legislative initiative lacking in formal and institutional capacity is the amending of law on rape in Liberia. This law, which came into force in January 2006, was largely a legislative procedure initiated by international NGOs and UN agencies together with local rights advocacy groups.[558] In this process, the discrepancy between international motivation and reality was striking. The weak Liberian judiciary and the low level of awareness among the population (combined with the social stigma associated with rape) resulted in weak enforcement. Because of this weakness many cases were settled out of court in customary justice procedures.[559]

This lack of strength in capacity could have been foreseen given the conditions of the Liberian justice sector following the civil war. Accordingly, greater caution should be exercised against launching ambitious law reform initiatives in the absence of an adequate institutional foundation. The enactment of the new rape legislation was followed by a nationwide Stop Rape Campaign, but came with the danger of encouraging already vulnerable people to report rape to the police, and thus creating expectations that could not be realised. The difficulties of adequate implementation of the new legislation eventually led to

---

555 Schoiswohl 2006 p. 859.
556 Miller 2004 pp. 16–17.
557 Miller 2004 p. 17.
558 An Act to Amend the New Penal Code, Chapter 14, section 1470–1471, and provisions against gang rape. Human Rights Council A/HRC/4/6 2007 paras. 16–17.
559 Human Rights Council A/HRC/4/6 2007 paras. 16–17.

the establishment of a specialised court with exclusive jurisdiction over rape and other sexual offences in order to properly implement the law.[560]

Substantive and resource-intensive law reform projects seem out of context considering the constrained environments in which they are intended to apply. One approach sometimes advanced in relation to anti-corruption strategies is the focus on so-called 'bright line rules' where discretion in interpretation and enforcement is minimised, and this could possibly be of advantage after war and crisis.[561] While this might also reduce flexibility in the bureaucracy and judiciary, it could be considered in extremely constrained environments. The direct infusion or enmeshment of international norms, particularly of a more substantive character, will most probably create confusion as to the interpretation of the meaning of certain rights and standards. As The World Justice Project asserted in relation to the development of a rule of law index, adherence to the full panoply of international human rights law is difficult to achieve, and a pragmatic balance could be that of limiting 'enmeshment' and international norm-creation to civil and political rights that "bear the most immediate relationship to rule of law concerns".[562] While 'bright line rules' have specific drawbacks, their use could be considered in particularly sensitive areas such as corruption and economic governance, or on questions of applicable law, at least in interim and volatile situations.

CONSULTATION AND LEGITIMACY

An inherent structural problem exists in the way that international organisations approach rule of law reform.[563] The need to consult with and allow for participation of national stakeholders in law reform and constitution making is a frequently touted principle and 'lesson learned' by international agencies, but in many cases local actors often end up in a position of being the recipients of legal knowledge produced elsewhere. This reception process can range from the simple copy-and-paste approach discussed above, where a predesigned package of laws is provided, to a situation where foreign legal experts end up writing and drafting new laws based upon a mismatch of international benchmarks and national standards. In many cases, the international influence and lack of local capacity creates laws that are ill-adapted to the local context.[564]

The UN Secretary-General has maintained that no rule of law reform, justice reconstruction, or transitional justice initiative imposed from the outside can ever hope to be successful or sustainable and that the UN must assist local

560 UNSG S/2009/86 p. 8.
561 See Messick 2001, and also, Kaplow 1992 p. 586f for a discussion on rules versus standards.
562 The American Bar Association & World Justice Project 2008 p. 7.
563 Bassu 2008 p. 32.
564 Bergling 2006 pp. 77–78.

partners to "develop their own reform visions, their own agenda, their own approaches to transitional justice and their own plans and projects".[565] A similar argument for a procedure that includes consultation and participation is put forward in the study by Berkowitz, Pistor and Richard. The authors argue that neither the transferred law's origin (common law or civil law), nor the specific content is important for the success of reforms. The crucial point is how reforms are carried out, since procedure matters more than substance.[566] The claim is founded on two notions: first, for the law to be effective, it must have meaning within the context in which it is to be applied. If it is perceived as meaningful, citizens then have an incentive to use the law and to demand its institutions to work to enforce and develop it. Second, judges, lawyers, politicians, and other legal intermediaries responsible for developing the law must be able to increase its quality in a way that is responsive to demand and legality.[567]

But there is also an added dimension to consultation and participation: international participants need the involvement of national actors because of their knowledge and information. As Miller puts it, most organisations or states "have lawyers that tend to have expertise in what their employers do. Running failed states or nation-building is not a common task".[568] International actors rarely possess any intimate knowledge of the legal and administrative systems of the war-torn and crisis societies in which they are requested to operate. Sometimes in the worst cases, not even local agencies possess a systemic and extensive knowledge. Under such circumstances, knowledge has to be gained and problems identified in order to construct rule of law reforms that are needs-based. Collecting such information is predicated upon the participation and consultation of local actors from all sectors of society.

The need for a demand, or 'meaningfulness', means that international actors should take care to invite legal intermediaries and various interests groups from the 'host' or 'recipient' society early on in law reform processes.[569]

The direct linking of law reform and constitution-making to the concepts of consultation and participation reflects a growing awareness that these concepts are essential to the viability of newly drafted laws and constitutions. A lack of participation and consultation is often held to affect the process and success of legal reform. The first report of the UN Secretary-General on the establishment of UNMIK in Kosovo stated that an essential requirement of success in the mission was that "the peoples of Kosovo be included fully and effectively [...]

565 UNSG S/2004/616 2004 p. 7.
566 Pistor, Berkowitz, & Richard 2003 p. 6.
567 Ibid., p. 7.
568 Miller 2004 p. 11.
569 Berkowitz, Pistor & Richard 2003 p. 8. In countries where there has not been political will or constituencies in favour of reforms, Berkowitz, *et al.*, conclude that such countries are much more likely to experience a lower level of functional effectiveness: these countries are referred to as being subject to the "transplant effect".

community leaders and professionals can make immediate and significant contributions in judicial affairs".[570]

There might also be a normative imperative behind consultation and participation of citizens in rule of law reform, in particular where international agencies substitute for national governments. A link between participation and consultation and the right to take part in the conduct of public affairs is laid out in article 25 (a) of the International Covenant on Civil and Political Rights. Elaborated by the UN Human Rights Committee, this might mean in relation to, for example legal drafting, a requirement on external actors to invite broad participation:

> The conduct of public affairs, referred to in paragraph (a), is a broad concept, which relates to the exercise of political, in particular the exercise of legislative, executive and administrative powers. It covers all aspects of public administration and the formulation and implementation at international, national, regional and local level.
> [...] Citizens also participate directly in the conduct of public affairs when they *choose or change their constitution or decide public issues through a referendum* or other electoral process [...] citizens may participate directly by taking part in popular assemblies which have the power to make decisions about local issues or about the affairs of a particular community and in bodies established to represent citizens in consultation with government.
> Citizens also take part in the conduct of public affairs by exerting influence through *public debate and dialogue* with their representatives or through their capacity to organize themselves.[571]

In rule of law interventions such as Kosovo and East Timor, where the UN assumed a governing authority, the right to take part in the conduct of public affairs could thus be interpreted as imposing certain conditions on international administrations in their legislative and administrative capacities.[572] If direct participation is not possible at the starting up of an international administration, it could be argued that international actors should, at least, be seen to have a responsibility to establish the means whereby citizens are able to exert influence through public debate and dialogue. This norm would be particularly imperative in relation to the introduction of codes of law on, for example, economic matters that fundamentally change social structures, or on constitutional reform.

In some cases international participants try forcefully to adhere to consultation and participation as principles of first importance in rule of law

570 UNSG. S/1999/672 p. 4.

571 Human Rights Committee General Comment No 25 CCPR/C/21Rev.1/Add.7 1996 paras. 5, 6 & 8 (Italics added).

572 See, also, Franck 1992 in positing that there is an emerging right under international law to democratic governance and participatory electoral processes, though the establishment of such right is disputed.

reform. Seemingly, in an effort to avoid the mistakes of Kosovo on the lack of such principles in functionally necessary areas – which caused UNMIK substantial criticism – the UNTAET tried constitutionally to impose a better relationship between international and national players. The first regulation in East Timor (1999/1) included a provision requiring the UN transitional administrator to consult and cooperate closely with the East Timorese people.[573] This led to the creation of the National Consultative Council, through UNTAET regulation 1999/2. The Council was set up as a joint consultative forum, consisting of both East Timorese and UNTAET personnel, and given the task of making policy recommendations on "significant executive and legislative matters".[574] The council, later renamed the National Council, consisted of an "elite group of hand-picked (not democratically elected) East Timorese".[575] This group was invited to review UNTAET legislation, but the level of discussion on legislative matters among the broader public was simultaneously kept to a minimum.

The events in East Timor have indicated that even when constitutionally supported, consultation and other mechanisms to secure accountability might still be reduced to meaningless catch-phrases unless the methods for achieving such objectives are carefully reviewed. Problems of a similar nature on the use of advisory councils or commissions have proved problematic in other state-building missions – that is, in Kosovo and Afghanistan.

Moreover, upholding the principles of consultation and participation in law reform and constitutional change also present challenges where it can be anticipated that local influence might provide an outcome unfavourable to international actors. This was evident in the process that established the Constitutional Commission in East Timor. In 2001 the National Consultative Council rejected the draft regulation proposed by the SRSG on the establishment of Constitutional Commissions. Though the Council only had advisory powers and did not have a mandate to veto legislation, the SRSG proceeded by promulgating the law on Constitutional Commissions as a directive, a subordinate form of legislation used in order to instruct on the implementation of regulations.[576] While the legality of the SRSG to issue directives without the scrutiny of the National Consultative Commission was not disputed, the use of a directive meant that there was no 'parent regulation' and that moreover, in the words of Morrow and White: "the irregular use of 'orphaned' subordinate legislation to avoid the difficulty of reaching a political consensus about how consultation should occur, was, therefore, at the expense of the observance of the hierarchy of legal norms, established in East Timor's case".[577] The circumvention

573 UNTAET/REG/1999/1.
574 UNTAET/REG/1999/2.
575 Linton 2001 p. 136.
576 UNTAET/DIR/2001/3 regarding the establishment of District Constitutional Commissions.
577 Morrow & White 2002 p. 20.

of resistance through the use of subordinate legislation, even when breaching rule of law principles, shows how international actors apply laws and legal institutions instrumentally in order to achieve other political ends.

In many such societies it remains unclear precisely who has the authority to draft new laws. Different documents such as peace agreements or UN Security Council resolutions might place law reform initiatives outside the traditional confines of legislative assemblies and processes. Law reform responsibilities can be granted to special national commissions, to the Special Representative of the Secretary-General, or in joint structures combining national and international experts and agencies.

There are frequent calls from scholars and practitioners alike that in law reform and constitutional reform, process matters just as much as substance.[578] From the perspective of the transplant effect, this is because the legitimacy of the resulting laws and constitutions is principally derived from participation in the formulation of common goals and policies, and that the process in which a new constitution or law is developed has a direct effect who has a voice in choosing the substantive terms. This suggest an urgency for finding ways in which local actors, on a broad level, can be made more responsible for both constitutional reform and law reform.

578 See Fuller 1958 p. 643f for an early argument on foreign assistance in constitutional reform.

5. INSTITUTION BUILDING

INTRODUCTION

As discussed in the previous chapter, the viability of law reform and constitutional reform together depend on a number of factors, such as inclusion and the pragmatic consideration of host country ownership. Another essential circumstance is the creation of an adequate institutional framework that can implement, monitor and manage structural legal reforms meeting the needs of end-users, the state and international donors. The international community has identified the construction of sound institutions as something central to the rule of law, and institutional reform has remained a core objective since the early activities of the law and development movement.

The building of institutions, and judicial reform in particular, is regarded by many commentators as being the most difficult of reform areas in rule of law promotion in war-torn and crisis societies. Yet international actors often approach the topic as a technical or practical matter – that is, translated into refurbishing court-houses and prisons, and merely the upgrading of technology.[579] However, the creation of institutions is, above all, a matter of enhancing capacity and changing behaviour, which is time-consuming and difficult, particularly since it involves changing procedures, mentalities and other often well-established institutional patterns and ways of working.[580]

This chapter examines methods of international support in the strengthening of capacity and integrity of legal and administrative institutions after war and crisis. In particular, it analyses how issues of organising the courts and bureaucracy, the selecting and vetting of public officials, and capacity-building initiatives and how the newly made or reformed institutions are supported.

The difficulty of institutional capacity has in some cases led to an internationalisation of institutional reform, a topic also discussed in this chapter. More often than not, structural legal reform, constitutional or ordinary law, lacks effect because of weakness in the institutions set up to enforce them. Here, too, as in relation to constitutional and law reform, the political economy – that is, commitment and ownership – play vital parts in the implementation of rule

579 Hammarberg & Gavian 1998 p. 11.

580 See Markovits 2004 and Bernasconi & Solotych 2003 on problems relating to the procedural reform of organisations that collide with traditions and notions of "we've always done it like this", and on conflicts with positions of power and vested interests.

of law reform, as well as the influences of international law, benchmarks and codes. Also under discussion are the methods and strategies adopted in order to both enhance access to justice and increase governmental compliance with rule of law principles through measures such as National Human Rights Institutions, anti-corruption commissions and by means of the offices of the ombudsman.

SEQUENCING AND POLITICAL WILL

Blair and Hansen stress in their 1994 report, Weighing in on the Scales of Justice, that institution-building should not be a first order priority for donors engaged in rule of law assistance.[581] This recommendation arises from an observation that in many countries "constituencies and coalitions may be so fragmented and fractious, and the political environment may be so inimical to judicial reform [...] as to eliminate any effective program activity".[582] According to their stylised sequencing model of rule of law reform, institution-building should follow after political and popular will has been established, and after the legal framework has been changed and prepared for institutional reform.[583]

Blair and Harry propose in this model that rule of law reformers should ultimately start by garnering political support. If gaining such support proves difficult, they recommend strategies that either circumvent or exert pressure on political leaders by creating support for reforms from below – from the rank and file, community-based organisations, and from advocacy groups. The next step in rule of law reform should be to first conduct an inventory of the legal framework and then to suggest appropriate reforms or amendments. Only after the conclusion of those two sequences should reformers concentrate on institutional reform and capacity-building. The last sequence of the model host interrelated strategies seeking to improve access to justice and accountability as a way of anchoring institutional reforms. A similar but less stylised approach is described in the UN Secretary-General's report Rule of Law and Transitional Justice, where law reform, institution-building and access creation activities are all emphasised.[584]

This ideal model of sequencing is rarely followed after war and crisis.[585] Given the time constraint, the lack of capacity of national actors, and the anatomy of legal and administrative systems in war-torn and crisis societies, it is

[581] Blair & Hansen 1994 pp. 55–57.
[582] Ibid., 1994 p. 51.
[583] Bergling 2006 p. 42. See, also, the Rule of Law Strategic Framework developed by USAID for a similar approach to sequencing and prioritisation, USAID 2008, Guide to Rule of Law Country Analysis.
[584] UNSG S/2004/616 p. 12.
[585] The authors also acknowledge that their sequencing model is an ideal, and therefore difficult to implement in full. Blair & Hansen 1994 p. 11.

more common for international actors simultaneously to pursue several reform initiatives.[586]

New approaches to institution-building have also evolved since the Blair and Hansen report was published and institutional reform in central and eastern Europe served as the main repository of empirical data for the author's conclusions. Nevertheless, the main conclusion from the sequencing model – the necessity of political will and constituency support – remains a valid observation for rule of law reform in war-torn societies. It is against this backdrop that local ownership and leadership are frequently called for, also in the 'technical' project of institution-building.[587]

POLITICAL, PROFESSIONAL AND CONSTITUENCY SUPPORT FOR INSTITUTIONAL REFORM

The need for political will and constituency support for rule of law reform has been repeated by scholars and practitioners alike as a condition for successful reform.[588] The difficulty is that there are few incentives for interim governments and other political actors in societies laid waste by war to agree to resolve differences according to the law.

In the study by Morlino and Magen on democracy promotion and rule of law reform in four European countries (Serbia-Montenegro, Ukraine, Turkey and Romania), the authors found that conditionality in the form of EU membership provided a leverage that might explain the success of reforms. The authors find that: "the credible promise of large and material benefits – particularly the 'golden carrot' of full EU membership [...] – is generally effective in persuading national governments formally to adopt rules and institutions they would otherwise resist".[589] Conversely, where the study found overtures of EU membership weak or absent "the achievement of formal compliance with externally mandated rules has proven generally more difficult and less complete".[590] While the conclusions are drawn from a European setting, the observation on credible and in turn tangible benefits should not be overlooked in relation to war-torn and crisis societies.

It is not only national ownership as a moral principle that emerges from the discussion on rule of law reform, but also pragmatism: without national involvement and a sense of influence and control over the whole procedure of law reform, externally promoted laws run the risk of 'rejection' and resistance.[591]

586 See Salas 2001 p. 37ff.
587 UNSG S/2004/616 p. 7.
588 Blair & Hansen 1994 pp. 16–18.
589 Morlino & Magen 2009 Conclusions p. 229. See, also, Schimmelfennig 2008 p. 920.
590 Morlino & Magen 2009 Conclusions p. 229.
591 Berkowitz, Pistor & Richard 2003 p. 167f.

Laws and institutions imposed upon countries and societies, without the benefits of an open and inclusive process, are less likely to enjoy the same amount of legitimacy and trust as national initiatives. The moral and pragmatic considerations of ownership are even more accentuated in institution-building, which is not only susceptible to 'failure' because of the caution inherent in the sequencing model for rule of law reform generally, but also because of the political economy in institution-building in particular. The political economy means the win-lose situation of rule of law reform, where vested interests are pitted against one another, or where one side stands to lose its political and financial position as a result of changes in the legal structure.[592]

This aspect of justice reform is often neglected or overlooked by international players, who tend to approach the objective of institution-building as if the judiciary and other legal institutions occupied an autonomous field, separated from political, social and economic spheres, and where the choice of reform is based upon rational deliberations as to the best outcome for the efficiency, fairness and effectiveness of the legal system as a whole.

Flowing from the difficulties of using credible conditionality and of acquiring political will, international agencies sometimes resort to civil society organisations and other non-state actors to create pressure groups that can push for reforms from below, leading to a strengthening in coalition-building and enhancing the capacity of local human rights groups and other advocacy associations.[593] This is based upon the assumption that "accountability enhancing reforms do not come forward without a clear 'public demand' for reform".[594]

The strategy of supporting the creation or financing of local NGOs in war to peace transitions was employed in the UN mission to Cambodia in the early 1990s.[595] Another relevant instance is the Ivory Coast where the UN Mission, with funding from the Office of the High Commission for Human Rights, started a programme to strengthen national human rights groups and their capacity to raise awareness of human rights within the population.[596] A similar approach was taken in Sierra Leone where UN agencies, in cooperation with the government, launched a nationwide consultation campaign in 2004.[597] Its ambition was to formulate national legislation for the implementation of the Convention on the Elimination of All forms of Discrimination Against Women, along with training some 3,587 members of the civil society. The overall result was presented as a way of furnishing these groups with a "grounded knowledge

592 See Daniels & Trebilcock 2004–2005 pp. 129–130.
593 Pouligny 2003 p. 374 fn. 5.
594 Schedler 1999 Conclusion p. 341.
595 Pouligny 2003 p. 361.
596 UNSG S/2006/2 p. 13.
597 Peacekeeping Best Practice Unit 2003, Lessons Learned from United Nations Peacekeeping Experiences in Sierra Leone p. 56.

of human rights principles as part of a gradual handover of the responsibility to monitor promote and report on the human rights situation in Sierra Leone".[598]

Consultation with civil society groups was also part of the strategy practiced by UNOSOM II in Somalia. Besides working with local lawyers on matters such as detention and criminal rehabilitation, UNOSOM also hand-picked a group of intellectuals and artists, community representatives and religious and traditional leaders in an effort to create a civil society in an environment where the concept of such a society had previously been wholly absent.[599] In similar fashion USAID supplied 25,000 Liberian families and schools with "simplified explanations of the constitution".[600] As a result, according to a USAID survey, some 10,000 private Liberian citizens "exercised at least one of their fundamental rights: association, fair trial, freedom of religion, and free speech".[601] However, the direct causality between distributing samples of the constitution and the actual exercise of individual rights is open to question.

A more formalised approach to the creation of civil society support and a pressure group from below has been adopted in Kosovo, where the Kosovo Law Centre and the Kosovo Judicial Institute, both independent bodies established by the OSCE, provide for the training of legal professionals, research and analysis, as well as legal awareness and education.[602] For the first five years of the international administration the Kosovo Judicial Institute was a formal part of the OSCE mission. It was later established as an independent institution with a specific mandate to provide training, to assess and organise the preparatory examination for judges and prosecutors, to hold basic training courses for lay judges, and to furnish instruction to other legal professionals working within the judiciary.[603]

Apart from the important part played by civil society support for 'planting' institutional reforms in society, it can also provide incentives for national ownership and participation in decision-making similar to that of consultation and participation in law reform. NGOs and the civil society in general are often employed as reform partners by international agencies in institutional reform because of their presumed watchdog functions, and as pressure groups able to move a recalcitrant government to act on certain matters.[604]

---

598 Commission on Human Rights E/C.N.4/2005/113 p. 15.

599 Pouligny 2003 p. 362.

600 USAID 2002 p. 131.

601 USAID 2002 p. 131.

602 OSCE 2005 Kosovo Judicial Institute Factsheet.

603 UNMIK/REG/2006/23.

604 An illustration is this 2003 law in Liberia: An Act to Govern the Devolution of Estates and Establish Rights of Inheritance for Spouses of Both Statutory and Customary Marriages. Women's rights under customary law on access and inheritance of land have been problematic. A group of Female Lawyers of Liberia assisted in passing the law that established equal rights in both the statutory and customary systems, despite resistance from some customary leaders and parliamentarians. See Unruh 2009 p. 428.

However, it remains unclear what effect the building of advocacy groups will have in the long term. On direct support or the creation or financing of local NGOs, there is also a risk of identifying credible reform partners. In some cases, NGOs or civil society groups did not exist prior to a UN or intervention, as with Somalia or Cambodia. With a sudden and continuing flow of external support some NGOs might be more motivated by money than by a genuine commitment to rule of law reform. NGOs can also become entangled in politics and are sometimes affiliated to a particular faction or ethnic group and might well utilise their civil society status to establish political platforms.[605]

LOW POLITICS AND HIGH POLITICS OF INSTITUTIONAL REFORM

A distinction can also be made between reforms in areas of 'low politics' and 'high politics'. As Morlino and Magen concluded in their case study of countries seeking EU membership, reforms with the aim of modernising courts and improving efficiency encountered a minimum of opposition from national governments, but reforms directed at strengthening judicial independence through the removal of executive control "met with potent resistance across all four case study countries".[606] The resistance against reforms aimed at areas involving 'high politics' is likely to be just as strong in war-torn and crisis societies where former warring factions often make up interim governments, and guarding their spoils of war.

The UN Secretary-General noted in relation to the transition in Sierra Leone, for example, that court-houses and prisons had been built or renovated throughout the country, but "progress has been slow in addressing such problems as undue delays in the trial and adjudication of cases and the lack of judicial personnel".[607]

Because of the political economy of institution-building in general, and in reform of the judiciary in particular, the difficulty of asserting political support for externally promoted rule of law reform is a specifically salient feature in war-torn societies, where many countries display a tradition of using the judiciary as a repressive force, or where there are parallel systems of justice, or where the result of prolonged fighting has led to widespread destruction of the legal structure. The political economy is also prominent owing to the fact that in the early phases of war to peace transitions the political terrain is unclear and demarcation lines between legislative, executive and judiciary remain blurred. Legal and administrative institutions are expected to operate independently in

605 See Pouligny 2003 p. 363.
606 Morlino & Magen 2009 Conclusions p. 255.
607 UNSG S/2005/273 p. 5.

environments where former parties to a conflict would now share parliamentary seats and ministerial posts, each guarding their own interests and with the ever-present threat of a return to violent conflict.[608]

JUDICIAL INDEPENDENCE

The report of the UN Special Rapporteur on the Independence of Judges and Lawyers made known that typical problems were to do with executive control, either through constitutional provisions or actions by the executive in contravention of constitutional guarantees of judicial independence. Other difficulties included tampering with judicial appointments and tenures as well as the use of the judiciary as a repressive arm of the executive by way of summary trials.[609] The problems of the political economy were also prevalent in the early stages of rule of law assistance to the former 'Eastern Bloc'.[610] The political economy, the soft side of institutional reform (or of any rule of law reform for that matter), also presents itself as a slow and cumbersome process subject to numerous pitfalls within other transitional contexts.[611] Independence is here taken to mean at least three forms of independence:

(1) from interest groups such as political parties;
(2) from peers within the judicial organisation, and;
(3) from other government agencies.

In relation to the judiciary, institutional reform represents, to some extent, an overzealous belief in the inclination of judges towards change, and assumption that legal professionals perform as 'social engineers'. This also characterised the early law and development movement. This assumption of 'reformers' is attended by difficulty in war to peace transitions. Where the judiciary has gained from a lack of supervision and legal 'chaos', they are not always a representative part of the solution, but that of the problem.[612]

Several reports from war-torn and crisis societies show that institution-building with the specific intention of strengthening the judiciary becomes

608 Hammarberg & Gavian 1998 p. 9 note that "several projects in Haiti – most prominently, judicial reform – have made little progress, principally as a result of lack of government support. Other missions – the human rights office in Cambodia, for example – has faced government officials openly hostile to human rights work".

609 Human Rights Council A/HRC/8/4/Add.1 28 May 2008.

610 The US General Accounting Office evaluation of US assistance to the former Soviet Union from 2001 p. 14 proclaims that a major impediment to judicial reform is that of essential actors failing to reach agreement on a coherent reform agenda. General Accounting Office 2001 p. 14.

611 Hammergren 2002, Fifteen Years of Judicial Reform in Latin America p. 2.

612 Dakolias 1995–1996 p. 170.

difficult, even where international participants have invested substantial resources over a long time.[613] Executive interference in particular is a frequently reported problem.

On Haiti, the US General Accounting Office stated in a 2000 report that the government lacked the necessary will to commit to judicial reform, and that the executive controlled the judicial budget, appointments, training, evaluation and removal of judges.[614] The US assistance to judicial reform in Haiti apparently never properly attempted to address long-standing structural and political problems. This is not unique to Haiti, but rather underlines an inherent obstacle to institution-building in the justice sector in war to peace transitions. Reforms in that sector are understood by international agencies to be of a technical nature. The assumption seems to be that training, technical equipment and increased financial support can mitigate vested interests.[615]

STRUCTURE AND ORGANISATION

Apart from the necessity of political will and constituency support, a first practical challenge to the building of effective, fair and sustainable institutions concerns questions of structure and organisation.

Decisions made on the organisation and structure of the judiciary in the initial phase of a state-building mission are motivated by the need to dispense justice effectively in order to deal with crimes committed during the transition, and for the overall organisation and restructuring of the particular state. Moreover, several sensitive questions of 'high politics' will also depend on the structure and organisation of the courts – for example, whether to establish separate administrative courts or to work through administrative chambers in the ordinary courts. Furthermore, questions on who will be granted authority to appoint judges and take decisions on the hierarchy of courts, including the establishment of a constitutional court, all have to be answered.

---

613 UNSG S/2008/458 p. 14. In Kosovo, the UNSG complained of backlog of disciplinary cases at the Kosovo Judicial Council, with a total of 57 outstanding.

614 US General Accounting Office 2000 pp. 15–17.The US assistance to Haiti at the time of the General Accounting Office evaluation extended over five years and involved 27m US dollars in assistance to the judiciary. Most of this assistance went to administrative enhancement: case registration and case management; training of judges and prosecutors; and the establishment of a magisterial school. US support did not manage to overcome weak political will and interference, corruption, cumbersome legislation and poor internal supervision within the judiciary.

615 See Domingo 1999 pp. 158–160. There are various ways of undermining judicial independence, even where constitutional guarantees exist. The executive and legislative bodies may abrogate judicial independence in a formal way, by either bypassing ordinary courts or establishing separate ones. Other ways of undermining judicial independence could be to dismiss, transfer and reassign judges.

Though institution-building embraces a number of different national agencies, the first order of institutional reform often centres predominantly on the judiciary. In many cases the previous structure of legal and administrative institutions becomes controversial, with courts and other institutions under the influence of the executive branch. In other cases, the institutional organisation concerned is found to be completely wanting in a legal framework, regulations, internal documents on the function and operation of the courts, prosecutorial offices and other interrelated parts of the state's bureaucracy. Courts, of various instances, also occupy for natural reasons a pivotal role in institution-building when considering rises in crime that bring a sense of urgency to the matter, and where international actors have invested substantial time and money on strengthening the judicial system. Moreover, courts are generally viewed as having a central function in rule of law assistance as vital institutions in order to ensure the lawful exercise of public authority by the executive and legislative branches. They are therefore illustrative of many of the difficulties attached to institutional reform on political and popular support, on ownership and consultation, and on participation.[616]

The overall aim of assistance to the building of institutions, and in particular judicial organisation, is to increase efficiency, to secure fair and high quality judgements, and to ensure judicial independence.[617] The idea also is to establish institutions with a dual function – that is, institutions providing public access and the resolution of disputes between private individuals, as well as acting as checks and balances on the actions of the state. In some instances the driving force behind institutional reform is influenced by the problems of the particular context, as with Kosovo where the Standards Implementation Plan of 2004 centred on the capacity of the courts to deal with organised crime as well as minority representation in the judicial organisation.[618] Similarly the 2005 Results-Focused Transitional Framework for Liberia noted a necessity for the "jump-starting of essential criminal courts" as well as laying the foundation for a "professional, independent and credible judiciary".[619]

The extent of international involvement in institutional reform depends ultimately on the mandate of donors and other agencies involved in the transition, as well as the framework of national constitutional documents and agreements. In many of the recent UN state-building missions the Security Council has made judicial reform a prioritised area of rule of law assistance. The imperatives for judicial reform tend to be vaguely formulated and concerned with the necessity of extending judicial authority throughout the particular country, to increasing impartiality, to improving effectiveness and independence, and providing instructions on modernisation and further technical support. The

616 Davis & Trebilcock 2004–2005 p. 119.
617 Reiling, Hammergren & Di Giovanni 2007 p. 9.
618 See the Kosovo Standards Implementation Plan 2004 p. 26f.
619 Results Focused Transitional Framework for Liberia 2005 p. 15.

restructuring of a judiciary is sometimes included as a specific condition in a peace agreement. In some, judicial reform and restructuring is only briefly mentioned, such as in the 1992 Addis Ababa Agreement for Somalia,[620] or in the 2004 Implementation Modalities for the Sudan.[621] Other agreements provide more detailed instructions, such as the 2000 peace agreement for Burundi. This agreement, choosing legal continuity where the previous laws in force were to apply, centres on the process of appointing judges, establishing a constitutional court in accordance with the 1992 constitution, and for ensuring ethnic and gender balances within the judiciary. The agreement for Burundi also establishes rules for amending the laws on the judiciary, requiring a two-thirds majority in the transitional assembly. Similarly in Afghanistan, the Bonn Agreement declared that judicial power should be independent and vested in the Supreme Court. As for other courts and their organisation, the Bonn Agreement only stipulates that the Interim Administration may take such measures.[622] A judicial commission was also to be established in accordance with the agreement, with the assistance of the UN, in order to "rebuild the domestic justice system in accordance with Islamic principles, international standards, the rule of law and Afghan legal tradition".[623]

Two main and interrelated difficulties confront the question of structure and organisation, particularly with the judiciary. One of them is that the dearth of judicial and other institutions at the beginning of a transitional period raises logistical and technical problems. In the anatomy of crisis states, governmental institutions have either ceased to function or are severely discredited by the population and the capacity of national agencies to embrace complex reform is therefore limited. The second is that these situations often require of international actors the capacity to either assume temporary judicial functions or to swiftly re-establish a local judiciary that is seen to be legitimate in the eyes of the people, and comporting with the standards and principles established for institutional reform.

Both difficulties might invoke significant trade-offs, all of which make decisions on structure and organisation of the judiciary a sensitive political matter. They also indicate that, as a general rule of guidance, judicial structure and organisation should be supported so as to 'fit' the absorptive capacity of the particular society.

Re-arranging the Existing Court System

In Bosnia and Herzegovina, following the signing of the Dayton Agreement in 1995, the international response to the problems within the judiciary was

620 Addis Ababa Agreement 1993 Art. IV (1), (3).
621 The Implementation Modalities of the Protocol on Power Sharing 2004.
622 Bonn Agreement Art. I.
623 Ibid., Art. II.

initially ad hoc, and sporadic measures aimed at strengthening both integrity and independence were implemented with few tangible effects. The structure and organisation of the judiciary was originally established through the constitution, which makes up Annex 4 of the Dayton Agreement. The complex constitutional structure of that agreement, with a three-person presidency (one from each of the major ethnic groups) was replicated in the organisation of the judiciary. Judicial authority fell largely under the Federation of Bosnia and Herzegovina and the Republika Srpska. Both were divided into semi-independent cantons or administrative entities, each of these of them with their own constitutions, independent ministries of justice and court systems.[624]

While the complex structure emanated from the political necessity of reaching an end to the civil war, a consequence of the creation of de facto distinct entities also meant that the judicial organisation was fractured and inconsistent with little overall guidance at state level. The different judiciaries were also vulnerable to political influences and suffered from considerable corruption and nepotism.[625]

Following meetings in 1997 and 1998 of the Peace Implementation Council, the international supervisory body created by the Dayton Peace Agreement, judicial reform was made a top priority in order to remedy persistent problems relating to limited supervision and organisation. The Office of the High Representative, the international agency established to oversee the implementation of the civilian aspects of the Dayton Agreement, was granted extensive powers, including the authority to remove public officials from office, and became responsible for the development of a comprehensive plan for judicial reform.[626]

The first measure taken by the High Representative was to establish a common court for all of Bosnia and Herzegovina through the Decision Imposing the Law on the State Court of BiH (often referred to as the State Court). The State Court was set up with original jurisdiction for criminal and administrative matters, with an appellate division. The objective was to provide a uniform and coherent judicial decision-making apparatus. The State Court was also given the power of reopening criminal proceedings for offences defined in the laws of the state of Bosnia and Herzegovina, in addition to deciding on conflicts of jurisdiction between the courts of the entities.[627]

Soon after the establishment of the State Court, the High Representative gave notice of a decision that would establish the Independent Judicial Commission (ICJ). The ICJ was accordingly set up and given the mandate to enforce standards

624 Brcko District became a self-governing district in 1999 with its own judiciary.

625 Bergling 2001 p. 492.

626 Peace Implementation Council 1997 para. XI and Peace Implementation Council 1998 para. 12 (1) and Annex para II.

627 Bergling 2001 p. 495.

of ethics and professionalism in the judicial and prosecutorial structure as well as guiding and coordinating reforms.[628]

The structure and organisation of the courts in Bosnia and Herzegovina, as initially provided for in the Dayton Agreement, reflected more a political compromise in the negotiations of the peace deal rather than adequate measures taken to create impartial, independent and effective judicial agencies. The initial and complex legal organisation, which persisted for five years, meant delayed justice for many in Bosnia and Herzegovina, with a stalling in state-building.[629] The setting out of complex jurisdictions has also impeded questions on structure and organisation for other institutions in Bosnia and Herzegovina. The Venice Commission critically noted that the "the human rights protection mechanisms foreseen in the legal order present an unusual degree of complexity".[630] What the Commission referred to was the duplication of judicial bodies entrusted to human rights protection – the Constitutional Court, the Commission on Human Rights and the Human Rights Chamber. Conflicts of competence between institutions responsible for human rights protection create problems of consistency and authority and can also affect constitutional authority and, as such, the state itself.

Creating New Judicial Structures

International participants initially took a more decisive approach to questions of structure and organisation in Kosovo and East Timor. The administration of justice also came under the direct authority of each respective administration from the start of the state-building missions. The UN initially treated the question of structure and organisation as a matter of weak judicial capacity. Thus early on in the UN administration over Kosovo, for the purpose of putting right the lack of judicial structures, the SRSG issued a regulation establishing two ad hoc bodies – a court of final appeal and an office of the public prosecutor.[631] That court was to function until the Supreme Court could be re-established. Parallel to this the Kosovar judiciary remained with its previous structure and organisation.

Reliance on a Kosovar judiciary was both symbolic and a practical. After a decade of discrimination under a Serb-dominated judiciary, the legitimacy of the courts had been eroded. But the attempt to satisfy local claims for a legitimate

---

628 OHR, Decision Providing the Independent Judicial Commission (IJC) with a Comprehensive Mandate 14/3/2001.

629 See e.g. ICG 2000, Denied Justice: Individuals Lost in the Legal Maze.

630 Venice Commission 1996, On the Constitutional Situation in Bosnia and Herzegovina with Particular Regard to Human Rights Protection Mechanisms para. 4.4.2. See, also, Pimentel 2008–2009 p. 111.

631 UNMIK/REG/1999/5 on the establishment of an ad hoc court of final appeal and an ad hoc office of the public prosecutor.

court structure and international principles and standards on judicial organisation and function proved difficult, with growing accusations of discrimination and failures to provide fair and impartial adjudication. This became manifest in particular in cases where the alleged offender had belonged to the former Kosovo Liberation Army (KLA), or when the accused came from the Serb minority group.[632] The situation eventually prompted the UN administration to adopt a unique measure in state-building missions by introducing international judges and prosecutors to serve within the Kosovo judicial system.[633]

The programme for international judges and prosecutors was later expanded through regulation 2000/64. This increased the number of judges so as to minimise the risk of being 'outvoted' when sitting with Kosovar judges.[634] The decision to use international judges and prosecutors sparked controversy and criticism from inside and outside Kosovo. The Ombudsperson Institution in Kosovo noted in its 2008 annual report that there was a lack of transparency regarding the appointment of international judges, as well as in case assignment, and argued that the principles applicable to Kosovar judges in respect of merit, appointment, and case assignment should apply equally to international judges.[635]

International judges were also employed in East Timor, but there the UN had to deal with a situation different from that of Kosovo. While the same reasons for employing a mainly 'local' judiciary applied equally in East Timor, the difficulty affecting judicial structure and organisation was primarily that of capacity. International judges served on the special Panels with Exclusive Jurisdiction over Serious Crimes.[636] Apart from this, the strategy of UNTAET was to maintain as far as possible a Timorese judiciary. This posed particular problems of capacity. Owing to the discriminatory policy that Indonesia practiced during its occupation from 1975 there was no existing legal infrastructure at the start of transition. The UN administration therefore had to build or rebuild one. In regulation 2000/11 the UN intended to establish two sets of courts: eight district courts and a court of appeal.[637] Moreover, the regulation on judicial organisation also stipulated detailed jurisdictional issues, giving Dili District Court exclusive jurisdiction over serious crimes (genocide, war crimes, crimes against humanity, murder, sexual offences and torture) committed between 1 January 1999 and 25 October 1999. The UNTAET regulation on

632 Hartman 2003 p. 5.

633 UNMIK/REG/ 2000/6 regarding the appointment and removal from office of international judges and international prosecutors.

634 UNMIK/REG/2000/64 on the issue of assignment of international judges and prosecutors.

635 Ombudsperson Institution in Kosovo 2008 p. 19.

636 UNTAET/REG/2000/15. The subject matter jurisdiction built upon the provisions contained in the Rome Statute of the International Criminal Court.

637 UNTAET/REG/2000/11.

judicial organisation also contained rules on conflicts of interest, administration of the courts, legal cooperation and rules on the rights and duties of judges.

The organisational system set out for the courts in East Timor was rather complex and expensive with regard to the number of judges serving on one panel, and was criticised for imposing standards that were too high in the transition period.[638] While regulation 2000/11 called for eight district courts, only four of them had been established after five months into the mission. Continuing logistical and practical difficulties finally led UNTAET to amend regulation 2000/11 and reducing the number of district courts to four.

The regulation on the organisation of the courts in East Timor also provided for the establishment of investigative judges for each of the district courts, but without clarifying their responsibilities. On the powers of investigative judges, the UNTAET regulation only referred to such powers as described in the Criminal Procedure Code and in relevant UNTAET regulations. This caused a problem: there were no provisions in the applicable Indonesian Criminal Code for the office of investigative judge, and neither were there any relevant UNTAET regulations on the subject. At the time of the UNTAET regulation establishing the organisation of the courts, the new Criminal Procedure Code had yet to be drafted.[639]

In both Kosovo and East Timor, international actors thus resolved some aspects of judicial organisation by temporarily internationalising it, but the reasons for bringing in international judges and prosecutors differed. In Kosovo, the decision was mainly motivated by increasing numbers of accusations of a biased Kosovo-Albanian judiciary, while in East Timor an acute and chronic lack of experience and capacity appears to have influenced the decision, combined with the need to ensure impartiality and fairness in the proceedings concerning serious crimes.

The measures taken in Afghanistan on the structure and organisation of the judiciary also exemplify the challenges of weak capacity and local legitimacy. The first appointments to the Supreme Court, particularly that of the Chief Justice, created fears among international participants of a politicisation and radicalisation of the judiciary. After his appointment, the Chief Justice expanded the number of Supreme Court judges from nine, as laid down in the 1964 constitution, to over 100, apparently without adhering to formal requirements regarding professional skills and educational qualifications (many of them lacking education in secular law).[640]

---

638 Ibid., Art. 9.

639 Linton 2001 p. 140. The International Civilian Police (CIVPOL) responsible for policing started working with the investigative judges rather than the prosecutors, mainly it seems because of language barriers, leading to investigative judges supervising and instructing CIVPOL on arrests and detentions.

640 ICG 2003 Afghanistan: Judicial Reform and Transitional Justice p. 10.

Moreover, the Afghan Supreme Court took upon itself the establishment of special national security courts, despite the Bonn Agreement declaring the establishment of courts to be the province of the interim administration. The perplexity surrounding the structure and organisation of the Afghan judiciary, a confusion predating the Bonn Agreement, sustains a layered complexity of law where ordinary courts, district and local, as well as special courts and Islamic courts, not only overlap one another but are in conflict. Added to this is the risk of politicisation of judicial restructuring efforts, including a politicisation of the second Judicial Commission[641] as well as confusion over the establishment of parallel judicial or semi-judicial institutions, such as the National Human Rights Commission.

Judicial restructuring and reorganisation raise several difficult matters for the continuation of rule of law reform. Questions on organisation and structure are sensitive, since they can thwart informal power-sharing arrangements or the grip on power of former warlords. Against this background, the process of how judicial reorganisation is pursued seems to matter, but conflict might arise between international standards and local claims for legitimacy and ownership.

In some instances local ownership is not possible, whereas in other cases it might be a functional necessity (not least symbolically) to allow for higher levels of ownership. It is also apparent that there is a risk associated with excessively ambitious proposals for institutional reform. Along the lines of the argument of 'good enough governance', an observation can be made that questions on structure and organisations should be raised in light of the absorptive capacity of the particular society.

CAPACITY, INTEGRITY AND PROFESSIONALISM

FINDING LEGAL PROFESSIONALS

In parallel with efforts to review and strengthen structural and organisational aspects of legal and administrative institutions comes the challenge of specifying those legal professionals able to serve in new or reformed institutions. In many war-torn societies a lack of educated personnel is a major difficulty for assembling the 'bare bones' structure of the legal and administrative system and getting it to function. Such deficiency has in some cases been a problem predating conflict and crisis. According to an assessment of the justice sector in Liberia in 2006, only three of the 130 magistrates were lawyers. Out of a total of 300 justices of the peace whose sole qualification was literacy, more than half

641 Ibid., p. 12. The second Judicial Commission had a more watered down mandate than the original commission which was disbanded after three months. For example, the decree establishing the new commission did not declare it as an independent commission.

were illiterate.[642] Burundi proved to be equally alarming. Before the establishment of the UN mission, the UN Secretary-General reported that there were only 60 defence lawyers available in the country, most of them located in the capital.[643]

A lack of judges, magistrates, and other legal professionals, including civil servants, creates many problems. One is that insufficient legal professionals causes backlogs of cases and prolonged times of detention, and places constraints on overall access to justice.[644] Such deficiencies also affect the organisation of the state as a whole. There is a risk that of separation of powers becoming affected if the adjudicative branch suffers acute in capacity. Moreover, where there is a shortage of legal professionals, government policies and parliamentary legislation cannot be adequately pursued and upheld.

Accordingly, among the first concerns of international and national actors working at the start of a war to peace transition is to make good such deficits. Compromise becomes essential in making appointments to quickly fill positions. For example, practical experience becomes acceptable in the absence of a formal qualification. In Cambodia at the beginning of the UN mission in the early 1990s, the shortage of legal professionals led to drastic measures that demonstrated such a trade-off. The interim code drafted by the UN, Provisions Relating to the Judiciary and Criminal Law and Procedure Applicable in Cambodia during the Transitional Period, stated in article 7 (2) that any person possessing a secondary school certificate could act as legal counsel in a criminal trial.[645]

Apart from such drastic measures, the international and national response to personnel recruitment early on in war to peace transitions typically consists of three steps. First is the identification of legal professionals. Second, for those legal professionals that are identified, or for those that have remained within the legal and administrative system, some form of qualification standard must be applied. This is necessary in order to ascertain a level of professionalism, and important for the removal from office anyone guilty of taking part in atrocities and human rights violations before and during the conflict in question. Third, when legal professionals have been identified and assessed, there is a need for comprehensive training. This is to bring legal professionals 'up to date' in cases where they have been unable to practice law for some time, and to enable legal professionals to come 'on stream' in line with any rule of law reforms being undertaken.

---

642 ICG 2006, Liberia: Resurrecting the Justice System p. 1.

643 UNSG S/2004/210 p.13.

644 In Kosovo and East Timor, while struggling with this type of problem, the UN was more successful in the appointment of judges. See e.g. Strohmeyer 2001, Collapse and Reconstruction.

645 United Nations Transitional Authority in Cambodia, Provisions Relating to the Judiciary and Criminal Law and Procedure Applicable in Cambodia During the Transitional Period, September 10 1992.

Judicial Councils and Commissions

In response to the finding of legal professionals, one frequent method has been to support the establishment of national judicial or civil service commissions and councils in the early stages of transition. Such bodies serve a dual purpose in war-torn societies.[646] One is to help identify legal professionals and the other to function as organisations ensuring quality and consistency in the judiciary and civil service through a range of measures over a longer-term perspective – that is, supervising, disciplining and providing education and training. The latter is the function most often associated with judicial councils and similar bodies in accordance with international best practice. Because of the anatomy of crisis states, however, the first function is often emphasised in the initial stages of transition. This is a pragmatic consideration, since the identification of national legal professionals is difficult to accomplish by outside agencies. Support extended to commissions and councils also serves to create ownership early on in rule of law reform.

In 1999, at the start-up of the mission, UNMIK created the Technical Advisory Commission on Judiciary and Prosecution Service. This comprised a mix of national and international experts.[647] In the creation of a judicial commission, and in its composition, East Timor followed the route established in Kosovo. One of the first regulations by UNTAET was the establishment of the Transitional Judicial Service Commission. That body was charged with recommending candidates for the positions of prosecutors and judgeships, and provide advice on the removal of judges as well as formulating a code of ethics for judges and prosecutors.[648] The composition of the commission reflected the direct international influence in the UN administration of East Timor: two of its five members were international experts.

In Afghanistan the Judicial Reform Commission established in 2002 was given a coordinating role with the task of not only recommending a selection of judges, but of acting in liaison with the UN and international donors that under the Bonn Agreement were given responsibility for rule of law reform. Though the commission itself did not comprise any international experts, because of the differences in mission type compared with those of Kosovo and East Timor, it was to report to the Afghan interim administration and to the UN mission, as well as other assistance providers if so requested.[649] Such a reporting responsibility ensured if not control, then at least supervision by international agencies in the selection of judicial candidates.

---

646 See Autheman & Elena 2004 for a discussion on best practices regarding judicial councils in comprehensive judicial reform.

647 UNMIK/REG/1999/7, Art. 2.

648 UNTAET/REG/1999/3 Art. 1.

649 Presidential Decree No. 153 2002, Formation of the Judicial Reform Commission and Its Duties.

Both Burundi and Liberia chose a similar approach to the above-mentioned cases, but with a more nationally owned process. The 2000 peace agreement for Burundi specified a list of legal and judicial reforms to be undertaken during the transition. For the supervision of those reforms, the peace agreement stipulated the creation of a commission of the transitional national assembly.[650] Similarly in Liberia, the 2003 peace agreement included a host of commissions and councils charged with governance and rule of law reform. Since all judges, in accordance with the peace agreement, were deemed to have resigned upon the installation of the transitional government, ways and means had to be found to reinstall or select new candidates for the judiciary.[651] For the appointment of judges the peace agreement declared that the national bar association would select candidates, which would be decided upon by the transitional government and the transitional parliament.[652]

The consequences of applying councils and commissions have been mixed. On the one hand, they have achieved results in quantity, in finding legal professionals during the early phases of transition, but on the other, the creation and composition of such councils and commissions has proved difficult from a qualitative perspective. Identifying legal professionals and other public officials touches upon a critical aspect of the rule of law on independence and control over judicial power. As recent research indicates, judicial councils and the way that their composition and competences influence judicial independence is complex and dependent on a number of factors, among them the regime type in which they operate.[653]

International best practice and norms – that is, as expressed in The Universal Charter of the Judge and the European Charter on the Status of Judges, stress the need for independence and impartiality on the part of councils and commissions, in particular judicial councils.[654] The 1994 Council of Europe Recommendation on the Independence, Efficiency and Role of Judges stipulates that the "authority taking the decision on the selection and career of judges should be independent of the government and the administration".[655] However, in practice many commissions and councils have faced criticism for alleged bias, or in lacking in independence of the executive and other influential political actors, including international agencies.

---

650 Arusha Peace Agreement Art. 17.

651 Accra Peace Agreement Art. XXVII (2).

652 Ibid., Art. XXVII (3).

653 Nuno & Ginsburg 2009 p. 126: "We predict that autocracies will feature councils with weak competencies (ineffectual council) or strong competences/fewer judges (for greater political control)".

654 See Autheman & Elena 2004 p. 17 on providing a list of benchmarks for judicial councils, including: developing accountability mechanisms for council members, transparency in council procedures, insulating the council from interference and increasing the levels of civil society participation.

655 Council of Europe Recommendation No. (94) 12 Art. 1.2.

In Kosovo the Advisory Judicial Council was intended to allow for national ownership in judicial reform by making long-term appointments to the courts on judges and prosecutors and in improving overall court administration. The constitution of the Council specifically designated a majority of posts to local people "to empower them to overrule the international members so as to build a strong sense of ownership over the new judiciaries and to inject as much domestic expertise as possible into the process".[656] The bias on appointing to the Advisory Judicial Commission (and its predecessor, the Joint Advisory Council on Provisional Judicial Appointments) undermined its legitimacy and independence. Moreover, the appointed members of the Commission with a minority background were accused of having collaborated with the Milosevic regime and were thus intimidated. Both Commission and Council members lacked qualifications, rendering them susceptible to outside interference and thus operational capacity. The Advisory Judicial Council, for example, was mandated to make suggestions to SRSG on the removal of judges, but was renowned for being averse to taking disciplinary actions against its nominees.[657]

Similar problems existed in the Afghan Civil Service Commission, with its legal basis under the Bonn Agreement, which ran into difficulties even before it could assume its mandate of appointing public officials. The establishment of the commission was delayed because of political bickering, which led the interim government to appoint candidates to a majority of the positions in the civil service. This measure later attracted criticism and allegations that ethnic or family ties had influenced several of the government appointments.[658] The Judicial Council in Afghanistan faced similar worries.[659]

The problems encountered in the approaches to putting right deficiencies in capacity illustrate the difficulties of external involvement – above all, the political economy of rule of law reform and particularly institutional reform. While international participants have had an influence on appointments in Kosovo and East Timor, pursuant to the particular mandates of those missions, they have nevertheless depended on local capacity, resources, and information. That dependence was manifest both in the establishment of commissions and councils, and in the selection of judges and legal professionals by those commissions.

---

656 Strohmeyer 2001, Collapse and Reconstruction p. 52.

657 O'Neill 2002 p. 77.

658 UNSG S/2002/278 p. 5. A Civil Service Commission was established in 2003 by Presidential Decree No. 26 2003 Regulation on the Functions and Activities of the Independent Administrative Reform and Civil Service Commission.

659 Thier 2004 p. 57.

VETTING AND SELECTING LEGAL PROFESSIONALS

The identifying of legal professionals in the early phase of a war to peace transition is further made difficult, for two reasons. First, legal professionals might be lacking in skills and capacity, and might not have practised law for a long time. Second, legal professionals as well as other public officials might have been implicated in repressive policies and acts under a previous regime or during conflict and crisis.

The test of assessing the integrity and skill of legal professionals in many war-torn societies is conducted through vetting programmes (or lustration, as it is known with regard to rule of law reform in central and eastern Europe). Vetting and personnel programmes in the immediate phase of war to peace transitions are typically focused on justice sector institutions and law enforcement agencies. The reason why international agencies home in on these areas is that the judiciary, intelligence services, and law enforcement are all perceived to be essential institutions underpinning the rule of law, and are "most directly responsible for maintaining stability and fundamental security and protecting human rights".[660] Vetting programmes may be based upon provisions in peace agreements, as with Liberia where all judges were required to resign and reapply at the installation of the transitional government,[661] an interim constitution, or a UN Security Council mandate.

Integrity and Legitimacy of Vetting Processes

Initiating vetting programmes in war-torn societies has met considerable challenges. One is the fundamental matter of what standards to apply. Vetting of legal professionals, in particular judges, must be implemented with due regard to judicial independence and the principle of the separation of powers. Vetting, therefore, juxtaposes the fundamental rule of law principles of judicial independence, judicial integrity, impartiality and fairness.

Experience in the field shows that the question of selecting and removing judges is a sensitive subject that is not easily resolved. The UNDP guide Vetting Public Employees in Post-conflict Settings and the UN OHCHR manual, Vetting – An Operational Framework, provide entry points into the establishment of vetting programmes, standards of assessment and procedural instructions.[662]

---

660 UNDP 2006, Vetting: An Operational Framework p. 10.

661 Accra Peace Agreement Art. XXVII. According to the constitution of Liberia Art. 71, removal of judges from office can only be effected following "impeachment and conviction of the Legislature based on proven misconduct, gross breach of duty, inability to perform the functions of their office, or conviction in a court for treason, bribery or other infamous crimes". The practice of removing and reappointing judges en masse, despite constitutional guarantees on judicial positions, is perhaps best viewed as an indication of the particular transitional legal order created in war-to peace transitions.

662 UNDP 2006, Vetting Public Employees in Post-Conflict Settings; and UN Office of the High Commission for Human Rights 2006, Vetting: An Operational Framework.

Both the UNDP vetting guide and the framework provided by the UN OHCHR establish that vetting should be undertaken against international standards of human rights.[663] This seems to be the general international agreement. Gross violations of human rights and serious crimes committed within the jurisdiction of international law thus provide a crude minimum standard for the removal of public officials.[664] In order to assess conduct integrity (beyond gross violations of human rights), vetting procedures should rely on internationally developed standards of conduct, including the standards discussed in relation to law reform – that is, the UNBPIJ, UNGRP, and the UN Code of Conduct for Law Enforcement Officials.

In this instance of institutional reform it is possible to observe the direct influence of international standards – just as in law reform and constitution-making. This time the international influence concerns non-binding points of reference standards for comparison in externally promoted personnel programmes.[665] Beyond these markers, it is difficult to establish general conditions. Even the UN Office of the High Commissioner for Human Right's basic structure for vetting acknowledges that the circumstances of authoritarian rule and conflict might extenuate past acts, and that the integrity of a disgraced public official can be restored over the course of time.[666]

Judicial Restructuring without Legal Safeguards

In both Kosovo and East Timor, vetting was built into the selection process of judges, perhaps a reflection of the fact that both territories started with a limited legal infrastructure and that large-scale vetting programmes were not deemed necessary in the initial phase. For the Advisory Judicial Commission in Kosovo, with responsibility to advise the SRSG on the appointment and removal of judges, the criteria for the selection of candidates insisted (apart from professional skills) that candidates had no criminal record, and furthermore were not registered with any political party or participating in any political activity, and that they had not "participated in discriminatory measures, or applied any repressive law or have implemented dictatorial policies".[667]

The question of disciplinary actions and removal of judges in Kosovo has been addressed on two occasions. The first followed UNMIK regulation 1999/7 on Appointment and Removal from Office of Judges and Prosecutors. This

663 UNDP 2006, Vetting: An Operational Framework p. 21 "individual integrity manifests itself in a person's adherence to international standards of human rights and professional conduct".

664 For example,torture, genocide, war crimes, extra-judicial executions.

665 See, for example, the standards annexed to the judicial commission in Afghanistan for the selection of legal professionals. The standards included the UN 1985 Basic Principles on the Independence of the Judiciary. Afghanistan Presidential Decree No. 153 2002.

666 UNDP 2006, Vetting: An Operational Framework p. 21.

667 UNMIK/REG/1999/7 para. 6.1.

programme of careful examination began in the early phase of transition, but generally fell short of compliance with international best practice – that is, to include reprimands, suspension and other disciplinary measures that could be employed before a final decision on removal was considered. These disciplinary measures were included following regulation in 2005/25 on the establishment of the Kosovo Judicial Council (which superseded the Advisory Commission). Thus not until five years after vetting was first initiated were provisions established allowing judges suffering removal the right of appeal.

The second vetting programme was initiated after UNMIK Regulation 2006/25, which established a comprehensive reappointment process for judges and prosecutors, with the particular aim of ensuring greater participation from minority communities.[668] Considering the experience of the first programme and the lack of due process guarantees, it is somewhat surprising that the second programme also failed to include proper safeguards. Among other things the Independent Judicial and Prosecutorial Council, charged with responsibility for overseeing reappointments, did not have to explain its reasons when deciding on candidates for the judiciary and prosecutorial offices. Moreover, there were no explicitly mentioned procedures for appealing decisions by the Independent Judicial and Prosecutorial Council.[669] For those candidates denied a position, the available option was to file a request for consideration within a reasonable time. A ground for appeal was also limited to either the material or on the grounds that new information had emerged that was unknown to the Commission when it made its decision.

The structure, competence and function of the Independent Judicial and Prosecutorial Commission in the second vetting programme went against established best practice for judicial councils, and those deficiencies were attended to eight months later.[670] A new UNMIK directive introduced more extensive grounds for appeal beyond a request for reconsideration, with the possibility open to submit an application to the Supreme Court for a judicial review of the decision.[671] These changes seem to have been successful in creating greater efficiency, openness and fairness judicial selection. The Judicial Reform Index produced by the American Bar Association for Kosovo in 2007, reported significant improvements in judicial reorganisation on integrity and impartiality in the procedures on reappointments.[672]

In East Timor the Judicial Service Commission, established in the early part of the UN administration in 1999 included the right to a hearing for judges

---

668 UNMIK/REG/2006/25.

669 UNMIK/DIR/2006/18.

670 Autheman & Elena 2004 p. 12: "if there are no objective criteria, transferring selection powers to the Judicial Council may only reproduce, or worsen, discretionary and politicized appointments".

671 UNMIK/DIR/2007/7 section 1.

672 American Bar Association 2007, Judicial Reform Index: Kosovo Volume III p. 1.

facing disciplinary action and possible removal from office.[673] From a rule of law perspective the integrity of judges is clearly important, but so too is their protection against arbitrary removal. Though the international administrator was the final arbiter in cases of removal in Kosovo and East Timor, it is nevertheless imperative that adequate safeguards are properly installed from the beginning.

In Bosnia and Herzegovina, vetting was approached on a broad scale, focusing on specific sectors of professionals, such as the judiciary. Following frustrated attempts to reform the judiciary, the High Representative created the IJC in 2001, consisting of both international and national legal experts. Together with the ICJ, the High Representative initiated a re-application procedure for judges.[674] This screening was motivated by a "widely-perceived pattern of corruption and incompetence throughout the system".[675] In addition, many of the judges had served in a previous system that had imposed upon them a minimum of expectations. This, too, prompted the establishment of clear standards of integrity, professional competence and performance.

In the re-appointment procedure, judges had to provide detailed applications and disclosures, including divulgence of any wartime activities.[676] Similarly, for the civil service in Bosnia and Herzegovina, the High Representative promulgated a law in 2003, providing for all existing civil servants to be subject to review by the Civil Service Agency (with a view to determining whether or not they had been appointed in accordance with the Law on Public Administration).[677]

What stands out in the vetting process in Bosnia and Herzegovina is that it was undertaken within a comprehensive judicial restructuring programme. In a decision by the High Representative in 2002 all relevant provisions of domestic law on the appointment of judges and prosecutors were suspended.[678] This enabled the High Representative and the IJC to remove *en masse* all judges without risk of contravening international human rights standards – for example, Article 6 of the European Convention on Human Rights.

The High Representative could thus effectively remove sitting judges and make them reapply for their positions, and also appoint judges to new and different judgeships from those that had previously existed.[679] For those judges and prosecutors already in office the High Representative's decision offered, from a rule of law perspective, a paradoxical solution in declaring that all judges

---

673 UNTAET/REG/1999/3 para. 13.4.
674 OHR 2001, Decision providing the Independent Judicial Commission (ICJ) with a comprehensive mandate.
675 Pimentel 2008–2009 p. 113.
676 See IJC 2004.
677 OHR Decision 2003 Art. 64.
678 OHR Decision 2002, Suspending all Judicial and Prosecutorial Appointments para. 1.
679 Pimentel 2008–2009 p. 115.

and prosecutors holding office "regardless of expiration of mandates, shall continue to perform judicial and prosecutorial functions in accordance with their mandate, and shall enjoy all rights under law until further provided by law as a result of restructuring of the judicial and prosecutorial system".[680] The reappointment operation ended in 2004, and more than 30 per cent of judges were not reappointed. Despite its controversial features, it was considered a success, according to the Judicial Reform Index of the American Bar Association.[681]

Large-scale Vetting Programmes

Vetting procedures face difficult compromises similar to the trade-offs involved in identifying legal professionals and civil servants. On the one hand, reformers may decide to examine an entire corps of civil servants or legal professionals and start anew. This can result in a further weakening of an already fragile bureaucracy. On the other hand, reformers face the uneasy course of allowing public officials continue in office because of their expertise and competence, or simply because there is nobody to replace them – despite suspicions of crimes committed under a previous regime or doubts on their professional skills and qualifications.

The de-Baathification process of Iraq, where more than 30,000 officials were vetted, undermined an already weak bureaucracy.[682] Large vetting programmes of public officials were initiated in 2003 under the leadership of the Supreme National de-baathification Council, established by the CPA, the temporary international governing body. The de-Baathification Council was endowed with strong authority to investigate affiliations with the Baath Party.[683] De-baathification was undertaken in broad strokes, removing large numbers of civil servants and security personnel from their positions. A later CPA order in 2004 allowed some of the previously scrutinised personnel back into office.[684]

The de-Baathification of Iraq has been widely criticised for being implemented in a crude and non-transparent way and thus threatened the legal security of those caught up in the process. Diamond, in his critical review of both the US intervention and the CPA, argued that vetting was implemented

680 OHR Decision 2002, Suspending all Judicial and Prosecutorial Appointments para. 2.

681 American Bar Association 2006, Judicial Reform Index for Bosnia and Herzegovina: Volume II p. 1.

682 Meierhenrich 2008.

683 CPA/ORD 2003/05 on Establishment of the Iraqi Council for de-Baathification. Section 4 stipulates that failure to comply with a Council request for information could result in imprisonment for up to one year. The de-baathification was undertaken in two broad strokes. The CPA/ORD/2003/1 made the Baath Party illegal and dismissed all senior members from government posts. CPA/ORD/2003/2 dissolved the military and security forces.

684 CPA/ORD/ 2004/100 dissolved the Supreme National de-Baathification Commission and allowed some of the former Baath Party members to return to their positions in government.

without considering the effect it would have on the capacity of the Iraqi bureaucracy. The de-Baathification campaign was much too broad, according to Diamond, in its "excluding from any meaningful role in the future state anyone who had held any kind of high-level position in the party, regardless of whether they were directly involved in serious crimes".[685]

For the judiciary specifically, a Judicial Review Committee was established in 2003 similar to the councils and commissions employed by the UN in Kosovo.[686] The Committee was mandated to review all judges and prosecutors in Iraq and to make recommendations to the CPA on removals from office. On completion of its review of 800 judges and prosecutors, the Committee recommended the removal of 170 on charges of corruption or human rights abuse. The vetting of the judiciary appears to have been largely well received by national actors for its transparency and the 'judicial nature' of the removal procedures, in particular when compared with the de-Baathification programme of the military, the police, and public administration.[687]

The sheer size of such vetting programmes threatens rule of law principles. It is simply not logistically possible to provide due process safeguards to such numbers and under the conditions that prevailed in the first year of the US occupation of Iraq. This indicates a need to consider different approaches to vetting, particularly where it is associated with an ideological party or on similar grounds affecting large numbers of people. Vetting should be individualised and not based upon group affiliations. As the UN High Commissioner for Human rights vetting guide emphasises the 'traditional' safeguards should apply to vetting: due process, burden of proof falling on the reviewing body, the right to a fair hearing, reasonable time for a hearing, notification of concerned parties, and a generally public review process.[688]

In Kosovo and East Timor a possible learning curve can be observed. The mistake of not properly instituting due process principles in the vetting programme in Kosovo was avoided in East Timor. This can be contrasted with the High Representative's decision in Bosnia and Herzegovina to initiate a broad vetting programme that raised concerns from the start, but where the careful consideration of due process principles and the way they were made was transparent, with the publication of decisions in the Official Gazette, managed to accord it both international and national support and approval.[689]

---

685 Diamond 2004 p. 43.

686 CPA/ORD/ 2003/15 on the establishment of the judicial review committee.

687 Williams 2004–2005 p. 238.

688 UN High Commissioner for Human Rights 2006, Vetting: An Operational Framework p. 26ff. See, also, Council of Europe 1996 Parliamentary Assembly Resolution 1096 regarding measures aimed at dismantling the former communist party structures para. 11.

689 ABA 2006, Judicial Reform Index for Bosnia and Herzegovina p. 12.

Arguably, vetting and comprehensive personnel reform should be 'owned' by national authorities.[690] However, both the standards of assessment (which include vague references to human rights, humanitarian law, and detailed international codes of conduct) and the fact that the sensitivity of the whole process might delay necessary reforms if completely managed and owned by weak and fragmented interim governments, make international support a necessity. This trade-off raises the question of viewing ownership in terms of where it might be functionally necessary to devolve decision-making to local authorities through 'localised' commissions or councils, and where the sensitivity of the matter makes it a dangerous and counter-productive policy.

SKILLS AND 'SENSITIVITY'

One of the challenges of institution-building is that of manpower and putting in place adequate schemes for the training of judges, prosecutors, lawyers and civil servants. In many societies that have suffered the disruption of war, the legal personnel serving as judges, lawyers or prosecutors often lack an adequate education or have been unable to practice law for a long time, or sometimes both. To improve matters training programmes are frequently implemented in the early phases of state-building missions.

Training often focuses on two topics: updating the knowledge of legal professionals working within the system, in particular in relation to the newly reformed legal structure, and 'sensitising' them to human rights, first and foremost on criminal procedure. A typical sensitising example was the workshop organised by the UN in 2005 in the DRC in which 130 lawyers and magistrates were 'informed' of the Convention on the Elimination of All Forms of Discrimination Against Women in order to "help ensure that the rights of women are effectively promoted and protected by the Congolese courts".[691]

In Somalia, the UNDP has been engaged in judicial reform for more than a decade through its Role of Law and Security programme. While several of the reform measures in this programme relate to physical reconstruction, such as supplying printers, registers, law books and the establishment of an official gazette, much judicial reform has also been based upon the extensive training and 'retraining' of judges by way of workshops and conferences.[692]

The importance of educating legal professionals and other public officials and providing them with modern knowledge is clear from what happened in Kosovo – for example, on the implementation of the Law on Access to Official

690 OHCHR 2006, Vetting: An Operational Framework p.7.

691 UNSG S/2005/832 p. 10.

692 See UNDP 2008 Somalia-BCPR: Strategic Framework July 2007-June 2009 p. 13.

Documents.[693] Three sub-laws in the form of administrative instructions were enacted subsequent to the law. These provided details on the implementation of the law, including how to set up archives, classification schemes and communications with citizens.[694] Yet, the OSCE review on the implementation of the law, vast gaps were identified between the ambitions of the law and its sub-laws and between the awareness and capacity of local municipal officers and their capability of implementing such laws.

Common to most training enterprises on the enhancement of professional skills are practical aspects such as language and access to adequate information. One illustrative example was the Portuguese-led training in East Timor. One of the difficulties that this judicial teaching programme faced was the holding of training in Portuguese (one of Timor-Leste's two official languages). Roughly 80 per cent of the legal professionals had only limited skills in Portuguese. Participants were offered a one-month intensive language course, which would seem insufficient to develop the skills necessary in order to follow a detailed course of legal training.[695] Rwanda provides another example. Following the post-genocide intervention, international actors centred on prosecuting the perpetrators of genocide. This prompted the need for comprehensive capacity-building and training programmes for the few remaining judges and other legal professionals left in Rwanda. Most of the international experts employed to assist the judiciary came from common law backgrounds, with little or no understanding of Rwanda's legal tradition (a mixture of French and Belgian civil law). This adversely affected capacity-building in a judiciary attempting to deal with a backlog of cases.[696]

For training programmes directed towards helping legal professionals to become sensitive to such things as international human rights standards and benchmarks, which are important aspects of institution-building, the long term the effect of such training is unclear. Neither, is it clear to what extent training in skills actually matters in places where judges continue to work unpaid, or where executive interference in the judiciary remains a significant fact.[697] The limited effect of the capacity development of legal training schemes has been emphasised by the US General Accounting Office in relation to several rule of law programmes. In an evaluation of US rule of law support to the former Soviet

693 UNMIK/REG/2003/32.

694 OSCE 2007, Report on Implementation of the Law on Access to Official Documents at the Municipal Level. UNMIK/DIR/ 2006/01; UNMIK/DIR/2006/03; and UNMIK/DIR/2007/07.

695 Commission on Human Rights E/CN.4/2005/115 p. 4.

696 Mburu 2001 p. 29.

697 It is difficult to assess the 'impact indicators' of training programmes. There are quantitative and qualitative factors that can be applied as entry points in an evaluation, such as higher quality of judgements, results from surveys and interviews, changes in judicial performances, the number of cases and length of proceedings. It is also difficult to determine whether the observable changes are permanent, or only in response to the presence of a donor during the project implementation phase. See USAID 1996.

Union, the US General Accounting Office stated that training initiatives had had limited results, and that the long-term viability of "improvements is questionable".[698]

Legal training in skills and sensitivity appear to be necessary but insufficient to solve problems in the legal institutional structure. The Judicial Reform Index for Kosovo, developed by the American Bar Association, points to the uncertain effects of training when it is not made part of a broader restructuring and judicial reform objectives. The Kosovo Judicial Institute is an independent body charged with implementing ongoing training programmes for judges. There is no legal rule requiring continuing legal education for judges, though the Ethics and Professional Conduct of Judges adopted by the Kosovo Judicial Council (KJC), declares that judges shall "engage in continuing legal education and training as determined by the KJC".[699]

A further observation is that the level of ownership of international participants in the training of legal and administrative personnel is influenced by how they define and understand the rule of law. The training of judges, lawyers and prosecutors tends to attract international attention and financial support while that of civil servants in the public administration, on the other hand, is often 'localised' – that is, such training is often the primary responsibility of national agencies. The poor implementation of the law on access to official documents in Kosovo indicates how similar rule of law problems on training are treated differently depending in which 'sector' they are found.

A training need within the justice sector in Kosovo is organised directly under UNMIK. This is an area where the international administration has retained direct control. In public administration, UNMIK devolved much of its initial authority to national actors. Through regulation 2005/15 the Kosovar authorities were made principally responsible for the training and supervision of the public sector – that is, the Ministry of Local Good Administration,[700] and the Kosovo Institute for Public Administration.[701] This has meant that training to secure the rule of law in public administration is almost completely dependent on national initiatives and management, while rule of law training in the justice sector receives substantial international attention.

Apart from the urgency of supporting progressive legal training in skills and sensitivity, it is also necessary to review the capacity and needs of more long

698 US General Accounting Office 2001 p. 18. At the same time, a USAID commissioned study holds that "one of the single most important aspects of USAID's ROL [rule of law] work in Africa has been capacity-building within the justice sector", USAID 2002 p. 22.

699 Code of Ethics and Professional Conduct for Judges adopted by the Kosovo Judicial Council April 25 2006 Art. III (a) (3). Cf. Bosnia and Herzegovina where all sitting judges must attend at least four days of mandatory continuing legal training. American Bar Association 2006, Judicial Reform Index for Bosnia and Herzegovina p. 2.

700 UNMIK/REG/2005/15.

701 UNMIK/DIR/2003/25.

term legal education. In many societies imperilled by war higher legal education is disrupted and suffers constraints similar to other institutions – that is, a weakness in capacity, a prevalence of corruption and the destruction of basic infrastructure. In some cases there might not even be a functioning higher legal education to start with.

These conditions create a capacity gap, which must be addressed early on in a transition. International actors have only sporadically approached the question of higher legal education. For example, in both Liberia and Somalia, the UN briefly mentioned the need of supporting higher legal education but the primary focus was on the continuing legal training of judges, prosecutors and lawyers. While quickly finding, training and appointing judges are necessary measures in the short term, such strategies will eventually fail adequately to address structural shortages of skilled people. Moreover, the potential of law faculties in contributing through their research and competence as interlocutors in rule of law reform is not seized upon.

Support for legal education, as with most areas of institutional reform, has been approach as a technical question.[702] There is a need for refurbishing and re-equipping universities and law schools in war to peace transitions, but the 'software' side tends to be neglected. Difficulties facing higher legal education concern how it is regulated, what laws there exist on examination, degrees, and the content of education – as well as the legal requirement of passing the bar examination or its equivalent. There is also a need for improving teaching methodologies, though this is also a question of financial support – that is, to break up large classes into units of seminar size and work groups where problem-based teaching can be applied. Teaching methodologies might be formal and archaic in nature, based upon applying formalistic models on hypothetical cases or problems. The syllabus of courses and the whole curriculum might require modernising to correspond with political, social, economic and legal changes.[703]

Supporting an enabling environment can also be achieved by establishing legal aid clinics where students can obtain practical experience as part of their curriculum and "come on stream"[704] in a legal transition. Law clinics can have an important function in rule of law reform in two ways. The first is by allowing students to practice law from a problem-based perspective where legal education integrates with real legal problems. This is always difficult to achieve with traditional lecturing styles. Second, while students refine their practical skills they can also work as legal intermediaries, providing legal aid for vulnerable

702 The European Commission has a Tempus Programme designed to provide assistance to higher education in a number of regions. Few of the individual programmes concern legal education. Two recent ones have been in Bosnia and Herzegovina, and Kosovo.

703 This is one of the key recommendations in the study by Tufts University in the review of Afghanistan's justice system. Nojumi, Mazuran & Stites 2004 p. 4.

704 See, generally, Waters 2005 for an overview of legal education in war to peace transitions.

groups. This also serves to alleviate the pressure and backlog of the courts and other institutions.

Similar to other forms of institution-building, there might be vested interests within law faculties where corruption has become entrenched. It is a misguided assumption that law faculties would unhesitatingly respond to reforms aimed at introducing European or American standards of legal education. It is therefore important in this area of institution-building to provide partners for reform, ideally in the form of established universities in other countries. Such partners could act as long term catalysts by supporting student organisations, pedagogic and curriculum reform under twinning-programmes or similar arrangements.[705] Socialisation in this way would also provide tangible benefits in the form of teacher, student and visiting scholar exchange programmes or in financial support to research publications and projects.

INTERIM INTERNATIONALISATION

In response to weak local capacity, or because of certain questions of 'high politics' – international experts are sometimes employed directly to support national institutions. Part of this so-called internationalisation approach has previously been briefly examined in relation to judicial councils and commissions, of which some comprise international experts established to oversee reforms of the organisational structure and in vetting programmes. Under discussion in this section is the employment of international experts to substitute or work alongside national legal professionals in designated institutions, or the creation of temporary international agencies to work on certain topics such as resolving mass claims in property rights. This is sometimes done through various twinning programmes or joint structures between national and international actors.[706]

Temporary measures of internationalisation seem generally to follow two objectives. One of them is to provide capacity-building at the point of operation. This is also a form of socialisation with international actors functioning as 'teachers' of norms. The second objective is to temporarily alleviate national

705 This was implemented in both Tempus programmes for Bosnia and Herzegovina, and Kosovo. In Kosovo one problem was of the donor intensity. Other donor agencies offered to hold seminars on teaching methodologies; problem-based learning; legal clinics; rather than the law faculty running them at Prishtina University. Originally intended as an internal capacity-building exercise of the law faculty, the activities were contracted out.

706 While interim measures of international experts being brought in to serve in the national administration of a war-torn society have been rather frequent in state-building missions over the past decade, it is noteworthy that this was also done in the United Nations Operation in the Congo in the 1960s. See Jacobson 1964 p. 84 for a discussion on the use of international experts and their status in the national bureaucracy of the Congo.

institutions, either from a weak capacity and backlog, or in matters too sensitive to be dealt with impartially within the existing institutional structure.

International Staff in National Institutions

The employment of interim international experts or institutions is not without controversy. Besides challenges to national sovereignty, interim internationalisation might postpone the capacity-building of local institutions. Using international experts can also lead to the feeling among local legal professionals of being considered unworthy in professionalism or integrity, or both. In East Timor a comprehensive national training initiative was started in 2004 with support from the UNDP. In order to provide on the ground training for the East Timorese judiciary, four international judges, together with international clerks and one international prosecutor, were deployed directly in the district courts. When more than 80 per cent of the cases were redistributed to the four international judges, this caused resentment.[707]

Furthermore, when international actors substitute for a weak government or for one yet to be formed, or perform tasks under the guise of assistance by putting in place technical advisers and contractors as staff at ministries and government agencies, the result is an inherent reduction in accountability. A report by the ICG in 2003 on Burundi noted a heavy influx of international technical consultants within the bureaucracy and pointed out that they seemed "to take on more responsibility than the government did".[708] In East Timor outsourcing institutional capacities to international actors has been more obvious than in Burundi. Acknowledging a local lack of capacity to maintain a functioning tax administration in East Timor, the government contracted out the High Administration, Taxation and Audit Court to private international management by way of Price Waterhouse Coopers.[709]

The experience of Kosovo illustrates another problem of how international players need to balance the objectives of local ownership and capacity with maintaining international control and influence. Seemingly acting on conventional wisdom on the necessity of ownership and participation in rule of law assistance, UNMIK at first rejected a proposal to use international judges in a co-location arrangement with the Kosovar judiciary. After a time, when several reports corroborated claims that the local judiciary had failed KLA members, UNMIK decided to use international judges.[710] The deployment of international judges and prosecutors in Kosovo met considerable criticism from Kosovar Albanians, particularly in relation to what was perceived to be executive

707 Commission on Human Rights E/CN.4/2005/115 22 March 2005 p. 4.
708 ICG 2003, A Framework for Responsible Aid to Burundi p. 8.
709 Bergling, *et al.*, 2008 p. 14.
710 Hartz, Mercan & Williamson 2006 p.164.

interference by UNMIK and an imbalance in prosecutions of Kosovo Albanians for war crimes.[711] The deployment of international judges in Kosovo remains controversial. For example, in the 2008 annual report of the Ombudsperson Institution, the lack of transparency and clarity on case assignment to international judges is criticised.[712]

International Institutions

Establishing international institutions directly in war-torn societies in order to attend to complex or politically sensitive matters is also an example of interim internationalisation. The Commission on Real Property Claims of Refugees and Displaced Persons (CRPC) in Bosnia and Herzegovina,[713] as well as the Housing and Property Directorate and the Housing and Property Claims Commission (HDP/HPCC) in Kosovo,[714] constitute examples of internationally backed attempts to facilitate the swift, fair and effective processing of similar cases. These institutions are characterised by a standardised mass claims procedure and serve as potential precedents for the settlement of refugee and displacement problems in many other conflict and post-conflict situations.

The Dayton Agreement foresaw the establishment of the CRPC as an internationally supervised institution, mandated to receive and decide on claims for restitution or compensation for lost properties that had not been voluntarily sold or otherwise transferred since the outbreak of war in 1992.[715] The CRPC consisted of six national members and three others appointed by the president of the European Court of Human Rights. The Commission applied both national and international legal norms in its decision-making. Enforcement, however, was the responsibility of local authorities, which posed a major challenge to the authority and effectiveness of the Commission.

In Kosovo the HPD/HPCC was set up with jurisdiction over property-related disputes arising between 1989 and the 1999 conflict. The HPD had responsibility for providing overall direction on matters concerning property rights in Kosovo and also received residential property claims. The HPCC was given exclusive jurisdiction over deciding claims received by the HPD. The rulings of the HPCC were final and not subject to review or appeal, other than to the HPCC itself.[716] At the end of 2007 the HPCC had decided on all of the 29,160 cases submitted to the HPD, which formally ended its mandate.[717]

711 Perriello & Wierdi 2006 p. 31ff.
712 Ombudsperson Institution in Kosovo 2008 p. 19.
713 Established through the Dayton Peace Agreement Annex 7 Art. XI.
714 Established through UNMIK/REG/1999/23.
715 Von Carlowitz 2004 pp. 601–602.
716 UNMIK/REG/1999/23 para 1.1.
717 OSCE 2009 Conflicting Jurisdiction in Property Disputes p. 2.

Though the interim internationalisation in Kosovo was successful with regard to the number of claims processed, its relationship with local authorities was always strained and marked by controversies on jurisdictional matters with the local authorities. Despite the finality of HPCC decisions, some aspects were open for court review. The HPCC could also refer issues arising in claims "which were not within its own jurisdiction" to the local courts.[718] This relationship has proven to be problematic. Courts receiving cases from the HPCC often arrived at conflicting decisions that competed with HPCC findings, leaving parties without an effective resolution. The situation was further complicated by the fact that courts were unaware of previous decisions of the HPCC or its predecessor, the Kosovo Property Claims Commission (KPCC). Moreover, as the OSCE legal monitoring team observed regarding contested property, even where local courts had been made aware of decisions made by the HPCC or KPCC, they were frequently ignored.[719]

Those difficult features, particularly the relationship between international agencies and national courts, put an obstacle in the way of people's access to justice. This hurdle will have to be cleared successfully in future similar situations considering the fact that property rights crises are often beyond either the will or the capacity of national governments to resolve alone. In 2005 the Special Rapporteur to the UN Commission on Human Rights on Housing and Property Restitution drafted the Principles on Housing and Property Restitution for Refugees and Internally Displaced Persons. This established benchmarks for resolving property and land disputes in war-torn areas. Though the primary responsibility under international law and as articulated in the principles, is that of the state to settle such matters, there is also a part to be played by international actors. Peace operations, according to the principles, should be "requested to support the protection of the right to housing, land and property restitution, including through the enforcement of restitution decisions and judgements. Members of the Security Council should consider including this role in the mandate of peace operations".[720]

Liberia: Anti-corruption Reform Through International Control

Liberia provides many examples of how the different objectives of a temporary internationalisation – capacity-building and dealing with sensitive issues – are translated into practical measures.

Two financial audits carried out by the EC and the Economic Community of West African States in 2004 revealed that the offences of theft and fraud within the transitional government were rife to the extent that they were sabotaging any

---

718 UNMIK/REG/2000/60 para. 22.1.

719 OSCE 2009, Conflicting Jurisdiction in Property Disputes p. 3.

720 Commission on Human rights E/CN.4/Sub.2/2005/17.

possibility of durable peace-building.[721] The auditing of state-owned enterprises met with resistance and several members of the Liberian government attempted to obstruct investigations.[722] The Liberian Institute for Certified Accountants filed a writ of prohibition with the Supreme Court seeking to restrain public officials from cooperating with the audits. The Supreme Court refused the writ after civil society groups filed an *amicus curiae* brief on behalf of the audits.[723]

Previous pressure from the donor community in Liberia had resulted in the formation of a Task Force on Corruption and a Cash Management Committee. The UN Security Council also adopted resolutions for the freezing of assets and the supervision of the trading in diamonds, but with limited results.[724] Similarly, the European Council took measures against Liberia in 2003 following reports that its government had failed to honour agreed standards on human rights protection and the rule of law and good governance, as stipulated in the Cotonou Agreement.[725] None of those measures proved sufficient in tackling the rule of law deficit within the transitional government in the area of economic governance.

In response, a group of international donors established the Governance and Economic Management Assistance Programme (GEMAP).[726] The agreement, which was signed by the Liberian Government in 2005, represented an intrusive and radical form of international control and supervision over a number of economic and governance issues. Its main objective was to improve governance and enhance transparency and accountability by targeting revenue collection, expenditure controls and government procurement practices.[727]

A special feature of GEMAP was that several components called for the deployment of international experts with binding co-signature authority. No major transactions could take place without being examined by both a Liberian manager and an international counterpart.[728] For example, under the financial management and accountability component, an international expert had

---

721 The audits involved the following revenue generating agencies: Liberia Petroleum Refining Company; Forestry Development Agency; National Port Authority; Roberts International Airport; Bureau of Maritime Affairs; and Central Bank of Liberia. See, also, the report of UNDP, The Dimensions of Corruption in Post-War Liberia (2006).

722 UNSG S/2005/376 p. 8.

723 See Dwan & Bailey 2006 for a full description of the events leading up to GEMAP.

724 See SC Res. 1521 (2003); SC Res. 1532 (2004); and SC Res. 1607 (2005).

725 See Council Decision of 25 August 2003.

726 International Contact Group for Liberia, 11 May 2005. Governance and Economic Management Assistance Program, Monrovia, 9 September. GEMAP was to run for 36 months, unless the completion Point under the Enhanced Highly Indebted Poor Countries Initiative was not reached.

727 GEMAP included six components: financial management and accountability; improving budgeting and expenditure management; improving procurement practices and the granting of concessions; establishing effective processes to control corruption; supporting key institutions; and capacity-building.

728 This was been put in place in the following institutions: Ministry of Finance; Central Bank of Liberia; Bureau of Budget; Ministry of Lands, Mines and Energy; National Port Authority;

co-signing authority over matters relating to banking and for ensuring that internal controls and audits are carried out in accordance with established rules.[729] International experts also had co-signing authority on financial management issues in various state-owned enterprises.[730] In one of the draft papers to the agreement was the provision of employing international judges in the same way as in Kosovo and East Timor. But this was obstructed by the transitional government, referring to legal requirements stating that only Liberians could serve in the judiciary.

GEMAP also included the establishment of the independent Anti-Corruption Commission to assist in the investigation of fraud and corruption, and various economic crimes.[731] The Commission, consisting of both Liberian and international experts, retained full prosecutorial powers. In addition, an independent prosecutor was installed to work on corruption charges. International technical assistance was also provided to enhance the investigative capacity of the prosecutorial office.[732] The international influence was notable in its anti-corruption strategy. International legal experts were to be called upon to support and advise the Liberian judiciary in the dispensation of justice, particularly in cases of corruption where international judges would advise national judges during court proceedings.

There were several difficulties with the agreement from the perspective of sovereignty that should be acknowledged, in particular, the intrusive measures of providing international experts with co-signing authority.[733] At the same time the implementation of the agreement gained momentum and saw tangible progress, particularly in relation to improved fiscal discipline and increased revenues during its first year of operation.[734]

The main difficulty with interim internationalisation, as with the cases of GEMAP in Liberia and international judges in Kosovo, is how to link such initiatives with other rule of law programmes and projects under implementation. For example, on GEMAP the programme was not fully incorporated within the comprehensive rule of law strategy of UNMIL. Another difficulty relates to the central dilemma of all internationally supported reform

---

Robert's International Airport; Liberia Petroleum Refinery Cooperation; and the Forestry Development Agency.

729 GEMAP p. 3.

730 ECOWAS originally proposed that judges from the region would be brought in to sit on the Liberian bench. The Liberian government rejected this proposal as being too intrusive and sovereignty-offensive, and it was withdrawn. Dwan & Bailey 2006 p. 23.

731 GEMAP p. 4.

732 This is in stark contrast to the previous Anti-Corruption Agency established under ACPA, Executive Order No. 6 in June 2005, where no prosecutorial powers were included. Any person or group can take a case to the Commission, including donor organisations suspecting their funds and assistance programmes have not been properly used by the government.

733 The ICG stressed that the agreement was sui generis and should not be seen as a template for other crisis states. ICG 2005 Liberia's Elections: Necessary but Not Sufficient p. 14.

734 Economic and Governance Steering Committee 2006 Status Report Year 1 p. 11.

programmes: how to ensure sustainability once external support is withdrawn. International actors must balance the need for international supervision and control with local ownership and influence over the programme agenda and its implementation. The real test for concepts like GEMAP, or for the employment of international judges, is whether or not national authorities continue with reforms, practices and standards after the completion of external rule of law promotion.

Employing international experts directly in national institutions involves a delicate balance between devolving power where it might be practically and functionally necessary, and retaining authority where it would be politically difficult to devolve. It could be presumed that national actors and agencies would benefit from co-location programmes and other forms of socialisation where international players are embedded in local institutions. The goal of co-location programmes seems important in this regard. If international actors are fixed firmly in position in order to bolster capacity and legitimacy in a long-term perspective, this could reasonably improve the chances of sustainable institutional capacity. If, on the other hand, international actors utilise co-location in a more ad hoc fashion in reaction to pressing needs and problems, without considering its long-term implications, the international influence could be short-lived and would only 'rub-off' as long as there was a tangible presence.

MONITORING INSTITUTIONS

Few institution-building reforms are adequately monitored, focusing on project inputs rather than output performance. As the US General Accounting Office noted in its review of UN peace-keeping, courts and institutions are used as measures of progress with a limited understanding of how these institutions really function and are made use of by citizens.[735] Monitoring the performance of the justice system is one way of promoting and ensuring respect for rule of law principles. It is most commonly directed towards the identifying patterns and trends that violate international standards, as well as pinpointing systemic issues that hinder compliance.

Justice sector monitoring is not just about supervision, and neither does its presence have to be a manifestation of distrust, or suggest ideas of 'us' versus 'them'. Rather, an 'on-going assessment' of laws and daily practices in the justice sector can provide national and international decision-makers with the accurate and specific information that they require for the strategic targeting of resources for the purposes of reform. For a fledgling domestic legal and administrative system struggling to comply with international standards and integrate them into reform and action plans, monitoring can be a particularly effective tool both

735 US General Accounting Office 2003 p. 32.

for highlighting specific compliance problems and indicating how to best tackle them when resources are scarce.

On monitoring of the justice or the administrative sector, there is no formal rule of law treaty or any other binding instrument against which to check or measure rule of law compliance. Nor is there any UN organ exclusively concerned with rule of law monitoring. Nevertheless, there are several indirect sources of normative guidance, notably international human rights instruments. It should be noted that almost all countries, including the group of post-war countries, are members of various international and regional organisations (UN, Council of Europe and African Union) and have ratified the most important human rights treaties. Additional guidance may be found in the decisions of the courts and commissions created to interpret these instruments and provide judgements or opinions concerning their application.

In a state-building mission there are often a number of parallel monitoring initiatives targeting aspects of human rights, judicial performance, and other topical matters. This monitoring capacity may be located either within the UN mission (for example, as a component of UN Mission in Bosnia and Herzegovina -UNMIBH, UNMIK and UNMIL) or with another international or regional organisation (for example, the OSCE). The UN OHCHR also provides support and technical advice to the human rights components of UN state-building missions.

There is constant work in the UN and other organisations to refine monitoring techniques and approaches. The UN OHCHR 2006 Monitoring Legal Systems focuses specifically on tracking human rights standards in the justice system in war-torn societies.[736] The report emphasises that the practice should be comprehensive. This would mean covering the whole array of topics concerned with establishing and maintaining legal and administrative institutions functioning in accordance with the rule of law – for example, budgetary allocations, supervision and accountability mechanisms, appointment processes, manpower policies, and training.[737]

Another important lesson for consideration is that monitoring should examine whether parallel informal or traditional structures exist and if so, how they function and interact with the formal system and to what extent they comply with rule of law and human rights standards.

736 OHCHR 2006, Monitoring Legal Systems.

737 See, also, OSCE 2008, Trial Monitoring: A Reference Guide for Practitioners in noting guidelines for the trial monitoring of criminal law proceedings but mindful that "the practical advice and tools the manual provides will still be of use for those who are considering organizing any form of trial-monitoring exercise, including civil or administrative justice or cases with strong political overtones or human rights concerns". The Trial Monitoring Guide, however, would then need to be adjusted in order to follow judicial review proceedings and appeals within the public administrative system.

Furthermore, in line with the human rights approach to legal system monitoring, both domestic law and domestic practice should be analysed for evaluating compliance with international standards. Where it is determined that the domestic law in question meets international standards, the accent should be shifted to whether or not actual practice conforms to the domestic law.

A successful mandate on monitoring was the Judicial System Assessment Programme in Bosnia and Herzegovina. UN Security Council resolution 1184 (1998) authorised the mission to undertake "monitoring and assessing the court system in Bosnia and Herzegovina, as part of an overall program of legal reform".[738] The resulting assessment programme had unhindered access to court proceedings and files.[739]

Though comprehensive monitoring is to be preferred, it is rarely possible to observe all aspects of legal and administrative practices. A more realistic approach might be to try to identify such things as representative practices, procedures, and policies in a particular system by monitoring groups of cases and by recognising trends and patterns within them so as to draw overall conclusions on the functioning of the system and to formulate recommendations for reform.

Monitoring can also provide a short-term 'injection' in attempting to remedy institutional deficiencies in sensitive areas. It might in this sense mean the creation of pressure for accountability by exposing and solving problems within the system and reinforcing its proper role and purpose. The Rule of Law Unit of the UN mission to the Ivory Coast provided advice to the local judiciary on issues such as deaths in custody, ill treatment, and arbitrary killings involving security forces. Bolstering weak local judiciaries through a visible international presence can deter intimidation and threats directed at the judiciary's independence. It is also easier for international actors to criticise sensitive areas of high politics. This form of monitoring can also promote legitimacy in a short-term build-up phase where a judiciary or other legal institution enjoying little or no confidence among the population might gain in reputation by aligning itself with international (and seemingly) 'neutral' experts.

Where there has previously been a scarcity of monitoring programmes, they are now becoming standard in rule of law schemes. Several large-scale programmes are now employed in war to peace transitions, including the Judicial System Assessment Program (JSAP) in Bosnia and Herzegovina, the Judicial System Monitoring Program (JSMP) in East Timor, and the Legal System Monitoring Project (JSMP) in Afghanistan. The OSCE also undertakes a continuing review of the criminal justice system in Kosovo.[740]

---

738 SC Res. 1184 (1998). See, also, Bergling 2006 pp. 54–56.

739 Carlson 2006 p. 5.

740 For a detailed in context manual for criminal law monitoring, see United Nations Mission to Afghanistan (UNAMA) Trial Monitoring Manual 2007.

Most programmes primarily cover criminal cases, rarely civil or administrative justice. However, of late the OSCE has included the administrative justice system in its monitoring activities.[741] Court monitoring has also given rise to a number of field guides and operational directives.[742] Though it is sometimes perceived as 'toothless' when its function is merely advisory, it has proved an effective way of identifying real problems on which to start a dialogue for future reform.[743]

ACCESS AND EMPOWERMENT

An interrelated question with institution-building and capacity development is that of how to empower people and ensure their access to newly reformed institutions.[744]

A common theme of legal and administrative systems in crisis societies is that of a failure to protect the constitutional rights of people within their jurisdictions. Sometimes abuses by legal and administrative institutions occur by omission owing to a lack of resources, capacity and management. But abuses also occur because institutions are often geared towards ends other than the public good. State agencies are frequent violators of legal rights and remain inaccessible. Remedies are too expensive or complicated. Other practical matters also impede empowerment and access, including weak judicial representation in rural areas and language differences. In many war-torn societies courts and other state agencies only exist in the cities. Court personnel, if any, are rarely paid and have to finance their positions by attaching a 'price tag' to proceedings. Lacking legal textbooks, judges have to rely on memory and adjudicate according to what seems to them to be fair.[745]

Court proceedings, under such circumstances, become ad hoc, unpredictable and vulnerable to outside influence. Such dysfunctional judicial and administrative processes undermine the citizen's faith in the state and its institutions. Endemic corruption in Afghanistan, for example, and the infiltration of former warlords into the judiciary has led to the perception among people that the Taliban regime provided a fairer administration of justice.[746]

741 OSCE 2007, Report on the Administrative Justice System in Kosovo.

742 OHCHR 2006, Monitoring Legal Systems.

743 OHCHR 2006 p. 2, states that publicised reports can not only influence behaviour in a certain direction but also motivate the political will to do so.

744 See e.g. UNSG S/2004/616 p. 12: "our programs must also support access to justice [...] independent national human rights commissions can play a vital role in affording accountability, redress, dispute resolution and protection during transitional periods".

745 UNSG S/2008/553 p. 10 describes the situation in Liberia as "lack of funding, shortage of qualified judicial officials, the lack of infrastructure [...] archaic rules of procedure [...] poor case management".

746 UNSG S/2006/935 p. 11.

Under such circumstances where people are denied the experience of using and trusting laws and legal institutions to protect their rights, or to challenge government actions, an important aspect of institutional reform lies in support aimed at enablement and the use of knowledge to 'anchor' rule of law reform.[747] It is also important that laws and legal institutions are established in such a way that citizens can make use of them individually or collectively.[748] Such vertical accountability mechanisms should also allow for people to challenge government actions or to report on breaches committed by public officials by way of a mobilisation of legal means.[749]

HUMAN RIGHTS AND 'WATCHDOG' INSTITUTIONS

A common form of institutional support directed towards enabling vertical accountability is the establishment of national human rights institutions and ombudsperson offices. Such institutions are regarded by international actors as having the potential to function as a repository of human rights knowledge within a country, and might also review legislation in light of international standards on human rights, and provide recommendations to the government in question on human rights affairs. National human rights institutions are also supported as essential institutions in order to enable citizens to complain when they feel their rights have been transgressed or flouted. Sometimes commissions are established as a complement to the formal judicial system, in that they can pass cases to the prosecutor, though they may also hold investigative and prosecutorial authority of their own. National human rights institutions are often part of a peace accord – for example, in El Salvador, Guatemala, and in Bosnia and Herzegovina.[750]

In the 1992 Commission on Human Rights resolution, Principles Relating to the Status of National Institutions (often called the Paris Principles), the main tenets of national human rights institutions are established. The central features of a human rights institution are described as having advisory and supervisory functions on a broad subject matter on human rights, and should strive for an amicable settlement through conciliation in a form of quasi-judicial competence.[751] These features were later elaborated in practical ways in the 2005 Handbook for National Human Rights Institutions.

747 UNSG S/2004/616 p. 12.
748 Afghan Human Development Report 2007 p. 100.
749 O'Donnell 2004 p. 37 distinguishes between three forms of accountability: vertical accountability through elections; vertical accountability by using legal means, i.e. challenging government actions through law; and horizontal accountability by institutional checks-and-balances.
750 See e.g. Reif 2000.
751 Commission on Human Rights E/C.N.4/1992/54 and UNGA, A/RES/48/134.

There has been great disparity in how countries in war to peace transitions have chosen to establish human rights institutions, and with what competencies and powers they are endowed.[752] The Afghan National Human Rights Commission, for example, is relatively weak compared with its equivalent in Sierra Leone. In Afghanistan, the investigative powers have remained unclear, as well as the competence to initiate legal proceedings on the basis of individual complaint.[753] Moreover, there is no law compelling courts to review cases referred to them by the Human Rights Commission.[754] Another constraint on the Afghan Human Rights Commission is that it does not encompass customary law resolutions such as *shuras* or *jirgas* in any official capacity. Its mandate stipulates that it shall monitor "the performance of those administrative systems, legal and judicial institutions, and national and international profitable and non-profitable organizations in the country that affect human rights".[755] While *shuras* and *jirgas* as customary institutions for dispute resolution clearly affect human rights, considering their dominant position in the legal system, it is unclear whether the Human Rights Commission can monitor them (or possesses the resources to do so) though claims have been made for expanding the monitoring mandate of the Commission.[756]

The Human Rights Commission in Sierra Leone, in contrast, was also established in the beginning of the transition but with substantially different powers. The Commission there was vested with powers and responsibilities similar to those of a high court of justice or a judge.[757] This means that the Commission can enforce the attendance of witnesses, compel the production of documents, or make requests to examine witnesses abroad.

The disparity between competences and powers among national human rights institutions is perhaps better understood against the background of a weak international normative support on national human rights institutions and other such agencies. The Paris Principles declare investigative powers to be an optional function.[758] Neither are they explicitly mentioned in the handbook

---

752 The OHCHR 1995 National Human Rights Institutions para. 39, refers to a national human rights institution as "a body which is established by a Government under the constitution, or by law or decree, the functions of which are specifically defined in terms of the promotion and protection of human rights".

753 President of the Republic of Afghanistan Decree No. 16 2005, Enforcement of the Law on Structure, Duties and Mandate of the Afghanistan Independent Human Rights Commission.

754 Moschtaghi 2006 p. 583.

755 President of the Republic of Afghanistan Decree No. 16 2005, Enforcement of the Law on Structure, Duties and Mandate of the Afghanistan Independent Human Rights Commission Art. 21 (3).

756 Afghan Human Development Report 2007 pp. 108–109.

757 The Human Rights Commission of Sierra Leone Act. 2004 No. 9 Art. 8 (1–3). The Lomé Agreement in Sierra Leone first called for the establishment of a national human rights commission no less than 90 days after the signing of the agreement.

758 The Paris Principles. There is an appendix to the Paris Principles including examples of offices with authority to hear individual complaints.

developed by the UN High Commissioner for Human Rights. Though it lists the six principles for ensuring effectiveness of national human rights institutions – independence, defined jurisdiction, adequate powers, accessibility and cooperation, operational efficiency, and accountability – investigative powers are omitted.[759]

Interrelated with human rights commissions are ombudsman institutions. It is sometimes difficult to categorise newly created institutions in war-torn societies as being either ombudsman or human rights commissions.[760] Sometimes this might lead to confusion and an overlapping of mandates that complicates the system of human rights protection. Contrasting the ambiguity on investigative powers of national human rights institutions, the power to investigate is more or less universally agreed upon in relation to ombudsman institutions in order to provide administrative accountability.[761]

The most common definition of an ombudsman is a person or office formally appointed by the parliament or government of a country to perform general and *in casu* supervision of executive or judicial authorities on behalf of citizens.[762] The ombudsman typically receives complaints from the public, and may then decide whether or not to initiate an investigation. The ombudsman may, alternatively, initiate an investigation *ex officio* if he discovers irregularities or malpractices within the administration. The most important role of the ombudsman is thus not to review every complaint *in casu*, but to supervise general legality and compliance with the principles of good administration within public agencies. In some systems the ombudsman has the right to alter decisions he finds wrong or illegal, but this construction carries the risk of conflict between the ombudsman and the formal appeals structure, typically the courts. In most systems the principle is therefore that the ombudsman should point out mistakes and structural problems in the application of the law by the administration, with the option open to take legal action against individual civil servants who have seriously violated the law or otherwise failed to execute their duties.

If the ombudsman is to be effective as an extraordinary institution in addition to the regular political, administrative and judicial authorities, he must not be bogged down by too many cases. The agency must also have the right to determine which cases should be investigated as being of principal or symbolical importance. It is also important for the authority of the institution that the

---

759 OHCHR 1995 National Human Rights Institutions p.13. In the handbook, 'adequate powers' are treated diplomatically, stating: "It is not useful to set out a list of basic or even minimal powers with which a national institution should be vested. Power can only ever relate to purpose".

760 Reif 2000 p. 11.

761 Schedler 1999, Conceptualizing Accountability p. 22.

762 Reif 2000 p. 8.

ombudsman is formally and *de facto* independent of all other branches of the state, and that his statements are respected and acted upon.

Resource and capacity issues are critical, particularly in post-crisis environments where even the most fundamental state agencies may lack sufficient resources to perform their functions properly. For example, ombudsperson institutions were established in Bosnia and Herzegovina and Kosovo early on in the international interventions. Both of these institutions were also international in the first phase, and had international experts acting as ombudsmen.[763]

The Ombudsman institution in Bosnia and Herzegovina retained much of the character of an "internal international actor".[764] According to the Dayton Agreement the mandates for the Human Rights Ombudsman and the Human Rights Chamber expired on 31 December 2000. When at the end of the mandate national authorities were unable to decide on an extension, the Office of the High Representative imposed one of three years and expressed its regret that "state authorities felt unable to adopt the law which protects crucial rights for all BiH citizens".[765] The law providing the new framework for the ombudsman, moreover, was drafted by the Venice Commission.[766]

The Ombudsperson Institution in Kosovo has been more successful in efforts at 'localisation'. The Kosovo ombudsman was also established with support from the OSCE but gained a more independent status from the OSCE and other pillars of support in UNMIK.[767] To a certain extent there were also overlapping mandates in Kosovo, with peculiarities such as the right of people to appeal to the SRSG directly if they believed that a judicial decision was founded on discriminatory grounds, but only on discrimination based upon community membership.

East Timor also established the Office of the Ombudsman for Human Rights and Justice, or *Timor-Leste Provedor de Direitos Humanos e Justica*.[768] The constitution provides for the independence of the *Provedor* enabling it "to examine and seek to settle citizens' complaints against public bodies, certify the conformity of the acts with the law, prevent and initiate the whole process to

763 Ombudsman of the Federation of Bosnia and Herzegovina 1996, Annual Report p. 1.

764 Aolain 1998 p. 984.

765 OHR Press Release 2000, High Representative Imposes Law on Human Rights Ombudsman of BiH 13712 2000. See also OHR Decision 2000, Decision Imposing the Law on the Human Rights Ombudsman of Bosnia and Herzegovina.

766 Venice Commission 2000, Law on the Ombudsman of the Federation of Bosnia and Herzegovina 140/2000.

767 UNMIK/REG/2000/38. The legal basis was later amended by UNMIK/REG/2006/6 in which the power to investigate claims made against international administrative bodies was abolished. The Ombudsperson Institution also received clear constitutional protection as an independent body through the new Kosovo Constitution of 2008.

768 Statute of the Office of the Ombudsman for Human Rights and Justice Law No. 772004 26 May 2004.

remedy injustice".[769] The particular areas of responsibility are human rights, good governance, and anti-corruption. There are ombudsmen with specific responsibilities for each subject area. In addition, it also functions as an anti-corruption commission.[770] The *Provedor* may undertake inspections and investigate any government or judicial authority, but has no authority to challenge the actions and decisions of the courts or parliament. Apart from supervision, it has also been given the task of providing education on human rights and justice, and of promoting 'good practice' in government bodies. Though the *Provedor* is a recent institution (it started operating in early 2006), it is well-known in Timor-Leste and has received many cases concerning good governance, violations of human rights, and corruption.[771]

The most difficult challenges to the functioning of the institution have been resource and capacity bottlenecks. The *Provedor* still struggles with finding sufficiently trained staff, acquiring and maintaining buildings and technology, and with generally obtaining the essential means to function adequately. Another significant difficulty relates to the overlapping mandates of the *Provedor* and other accountability institutions. This concerns in particular its mandate to function both as an anti-corruption agency and a national human rights institution. Besides technical and capacity problems, as well as the security concerns of the staff when investigating corruption allegations, the mandate conflicts with the Office of the Prosecutor General and the Office of the Inspector General. Along the lines of the argument by the Venice Commission, expressing concern on overlapping mandates for human rights bodies in Bosnia and Herzegovina, there is a risk here that creating new institutions or adding new competences to established institutions, will be counter-productive.

Ensuring financial accountability in war-to peace transitions forms a crucial step in the proper management of state finances and for weak interim governments to effectively receive, coordinate and implement international assistance and humanitarian aid. Though corruption is generally considered to be among the most grievous impediments for social and economic development, there are indications that its effect in war-torn societies is even more dramatic, posing a direct threat to national security, and undermining financial and manpower capacity in state institutions, including the justice sector.[772]

Though not set up as human rights institutions, anti-corruption commissions or agencies, such as the *Provedor* frequently allow for, and even depend on for their function, appeals and reports from individuals similar to that of human rights bodies.[773] These agencies are one the most favoured instruments for

---

[769] Constitution of East Timor Art. 27.
[770] Commission on Human Rights E/CN.4/2005/115 p. 7.
[771] Bergling, *et al.*, 2008 p. 34.
[772] Rose-Ackerman 2008 p. 405.
[773] Schedler 1999, Conceptualizing Accountability p. 22: "financial accountability subjects the use of public money by state officials to norms of austerity, efficiency, and propriety".

fighting corruption, and have been established in a variety of countries, often modelled on the Hong Kong Independent Anti-Corruption Agency (IACA). While this is an ideal type, with a sound financial base, social trust, and broad powers and competencies, emulations of this type of commission have by and large failed to reach similar standards in most other countries.[774] Commissions often end up with a weakened mandate, overlapping mandates with national human rights institutions or ombudsman agencies, or are in other ways undermined by lack of money. In some circumstances the commissions are solely under the auspices of the executive.

The lessons learned from supporting access-creating and accountability institutions boils down to this: the need for political will guaranteeing institutional independence. A broad-based support spanning different political parties and fractions is necessary, and not just that of the government. The Liberian Executive Task Force against Corruption, created after the peace agreement in 2003 following international pressure, is an illustrative example. The 'Task Force' distinguished itself by its being too close to the executive interim government and by not publishing a single investigation or supporting a single prosecution, despite operating in a country ruled by one of the most corrupt governments in its history.[775]

Governments sometimes create national human rights commissions or ombudsman institutions in response to international pressure, while lacking the political will to provide these organisations with adequate resources and money to operate independently. In war to peace transitions a broad political and public support might be difficult to generate owing to the sensitivity of human rights and accountability questions, and it should be considered what effects non-committal reforms might have on the trust and legitimacy of the state.

INTERIM MASS CLAIMS COURTS AND COMMISSIONS

A frequent concern with the judiciary in a war to peace transition is how it manages massive backlogs of cases. Delays create a serious problem of access to justice for individuals.[776]

The establishment and support of courts and administrative agencies is important in promoting and safeguarding rule of law standards, and for remedying problems on access to justice. At the same time, structural and institutional features of post-crisis societies (such as weak and manipulated

774 Nichols, Daniel, Polaine & Hatchard 2006 p. 475.

775 Governance Reform Commission 2006 p. 6.

776 Attempting to enhance the effectiveness of court administration, in particular the management of cases and records, to decrease the administrative tasks of judges are typical approaches. This area has seen a number of guides and best practices. See, for example, USAID 2001 Case Tracking and Management Guide.

courts and long distances) often prevent or discourage people from gaining access to courts and other formal institutions. Moreover, capacity-constrained ordinary courts and other institutions might be ill-suited to address complicated matters involving large numbers of claims.

An alternative route is to support the establishment of temporary mass claims courts and quasi-judicial commissions in order to solve the problem of access. Examples can here be drawn from international property restitution claims commissions and courts for the delivery of basic utilities.[777] Another example is the establishment of the Case Flow Management Committee by UNMIL to resolve the difficulty of pre-trial detainees held for long periods,[778] and similar such bodies. The UN also proposed to the government of the Ivory Coast the establishment of mobile criminal courts to "hear criminal cases involving deprivation of liberty and deal with pressing matters of justice".[779] Interim mass claims commissions and courts are thus applied in circumstances involving large numbers of grievances, often pressing in nature, related to the conflict to begin with, and which ordinary institutions cannot handle.

For example, in the Ivory Coast, where questions of who is and who is not an Ivorian have been at the heart of the conflict, mass claims agencies were established to deal with matters of citizenship, identification and for the issuing of citizenship identification documents. Determination to address properly the citizenship issue gained momentum through the Ouagadougou peace accord concluded in March 2007. Mobile courts were part of this initiative since the agreement entered into effect and were deployed around the country to settle affairs of nationality.

At the official closure of the programme in September 2007, the mobile courts had managed to issue 622,523 declaratory judgements in lieu of birth certificates and some 533,789 documents that would serve as valid identify papers, enabling those concerned to register on the electoral roll.[780] At the same time, the employment of these extensive mobile courts meant that the redeployment of ordinary courts and other institutions of the state slowed down throughout the country. In 2008 the government announced that it would not be able to redeploy the judiciary until the mobile courts operation ended, where it was estimated more than 50 per cent of all judges worked.[781]

There are numerous examples of initiatives to establish ad hoc agencies and institutions as being 'demand-driven' and thus difficult to implement and sustain in light of existing legal and administrative frameworks. Often their

---

777 See Von Carlowitz 2004 on discussing the challenges facing the two international interim bodies established to deal with conflict-related property rights in Bosnia and Herzegovina, and Kosovo.

778 UNSG S/2005/177 p. 7.

779 UNSG S/2005/186 p. 9.

780 UNSG S/2008/451 p. 6.

781 UNSG S/2008/250 p. 6.

establishment presupposes the existence of certain legal and institutional features. For example, effective processing of mass claims requires deep and extensive knowledge on a number of areas and on systemic problems – such as accurate claims registration, computerised processing, written procedures, offices, staff, salaries, enforcement mechanisms, and making decisions public.[782]

Such agencies and processes also risk becoming detached and atypical branches of the state, operating on the basis of different paradigms and sustained by other sources. There is a risk, as the mobile administrative units in the Ivory Coast have shown, that interim mass claims mechanisms undermine capacity-building in the permanent and ordinary institutions, just as with the temporary use of international legal experts to serve in national institutions.

'BOTTOM-UP' INITIATIVES

Another approach to creating and improving on access and empowerment is to support so-called 'bottom-up initiatives'. One example is legal empowerment programmes and projects, which have gained increasing momentum on the development agenda, in particular due to the work of the Commission on Legal Empowerment of the Poor, established in 2005.[783] Legal empowerment is a broad concept involving many different strategies. The Commission presents it as "a process of systemic change through which the poor and excluded become able to use the law, the legal system, and legal services to protect their rights and interests as citizens and economic actors".[784] In the conceptualisation of legal empowerment the Commission emphasises two key ideas: voice and identity.

In general terms, legal empowerment often focuses on legal literacy and information on rights, the simplifying of administrative procedures and costs, mediation, counselling and negotiation, as well as more sophisticated support to public interest litigation.[785] While the notion of legal empowerment is gaining recognition as an important rule of law strategy on the development agenda, initiatives in war-torn societies in this field remain ad hoc and compete with the more conventional institution-based approaches.[786] This might be a consequence of the fragility of civil society in many of these devastated areas, making it difficult for outside actors to identify intermediaries at community level. In Kosovo, the OSCE published the Remedies Catalogue early on in its mission

782 Bergling, *et al.*, 2008 p. 36.

783 For short reviews of the work of the Commission see Golub 2009, The Commission on Legal Empowerment of the Poor, and Stephens 2009.

784 Commission on Legal Empowerment of the Poor 2008 p. 3.

785 Golub 2003 p. 26.

786 See, for example, on Kosovo, the Venice Commission 2004 Opinion on Human Rights in Kosovo – Possible Establishment of Review Mechanisms para. 60. "In respect of human rights specifically, there is no effective mechanism enabling individuals whose rights have been breached to initiate proceedings against the respondent authorities and to obtain just compensation."

with a view to disseminating information on the rights and duties of the emerging state agencies, as well as courses of action people could take if their rights were infringed.[787] The catalogue dealt with criminal justice, UNMIK police, Kosovo police forces and KFOR, as well as non-discrimination laws and the legal framework available for victims of crime, and property rights violations.

Legal empowerment may be promoted through support to paralegal programmes. Paralegals, or 'barefoot layers' as they are sometimes called, function as intermediaries between communities and the state by offering free or inexpensive legal services. They tend to have a rudimentary training in law, but a good understanding of the problems of the communities in which they serve. As such they provide a sort of 'gap filling', and fulfil an important function in access creation.

There are three broad roles for paralegals. The first is to function as repositories of information. Considering the abysmal state of the legal and administrative systems in many war-torn societies, and the lack of awareness among insiders and users of rules and functions, they contribute with knowledge and guidance to citizens seeking advice. Their second function is to assist in appeals and reviews of decisions made by courts or administrative agencies. Their third is to act as points of contact between the state and the person by facilitating and promoting communication, information and awareness – for example, by supporting community campaigns and civic education.

The paralegal programme called Timap for Justice in Sierra Leone started as a joint first step between the Sierra Leonean National Forum for Human Rights and the Open Society Justice Initiative. The objective was to advance the cause of justice at the local (chiefdom) level by using community paralegals. The paralegal project was motivated after initial needs assessments in several chiefdoms revealed that justice problems existed on two levels: between citizens (for example, in cases of domestic abuse) and between citizens and the authorities (for example, on corruption in government services and favouritism among customary officials). In individual cases, the paralegals provided information on rights and procedures, mediated in conflicts, and assisted in dealings with the authorities. In community cases, they engaged in education and dialogue and supported people in undertaking collective action. In order to ensure accountability on the part of the paralegals, bodies known as community oversight boards were set up at local level. An interesting feature of the programme is its straddling of both the formal and informal, or customary systems, in Sierra Leone with its dual function as an intermediary between the ordinary state courts and the common practice that most people use.[788]

---

787 OSCE 2003, Remedies Catalogue. See also Venice Commission 2004, Opinion on Human Rights in Kosovo – Possible Establishment of Review Mechanisms para 73 on supporting the Remedies Catalogue and the work of the OSCE in the establishment of human rights mechanisms within each of the municipalities of Kosovo.

788 See Maru 2006.

In Bosnia and Herzegovina the Administrative Justice Initiative was implemented by the local NGO, *Vaša Prava* (VP) with international support.[789] This initiative provides an interesting perspective on how legal aid and paralegal activities can be employed in relation to public administration and administrative justice. VP officers assist or represent citizens in procedures and disputes. VP has also developed a strategic plan to assess the most common administrative problems faced by its clients together with a country-wide media and public education plan. VP lawyers have made a total of 16 radio and television appearances. Written and electronic public education materials and a radio and television 'jingle' on administrative rights have also been produced.[790]

Paralegal initiatives may provide temporary relief by helping people gain access to systems that are closed or dysfunctional. But paralegals are not particularly effective in attending to the underlying structural and institutional problems that prevent access in the first place. Furthermore, they often represent or promote one specific interest at a time (for example, women's rights or migrant workers), rather than general rights. This tends to accord priority to 'high profile' issues over more mundane grievances against the administration. The long-term effects of 'bottom-up' initiatives such as paralegal programmes are difficult to assess properly when they are implemented ad hoc or in isolation from more comprehensive state-institutional reform programmes.[791]

INSTITUTIONAL REFORM OUTSIDE THE JUSTICE SECTOR

TRADITIONAL INSTITUTIONS

While the common understanding of institution-building and of access and empowerment is often "to get people and their grievances into court",[792] this apprehension is too narrow and somewhat misleading. Courts have to be enlarged to include a variety of organisations ranging from civil, criminal and administrative dispute resolution agencies as well as informal or traditional 'courts'. Formal mechanisms for dispute resolution are often not a realistic alternative for people in societies in transition from war. Apart from a lack of trust towards formal institutions, other circumstances often create solid barriers. These things might be costs relating to litigation, a scarcity of legal professionals, or long distances from courts, all of which create logistical and practical problems when starting a legal proceeding that might extend over months, even

789 USAID 2007, Assessment of the Administrative Legal System in Bosnia and Herzegovina p. 21ff.
790 IRIS Center 2006.
791 See Khair 2009 p. 36.
792 Galanter 1981 p. 2.

years. In most war-torn societies, citizens are not accustomed to making use of formal legal institutions or to expect any results if they actually do use them, especially in challenging political leaderships. To support and enable citizens to use and take advantage of the rule of law, to support human agency in a sense, could therefore be viewed as a shift in perception and an "immense metamorphoses" for individuals to move from subjects to "accountability-demanding citizens".[793]

Many war-torn societies have a bifurcated legal and administrative system. Generally the so-called 'formal state law' – that is, law enacted by parliament – has limited reach. Beyond the capital and major cities it is not unusual to find legal and administrative systems based either upon religious or customary traditions.[794] Dispute resolution through traditional justice mechanisms may be cheaper, more efficient and enjoy a higher degree of legitimacy than formal dispute resolutions provided by state agencies. Non-state justice systems, according to some estimates, account for most 'justice delivery', perhaps as much as 80 to 90 per cent in some parts of Africa, according to a 2006 World Bank study.[795] Customary systems are preferred for a variety of reasons, including cost, speed, accessibility, and cultural relevance.[796] Customary systems are often treated as substitutes or complements to the formal state judiciary, adjudicating in minor criminal offences, community, and family disputes. The Gacaca trials in Rwanda offer one example, though extraordinary, of how local informal dispute resolution systems can be employed in order to address access to justice issues in a war to peace transition. The Gacaca courts are used as community forums, with judges chosen by the communities, to adjudicate in cases of suspected perpetrators of the 1994 genocide. Besides dispute resolution in criminal and family matters, customary systems generally also perform a number of tasks that typically fall within the public administration and it is difficult to distinguish between judicial and public administrative (executive) functions.

In view of the deficiencies of the formal system, and the prevalence of customary law, it is thus essential that rule of law reform is directed towards enhancing access to justice and legal empowerment. Systems of traditional or religious law often become solidified in war to peace transitions. As the only functional institutions, providing for at least some form of rudimentary justice, these systems garner legitimacy and popular support.

---

793 Bratton & Logan 2006 p. 4.

794 There are different views on how customary systems should best be described. The term informal is sometimes used, in order to denote a difference from formal law. Similarly, references to non-state justice are also frequent. The schematic distinction is not employable in cases such as Liberia where the state has attempted to regulate customary law.

795 Chirayath, Sage & Woolcock 2006 p. 3. Exact percentages are difficult to confirm, perhaps a reflection of the ambiguities surrounding the classification of customary systems.

796 Cooter 1998, for example, argue for the usefulness of making legal norms resemble informal norms and institutions in order to incorporate the flexibility of the informal sector.

The importance of recognising and incorporating customary systems in the rule of law strategies of international actors is emphasised in the 2004 UN Secretary-General report, Rule of Law and Transitional Justice, in which it is stated: "due regard must be given to indigenous and informal traditions for administering justice or settling disputes". It continues by asserting that international actors should assist local dispute institutions for dispute resolution in their vital role, but to do so in "conformity with both international standards and local tradition".[797]

An illustrative instance of the dangers of failing to acknowledge customary systems is presented in the 2006 World Bank assessment report on community empowerment and local governance in East Timor. The World Bank project centred on strengthening local level 'social capital' and in building inclusive institutions capable of resolving disputes at village level, adhering to a village 'code of conduct'.[798] UNTAET enacted regulations in support of the World Bank project, attempting to regulate favourable conditions for the purpose of promoting "effective village and sub-district level participation in the disbursement of funds for development activities [...] which is representative and accountable".[799] The objective of the project thus had a clear mandate to "socialize democratic principles".[800] That socialisation was further supported by the fact that UNTAET regulations enabled the direct implementation of the World Bank project by establishing new procedures for nominating and electing members to village councils and introducing the requirement that those councils and sub-district councils should consist of equal numbers of men and women.[801]

The World Bank assessment report, however, concluded that the local governance empowerment project was both premature and unrealistic. The project had assumed that in supporting institutions that consisted of elected village councils it would be "an effective way of setting up democratic institutions and bypassing traditional leaders".[802] The expectations placed on the elected village councils, in terms of inclusive, transparent and democratic gains, turned out the opposite to what was intended. Instead, village councils were regarded as lacking in legitimacy and the traditional leaders continued to exercise *de facto* political leadership.

---

797 UNSG S/2004/616 p. 12.

798 World Bank 2006, Timor-Leste Project Performance Assessment Report p 7.

799 UNTAET/REG/2000/13. At first the World Bank asked UNTAET to enact a regulation making the village groups into government agencies. This was eventually resisted by UNTAET and some East Timorese leaders, since it would mean a pre-emption of a constitutional discussion on the structure of the East Timorese state. Morrow & White 2002 p. 30.

800 Rawski 2005 p. 933. See, also, World Bank 1999, Building a Nation: A Framework for Reconstruction and Development.

801 UNTAET/REG/2000/13 2.1, 3.1.

802 World Bank 2006, Timor-Leste Project Performance Assessment Report p. 11.

A first step for international actors in support of access to justice in customary systems is to base interventions upon adequate and accurate information. This requires in-depth studies and the necessity of working with new partners both inside and outside the formal system. There is also a need for an appraisal of the institutional structure so as to understand fully what functions the customary system performs with regard to judicial and executive responsibilities. This should be combined with a risk assessment. It is necessary to identify resistance and reaction among those on the inside and the outside.

The tools developed by donor agencies for mapping and assessing the justice sector might require certain modifications before they can be used within the field of customary law. As a case in point for local ownership, the gathering of data must be a participatory project shared jointly between donor agencies and local interlocutors. This is because of the 'informality' of customary systems with their lack of written laws, judgments, and other documents that are necessarily used for assessments in the formal justice sector. Depending on the prevalence of the particular customary system, what functions it performs, and how well they are executed, there are various strategies for states and peace-builders to pursue. These include:

(1) incorporating the customary system into the formal public administration;
(2) codifying or standardising customary governance functions;
(3) building capacity within the customary system to perform certain functions; and
(4) establishing supervisory and accountability mechanism to protect human rights.[803]

Providing for some kind of regulation of the mandate and organisation of the informal system is probably the most effective way of safeguarding and supervising access to justice. The mandate and relationship to the formal system should ideally be regulated with constitutional provisions. Openness and access to justice in the customary system may also be promoted by introducing rules and procedures for basic record keeping. Systematised and reliable record keeping is particularly essential when the system concerned deals with, for example, property rights on a large scale. Record keeping is also important in facilitating appeals to formal state agencies, and serves as an entry point for quality monitoring.

Liberia exemplifies the difficulties of access to justice that are encountered in many customary systems. There are two different forms of legal authority in Liberia. One is the customary administrative practice, consisting of districts controlled by commissioners, followed by a line of chiefs, from the paramount chiefs who head the chiefdoms, to clans, towns, and quarters. The other form is

[803] See e.g. Penal Reform International 2001 pp. 129ff.

based upon municipal authority, with cities (presided over by mayors), and towns (led by township commissioners). For the all the different counties, the president appoints superintendents, accountable only to the president.

Under the Liberian constitution, paramount chiefs, clan and town chiefs are elected in their respective localities. Though local customary administration is in dire need of revision, direct interference by the executive has resulted in a problematic relationship between local and central authorities. There is no mention in the constitution of the complex bifurcated system of statutory districts and cities. Only counties are mentioned. Statutory districts and cities are instead regulated under the Revised Rules and Administrative Regulations Governing the Hinterland.[804]

This creates an overall problem of access to justice. The 2006 National Human Development Report of Liberia observed that the customary system was "confusing [...]. There are currently 15 major administrative subdivisions called counties. Within each county there are at least two statutory districts. At this level and downwards the government structure becomes ambiguous and difficult to manage".[805] The confusion within the customary administrative system seems to be exacerbated in the area of property rights. This, according to some accounts, occupies between 75 to 90 per cent of all cases in statutory and local courts.[806]

There is a procedure for individuals to take complaints and charges to the Provisional Commissioner against officials of the province (decisions taken by paramount chiefs are appealed to district commissioners and superintendents, and finally to the Office for Tribal Affairs at the Ministry of Internal Affairs) but this procedure is generally not applied.[807] Because of the existing gap between statutory and customary law, there is no functioning judicial review procedure on decisions made by officials in the customary system. This affects access to justice, since it is within this system that a majority of individuals interact with state authorities.

When considering the fact that some customary systems deal with almost all 'justice delivery', any attempt to circumvent and import outside solutions to local problems is likely to face resistance.[808] At the same time, active engagement of local customary systems can be attended by difficulty. For one thing the conflict in question might have distorted the legitimacy of the system. In some cases, those directly involved in the conflict have replaced traditional chiefs by

---

804 Revised Laws and Administrative Regulations for Governing the Hinterland 1949.

805 Liberia National Human Development Report 2007 p. 34.

806 Unruh 2009 p. 427.

807 Revised Laws and Administrative Regulations for Governing the Hinterland 1949 Art. 4 (c). See Liberia National Human Development Report 2006 p. 34.

808 Prior to the UNSG's 2004 report the UN did not devote much attention to customary systems. Greenfell 2009 p. 171.

force.[809] In addition, there tends to be a romanticised view of a customary system that does not always reflect contemporary practice. The Hinterland Regulations in Liberia still use the terms 'natives' and 'civilized peoples', thereby distinguishing between Americo-Liberians and indigenous Africans. Finding the way back to a 'golden age' of customary systems is perhaps an unrealistic alternative.[810]

Adding to the problems of access to justice in customary systems, frequent reports provide insights into human rights violations associated with these systems, as well as a gender bias. The Hinterland Regulations still allow for trial by ordeal (provided the trial does not endanger life), though in 1940 the Liberian Supreme Court declared the practice unconstitutional.[811] Of particular concern is the status of vulnerable groups having limited social influence. Gender discrimination is well-documented. Many customary systems, including that of Liberia, fail to grant women equal standing with men. They also tend to discriminate in cases of land, property or family disputes.[812]

PUBLIC ADMINISTRATION

Similar to the necessity of recognising the part played by customary systems, the public administrative sector also affects matters of access to justice and empowerment. The ICG noted on legal reform in Bosnia and Herzegovina that most international rule of law programmes focused on justice sector problems, while neglecting similar concerns in public administration, despite the fact that relatively few people encounter a court of law. In contrast, most people interacted with the public administration. Whether to obtain a birth certificate, identity papers, or to register a property "virtually all BiH citizens queue in front of municipal and cantonal offices at some point".[813]

A claim for an increased attention to enhance access to justice and accountability in relation to administrative agencies is supported by reports in the field. As the UNDP report on governance in war to peace transitions observed, public administration often suffers from a lack of regulatory framework for the delegation of authority and accountability, leading to overlapping jurisdiction, poor articulation between branches of government, in

809 Unruh 2009 p. 430.

810 See Commission on Human Rights E/C.N.4/2006/11 and the ICG 2006, Liberia: Resurrecting the Justice System p. 9. See, also, Afghan Human Development Report 2007 p. 97.

811 Tenteah *et al.* v. Republic of Liberia, 1940, reported in ICG 2006, Liberia: Resurrecting the Justice System p. 9 fn. 59. Revised Laws and Administrative Regulations for Governing the Hinterland 1949, Art. 73.

812 Human Rights Council A/HRC/7/67 pp. 11–12.

813 ICG 1999, Rule of Law in Public Administration p. 1. See, also, American Bar Association 2006, Judicial Reform Index for Bosnia and Herzegovina p. 18.

particular between the executive and parliament, together with little official documentation and unclear or obsolete bureaucratic rules and regulations.[814] Supporting access to justice by enhancing the capacity of the judiciary, police and prisons only responds to a part of the range of problems exhibited by post-crisis states. Serious rule of law deficiencies are also found within the executive, administrative agencies, and in the often unintelligible administrative and civil law framework.

A case in point of how rule of law access to justice within the administrative sector tends to be neglected is that of the organisation of the judiciary in Afghanistan. In the Bonn Agreement, the establishment of a judiciary in accordance with the rule of law was an explicit objective. Subsequent reforms, including the new constitution and the Law of Organisation and Jurisdiction of Courts of the Islamic Republic of Afghanistan (LOJC),[815] have established a judicial structure and hierarchy, including commercial courts, criminal courts, juvenile courts and urban primary courts.

What is omitted in the constitution and the LOJC is how executive acts that violate individual rights should be dealt with. A reading of the LOJC in conjunction with the constitution indicates that the Chamber of Public Rights of the Urban Primary Courts, Appeals Court and the Supreme Court are competent to review administrative acts.[816] While this perhaps establishes their competencies, there is no regulation to do with how citizens should file a complaint, which creates a rule of law vacuum in administrative justice.[817] In the high profile area of rule of law reform in Afghanistan it appears that the rule of law in relation to administrative agencies has fallen behind.

Kosovo is a relevant instance of how questions of access to justice are addressed differently following from how the concept of the rule of law is understood. There, UNMIK distinguished between those matters relating to 'core institutions' (judiciary, police and the rest) and more peripheral institutions such as public administration, administrative law and regulatory mechanisms.

At an early stage in the UN administration it was decided that with a view to preparing for substantial autonomy, the Provisional Institutions of Self-Government (PISG) should be allowed to take a broader responsibility in the administration of the territory. In the Constitutional Framework for Provisional Self-Government, certain areas were devolved from international control to local authorities, among them a major part of the public administrative system.[818] The SRSG kept core functions within the international domain, in what was called

814 UNDP 2004, Governance in Post-Conflict Situations p. 66 et seq.
815 See Moschtaghi 2006 p. 555ff.
816 Moschtaghi 2006 pp. 581–582.
817 The only possible venue is the Independent Human Rights Commission. Moschtaghi 2006 p. 583.
818 UNMIK/REG/2001/9.

'reserved powers', including the administration of justice – that is, the appointment of judges and control over law enforcement.[819]

With the formation of the PISG, UNMIK withdrew from direct management of the administration. In an earlier regulation, UNMIK had previously accorded vast responsibilities to 30 municipalities.[820] While the constitutional framework stated that the UN still retained responsibility to ensure that the system of local municipal administration functioned effectively, based upon international standards, the actual control was primarily to be within the competence of domestic authorities.[821]

From the perspective of functional necessity, this would meet with approval. The administration of justice is kept within the reserved powers based upon the argument that those issues that it includes deal with sensitive core questions central to the process of recovery, such as access to justice.

Commonsensical as this devolution of power might seem, it has constrained possibilities of access to justice reforms in public administration and fails to address two crucial matters. The first is that problems of access to justice might be caused by circumstances beyond the control of justice sector institutions and others within the reserved powers. Second, devolution of power poses difficulties in answering questions on how to deal with multidimensional problems – of how to avoid bias towards justice sector institutions, so that a duality in the system is created. This is the duality of criminal justice excelling while widespread discrimination, corruption and a lack of access to justice permeates administrative law.

The issue of civil registration of ethnic minorities in Kosovo illustrates the need for concerted access to justice in public administration. In 2006 the Office of the Prime Minister in Kosovo issued Recommendations Updating Return Policy and Procedures. This instructed the PISG and the municipalities to "ensure that pending registrations of Roma, Ashkali and Egyptian were completed in the next six months". The civil registration process is essential for people to gain access to basic civil, political, economic, social and cultural rights. In several cases municipal offices simply refused to follow the recommendations, or claimed not to be aware of their existence. Moreover, the recommendations were never followed by a written detailed instruction on how to implement the civil registration, allowing responsible agencies to adopt a lax approach to the on

819 The Constitutional Framework created 11 ministries. Seven of them came to deal with competencies within the civil administrative framework previously belonging to UNMIK. Constitutional Framework for Provisional Self-Government Chapter 5.

820 UNMIK/REG/2000/45.

821 For a review of the performance of administrative agencies in Kosovo see, e.g., OSCE 2007, Report on the Administrative Justice System in Kosovo and OSCE 2007 Report on Implementation of the Law on Access to Official Documents at the Municipal Level.

the affair, further compounding the exclusion of minority groups in Kosovo from basic civil and economic rights and access to justice.[822]

There are tentative signs of international recognition of this problem. The UN High Commissioner for Human Rights noted in a 2005 report on Sierra Leone that while substantial progress had been made in human rights, that progress was lopsided in favour of rule of law in the justice sector with few improvements in public administration.[823] At the close of the UN peace operation in 2006, and the establishment of a UN Integrated Office in Sierra Leone, the UN Secretary-General concluded that economic progress would gain traction as peace became more consolidated, but that the elimination of administrative barriers was an essential prerequisite for further reconstruction efforts. Among other things, the UN Secretary-General noted that external technical assistance was necessary to achieve adjustment of a more consolidated regime for legal, administrative and regulatory measures and the fight against corruption.[824]

822 OSCE 2007, Civil Registration in Kosovo of Persons Belonging to the Roma, Ashkali and Egyptian Communities p. 4.

823 Commission on Human Rights E/CN.4 2005/113 para. 33.

824 UNSG S/2006/269 p. 9.

6. EFFECTIVENESS AND INTERNATIONAL ACCOUNTABILITY

INTRODUCTION

The two preceding chapters were the subject of discussion on methods applied in law reform, constitution-making and institutional reform. This chapter examine the question of accountability and effectiveness of rule of law reform.

There is a fundamental paradox in rule of law assistance, particularly in situations where international actors exercise a form of executive power. While they promote reforms with intent to achieve judicial independence, the supremacy of law, the separation of powers and increased access to justice, state-building missions often perform in ways that contradict those very principles.

This is explained partly by the idea itself of state-building missions. International actors substitute for local governments, or assume responsibility for legal and judicial reform, because of weak domestic capacity. International participants are not elected officials, and often the local interlocutors with which they cooperate are transitional governments, but interventions are accepted on the basis of necessity or out of human rights and humanitarian imperatives in order to redress past abuses and violations and for the maintenance of peace and security.

But while there might be acceptance towards the idea of state-building, there are deficiencies in the structure and methods that undermine effectiveness and accountability. One such deficiency arises from the employment of vague or excessively ambitious mandates as constitutional foundations for rule of law assistance. This aspect, together with the existence of weak coordination mechanisms for multilateral interventions, is discussed first in this chapter. The multitude of donor agencies is one impediment to effectiveness and accountability. Each comes supplied with their own policies, procurement procedures, contracts, and lines of accountability, and in the starkest cases "each organization asks for exemptions from prevailing law; and each drains the talent of the government and the private sector while lamenting the government's lack of capability".[825]

---

[825] Ghani & Lockhart 2008 p. 92. That donor agencies wish to retain control over the disbursement of their money is not controversial in itself, but as Chesterman 2004 p. 191 points out: "Although donor behaviour may be rational from the donor government's perspective, however, the sum total of donor policies rarely presents a rational whole".

Such attitudes and habits give rise to tensions and disagreements between international and national actors. The president of East Timor, for example, tired of constant suggestions from international agencies on what his country was required to accomplish in the transitional period, stated: "We are not interested in a legacy of cars and laws, nor are we interested in a legacy of development plans for the future designed by [people] other than East Timorese".[826] Such rebukes to international donors, pushing their agendas in environments weakened by conflict, reveal the tensions that mount up in some rule of law interventions, and highlight the question of legitimacy, effectiveness and donor accountability.

Second, no regulatory regime exists for ensuring accountability of international agencies specifically adapted to state-building missions. This is particularly problematic to situations where the UN or some other agency assumes a governance role. The question of "who guards the guardians" is discussed in the second half of this chapter by way of an examination of some of the methods employed by international actors that contradict fundamental rule of law principles. Improvements in minimising the accountability gap in recent state-building missions, as well as guidelines for rule of law reform, are also analysed.

POLICIES, MANDATES AND COORDINATION

The 'multilateralism' inherent in state-building missions – that is, the proliferation of agencies ranging from multilateral organisations such as the UN, to bilateral assistance from small NGOs – is a result of the costs and logistics of involvement. It is simply too much for one organisation to bear, especially if the international presence becomes protracted. This multilateralism is also a consequence of the ideologies that underpin the whole of rule of law assistance – that in order to achieve human rights protection, economic development and international and national security, laws and legal institutions subscribing to rule of law principles are a necessity. This should also be read in conjunction with a broader interpretation of international peace and security by the UN Security Council since the end of the cold war.[827]

At the same time, the proliferation of donor agencies might also create a competitive environment, necessitating the establishment of new competencies in rivalry with other organisations and interests.[828] Under such conditions it is difficult to formulate and apply consistent and transparent standards for

826 Sydney Herald Tribune 10 October 2000.

827 See Österdahl 1997 and 2005 on UN Security Council activism since the early 1990s and the application of the concept 'international peace and security'.

828 Caplan 2002 p. 22.

effectiveness and accountability. That there is a need for better cooperation and coordination in state-building missions is no new insight. The UN Secretary-General considered the matter in the 1995 report, Supplement to an Agenda for Peace.[829] Lack of co-ordination among the fora of organisations was noted as a point of concern because weak coordination might signal to local players a reduced degree of commitment on the part of the international community to the task of state-building.[830]

Another problem was the duplication of rule of law efforts – for example, parallel and overlapping training initiatives delivered by different international agencies.[831] Though rule of law assistance may take place under the auspices of a UN Security Council mandate, actual transformation and reconstruction is undertaken by a number of interested parties which makes coordination difficult. The SRSG of UNMIBH, Jacques Klein, described the situation of UN efforts to support the local police in Bosnia and Herzegovina being marred because police reform was not matched by equal improvements in the judicial sector, which was under the reform of another international agency.

The duplication of efforts is partly a structural problem with large organisations. In the 2006 UN inventory report on peace-building capacities, segmentation, competition and atomisation of efforts in the field of rule of law was noted. Despite a growing number of units and experts within the various UN departments working on rule of law matters, there was found among them a lack of direction and delineation of responsibility.[832]

It is possible to observe a tentative learning curve on the part of international agencies on coordination. In Bosnia and Herzegovina, the issue of coordination became emphasised when a few years after the Dayton Agreement was signed in 1995, it became apparent that considerable overlaps between the policies and programmes of the different international actors existed. According to the Dayton Agreement, reconstruction and state-building was to be a multilateral undertaking, split between various organisations responsible for different sectors. Installed to supervise reconstruction was the High Representative, the highest international civilian authority in the territory. The contracting out of tasks was set out in the 11 annexes to the Dayton Agreement. These concern fundamental areas for reconstruction and reform, including ensuring regional stability, the return of refugees and displaced persons, elections, human rights development, economic reconstruction and arbitration on inter-entity boundary lines.

---

829 UNSG S/1995/1.

830 UNSG S/2001/394 p. 7.

831 Hurwitz & Studdard 2005 p. 3.

832 Executive Office of the Secretary-General Inventory, United Nations Capacity in Peacebuilding 2006. In response to the challenges of coordination and planning, the UN has now introduced within the Secretariat a Criminal Law and Advisory Unit at the DPKO and a Rule of Law Unit.

The principal international actors according to the Dayton Agreement were the Office of the High Representative, the OSCE, the UN Mission in Bosnia and Herzegovina and the UN High Commissioner for Refugees, while a NATO-led force directed military security. A Peace Implementation Council (PIC) was also established, consisting of 55 states and agencies, functioning as an instrument through which the international community could monitor implementation of the peace agreement and develop policy and instructions for the High Representative.

At an early stage in the transition, functional overlaps became evident, in particular between the High Representative and the OSCE. Five years after the Dayton Agreement the lack of effective coordination led the High Representative to conduct an internal audit to determine precisely what international participants actually did in Bosnia.[833] The High Representative was also granted extensive executive powers by the PIC in response to recalcitrant national authorities and began a streamlining of international projects and programmes.[834]

The nature of the coordination problem in Bosnia and Herzegovina was not the number of international agencies involved, but that of no all-embracing coordinating power or framework. The only guiding framework, the Dayton Agreement, was explicitly clear on the point that the High Representative should respect the spheres of interest of each principal organisation and merely give "general guidance to them about the impact of their activities on the implementation of the peace settlement".[835]

After Bosnia and Herzegovina there have been different attempts at providing for improved coordination. One approach was the UN Security Council resolution 1244 (1999) on the establishment of a temporary UN administration in Kosovo. The mission structure adopted there represents an idea of empowering regional organisations to assume state-building responsibilities based upon a pillar structure with clear outlines of tasks and responsibilities.

Resolution 1244 established the SRSG as the Transitional Administrator with executive authority. Below that administrator different areas of responsibility were allotted to each of the organisations involved – the UN was accorded responsibility for civil administration; the OSCE for organising elections and human rights promotion; with economic reconstruction going to the EU. In addition, different special agencies and departments of the UN were given administrative duties.[836] The military presence was to be maintained by KFOR – a force combining NATO and non-NATO countries.

833 ICG 2001, Bosnia: Reshaping the International Machinery p. 29.
834 See Chesterman 2004 p. 128f, and Caplan 2005 p. 180f.
835 Dayton Agreement Annex 10 Art. II.1 (c).
836 See UNSG S/1999/672 p. 2 and UNSG S/1999/779 p. 9.

UNMIK also allowed for co-administration early on in the mission through the establishment of the Kosovo Transitional Council. This policy appears to have drawn upon lessons learned from the High Representative where no such consultative body was established.[837]

While this pillar structure to some extent managed to pool resources and expertise, it caused other problems in the working relationship between different actors. For example, the UN was primarily responsible for setting up and administering the justice sector and in the overall administration of justice, whereas the OSCE was appointed the responsibility of supervising and monitoring the functions of the justice system. This meant, in effect, that one international organisation was responsible for monitoring the work of another.

Though at first sight this could be taken as a step towards increasing accountability and effectiveness through checks-and-balances, the overlapping mandates led to 'turf wars' and strained relationships between the OSCE and the UN.[838] Moreover, the division of powers seems equally to have been about international politics rather than an actual reflection of each organisation's capacity and competence.[839]

As noted above, there is no hierarchy of organisation able to guide this kind of multi-organisational cooperation. Conflicts of interest arising between organisations must therefore be resolved by consent, since there is no prevailing framework for doing otherwise.[840] This may lead, as it has done repeatedly, to a lack of policy coherence among major actors "even to the extent of agencies occasionally working at cross-purposes".[841] However, caution should be exercised on the adoption of solutions that provide one organisation or country with too strong an influence. One example is the 'lead nation' approach in Afghanistan, replicating to some extent UNMIK's pillar structure where a select group of states were given sector responsibilities. This lead nation approach has been criticised, among others by the ICG, for insulating decision-making on strategic matters in judicial reform.[842] Italy has retained overall responsibility for the justice sector. While funding and coordination was expected to improve under a single 'command', trade-offs involved a donor-oriented system where legal and institutional reforms were influenced by the lead nation.[843]

In light of this, integration is perhaps an alternative, and many UN missions have improved in that regard. In integrated missions, the Deputy Special Representative of the Secretary-General often assumes the functions of UNDP

---

837 Caplan 2005 p. 94.

838 Baskin 2001 p. 32.

839 Stromseth, *et al.*, 2006 p. 360.

840 Ruffert 2001 p. 619.

841 Caplan 2002 p. 36.

842 ICG 2003, Afghanistan: Judicial Reform and Transitional Justice p. 8.

843 Dobbins *et al.*, 2007 p. 101: "Italy simply lacked the expertise, resources, interest and influence needed to succeed in such an undertaking".

resident representative, UN resident coordinator and humanitarian coordinator (but these responsibilities can also be separated) and in this sense allow for attending to questions that are cross-cutting in a more effective way. In Liberia the substantial rule of law focus of the mission mandate was reflected in the pillar structure. The two pillars of UNMIL, each with a Deputy SRSG consisted of the rule of law and recovery and governance.

A plurality of international actors can also provide some form of rudimentary accountability mechanism. National authorities can, and sometimes do, play donors off against one another. Such lack of coordination means that national authorities thus have the possibility open to them of 'donor shopping'. This might sometimes be the only way of asserting at least a minimal form of donor accountability.

Problems with coordination also depend in part on the expanding state-building agenda in war-torn societies. International players are not only expected to focus on the maintenance of peace and security in the aftermath of conflict, but to engage in judicial reform, the capacity-building of civil society and in providing support to vertical accountability mechanisms. A weak national capacity to initiate, implement and manage international rule of law assistance, is therefore conducive to the "wholesale importation of governmental infrastructures" through arrangements with a multitude of different international agencies.[844] The objectives of a rule of law intervention are sometimes clogged by the sheer weight of UN Security Council resolutions aimed at revising operational concepts, adding new objectives and eliminating others. In Bosnia and Herzegovina, for example, the UN peace-keeping force was based upon no less than 70 resolutions in its short time between 1992 and 1995.[845]

The content and formulation of legal mandates for state-building missions can further compound the issue of effectiveness and accountability. UN Security Council mandates are often fraught with difficulties of interpretation and they are being increasingly challenged from an operative standpoint by the growing reform menu they impose for rule of law reform.[846]

UN Security Council resolutions are therefore sometimes unworkable as blueprints for what international actors should and should not do within complex state-building arrangements. In the Brahimi Report, the importance of a clear and enforceable mandate was emphasised. It is said that operations with ambiguous mandates and political goals should not be established at all.[847] The

844 Baskin 2001 p. 22.

845 Starting with SC Res. 743 (1992).

846 Brahimi Report 2000 p. 8 para. 47 (b).

847 In subsequent UN Security Council discussions on the Brahimi report, the need for clear and unambiguous mandates was stressed – indicating a doctrinal shift in the establishment of peace operations. The Council resolution stated that UN operations should have "where

Brahimi Report also noted a lack of preparation for wider rule of law responsibilities in rule of law reform within the UN system.[848] The UN Secretary-General's high-level panel, Threats, Challenges and Change, argued along similar lines. The main demand, according to the report, was to make secure an "appropriate, clear and well understood mandate, applicable to all the changing circumstances that might reasonably be envisaged".[849]

This recommendation was echoed in a later report of the UN Secretary-General in stating that priority must be given by the UN Security Council to the restoration of, and respect for, the rule of law. That support should be explicit in Council resolutions in order to make resources available at an early stage. Furthermore, according to the report, the UN system must be enhanced so as to provide arrangements supporting the rule of law in war-damaged societies, so as to become an integrated part of strategic and operational planning for peace operations.[850]

Another factor that makes effectiveness and coordination difficult is the shortage of personnel and institutional resources within the UN. This was noted in the country studies of the King's College review of peace operations in 2003 in describing a lack of coherent strategy and planning, even in areas where the mandate was clear.[851] In East Timor, despite both the fact that widespread post-ballot violence was anticipated in 1999 and the acknowledgement that the UN would play a crucial part in the country's administration and reconstruction, no plans were made for how to rebuild the judicial and police services until sometime after the UN administration had been established.[852] In Bosnia and Herzegovina and Kosovo the concerted planning and elaboration of the concept of the operations took a considerable time to develop. For the first seven years the Office of the High Representative lacked a Mission Implementation Plan. In Kosovo, UNMIK's first strategic planning document was not produced until six months into the mission.[853]

The tests of effectiveness and accountability are therefore not only matters of vague mandates, but also of resources and the capacity to appreciate the difficulties of externally promoted reforms in order to prepare rule of law assistance within a war-torn society context and dynamics.

---

appropriate and within their mandate, a credible deterrent capability". SC Res. 1327 (2000) Annex I.

848 Brahimi Report 2000 p. 13.

849 A More Secure World: Our shared responsibility 2004 p. 68.

850 UNSG S/2004/616 p. 21.

851 King's College 2003 p. 12.

852 Caplan 2005 p. 161.

853 Ibid., pp. 172–173.

WHO GUARDS THE GUARDIANS?

INTERNATIONAL ACCOUNTABILITY AND LEGITIMACY

While overriding structural problems such as unclear mandates and a lack of coordination make serious demands on accountability and effectiveness, there are also certain specific legal and methodological points at issue on how donors conduct themselves that affect accountability.[854]

On international accountability there is a form of constitutional framework. International transitional administrators, as in Kosovo, or the mission leadership in other state-building missions, are accountable to the body that authorised their presence. This is evident from the first regulations enacted in Kosovo and East Timor by the respective administrations where the constituting UN Security Council resolutions functioned as acts of foundation. This horizontal accountability framework means that the Security Council, or the Peace Implementation Council in Bosnia and Herzegovina, performs a supervisory role. For example, the UN Secretary-General is often required to report to the Security Council, and sometimes SRSG are also asked to brief the Council directly. Rudimentary as this accountability structure is, it provides some form of superintendence. Moreover, the legality and legitimacy of the UN to establish state-building missions, including international administrations as in Kosovo and East Timor, has been firmly established.[855]

Instead it is the actions taken within such missions and weak vertical accountability systems that constitute an accountability deficit. Vertical accountability mechanisms mean those institutions that allow for people to legally challenge government actions or to report violations of rights committed by public officials by enabling them access to the law. As opposed to horizontal accountability mechanisms, the following sections in this chapter concentrates on the existence of institutions and norms capable of functioning as independent accountability systems to prevent, redress, or punish any illegal actions or

[854] The question of accountability is here approached from a governance perspective. That is, accountability in situations where the UN or other international actors assume some form of governance and responsibility, either explicitly as in Kosovo and East Timor, or more by default owing to weak capacity within interim government institutions. The question of individual accountability for peace-keeping soldiers and UN personnel recently highlighted, for example, through the number of sexual abuses by peace-keepers, falls outside the scope of this study.

[855] Chapter VI and VII of the UN Charter provides adequate legal grounds for the establishment of an international transitional administration or other forms of state-building, provided that it is necessary in order to maintain or restore international peace and security. Article 41 of the UN Charter includes a non-exhaustive list of non-military measures that the UN Security Council can employ. Within this non-exhaustive list also lies the right to establish, in accordance with Art. 29, subsidiary organs to the Security Council such as UNMIK or UNTAET. Kondoch 2005 pp. 24–25 and Ruffert 2001 p. 621.

inactions of international organisations, in the same way that individuals would challenge and report on national authorities.[856]

Decisions and policies are increasingly being adopted by international actors that later affect states, groups and individuals.[857] This form of international governance and norm creation is particularly evident in relation to rule of law reform in war-torn societies and it derives its legitimacy and acceptance from international law, standards and benchmarks.[858] The idea that international actors have a legitimate role as norm promoters seems to flow from the perception that they are intrinsically benign, with altruistic motives in state-building.

However, they come equipped with their own interests, agendas and objectives that guide their mandates and action. This also applies to rule of law assistance, and the benign nature of international governance and law-making has to be carefully scrutinised from the perspective of proportionality of the imposed or proposed reforms in relation to mission objectives.

MECHANISMS OF ACCOUNTABILITY IN THE FIELD

The question of accountability in rule of law reform and state-building is particularly emphasised with regard to the lack of judicial review of regulations, decrees and orders issued by international actors. Knaus and Felix compare the High Representative in Bosnia and Herzegovina to that of a European Raj, owing to the lack of legal redress.[859] Chopra likens UNTAET to a UN kingdom.[860] Other commentators point to the inherent paradox in promoting the rule of law by substituting for national authorities, including judicial authority.

In both Kosovo and East Timor, the respective UN administrations ruled by decree and executive order. In Kosovo, even after power was devolved to Provisional Institutions for Self-Governance in accordance with the objective of establishing local ownership, the SRSG still had the "final authority to interpret the scope and any other parameters of the executive responsibilities".[861] Similarly, the High Representative in Bosnia and Herzegovina has seen its mandate extended since it was established in 1995.

Under such circumstances, where international agencies carry out tasks more similar to those of a state than an international organisation, the Venice Commission argued "it is inconceivable and incompatible with the principles of

856 O'Donnell 2004 p. 37.

857 See Woods & Narlikar 2001 for a discussion on accountability in relation to international organisations, in particular international financial institutions.

858 UNSG S/2004/616 SG p. 5.

859 Knaus & Martin 2003 pp. 61–62.

860 Chopra 2000.

861 UNMIK/REG/2001/19.

democracy, the rule of law and respect for human rights that they could act as State authorities and be exempted from any independent legal review".[862] While UNMIK, the High Representative and other such state-building missions have been established for the purposes of preserving international peace and security, and while due consideration must be given to their legal characters, a complete disregard of typical domestic standards pertaining to the exercise of authority seems both "technically unwarranted and politically dangerous".[863]

Detentions and Executive Decrees in Kosovo

It is on detentions founded upon executive decrees where the lack or absence of judicial review has been particularly noted. In the early stages of the UN mission to Kosovo arrears of uncompleted cases caused the SRSG to issue Regulation 1999/26 On the Extension of Periods of Pre-trial Detention, thereby prolonging the term of pre-trial detention for serious offences to up to one year.[864] That regulation was criticised for failing to allow for the independent review by a court of the grounds for detention. In practice the new detention regime meant that a person could be held by KFOR if deemed to be a threat to peace and security, even in the presence of a judicial release order.

In an attempt at justifying the extension of detention periods the UNMIK police stated that Article 13 of the European Convention on Human Rights allowed for an exception (derogation) in relation to certain emergencies, and that the situation in Kosovo was analogous to such an emergency situation as envisaged in the convention. Deprivation of liberty by executive order was held to be temporary and extraordinary. UNMIK also emphasised that its mandate was adopted under Chapter VII of the UN Charter "which means that the situation calls for extraordinary means and force can be used to carry out the mandate".[865]

Shortly afterwards, UNMIK adopted Regulation 2001/18 establishing the Detention Review Commission for Extra-Judicial Detentions Based on Executive Orders.[866] This consisted of three international experts with a mandate to decide upon whether or not extra-judicial detention was justifiable. The regulation also stipulated a time limit on the Commission's decision-making. Decisions were to be made as speedily as possible and no later than seven days after hearing submissions from the detained, person or from counsel.

Despite the initiative to establish the Commission, the issue has continued to spark controversy and has on several occasions been criticised by the

862 The Venice Commission 2004, Opinion on Human Rights in Kosovo para. 91.
863 Knoll 2008 p. 428.
864 UNMIK/REG/1999/26.
865 Press Briefing, Susan Manuel, UNMIK Police, July 2 2001.
866 UNMIK/REG/2001/18.

Ombudsperson Institution in Kosovo.[867] The UN Human Rights Committee, in its concluding observations on Serbia (Kosovo) in 2006, also noted that criminal suspects were being arrested under a detention directive of the Commander of KFOR, and under executive orders of the SRSG, without appearing before a judge and with no access to any independent judicial body with authority to determine the lawfulness of detentions. The Human Rights Committee called on UNMIK to revoke the regulation and furthermore instructed UNMIK that any person arrested under the discretionary powers of the UNMIK police or under a court orders should be informed of the reasons for such arrest and full details of any charges against them and then to be brought promptly before a judicial authority.[868]

Selective Judicial Review

While failing to provide proper judicial review and accountability mechanisms on executive detentions, UNMIK addressed this question in relation to other areas of governance. One example, the Kosovo Trust Agency (KTA), was established as an independent body in 2002 with "full juridical personality and in particular the capacity [...] to sue and be sued in its own name".[869] The KTA was primarily responsible for privatisation with authority to create subsidiary corporations from socially-owned enterprises.[870] Though the SRSG established immunity for all UNMIK personnel against "legal process in respect of words spoken and all acts performed by them in their official capacity",[871] an exception was made for the KTA. By establishing it as an independent body, UNMIK also limited liability claims against itself by owners and creditors affected by privatisation.[872]

Decisions of the KTA were subject to judicial review, perhaps as an acknowledgement that resolutions made under privatisation involved legal aspects affecting individual rights, including creditors' rights, labour rights and

867 See Ombudsperson Institution in Kosovo 2001, Special Report No. 3.

868 Human Rights Committee CCPR/C/UNK/CO/1 (2006) para. 17.

869 UNMIK REG/2002/12.

870 Ibid.

871 UNMIK/REG/2000/47. UNMIK comprehended the "international civilian presence established pursuant to Security Council Resolution 1244 [...] integrating the Interim Civilian Administration (United Nations), Humanitarian Affairs (UNHCR), Institution-building (OSCE), and Reconstruction (EU) components". The regulation also stated that immunity "from legal process of KFOR and UNMIK personnel and KFOR contractors is in the interests of KFOR and UNMIK and not for the benefit of the individuals themselves. The Secretary-General shall have the right and the duty to waive the immunity of any UNMIK personnel in any case where, in his opinion, the immunity would impede the course of justice and can be waived without prejudice to the interest of UNMIK".

872 As a result, fearing personal liability, the KTA's management board failed to assume responsibility between 2004 and 2005. See Knoll 2008 p. 239.

housing rights linked to former state-owned enterprises.[873] The Special Chamber of the Kosovo Supreme Court was granted jurisdiction over the review of KTA acts.[874] Allowing for judicial review of decisions taken by the KTA thus represented a significant improvement in the faltering accountability regime in Kosovo.

Another improvement in Kosovo was the early establishment of an Ombudsperson. Though this office had competence to investigate UNMIK, it was withdrawn in 2006.[875] Moreover, such competence throughout the period of the establishment of the Ombudsperson in 2000 was the subject of controversy. Furthermore, and in accordance with the Constitutional Framework for Kosovo, the courts were not accorded authority to review UNMIK decisions or actions (though they could review the decisions and acts of local government institutions).[876] Nevertheless, the office received more than 900 formal applications between 21 November 2000 and 30 June 2003, where in excess of 800 concerned alleged violations by UNMIK and KFOR. Most of the applications concerned property-related matters, lack of rights of access to court, failure of administrative agencies to respond to requests, and arbitrary or discriminatory administrative decisions.[877]

Balancing the limited authority of the Ombudsperson, steps were taken towards the establishment of a more comprehensive accountability regime through UNMIK Regulation 2006/12, seven years into the missions.[878] The regulation established a Human Rights Advisory Panel, with competence to accept complaints against actions by UNMIK for failing to comply with the catalogue of international human rights instruments listed in UNMIK Regulation 1999/24.

The Advisory panel retains jurisdiction over complaints "relating to alleged violations of human rights that had occurred not earlier than 23 April 2005 or arising from facts which occurred before this date where these facts give rise to a continuing violation of human rights".[879] Moreover, the Advisory Panel has the competence to request the participation of UNMIK personnel, and to order the disclosure of its documents, though the SRSG has leave to deny participation or disclosure based upon "the interests of justice, the promotion of human rights and the interests of UNMIK and the United Nations as a whole".[880]

---

873 OSCE 2008, Privatization in Kosovo: Judicial Review of Kosovo Trust Agency Matters by the Special Chamber of the Supreme Court of Kosovo p. 17f.

874 Constitutional Framework for Provisional Self-Government in Kosovo Art. 30. The Special Chamber was established through UNMIK/REG/2002/13.

875 See UNMIK/REG/2000/ 38 and UNMIK/REG/2006/06.

876 UNMIK/REG/2001/9.

877 Ombudsperson Institution in Kosovo 2003 p. 8.

878 UNMIK/REG/2006/12. The advisory panel comprises three international jurists.

879 Ibid., Section 2.

880 Ibid., para. 15.3.

The Advisory Panel represents a step forward towards ensuring accountability of international actors in Kosovo, but the institutional limitations makes it generally weak and exclude important issues such as the judicial review of administrative decisions made by UNMIK. The advisory panel is also weak in the sense that it can only make findings of a non-binding character, which is an enfeebled form of mandate compared with the Human Rights Chamber in Bosnia and Herzegovina, with its authority to promulgate binding decisions.[881] An explanation for the limited mandate might be that it represents a compromise in having the competence to deal with complaints involving acts and omissions by international actors. In 2006 UNMIK also agreed to submit a report to the UN Human Rights Committee on its activities in Kosovo, thereby opening up the way for an expanded international review function at horizontal level.

There seems to have been an attempt, drawing upon the lessons of Kosovo, at addressing such accountability deficiencies in the set-up of the UN mission in East Timor. In 2000 the SRSG provided for a special *habeas corpus* procedure to challenge unlawful arrest and detention.[882] UNTAET also allowed for decisions of UNTAET organs, or policies of the UNTAET Policy Committee, to be challenged in the courts on a number of sensitive areas. The regulation establishing protected places allow for the review of decisions of the Deputy Transitional Administrator by "competent judicial authorities in East Timor".[883] A form of judicial review was also set up through the regulations on public procurement.[884]

The use of executive detention orders and other regulations lacking correlating judicial review procedures might perhaps be taken as being indicative of differences in the mandates of international actors. In Kosovo, for example, OSCE officials were concerned with establishing the rule of law on the basis of international standards under their human rights pillar, while UN officials with an executive responsibility for law and order were forced to create a system that could provide justice in a crisis environment where the upholding of such standards is frequently challenged because of insecurity.[885] Under such circumstances rule of law becomes instrumental to the organisational mandates, the mission objectives and the dynamics of the conflict in question.

The complexity of state-building, together with the unchecked powers of international actors, raises the question of legal remedies available against them. The Venice Commission noted on the situation in Bosnia and Herzegovina: "the High Representative is not an independent judge and he has no democratic

881 See Aybay 1997 pp. 529–545.
882 UNTAET/REG/2000/30.
883 UNTAET/REG/2000/19 art. 8.1, and art. 8.4.
884 UNTAET/REG/2000/10 Art. 42.
885 Baskin 2001 p. 16.

legitimacy derived from the people of BiH".[886] The Commission, therefore, suggested that it seemed "unacceptable that decisions directly affecting the rights of individuals taken by a political body are not subject to a fair hearing or at least the minimum of due process and scrutiny of an independent court".[887]

The lack of accountability of international players is partly attributed and justified in light of security concerns. In some cases it might be difficult in practice or even dangerous in a fragile peace process to, for example, allow for 'localisation' or for extensive accountability mechanisms. Nevertheless, this argument must be constantly re-evaluated as the war to peace transition progresses and gains momentum. In situations of prolonged international involvement, in particular where international actors substitute for national governments, there is a need to ensure minimum rule of law guarantees as to the decisions they make, particularly where they concern individual rights and freedoms or questions on the structure and organisation of the state.

International actors also need to base their decisions upon transparent criteria – that is, to be able to justify difficult decisions by reference to well-established legal principles and standards of governance. By applying transparent criteria, international participants might then behave with greater sincerity both as norm promoters and as teachers of norms. While the apparent willingness in the case of East Timor to follow from the start rule of law principles by providing for judicial review (at least to a certain degree) represented an improvement compared with the UN governance in Kosovo, such improvement nevertheless reveals the inconsistency and lack of regulatory framework intrinsic to these types of situation.

SOURCES OF ACCOUNTABILITY

Several scholars have suggested that international humanitarian law, in particular the law on occupation, should apply in settings where the UN substitutes for national governments.[888]

The law of occupation entails a complex framework that occupying powers must work within to minimise possible contraventions.[889] At the same time, the law on occupation would, as it is presently understood, prohibit many of the

886 Venice Commission 2005, Opinion on the Constitutional Situation in Bosnia and Herzegovina and the Powers of the High Representative, para. 96.

887 Ibid.

888 See e.g., Kelly 1999 in suggesting that international humanitarian law, and more precisely, the law on occupation, should apply to 'complex' peace operations. The UN has refrained from calling itself an occupying power, even in the cases of Kosovo and East Timor where it held executive authority.

889 Some of the major principles of occupation law are to be found in Art. 43 of The Hague Regulations and Arts. 61 to 70 in the Geneva IV Convention.

decisions taken by international actors for the purpose of promoting the rule of law: "indeed, virtually every type of reforms proven vital to state-building operations from the post-war Germany and Japan through Kosovo and Iraq are arguably precluded by the law of occupation".[890] Article 43 of The Hague Regulations explicitly compels an occupying power to respect existing laws unless absolutely prevented. The IV Geneva Convention, furthermore, set strict limitations on the changing of penal laws in an occupied territory, unless they constituted a threat to the security of the occupying power or an obstacle to the application of the present convention.

A society in political turmoil seeking to radically transform political, legal and socio-economic structures would not benefit from the application of the law on occupation to govern an international presence, since this would explicitly prevent international support in several areas, not least within rule of law reform.[891] Neither does it seem likely that international actors would benefit from adhering to the obligations imposed upon an occupying power.

Besides the legal and political opprobrium associated with the application of occupation law in multilateral state-building missions, there is also a clear virtue in distinguishing between situations where the law on occupation should be applicable and places where other norms are relevant. The virtue of such distinction is to retain occupation law "in order to discipline aggressor armies and hold them accountable for their actions on foreign territories".[892] Occupation law was never designed for measures such as complex state building missions.[893]

Furthermore, the law on occupation does not encompass the core of the discussion on accountability in rule of law assistance – that is, a notion of a relationship between international and national actors founded upon on trust. The basis for this notion is that international participants, because of their special position, have to carefully model and anchor their authority with regard to the well-being of the people in war-torn societies. As argued by Chesterman, when the UN and other agencies assume state-like functions, they "must not lose sight of their limited mandate to hold that sovereign power in trust for the population that will ultimately claim it".[894]

---

890 McGurk 2005 p. 454.

891 The argument that the law on occupation is impractical in situations of state-building is further supported by the fact that the UN mission in Kosovo took its constituting decisions in light of the restrictions of the law on occupation. The former Principal Legal Officer at the UN Office of Legal Affairs, Miller, said that for international lawyers it was 'normal' to decide that the applicable law in Kosovo should be the law in force at the start of the UN mission: "this has a solid foundation in the laws of occupation where The Hague Regulations require the occupying power to respect, 'unless absolutely prohibited' the law in force in the country".

892 Scheffer 2003 p. 851.

893 Danchin 2009 p. 73.

894 Chesterman 2004 p. 257.

Trusteeship Models

Following the reasoning of trust, it could be argued that when international bodies assume executive responsibility under a UN Security Council mandate, they possess a dual function "constrained in its articulation by the operation of fiduciary trust bound between it and the ones it govern".[895] As such, international interventions, particularly where they are involved in rule of law assistance, could be seen as 'political trustees', and that because of this, international players should also provide for adequate checks and balances.[896] The reason for such checks further appears as an imperative simply because international organisations make decisions that produce winners and losers.[897] Apart from the direct responsibility incurred in relation to executive detentions international agencies also develop new legislation, reorganise the judicial structure, and influence constitutional reform with implications for the dissemination of power and authority.

Similar to the proposals for an application of the law on occupation, contentions have been made that useful guidelines for regulating intervening authorities might be found in a constructive adaptation of Chapters XII and XIII of the UN Charter. These contain the structure and function of the International Trusteeship System and the Trusteeship Council, a principal organ of the UN. While the Trusteeship System is now obsolete (following the termination of the last trusteeship of Palau in 1994), it was created as a regulatory mechanism for the UN to manage and supervise countries placed under 'trust' –that is, administered by another state.[898] The all-embracing principle of the Trusteeship System was the promotion of political, economic, social and educational advancement with a view to enabling "self-government".[899]

A constructive adoption of the trusteeship principles would, according to the International Commission on Intervention and State Sovereignty, allow for a "reconstruction and rehabilitation to take place in an orderly way".[900] A similar argument is put forward in the King's College report A Review of Peace Operations: A Case for Change. It suggests that in areas where an SRSG or a similar institution wields extraordinary and far-reaching powers, a group of countries (where at least one is a permanent member of the UN Security

---

[895] Knoll 2008 p. 179.

[896] Perritt 2003 p. 389 suggests a political trusteeship concept modelled on common law 'trust' and inspired by the UN trusteeship system.

[897] Perritt 2003 p. 419.

[898] Art. 78 explicitly prevents the trusteeship system from applying to territories that have become members of the United Nations. To provide more than just guidelines this would require Charter amendments. See Chesterman 2004 p. 222.

[899] UN Charter Art. 76 (b).

[900] International Commission on Intervention and State Sovereignty 2001 p. 43.

Council) could function as a supervisory body, similar to business management structures where executives are accountable to a board of directors.[901]

While a revival of the Trusteeship System might not be realistic for primarily political reasons, as well as practical, the underlying principles of the system are worth noting. In Chapter XIII on the Trusteeship Council, a set of review mechanisms are included. These involve such things as considering reports submitted by the administering authority; accepting petitions and examining them in consultation with the administering authority; and providing for periodic visits to the respective trust territories at times agreed with the administering authority.[902] Moreover, the Trusteeship Council was to "formulate a questionnaire on the political, economic, social and educational advancement of the inhabitants for each trust territory, and the administering authority for each trust territories".[903] On the basis of these questionnaires an annual report was submitted to the General Assembly. This report, together with the apparatus of individual petitions, enabled the Trusteeship System to provide a form of judicial review of actions taken by the administering authority.

Compared with the review system today, there are substantial differences. Though both SRSGs and the UN Secretary-General report to the UN Security Council on the basis of progress and problems in the course of present-day state-building, this represents less extensive review devices compared with the principled structure of review in the Trusteeship System.[904] In this sense, drawing upon the principles of the Trusteeship System could have the potential to improve upon horizontal accountability.

A formalisation of the relationship between national and international actors in spheres where the UN or other international players substitute for national governments – for example, through review bodies such as the Human Rights Advisory Panel in Kosovo, the Human Rights Chamber in Bosnia and Herzegovina, or through the application of the law on occupation or the trusteeship system, could be one way of improving accountability. On the international level, an extended reporting regime for UN administrators, for example, to the UN Human Rights Committee, could also be another means to that end.[905]

---

901 King's College 2003, A Review of Peace Operations: A Case for Change – Overall Introduction and Synthesis Report p. 10.

902 Art. 76 of the UN Charter lists the rights and responsibilities of trusteeships. This could, according to Stahn 2008 p 456, be read as a "mini-charter" for present day international administrations.

903 UN Charter Art. 88.

904 The UNSG, for example, annexed key legislation enacted by UNMIK in his mission progress reports to the Security Council.

905 Knoll 2008 p. 425–433 suggests a set of Accountability Guidelines for when the UN assumes a governance role, including the use of hybrid commissions and bodies to review international law making.

Nevertheless, there is still no framework in existence accountability that would apply from the start of an international administration. Though the improvements in accountability in Kosovo and East Timor were important, they represented developments that emerged in the field, in reaction to problems within those particular contexts.

State-building missions where the mandate is to provide advice and assistance present further challenge. The responsibility and accountability for rule of law reform resides with the national government, even though it might not actually function. In such situations UN agencies and programmes may by default assume a de facto governance responsibility, with the consequence that "their de facto exercise of administrative, and even governmental, functions in post-conflict territories is not justiciable in local courts, and is in practice exempt from the control of the political organs of the UN".[906] Such positions would arguably not be possible to regulate and formalise in the same way as temporary UN administrations.

Normative Guidelines

An alternative to the regulatory approach could be to work proactively and develop more detailed guidelines for the UN and other agencies involved in rule of law reform.

Some scholars and practitioners have argued for the development of a normative structure for state-building missions. Normative sources and support for such a framework could be drawn from the discussion on good governance and rule of law, and applied in relation to international agencies. Attempts have been made at international level to provide some form of essential support for international interventions.

One such example is the 2005 Paris Declaration.[907] The principles contained in it maintain that state-building rests on three pillars: "the capacity of state structures to perform core function; their legitimacy and accountability; and ability to provide an enabling environment for strong economic performance to generate income, employment and domestic revenues".[908] The Paris Declaration also advances five principles for effectiveness, legitimacy and sustainability of aid delivery to 'fragile states':

(1) ownership;
(2) harmonisation;
(3) alignment;
(4) results;
(5) and mutual accountability.

---

906 Verdirame 2005 pp. 88–89.
907 OECD/DAC 2005, Principles for Good International Engagement in Fragile States.
908 Ibid.

It remains unclear what effect such broad principles have in the field. Without further clarification as to a more detailed function of ownership or mutual accountability, it is difficult to envisage how such principles could be translated into practical guidelines.

Within the UN system the practical guide entitled Primer for Justice Components in Multidimensional Peace Operations: Strengthening the Rule of Law, was issued by the Department for Peacekeeping Operations. It lists six central principles for rule of law reform.[909] It is intended as a 'tool-kit' and guide for 'judicial officers' about to be deployed, or who are already working in a peace operation, and includes 'best practices' such as respecting national ownership and leadership; ensuring that legal reform is driven by national counterparts sensitive to the culture and legal traditions of the host country; that legal reforms take on a human rights-based approach where human rights standards form part of all analysis, assessment and programming; the promotion of gender equality in all programme activities, including the attempt to eliminate discriminatory laws, policies and practices; managing expectations and openness on constraints, while avoiding predictions about future assistance; ensuring participatory approaches to encourage the participation of all stakeholders, in particular civil society and the marginalised.

The principles in the primer encapsulate the discourse of international actors on ownership, transparency, effectiveness and accountability. However, the challenges that the primer (as well as other guideline approaches, such as the Paris Declaration) tries to address do not seem to be those of knowledge. Rather, the difficulty is that they fail to be properly respected in the implementation of complex rule of law reforms. Reasons for their lack of application seem to be influenced by both actual difficulties of adhering to such principles in war-torn societies, and their lack of normative weight. Broad principles calling for human rights observance, participatory approaches, or ownership, for the most part do not acknowledge the pitfalls encountered in the putting into effect of the rule of law concept in war-torn societies. Without criteria for determining when it is practically possible or politically difficult, for example, to work through joint structures that allow for local ownership, there will continue to be a gap between standards and principles and their implementation.

On the normative weight of primers and general guidelines, there is no equivalent document setting out rights and duties as in humanitarian law. With regard to humanitarian law the Secretary-General in 1999 developed the Bulletin on the Observance by United Nations Forces of International Humanitarian Law.[910] Deveraux suggests that as an interim measure, while a more formalised

909 UN Peacekeeping Best Practice Unit 2006, Primer for Justice Components in Multidimensional Peace Operations.

910 Secretary-General's Bulletin on the Observance by United Nations Forces of International Humanitarian Law 1999. See, also, Kondoch 2005 p. 41.

approach to accountability is developed, the UN Secretary-General could issue a similar bulletin on the application of human rights and governance norms.[911] More important, such a bulletin should also include a specific focus on state-building missions where the UN assumes a governance function and, in terms of rules for observance, not only deals with human rights, but also make use of the discourses on good governance and good administration in order to establish clearly structured principles for the administration of justice. Such a bulletin could also introduce an extended reporting system of the SRSG.

Another attempt at defining accountability standards for international organisations engaged in state-building missions is to be found in the work of the International Law Association (ILA). The accountability regime suggested by the ILA consists of a number of principles intended to function as yardsticks for international organisations.[912] Some of them include proposals that international actors should stick to the principle of good faith; the principles of constitutionality and institutional balance; of supervision and control; of stating the reasons for decisions or a particular course of action; the principle of procedural regularity; of objectivity and impartiality; of due diligence; and the principle of promoting justice.

The ILA also discussed the matter of accountability of international actors in state-building more directly and maintained that such players should incorporate basic human rights obligations into their operational guidelines and procedures "particularly when exercising governmental authority in the conduct of temporary administration over a particular territory".[913] Furthermore, the ILA went on to argue, any international organisation, particularly when designing and implementing decisions such as structural adjustment programmes and development projects, should observe basic human rights obligations. This could, for example, be translated into respect for indigenous peoples when planning for construction projects in infrastructure programmes in particularly sensitive environments, or to take responsibility for the consequences of economic adjustment programmes intended to rationalise and privatise parts of the public sector.

The question to what extent human rights law is binding (if at all) upon the UN remains contested. The UN possesses an international legal personality, and is thereby capable of bearing rights and duties under international law.[914] Thus,

---

911 Devereux 2009 p. 215.

912 International Law Association 2002.

913 International Law Association 2004 p. 23.

914 Devereux 2009 p. 205 lists five arguments in favour of the UN being subject to human rights obligations: the inherent obligation; delegated responsibility; constitutional obligation; the functionality view; and the derivative view. Zwanenburg 1998 p. 232 contends that: "In principle one should search for the norms that are applicable to the conduct of peace forces, including human rights and International Humanitarian Law norms, in the law applicable to the UN".

as a legal person the UN is bound by customary law.[915] Arguments for human rights obligations based upon a 'dual functionality' also carry some weight in this regard – that is, international administrations act both as subsidiary organs of an international agency and as national authorities.[916] Moreover, in the first regulations issued by UNMIK and UNTAET it was declared that public officials were to observe international human rights law. At the same time, it is not clear to what extent respective UN administrations sought to apply this to UN officials, and the practice of immunity and a minimal judicial review mechanism speaks against the interpretation that these conventions would also apply directly to UN administrations.[917]

In addition, the arguments for the applicability of human rights norms to the UN, if accepted, are lacking in clarity and still leave open the question of what rights this would include and what, in practical terms, it would mean for the UN in a governance function.[918] It is equally unclear who would possess the authority to interpret human rights contraventions by the UN or other international agencies in a similar position in war-torn societies, particularly when considering that in most such cases the national judicial and bureaucratic systems would not be functioning.[919]

This raises the question of a standing human rights or ombudsman institution within the UN system. The World Bank instituted an innovative precedent through the creation of the World Bank Inspection Panel in 1993. The panel is mandated to receive petitions of grievances from citizens affected by the World Bank's projects and to ensure that it follows its operational principles and policies in the design, preparation and implementation phase.[920]

An equivalent in the UN system, but not quite, would be the Office of Internal Oversight Services (OIOS). The OIOS is mandated to ensure compliance with the resolutions of the General Assembly and with the regulations, rules and policies of the United Nations.[921] But despite the broad mandate the OIOS has mainly focused on internal audits and investigations into the conduct of the UN system. This has also included peace operations, but with a focus exclusively on management and the servicing of ration contracts, allegations of fraud and corruption.[922] The OIOS would need a substantial increase in capacity in order

---

915 It remains debatable, however, what human rights that are considered to form customary law. See, for example, Meron 1989 pp. 95–97, in arguing that a core number of due process rights are included in customary law.

916 Knoll 2008 p. 213.

917 See Cerone 2005 p. 64.

918 See Kondoch 2005 p. 41.

919 A deeper discussion on the question of whether or not human rights apply to the UN falls outside the scope of this work. Sufficient to say is that the complexity of this matter, particularly on review and legal redress.

920 See e.g., Fox 2000.

921 See UNGA A/RES48/218 p. 2.

922 Hoffman & Mégret 2005 p. 52.

to effectively work as a supervisory body in relation to the growing responsibility of the UN in conflict management.[923]

What the considerations of the ILA have attempted to do, both in terms of the principles of good governance and human rights obligations, is to identify a set of norms possibly having the potential to affect and mitigate a growing accountability deficit. These principles could, arguably, form part of a more concerted effort towards the development of standard-setting similar to the Secretary-General's bulletin on humanitarian law, as noted above, applicable to missions with executive responsibility and to advice and assistance missions where international actors assume executive powers by default.

923 Ghani & Lockhart 2008 p. 93.

PART III

A RULE OF LAW FOR STATE-BUILDING

7. A RULE OF LAW FOR STATE-BUILDING

CASUAL ASSUMPTIONS AND STANDARD PRESCRIPTIONS

From the examination of how international actors treat the rule of law at policy and 'field' level, a distinct model emerges: *rule of law after war and crisis*. The distinct character of this model is the adaptability to post-war and crisis situations and how the rule of law has been made to 'fit' established practices. Before the rule of law became an architectonic ideal, justice sector reforms were already standard components of crisis management. When the UN and other international agencies eventually adopted the rule of law as an overriding objective, they did so without clarifying what it would mean in relation to an already established practice. Thus, organisations previously focusing on police and law enforcement reform, judicial reform, or criminal law reform started to rename and re-phrase activities under a rule of law banner. This means that the rule of law model that has emerged is fragmented and sectorised with little overall coherence. It makes more sense to speak of rule of law reform in the judicial, law enforcement or human rights sector, than general support to rule of law as a systemic concept.

The casual assumptions constituting the rule of law model in the aftermath of war and crisis would not be a cause for worry, lest it be shown that they create contradiction, confusion and goal displacement. Considering the challenges facing rule of law reform, the concept appears to have become, at best, nothing more than an "honorific title for an amalgam of values".[924] At worst, the rule of law resembles the confusion characterising law in war-torn societies, and the reason why international assistance is needed in the first place.

The methods employed in rule of law reform testify to the attendant conceptual difficulties. International agencies mostly work within three broad categories – legal and constitutional reform; institution-building; and access-creation. While the methods vary depending in part on the particular mandate of the international actors concerned, some common denominators of rule of law reform are possible to identify.

---

924 Fallon 1997 p. 41.

On law reform and constitutional reform, one typical method is the technical 'importation' of laws and institutions. In the context of such societies the 'importing' comes chiefly from international law and standards, but there are also frequent borrowings from participating nations and other state-building missions. International law functions here as both a standard-setting instrument (for example in the purging or updating of criminal law) and as an act of foundation in constitutional arrangements.

Institutional reforms also display similar references and applications to international law. Vetting programmes and capacity-building both use international standards. Access-creation is a less developed area of reform. The methods are also more ad hoc and contextual, and not necessarily confined to the justice sector. International law and standards are employed here as well, but more as instruments of advocacy than as standard-setting tools. The actors typically involved in access-creation are international non-governmental organisations, serving as socialising and supporting networks for national counterparts. Reform activities include the establishment of human rights institutions, ombudsman offices and awareness and empowerment initiatives.

Combining all of the methods is that ownership, participation and consultation are ambiguously approached, without any apparent criteria on when it becomes necessary to allow for a greater 'localisation', or on how to balance international control and responsibility with the need for national knowledge and support.

The causal assumptions underpinning the rule of law after war and crisis, and the standard prescriptions applied, give rise to several difficulties. These include the adoption of a check-list approach for remedying a perceived 'lack' of laws and institutions; promoting a value-laden concept that places high demands on commitment and capacity; the selective applicability of the rule of law concept in war-torn societies; the weak anchoring of reforms; and the lack of accountability of international agencies.

From the analysis of concepts and methods in this book, it appears that a substantial part of rule of law assistance rests upon the assumption of 'a lack'.[925] States moving from violent conflict are assumed to be in a transitory phase because they lack the proper laws and institutions.[926] Accordingly, the prescribed remedy is to establish the necessary state institutions and normative frameworks for constraining the arbitrary exercise of power, to define breaches and actual violations and to enforce punishments for such transgressions, as well as increasing the effectiveness and control of the state.

Though this perspective responds to the anatomy of societies torn apart by war and crisis, it says little about precisely what laws and institutions are in want

925 See Mattei & Nader 2008 where the 'lack' argument is described at length.

926 Societies in a transition from war and crisis are assumed not only to lack the proper institutions, but also to have the wrong type to begin with.

and may work. This 'lack' perspective prompts international agencies to employ pre-set models and to follow established practices – that is, they promote that with which they are familiar, in particular normative and institutional constraints that appear to have worked elsewhere, or are assumed to have acquired a certain normative superiority. The remedy to the difficulties identified in this work lies not in the launching of yet another 'common definition' (there is sufficient theorising on the rule of law).[927] Instead, it is argued here that a reorientation of rule of law assistance is necessary and a return to the core attributes of the concept. This means, in essence, adopting an ends-based approach to the rule of law. If international actors are genuinely committed to promoting the rule of law, and not merely established practices that have been absorbed under a rule of law concept ad hoc there is need for reorientation and focus. Thus, strategic policy should be informed by the broader consideration of how to restrain the arbitrary exercise of power and how to enable human interaction.

While these attributes are sufficiently broad to include many different rule of law reform initiatives their usefulness lies in formulating questions that are not affected by a particular legal and institutional bias. For example, by asking what problems there are in relation to rule of law (and only then beginning to develop legal and institutional responses) reformers can avoid confining the rule of law to the formal judiciary while most of people turn to informal dispute resolution, or avoid focusing the bulk of attention and resources on drafting laws that match international standards, while failing to provide the same consideration with regard to how those standards should be properly implemented.

TRANSITIONAL LEGAL ORDERS

Externally supported rule of law reform creates a particular form of transitional legal order in war-torn and crisis societies. Form and content of these legal orders varies depending on the mandate of international assistance, but a common feature is that transitional orders display a high degree of legal plurality. They are best described as a form of 'hybrid' regime with a mix of international, foreign and local laws, and institutions. Through post-war treaty ratification, the incorporation of international law in constitutions, the establishment of institutions based upon international models, or the employment of standards directly in law-making, war-torn societies are subject to rapid internationalisation. This is also evident from the use of international personnel in national institutions. The way law travels between state-building

[927] There are already existing rule of law definitions from international actors that are broad enough to encompass the core attributes of the rule of law and to allow for a systemic approach to the concept. The common definition launched by the UNSG is one example.

missions and international and national levels, creates a unique field of comparative law.

The 'exposure' to international law, standards and models from donor countries provides platforms and leverage for rights-advocacy groups, and also influences public and political discourse. It is possible to discern a growing interest in constitutionalism, the importance of an independent judiciary, the role of fundamental rights and freedoms, and the expression of grievances in the form of legal entitlement. The rule of law discourse and rhetoric of international actors is employed by national interlocutors. Moreover, communities of legal academics and practitioners are becoming more intertwined with similar actors in donor countries through international professional networks, which can function as reinforcing mechanisms of the rule of law in the future.

The internationalisation of transitional legal orders is also evident in the way that reforms and changes at national level reflect the specific mandates and objectives of particular international participants. This leads to a disproportionate legal and institutional development, where certain matters within the justice sector receive international assistance, for example criminal law, and where other areas (such as civil, administrative or customary law) lag behind. The transitional legal regimes also mean that legal professionals and other public officials have to interpret national law through the lens of international law and standards, which poses a challenge to resource-weak legal and administrative systems. Furthermore, while many post-war and crisis legal systems exhibit changes in substance in certain high profile matters – that is, on fundamental rights and freedoms and in criminal law – the procedural and institutional capacities required to put them into effect are often underdeveloped, creating a gap between law on books and law in reality.

THE DEVIL IS IN THE DETAILS

It is known from past experience that certain conditions must be considered in order to secure sustainable and well-anchored reforms. Chief among the conditions is that rule of law reform is not merely about law, but involves other factors. This means that context is of consequence for the reception and viability of rule of law reform. International assistance must be adjusted to the particular context in terms, for example, of social norms, expectations, demands and capacity.

Model laws and standards are valuable for reformers because they can provide reasonable approximation and calculability. Employing the UN Basic Principles on the Independence of the Judiciary as a code of conduct for the judiciary in Afghanistan, for example, allowed for a more immediate standard-setting. Neglecting international standards can also adversely affect reform efforts, as with Kosovo where the vetting programme was compromised owing to repeated failures to include international standards in order to secure judicial independence.

The crucial issue is how standards and models are applied. Assistance providers need to be aware that 'transplanted' laws and institutions will always be subject to detours, resistance and local adjustment, which means that the content and the function of a reformed law or institution will change. Thus reformers may be more helped by concentrating on the process of legal and institutional reform than on the particular content that they wish to support.

Above all, while international standards, benchmarks and models are perceived to hold a greater legitimacy than national laws and institutions, they should be used when it is necessary, and not as an automatic gap-filling function when there might be national alternatives. Rule of law reformers are perhaps more assisted by applying international law and standards as transitional trial and error experiences rather than as direct 'imports' of laws and institutions.[928] Effectively incorporating international treaty obligations or model laws directly into constitutional arrangements, or supporting treaty ratifications, might require a process of selectivity, and on sequentially anchoring only a few treaties and norms that support core rule of law principles. Quality rather than quantity in a transition can enable informed discussions on rule of law reform in the national arena.

Past practice consistently demonstrate that legal, judicial and administrative reform is most likely to succeed in cases where there is a genuine demand for reform. Such demand is essential, since the rule of law requires a commitment to the central values and principles of the concept on the part of the political elite to be bound by legal rules. The question to be considered is what factors can generate such demand and a desire to follow 'the rules of the game', particularly in those situations where the 'rule of the gun' has been the norm.

Demand for and commitment to a rule of law project can be supported by allowing national actors a say in the setting of reform priorities and deciding on the sequencing of their implementation, as well as through participation in such implementation.

For international actors to successfully support the 'anchoring' of rule of law reform, assistance must be seen as a long-term undertaking with objectives that extend beyond a single project outcome. Capacity-building might only be sustainable so long as the particular international presence is tangible. Despite training programmes, education initiatives and comprehensive legal drafting, there is a risk that public officials will resort to old patterns of behaviour unless both international and national checks and balances for monitoring are made effective.

928 Davis & Trebilcock 2008 p. 919.

CONTENT OVER FORM

Past experience emphasises that it is essential to match reforms to the absorptive capacity of the receiving national actors. That is, rule of law reforms should not overburden recipients with unrealistic demands on standards, nor require complex institutional reforms or arrangements that are unlikely to be implemented. Such initiatives might undermine rather than strengthen the rule of law.

Rule of law reform often emphasise compliance with a material standard, often a very high standard, by which progress in rule of law reform is measured. Too many rule of law initiatives are complex and resource-demanding beyond the absorptive capacity of these fractured societies. When the rule of law becomes integrated with human rights and the rhetoric of democracy, the conflicts and arguments in these spheres – for example, universalism and relativism – are transferred to rule of law assistance.

There are significant strands of instrumentalism in rule of law reform – international actors apply the rule of law to fit state-building ideologies that make the concept contingent upon the realisation of other political ends. In this way the rule of law model is stretched and bent to fit a legal, political or moral objective. This creates tension and controversies in the field since there are no well-established criteria for informing on the decisions made by international actors – that is, why certain reforms are pursued and not others, why some principles such as independence and accountability seem to hold relevance in one sector, and not another, or why there are frequent references to, and application of, international law while the development of national law reform lags behind.

Such concentration on material content leads to a neglect of procedure and form. Several examples from the field testify to this, such as international actors pushing for human rights inclusion in the Afghan constitution while it remains unclear how those rights can be realised or the creation of a 'new' transitional legal order in East Timor by circumventing the applicable (Indonesian) law through the employment of UN regulations and international standards. All in all, the value-laden and instrumental approach to the rule of law creates a mix of ideas and conceptions that can, at times, reflect contradictory values and aspirations.

International players seem to assume that their national interlocutors will respond with logic of appropriateness to the proposed laws and institutions. National actors are assumed to support reforms founded upon the rationally best option in terms of modernity, universality, efficiency and cost. Experience from war-torn and crisis societies reveal difficulties in applying international law and models as automatic gap-fillers. National agencies are equally, sometimes more so, influenced by choices that from an external perspective seem 'irrational'.

Even for environments that are recognised as lacking in capacity for upholding and enforcing complicated legal transplants, or implementing international agreements, there appears to be an implicit hope that once transferred, legal and institutional changes will take on an 'irritating' effect. It seems clear that the expectations on the potential of international law based upon assumptions of moral superiority, modernity or efficiency must be recalibrated and adjusted to post-war and post-crisis realities.

International law and standards are easily transferred – that is, initially and sometimes noncommittally received – but it is questionable what the effect is unless they are carefully applied. Undermining the usefulness of standards and models founded upon international law best practices is the absence of monitoring. Typically, there are mechanisms in a project cycle involving monitoring and evaluation, but since rule of law reform is a long-term process they are not often accessible after the closure of a project or programme. The effect of the import of international norms is therefore not fully clear, considering the lack of adequate assessments and more long-term perspectives.

FOCUS ON MATTERS OUTSIDE THE JUSTICE SECTOR

The conceptualisation made by international actors lends itself to reinforce a misinterpretation of the rule of law as a concept with exclusive sector relevance. The principles of legality, equality before the law, legal certainty and individual rights and freedoms are all, it appears, hand-picked to apply in the justice sector. As by one observer stated, today's heavy emphasis on judges, lawyers, and courts, is analogous to how the health sector would look if it focused only on hospitals and doctors, while failing to extend itself to rural areas and include nurses and hospital administrators.[929]

The exclusion of principally important areas such as public administration is a telling example of the results arising from the application of the rule of law to an already established practice of justice sector reform. The blind spot in the rule of law model to issues outside the justice sector is reflected in the mandates of international agencies. The DPKO, for example, which has overall responsibility for putting the rule of law into effect in UN missions, emphasises four areas: police, corrections, the judiciary and human rights. Governance and public administration fall outside of this focus and in essence they become someone else's job. An inclusive approach and understanding involving, for example, public administration, is perceived by many international actors to be something further down the line in state-building. Moreover, supporting rule of law reform in the public administration is not as 'prestigious' as the drafting of a constitution or revising the criminal justice code. It is not merely altruistic

929 Golub 2006 p. 106.

motives that prompt international agencies to work within the justice sector. This sector attracts funding more easily than reforming the regulatory framework governing wastewater, or in attempting to reform land laws, or the training of municipal officials in administrative procedures.

The current selective rule of law agenda tends to produce a dualism in the state system. Investment in criminal justice and the judiciary is good for increasing the protection of individuals. But corruption, administrative inertia, low levels of access to justice and a lack of accountability reign supreme in other areas – and a persistent lack of resources and infrastructure becomes the norm.

There are many legal and policy sources for rule of law in public administration, not least the CoE recommendations, but the development of practical handbooks, guidelines and benchmarks is lagging behind the development of 'justice sector tools'. The rule of law instruments developed by the UN mentions briefly that it is important to initiate reforms in public administration, but does not provide any practical guidance on how to do so.

Public administration and administrative law are only now beginning to attract attention in terms of rule of law, despite the fact that rule of law problems in this area have been widespread and frequently reported from several war-torn and crisis societies. Far-reaching reforms aimed at ensuring the rule of law in public administration might be perceived as threatening and intrusive by interim governments.

At its most basic level, strengthening the rule of law in public administration entails a shift from monitoring and control from the executive to the judiciary, civil society and other vertical accountability mechanisms. External pressure on the state on how it organises its agencies, they way it confers powers, competencies and responsibilities, and on how it responds to its citizens, are in many ways more politically sensitive than the restructuring of a fledging criminal justice system with the overall objective of creating law and order.

A USER FRIENDLY RULE OF LAW

Throughout the entire rule of law assistance there is a lack of concerted effort towards making the law 'user friendly' – that is, for law to have the potential of enabling ordinary people to challenge government actions. This must be considered one of the most serious challenges to the sustainability of rule of law reforms in war-torn societies. The viability and existence of laws and institutions is largely dependent on whether or not they are applied or used. Nominal changes run the risk of becoming cosmetic alterations unless care is taken to truly enable citizens to become 'consumers' of the reformed system.

Reformers should focus on 'anchoring' reforms more clearly in order to consolidate the gains created, for example, by law reform or institution-building.

Rule of law reform today is mainly reactive. Many of the reforms promoted concentrates on abuses and crimes arising in the immediate phase of war to peace transition. This is an essential strategy since many war-torn societies display a rise in crime and corruption after a peace settlement has been brokered. At the same time, there is a need to support environments that can function proactively and to avoid situations where rule of law reform gains momentum during an international presence, but fades when the focus of attention moves on. The means of conditionality as leverage is temporary in most war-torn societies and the 'end consumer' is only vaguely defined. In the absence of strong forces of conditionality as well as monitoring possibilities, pressure for sustainability must reasonably come from within.

While measures employed to anchor reforms must be contextual, inspiration can be drawn from experience in supporting local advocacy groups and constituencies to monitor, criticise, and engage with state actors on rule of law issues, the use of paralegals, legal literacy programmes and other such that fall under the heading of legal empowerment and access creation. Past experience tends to support the idea that public demand and pressure from below are important components in anchoring reforms aimed at enhancing accountability.

It is also clear that such measures are limited unless they are accompanied by formal structural and institutional reforms. Bottom-up strategies remain ad hoc, underfunded and driven by international NGOs, making them both financially and politically vulnerable. These initiatives cannot be standalone reforms but must be pursued in conjunction with overriding changes of legal and institutional frameworks and institutions.

International actors are not oblivious to the difficulties of making the rule of law a practical reality, primarily in the area of access-creation. Ombudsman institutions have been established in Bosnia, Kosovo and East Timor and national human rights institutions in Sierra Leone and Afghanistan. But these efforts are uneven. Access-creation institutions and other initiatives such as paralegal programmes and informal dispute resolution systems are often only tentatively included in rule of law strategies by international actors. To some extent this can be because legal empowerment strategies and informal systems lack the technical and measurable side of judicial reform and legal drafting. The effects of legal empowerment are difficult to assess and quantify. What is argued here is not the substituting of formal legal structures with the informal, or institution-building with 'bottom-up' empowerment strategies, but that greater care should be taken to strengthen mechanisms that are close to people, that are easy to use and which can play a significant part in access to justice and accountability.

Supporting a system that makes it possible for ordinary people to make use of laws and institutions to protect their rights, and in holding government officials accountable, requires the establishment of checks and balances at the early stages of transition. This should not merely include actions and decisions in the justice sector, but also in public administration and traditional systems of law.

On this note, the arguments for a 'good enough' approaches and a scaled-down rule of law concept stand as being potentially more beneficial towards the making of a 'user-friendly' and adaptable system as opposed to an instrumental and value-laden concept. Concentrating selectively on strengthening rule of law attributes through a more modest approach provides the concept with an independent 'analytical bite', making it easier for people and civil society organisations to identify transgressions in rule of law principles by state officials. Adopting a 'good enough' rule of law perspective offers the potential to allow international actors to concentrate their assistance more effectively on meeting the demands of war-torn societies and to be adaptive to dynamics as the transition progresses.

ROBBING PETE TO PAY PAUL

An overriding difficulty with the whole rule of law enterprise is that the function of international actors as norm-entrepreneurs tends to create an accountability deficit.[930] This is caused by several factors. The increased responsibility of (chiefly) the UN and the EU in large-scale state-building mission is one. The UN and the EU have been called upon to assume a larger share of duties in conflict management while lacking the organisation, the resources and the supervisory apparatus for doing precisely that. International actors – both bilateral and multilateral – are not organisationally prepared for the complex tasks that they perform in rule of law assistance to war-torn societies.

Furthermore, there is no equivalent to a fiduciary trust relationship in national legislation, nor any other form of agreement or contract similar to a lawyer-client relationship by which international assistance providers can be held responsible to constituents in war-torn societies. The function of international agencies as 'teachers of norms' is compromised by a discrepancy between what they say and actually do. The international response has been if not irreverent, then at least hesitant on finding appropriate solutions to this deficit in accountability.

The challenge with regard to lack of accountability is often framed in terms of ownership, participation and consultation. In rule of law reform the process of implementation is often initiated by donors, with little participation from actors and interests ultimately responsible for managing and sustaining legal reforms.

[930] This could also be said to apply to development cooperation, though certain aspects such as more constrained mandates of donors and a generally stronger role of national authorities speak for a smaller gap.

The institutional and organisational structures of international actors, combined with the anatomy of war-torn societies, create a situation conducive to donor influence and laws on demand.

Naturally there are several exceptions to such a one-sided process, and there is also a critical discourse within the international community on the dangers of neglecting national and local input. But calls for ownership, participation and consultation might also result in misleading simplifications. Some situations require that principles of ownership are temporarily sacrificed. The real problem is therefore not that international experts draft laws for a war-torn society, but that there is limited official recognition that this type of reform takes place (other than in anecdotal and informal discussion). International actors do not explicitly acknowledge their roles as 'norm-creators' and fail to be transparent when they deem it necessary to keep direct control, and when it is possible to allow for increased national ownership and lead.

In most UN Security Council resolutions, the basis for international involvement is assistance, support, and advice, yet in practice this often translates into actual decision-making by international actors. Where foreign experts are mandated to advise on court reform, or assist in constitutional reform, the input often exceeds the mandate because their national counterparts lack the capacity to take an effective lead on such matters. It is this gap that produces an accountability deficit. The question is no longer, as provocatively put in one seminal UN report, whether the UN should "be in this business at all". The UN is involved, and so are many other organisations and donor agencies. The question now is how best to regulate, monitor and implement this responsibility.

On the issue of international control and responsibility, it is necessary to develop the methodology for when and in what situations rule of law reform should be 'localised' and when it becomes necessary to keep international 'ownership' and international influence. At present the approach that international actors have taken to the conditions most commonly seen as conducive to effective rule of law assistance – a process respecting the need for ownership, participation and consultation – is best described as ambiguous. The approach also fluctuates. In one and the same mission international actors devolve areas of responsibility to local authorities though there might be a lack of political commitment to rule of law principles on the part of national actors, while deciding unilaterally on issues where ownership, participation and consultation appear functionally necessary to respect. The neglect of rule of law perspectives in public administration, or the failed attempts of deciding on applicable law from the outside, represents two examples of this ambiguous stance.

Guidance on when to devolve responsibility is required. Legal and normative support for such guidance can be drawn from the discussion on good governance and accountability of international actors, including the principle of legality, the need to motivate decisions, the need to inform concerned parties, and proportionality of any measures adopted.

Combined with a perspective of functional necessity – that is, international actors performing such tasks that are necessary in order to best achieve rule of law values – rule of law reform could become more transparent. The format for such principles must be adjusted to the mandates of international actors. In executive missions an institutionalisation of ownership, participation or accountability could be one approach. The main point is to achieve greater transparency on key issues: on the objectives of rule of law reforms; on the relationship between international actors and their national interlocutors; and on the measures adopted in order to secure the stated objectives. Applying such criteria will not be able to resolve lingering doubts on the international 'imposition' of a rule of law agenda, and it will not stop national political actors from criticising assistance providers in order to position themselves in their national arenas, but they might provide a more transparent rule of law reform process.

Ultimately, careful consideration of good governance principles should also be followed by an acknowledgement that international actors (both in situations based upon executive mandate and in cases where it is founded upon assistance and advice) act in the end on behalf of the people in any society struggling with the after-effects of war.

BIBLIOGRAPHY

INTERNATIONAL ORGANISATIONS AND STATE-BUILDING MISSIONS

COUNCIL OF EUROPE

Statute of Council of Europe, London, 5 May 1949, 87 UNTS 103
CoE (76) 5 on Legal Aid in Civil, Commercial and Administrative Matters (18 February 1976)
CoE (77) 31 on the Protection of the Individual in Relation to the Acts of Administrative Authorities (28 September 1977)
CoE (94) 12 on the Independence, Efficiency and Role of Judges (13 October 1994)
CoE (95) 5 concerning the Introduction and Improvement of the Functioning of Appeal Systems and Procedures in Civil and Commercial Cases (7 February 1995)
CoE Parliamentary Assembly Resolution (96) 1096 on Measures to Dismantle the Heritage of Former Totalitarian Systems (26 June 1996)
CoE (1996) The Administration and You
CoE DAJ/DOC (98) 23 European Charter on the Statute for Judges (1998)
CoE Recommendation (01) 9 on Alternatives to Litigation between Administrative Authorities and Private Parties (5 September 2001)
CoE Resolution (02) 3 Revised Statute of the European Commission for Democracy Through Law (21 February 2002)
CoE (2003) Working Together to Build Europe on the Rule of Law, Directorate General of Legal Affairs
CoE Recommendation (03) 16 on the Execution of Administrative and Judicial Decisions in the Field of Administrative Law (9 September 2003)
CoE Recommendation (04) 20 on the Judicial Review of Administrative Acts (15 December 2004)
CoE Recommendation (07) 7 on Good Administration (20 June 2007)
CoE (1985) European Charter on Local Self-Government ETS No. 122 1985
Venice Commission (2000) Law on the Ombudsman of the Federation of Bosnia and Herzegovina 140/2000
Venice Commission (2004) Opinion on Human rights in Kosovo: Possible Establishment of Review Mechanisms 280/2004
Venice Commission (2007) Opinion On the Draft Law on the People's Advocate of Kosovo 434/2007
Venice Commission (2008) Opinion on the Law on Conflict of Interest in Government Institutions of Bosnia and Herzegovina 466/2008

Venice Commission (1996) Constitutional Situation in Bosnia and Herzegovina with Particular Regard to Human Rights Protection Mechanisms 9/1996

Venice Commission (2004) Opinion on Human Rights in Kosovo – Possible Establishment of Review Mechanisms 33/2004

Venice Commission (2005) Opinion on the Constitutional Situation in Bosnia and Herzegovina and the Powers of the high Representative 4/2005

Venice Commission (2011) Report on the Rule of Law, Adopted by the Venice Commission at its 86th Plenary Session, 25–26 March 2011

European Court of Human Rights

Winterwerp v. the Netherlands [1979] No. 6301/79, 25 October 1979 (Judgement)

Zimmerman and Steiner v. Switzerland [1983] No. 8737/79, 13 July 1983 (Judgement)

Malone v. the United Kingdom, [1984] No. 8691/79, 2 August 1984 (Judgement)

Duclos v. France [1996] No. 20940/92, 20941/92, 20942/92, 17 December 1996 (Judgment)

Serghides and Christotoforou v. Cyprus [2000] No. 44730/98 5 November 2000 (Judgement)

EUROPEAN UNION

Council of the European Union, Copenhagen 21–22 June 1993, Conclusions of the Presidency SN 180/1/93 REV 1

European Commission Communication to the Council and Parliament COM (98) 146 Democratization, the Rule of Law, Respect for Human Rights and Good Governance: The Challenges of the Partnership between the European Union and the ACP States, 12 March 1998

Charter of Fundamental Rights of the European Union 2000/C 364/01 Official Journal of the European Communities

Partnership Agreement Between the Members of the African, Caribbean and Pacific Group of States of the One Part, and the European Community and Its Members of the Other Part, Cotonou (23 June 2000)

Council of the European Union (2002) Council Decision of 25 March 2002 Concluding Consultations under Articles 96 and 97 of the ACP-EC Partnership Agreement (2002/274/EC)

Council of the European Union (2003) Council Decision of 25 August 2003 adopting Measures Concerning Liberia Under Article 96 of the ACP-EC Partnership Agreement in Case of Special Emergency

Council of the European Union (2004) Council Joint Action on the European Union Rule of Law Mission in Georgia, EUJUST THEMIS 2004/523/CFSP (28 June 2004)

Council of the European Union (2005) Council Joint Action on the Integrated Rule of Law Mission for Iraq, EUJUST LEX, 2005/190/CDSP (7 March 2005)

Council of the European Union (2008) Council Joint Action on the European Union Rule of Law Mission in Kosovo, EULEX 2008/124/CFSP (4 February 2008)

Council of the European Union (2001) EU Concept for CSDP Justice Missions, 1873/10

ORGANISATION FOR ECONOMIC COOPERATION AND DEVELOPMENT

OECD/DAC (1995) New Global Context
OECD/DAC (2005) Principles for Good International Engagement in Fragile States: Paris Principles
OECD/DAC (2007) Security Sector Reform Handbook: Supporting Security and Justice
OECD/DAC (2010) Security System Reform: What Have We Learned?

ORGANIZATION FOR SECURITY AND COOPERATION IN EUROPE

CSCE/OSCE (1990) Charter of Paris for A New Europe, 19–21 November 1990
OSCE (1990) Copenhagen Meeting of the Conference of the Human Dimensions of the CSE
OSCE Permanent Council Decision No. 305 PC Dec. 305 1 July 1999
OSCE (2003) Remedies Catalogue
OSCE (2005) OSCE Human Dimension Commitments Volume 1: Thematic Compilation
OSCE (2005) Handbook for Mayors and Municipal Council Members of the Republic of Macedonia
OSCE (2005) Kosovo Judicial Institute Factsheet
OSCE (2007) Report on the Administrative Justice System in Kosovo
OSCE (2007) Civil Registration in Kosovo of Persons Belonging to the Roma, Ashkali and Egyptian Communities: Findings of a Monitoring Exercise
OSCE (2007) Report on Implementation of the Law on Access to Official Documents at the Municipal Level
OSCE Ministerial Committee Decision No. 7/08 Further Strengthening the Rule of Law in the OSCE Area MC. DEC./7/09 5 December 2008
OSCE (2007) Guide to Municipal Participatory Government
OSCE (2008) Trial Monitoring: A Reference Guide for Practitioners
OSCE (2008) Privatization in Kosovo: Judicial Review of Kosovo Trust Agency Matters by the Special Chamber of the Supreme Court of Kosovo
OSCE (2009) Conflicting Jurisdiction in Property Disputes

UNITED NATIONS

Charter and Treaties

Charter of United Nations, San Francisco, 26 1945 1 UNTS 68
International Covenant on Civil and Political Rights, 999 UNTS 171, 6 ILM 268 16, December 1966
Convention on the Elimination of all forms of Discrimination Against Women, 1249 UNTS 13, 18 December 1979

General Assembly

UNGA A/RES/40/32 Procedures for the Effective Implementation of the Basic Principles on the Independence of the Judiciary 7th UN Congress on the Prevention of Crime and the Treatment of Offenders (29 November 1985)

UNGA A/RES/48/134 National Institutions for the Promotion and Protection of Human Rights (20 December 1993)

UNGA A/RES/48/218B Review of the Efficiency of the Administrative and Financial Functions of the United Nations (12 August 1994)

UNGA A/49/512 Strengthening the Rule of Law: Report of the Secretary-General (14 October 1994)

UNGA A/55/305/S/2000/809 Report of the Panel on United Nations Peace Operations (21 August 2000), (Brahimi Report)

Human Rights Council, Commission on Human Rights, and Human Rights Committee

Commission on Human Rights E.CN.4/1992/54 Principles relating to the Status and Functioning of National Institutions (3 March 1992)

Commission on Human Rights, Resolution E.CN.4/2000/64 on the Role of Good Governance in the Promotion of Human Rights (26 April 2000)

Commission on Human Rights E.CN.4/2004/48/Add.2 Adequate Housing as a Component of the Right to an Adequate Standard of Living, Report by the Special Rapporteur, Milon Khotari (4 March 2004)

Commission on Human Rights E/CN.4 2005/113 Situation of Human Rights in Sierra Leone (2 February2005)

Commission on Human Rights E/CN.4/2005/115 Report of the United Nations High Commissioner for Human Rights on Technical Cooperation in the Field of Human Rights in Timor-Leste (March 22 2005)

Commission on Human Rights E/CN.4 RES/2005/32 Democracy and the Rule of Law (19 April 2005)

Commission on Human Rights E/CN.4/Sub.2/2005/17 Final Report of the Special Rapporteur, Paul Sergio Pinheiro Principles on Housing and Property Restitution for Refugees and Displaced Persons (28 June 2005)

Commission on Human Rights E/CN.4/2006/114 Situation of Human Rights in Liberia: Report of the Independent Expert on Technical Cooperation and Advisory Services in Liberia, Charlotte Abeka (6 February 2006)

Human Rights Committee General Comment No 25 CCPR/C/21Rev.1/Add.7 1996 The right to participate in public affairs, voting rights and the right of equal access to public service (7 December 1996)

Human Rights Committee CCPR/C/BIH/CO/1 Concluding Observations of the Human Rights Committee: Bosnia and Herzegovina (22 November 2006)

Human Rights Committee General Comment No 25 CCPR/C/21Rev.1/Add.7 The Right to Participate in Public Affairs, Voting Rights and the Right of Equal Access to Justice (12 July 1996)

Human Rights Committee CCPR/C/UNK/CO/1 Concluding Observations of the Human Rights Committee: Kosovo (Republic of Serbia) (14 August 2006)
Human Rights Council A/HRC/4/6 Report of the Independent Expert on Technical Cooperation and Advisory Services in Liberia (28 February 2007)
Human Rights Council A/HRC/7/67 Report of the Independent Expert on Technical Cooperation and Advisory Services in Liberia, Charlotte Abaka (14 February 2008Human Rights Council A/HRC/8/4/Add.1 Report of the Special Rapporteur on the Independence of Judges and Lawyers, Leandro Despouy (28 May 2008)

Office of the High Commissioner for Human Rights

OHCHR, Rule of Law Tools for Post-Conflict states: Truth Commissions, HR/PUB/06/1, 2006
OHCHR, Rule-of-Law Tools For Post-Conflict States: Mapping the Justice Sector, HR/PUB/06/2, 2006
OHCHR, Rule of Law Tools for Post-Conflict states: Monitoring Legal Systems, HR/PUB/06/3, 2006
OHCHR, Rule of Law Tools for Post-Conflict states: Prosecution Initiatives, HR/PUB/06/4, 2006
OHCHR, Rule of Law Tools for Post-Conflict states: Vetting: An Operational Framework, HR/PUB/06/5
OHCHR, Rule of Law Tools for Post-Conflict states: Reparations Programmes, HR/PUB/08/1
OHCHR, Rule of Law Tools for Post-Conflict States: Maximizing the Legacy of Hybrid Courts, HR/PUB/08/2

Secretary-General

UNSG S/25354 Further Report of the Secretary-General Submitted in Pursuance of Paragraphs 18 and 19 of Resolution 749, Proposing that the Mandate of UNOSOM II Cover the Whole Country and Include Enforcement Powers under Chapter VII of the Charter (3 March 1993)
UNSG S/1995/1 Supplement to An Agenda for Peace: Position Paper of the Secretary-General on the Occasion of the Fiftieth Anniversary of the United Nations (3 January 1995)
UNSG S/1999/672 Report of the Secretary-General Pursuant to Paragraph 10 of the Security Council Resolution 1244 (1999) (12 June 1999)
UNSG S/1999/779 Report of the Secretary-General on the United Nations Interim Administration Mission in Kosovo (12 July 1999)
UNSG, Secretary-General's Bulletin on the Observance by United Nations Forces of International Humanitarian Law 1999
UNSG S/2001/228 Ninth Report of the Secretary-General on the United Nations Operation in Sierra Leone (14 March 2001)
UNSG S/2001/394 No Exit without A Strategy: Security Council Decision-Making and the Closure or Transition of United Nations Peacekeeping Operations (20 April 2001)

UNSG S/2002/278 Report of the Secretary-General on the Situation and Its Implications for International Peace and Security (18 March 2002)
UNSG S/2002/1300 Report of the Secretary-General to the Security Council on the Protection of Civilians in Armed Conflict (26 November 2002)
UNSG S/2004/210 Report of the Secretary-General on Burundi (16 March 2004)
Secretary-General S/2004/300 Report of the Secretary-General on Haiti (16 April 2004)
UNSG S/2004/616 Rule of Law and Transitional Justice in Conflict and Post-Conflict Societies (23 August 2004)
UNSG S/2004/650 Third Special Report of the Secretary-General on the United Nations Organization Mission in the Democratic Republic of the Congo (16 August 2004)
UNSG S/2004/972 Fifth Progress Report of the Secretary-General on the United Nations Mission in Liberia (17 December 2004)
UNSG S/2005/177 Sixth Progress Report of the Secretary-General on the United Nations Mission in Liberia (17 March 2005)
UNSG S/2005/186 Fourth Progress Report of the Secretary-General on the United Nations Mission in Côte d'Ivoire (18 March 2005)
UNSG S/2005/273 Twenty-Fifth Report of the Secretary-General on the United Nations Mission in Sierra Leone (26 April 2005)
UNSG S/2005/376 Report of the Secretary-General Pursuant to Security Council Resolution 1579 (2004) Regarding Liberia (7 June 2005)
UNSG S/2005/391 Seventh Progress Report of the Secretary-General on the United Nations Mission in Liberia (16 June 2005)
UNSG S/2005/832 Twentieth Report of the Secretary-General on the United Nations Mission in the Democratic Republic of the Congo (28 December 2005)
UNSG S/2006/2 Seventh Progress Report of the Secretary-General on the United Nations Operation in Côte d'Ivoire (3 January 2006)
UNSG S/2006/269 First Report of the Secretary-General on the United Nations Integrated Office in Sierra Leone (28 April 2006)
UNSG S/2006/980 Uniting Our Strengths: Enhancing United Nations Support for the Rule of Law (14 December 2006)
UNSG (2008) Guidance Note of the Secretary-General: UN Approach to Rule of Law
UNSG (2008) Guidance Note of the Secretary-General: UN Approach to Justice for Children
UNSG S/2008/39 Securing Peace and Development: The Role of the United Nations in Supporting Security Sector Reform (23 January 2008)
UNSG S/2008/250 Sixteenth progress report of the Secretary-General on the United Nations Operation in Côte d'Ivoire (15 April 2008)
UNSG S/2008/451 Seventeenth Progress Report of the Secretary-General on the United Nations Operation in Côte d'Ivoire (10 July 2008)
UNSG S/2008/458 Report of the Secretary-General on the United Nations Interim Administration in Kosovo (15 July 2008)
UNSG S/2008/553 Seventeenth Progress Report of the Secretary-General on the United Nations Mission in Liberia (15 August 2008)
UNSG (2009) Guidance Note of the Secretary-General: United Nations Assistance to Constitution-Making Processes

UNSG S/2009/86 Eighteenth Progress Report of the Secretary-General on the United Nations Mission in Liberia (10 February 2009)

UNSG S/2009/149 Report of the Secretary-General on the United Nations Interim Administration Mission in Kosovo (17 March 2009)

UNSG (2010) Guidance Note of the Secretary-General: United Nations Approach to Transitional Justice

Security Council

SC Res. 693 (20 May 1991) El Salvador

SC Res. 743 (21 February 1992) Socialist Federal Republic of Yugoslavia

SC Res. 751 (24 April 1992) Somalia

SC Res. 794 (3 December 1992) Somalia

SC Res. 814 (26 March 1993) Somalia

SC Res. 865 (22 September 1993) Somalia

SC Res. 997 (9 June 1995) on Extension and Adjustment of the UN Assistance Mission for Rwanda and Reconciliation and Rehabilitation Process

SC Res. 1012 (28 August 1995) on Establishment of an International Commission of Inquiry in Burundi

SC Res. 1037 (12 January 1996) the Situation in Croatia

SC Res. 1040 (29 January 1996) the Situation in Burundi

SC Res. 1173 (12 January 1998) on the Situation in Angola

SC Res. 1149 (27 January 1998) on the Situation in Angola

SC Res. 1157 (20 March 1998) on the Situation in Angola

SC Res. 1168 (21 May 1998) on the Situation in Bosnia and Herzegovina

SC Res. 1170 (28 May 1998) on the Situation in Africa

SC Res. 1180 (29 June 1998) on the Situation in Angola

SC Res. 1184 (16 July 1998) on the Situation in Bosnia and Herzegovina

SC Res. 1265 (17 September 1998) on the Protection of Civilians in Armed Conflict

SC Res. 1202 (15 October 1998) on the Situation in Angola

SC Res. 1213 (3 December 1998) on the Situation in Angola

SC Res. 1244 (10 June 1999) on the Situation Relating to Kosovo

SC Res. 1272 (25 October 1999) on the Situation in East Timor

SC Res. 1327 (13 November 2000) on the Implementation of the Report of the Panel on United Nations Peace Operations

SC Res. 1345 (21 March 2001) on the Letter dated 4 March from the Permanent Representative of the former Yugoslav Republic of Macedonia to the United Nations Addressed to the President of the Security Council

SC Res. 1346 (30 March 2001) on the Situation in Sierra Leone

Sc Res. 1370 (18 September 2001) on the Situation in Sierra Leone

SC Res. 1417 (14 June 2002) the Situation in the Democratic Republic of the Congo

SC Res. 1433 (15 August 2002) the situation in Angola

SC Res. 1436 (24 September 2002) the Situation in Sierra Leone

SC Res. 1470 (28 March 2003) the Situation in Sierra Leone

SC Res. 1483 (22 May 2003) the situation between Iraq and Kuwait

SC Res. 1493 (28 July 2003) the Situation Concerning the Democratic Republic of the Congo
SC Res. 1503 (28 August 2003) International Criminal Tribunal for the former Yugoslavia and International Criminal Tribunal for Rwanda
SC Res. 1509 (19 September 2003) the Situation in Liberia
SC Res. 1521 (22 December 2003) the Situation in Liberia
SC Res. 1529 (24 February 2004) the Question Concerning Haiti
SC Res. 1528 (27 February 2004) the Situation in Côte d'Ivoire
SC Res. 1532 (12 March 2004) the Situation in Liberia
SC Res. 1542 (30 April 2004) the Question Concerning Haiti
SC Res. 1545 (21 May 2004) the Situation in Burundi
SC Res. 1562 (17 September 2004) the Situation in Sierra Leone
SC Res. 1577 (1 December 2004) the Situation in Burundi
SC Res. 1580 (22 December 2004) the Situation in Guinea Bissau
SC Res. 1589 (24 March 2005) the Situation in Afghanistan
SC Res. 1590 (24 March 2005) Reports of the Secretary-General on the Sudan
SC Res. 1593 (31 March 2005) Reports of the Secretary-General on the Sudan
SC Res. 1594 (28 April 2005) the Situation in Côte d'Ivoire
SC Res. 1602 (31 May 2005) the Situation in Burundi
SC Res. 1606 (20 June 2005) the Situation in Burundi
SC Res. 1607 (21 June 2005) the Situation in Liberia
SC Res. 1608 (22 June 2005) the Question Concerning Haiti
SC Res. 1609 (24 June 2005) the Situation in Côte d'Ivoire
SC Res. 1610 (30 June 2005) the Situation in Sierra Leone
SC Res. 1620 (31 August 2005) the Situation in Sierra Leone
SC Res. 1621 (6 September 2005) the Situation Concerning the Democratic Republic of the Congo
SC Res. 1635 (28 October 2005) the Situation Concerning the Democratic Republic of the Congo
SC Res. 1637 (11 November 2005) the Situation Concerning Iraq
SC Res. 1649 (21 December 2005) the Situation Concerning the Democratic Republic of the Congo
SC Res. 1653 (27 January 2006) the Situation in the Great Lakes Region
SC Res. 1658 (14 February 2006) the Question Concerning Haiti
SC Res. 1671 (25 April 2006) the Situation Concerning the Democratic Republic of the Congo
SC Res. 1662 (23 May 2006) the Situation in Afghanistan
SC Res. 1689 (16 June 2006) the Situation in Liberia
SC Res. 1693 (30 June 2006) the Situation Concerning the Democratic Republic of the Congo
SC Res. 1702 (15 August 2006) the Question Concerning Haiti
SC Res. 1706 (31 August 2006) Reports of the Secretary-General on the Sudan
SC Res. 1711 (29 September 2006) the Situation Concerning the Democratic Republic of the Congo
SC Res. 1719 (25 October 2006) the Situation in Burundi
SC Res. 1723 (28 November 2006) the Situation Concerning Iraq

SC Res. 1734 (22 December 2006) the Situation in Sierra Leone
SC Res. 1739 (10 January 2007) the Situation in Côte d'Ivoire
SC Res. 1746 (23 March 2007) the Situation in Afghanistan
SC Res. 1756 (15 May 2007) the Situation Concerning the Democratic Republic of the Congo
SC Res. 1776 (19 September 2007) the Situation in Afghanistan
SC Res. 1777 (20 September 2007) the Situation in Liberia
SC Res. 1778 (25 September 2007) the Situation in Chad, the Central African Republic and the Sub Region
SC Res. 1780 (15 October 2007) the Question Concerning Haiti
SC Res. 1793 (21 December 2007) the Situation in Sierra Leone
SC Res. 1794 (31 December 2007) the Situation Concerning the Democratic Republic of the Congo
SC Res. 1797 (30 January 2008) the Situation Concerning the Democratic Republic of the Congo
SC Res. 1806 (20 March 2008) the Situation in Afghanistan
SC Res. 1807 (31 March 2008) the Situation Concerning the Democratic Republic of the Congo
SC Res. 1812 (30 April 2008) Report of the Secretary-General on the Sudan
SC Res. 1833 (22 September 2008) the Situation in Afghanistan
SC Res. 1836 (29 September 2008) the Situation in Liberia
SC Res. 1840 (14 October 2008) the Situation Concerning Haiti
SC Res. 1867 (26 February 2009) the Situation in Timor Leste
SC Res. 1870 (20 May 2009) Report of the Secretary-General on the Sudan
SC S/PRST/2003/26 SC Res. 1160 (1998), 1199 (1998), 1203 (1998), 1239 (1999) and 1244 (1999) (12 December 2003)
SC S/PRST/2004/13 SC Res. 1160 (1998), 1199 (1998), 1203 (1998), 1239 (1999) and 1244 (1999) (30 April 2004)
SC S/2006/935 Report of the Security Council Mission to Afghanistan 11 to 16 November 2006 (4 December 2006)

UN Agencies and Departments – Reports and Documents

ECPS Task Force for the Development of Comprehensive Rule of Law Strategies for Peace Operations (2002) Final Report 15 April 2002
Eight United Nations Congress on the Prevention of Crime and the Treatment of Offenders, Basic Principles on the Role of Lawyers and Guidelines on the Role of Prosecutors, Havana Cuba (1990)
Executive Office of the Secretary-General (2006) Inventory, United Nations Capacity in Peacebuilding
Peacekeeping Best Practice Unit (1995) The Comprehensive Report on Lessons Learned from United Nations Operation in Somalia (UNOSOM)
Peacekeeping Best Practice Unit (2003) Lessons Learned from United Nations Peacekeeping Experiences in Sierra Leone
Peacekeeping Best Practice Unit (2004) Operation Artemis: Lessons Learned of the Interim Emergency Multinational Force

Peacekeeping Best Practices Unit (2003) Handbook on UN Multidimensional Peacekeeping Operations
Report of the Secretary-General's High level Panel on Threats, Challenges and Change (2004) A more secure world: Our shared responsibility
The Report of the Commission of Inquiry Established Pursuant to Security Council Resolution 885 (1993) to Investigate Armed Attacks on UNOSOM II Personnel Which Led to Casualties Among Them S/1994/653 (1 June 1994)
Treaty Event during United Nations Summit Receives Record Number of Treaty Actions Press Release 22 September 2005)
UN Office for the Coordination of Humanitarian Affairs Press Release, Liberia: Interview with President Ellen Johnson Sirleaf, 29 June 2006
UNDP (2004) Access to Justice: Practice Note
UNDP & Chr. Michelsen Institute (2004) Governance in Post-Conflict Situations, Bergen 5–7 May
UNDP (2003) Civil Service Training in the Context of Public Administration Reform: Lessons on Best Practices in the Approach to Effective Civil Service Training
UNDP (2006) Evaluation of UNDP Support to Conflict-affected Countries
UNDP (2006) The Dimensions of Corruption in Post-War Liberia: Rebuilding the Pillars of Integrity and Strengthening Capacities
UNDP (2006) Vetting Public Employees in Post-Conflict Settings: Operational Guidelines
UNDP (2008) Human Development Report 2007–2008. Fighting Climate Change: Human Solidarity in a Divided World
UNDP (2008) Somalia – BCPR: Strategic Framework, July 2007-June 2009
United Nations (1992) Cambodian Humanitarian Assistance and the United Nations (1979–1991)
United Nations (1994) United Nations Criminal Justice Standards for Peace-keeping Police
United Nations (1995) Guidelines for the Conduct of United Nations Inquiries into Allegations of Massacres
United Nations (1995) National Human Rights Institutions: A Handbook on the Establishment and Strengthening of National Institutions for the Promotion and Protection of Human Rights, Professional Training Series No. 4
United Nations Department of Economic and Social Affairs & United Nations Development Program (2007) The Challenges of Restoring Governance in Crisis and Post-Crisis Countries, 7*th* Global Forum on Reinventing Government: Building Trust in Government 26–29 July 2007
United Nations Mission to Afghanistan (April 2007) Trial Monitoring Manual
UNPAN Twelfth Meeting of Experts on the United Nations Program in Public Administration and Finance ST/SG/AC. g/1995/L.4 The Legal and Regulatory Framework of Public Administration (20 July 1995)

WORLD BANK

International Bank of Reconstruction and Development, Articles of Agreement 27 December 1945, 2 UNTS 134
World Bank (1992) Governance and Development, D.C.: World
World Bank (1999) Building a Nation: A Framework for Reconstruction and Development
World Bank (1999) Joint Assessment Report
World Bank (2000) Legal and Judicial Reform: Strategic Directions, Washington D.C.: World Bank
World Bank (2002) Legal and Judicial Reform: Observations, Experiences and Approach of the Legal Vice Presidency, D.C.: World Bank
World Bank (2003) Conflict-Affected Countries: A Comprehensive Development Framework Approach: Lessons From a Roundtable Discussion
World Bank (2004) Initiatives in Legal and Judicial Reform, D.C.: World Bank
World Bank (2004) The Role of the World Bank in Conflict and Development: An Evolving Agenda, Washington D.C.: World Bank
World Bank (2006) Emergency Public Administration Project Report, No. 35264 27
World Bank (2006) Timor Leste Project Performance Assessment Report, No. 36590
World Bank (2008) Doing Business 2008, D.C.: World Bank

INTERNATIONAL ADMINISTRATIONS: LEGISLATION, CASES AND DOCUMENTS

COALITION PROVISIONAL AUTHORITY – IRAQ

Orders and Regulations

CPA/ORD/2003/1, De-baathification of the Iraqi Society (16 May 2003)
CPA/ORD/2003/2, Dissolution of Entities with Annex A (23 August 2003)
CPA/ORD/2003/25 on the Establishment of the Iraqi Council for de-Baathification (25 May 2003)
CPA/ORD/2003/94, Banking Law (7 June 2004)
CPA/ORD/2004/ 100, Transition of Laws, Regulations, Orders, and Directives Issued by the CPA (24 June 2004)
CPA/REG/2003/1, Coalition Provisional Authority (16 May 2003)

OFFICE OF THE HIGH REPRESENTATIVE – BOSNIA AND HERZEGOVINA

Office of the High Representative Decision (14 December 2000) Decision Imposing the Law on the Human Rights Ombudsman of Bosnia and Herzegovina

Office of the High Representative Press Release (13 December 2000) High Representative Imposes Law on Human Rights Ombudsman of BiH
Office of the High Representative Decision (14 March 2001) Providing the Independent Judicial Commission (IJC) with a Comprehensive Mandate
Office of the High Representative Decision (4 April 2002) Suspending all Judicial and Prosecutorial Appointments in BiH (Except to the BiH and the Entity Const. Courts, the BiH H. Rights Chamber, the BiH Court, and all Courts in the Brcko District) Pending the Restructuring of the Judicial System

Ombudsman of the Federation of Bosnia and Herzegovina

Ombudsman of the Federation of Bosnia and Herzegovina (1996) Annual Report

Peace Implementation Council

Peace Implementation Council (1997) PIC Bonn Conclusions. Bosnia and Herzegovina 1998: Self-Sustaining Structures (10/12 1997)
Peace Implementation Council (1998) PIC Madrid Conclusions. Madrid Declaration (16/12 1998)

Independent Judicial Commission

Independent Judicial Commission (2004) Final Report of the Independent Judicial Commission

UNMIK – KOSOVO

Kosovo Standards Implementation Plan 31 March 2004
Kosovo Judicial Council (2006) Code of Ethics and Professional Conduct for Judges

Ombudsperson Institution

Ombudsperson Institution in Kosovo (2001) Special Report No. 3
Ombudsperson Institution in Kosovo (2003) Third Annual Report
Ombudsperson Institution in Kosovo (2004) Fourth Annual Report
Ombudsperson Institution in Kosovo (2007) Seventh Annual Report
Ombudsperson Institution in Kosovo (2008) Eight Annual Report

UNMIK Directions and Regulations

UNMIK/DIR/2003/25 implementing UNMIK Regulation No. 2001/19 on the Executive Branch of the Provisional Institutions of Self-Government in Kosovo (1 October 2003)

UNMIK/DIR/2006/1 implementing UNMIK Regulation 2002/13 on the Establishment of a Special Chamber of the Supreme Court of Kosovo on Kosovo Trust Agency Related Matters (11 January 2006)

UNMIK/DIR/2006/3 amending UNMIK Administrative Direction No. 2003/3, As Amended, Implementing UNMIK Regulation No. 1999/1, on the Authority of the Interim Administration in Kosovo (18 January 2006)

UNMIK/DIR/2007/7 amending UNMIK Direction No. 2006/18, implementing UNMIK Regulation No. 2006/25 on a Regulatory Framework for the Justice System in Kosovo (3 August 2007)

UNMIK/DIR/2006/18 Implementing UNMIK Regulation No 2006/25 on a Regulatory Framework for the Justice System in Kosovo (28 December 2006)

UNMIK/DIR/2007/7 Amending UNMIK Administrative Direction No 2006/18 Implementing UNMIK Regulation No 2006/25 on a Regulatory Framework for the Justice System in Kosovo

UNMIK/REG/1999/1 on the Authority of the Interim Administration in Kosovo (25 July 1999)

UNMIK/REG/1999/5 on the Establishment of an Ad hoc Court of Final Appeal and an Ad hoc Office of the Public Prosecutor (4 September 1999)

UNMIK/REG/1999/7 on the Appointment and Removal From Office of Judges and Prosecutors (7 September 1999)

UNMIK/REG/1999/23 on the Establishment of the Housing and Property Directorate and the Housing and Property Claims Commission (15 November 1999)

UNMIK/REG/1999/24 on the Applicable Law in Kosovo (12 December 1999)

UNMIK/REG/1999/26 on the Extension of Periods of Pre-trial Detentions (22 December 1999)

UNMIK/REG/2000/16 on the Registration and Operation of Political Parties in Kosovo (21 March 2000)

UNMIK/REG/2000/ 38 on the Establishment of the Ombudsperson Institution in Kosovo (30 June 2000)

UNMIK/REG/2000/45 on Self-Government of Municipalities in Kosovo (11 August 2000)

UNMIK/REG/2000/47 on the Status, Privileges and Immunities of KFOR and UNMIK and Their Personnel in Kosovo (18 August 2000)

UNMIK/REG/2001/9 on a Constitutional Framework for Provisional Self-Governance in Kosovo (15 May 2001)

UNMIK/REG/2001/18 on the Establishment of a Detention Review Commission for Extra-Judicial Detentions Based on Executive Orders (25 August 2001)

UNMIK/REG/2001/19 on the Executive Branch of the Provisional Institutions of Self-Government in Kosovo (13 September 2001)

UNMIK/REG/2002/12 on the Establishment of Kosovo Trust Agency (13 June 2002)

UNMIK/REG/2002/13 on the Establishment of a Special Chamber of the Supreme Court of Kosovo for Trust Agency Related Matters (13 June 2002)

UNMIK/REG/2003/32 on the Promulgation of a Law Adopted by the Assembly of Kosovo on Access to Official Documents (6 November 2003)

UNMIK/REG/2005/15 amending UNMIK Regulation No. 2001/19 on the Executive Branch of the Provisional Institutions of Self-Government in Kosovo (16 March 2005)
UNMIK/REG/2006/12 on the Establishment of the Human Rights Advisory Panel (23 March 2003)
UNMIK/REG/2006/6 on the Ombudsperson Institution in Kosovo (16 February 2006)
UNMIK/REG/2006/23 on the Promulgation of the Law on the Establishment of the Kosovo Judicial Institute Adopted by the Assembly of Kosovo (24 April 2006)
UNMIK/REG/2006/25 on a Regulatory Framework for the Justice System in Kosovo (27 April 2006)

UNTAET – EAST TIMOR

Directives and Regulations

UNTAET/DIR/2001/3 on the Establishment of Constitutional Commissions for East Timor (31 March 2001)
UNTAET/REG/1999/1 on the Authority of the Transitional Administration in East Timor (27 November 1999)
UNTAET/REG/1999/3 on the Establishment of a Transitional Judicial Service Commission (3 December 1999)
UNTAET/REG/2000/8 on Bank Licensing and Supervision (25 February 2000)
UNTAET/REG/ 2000/10 on Public Procurement for Civil Administration in East Timor (6 March 2000)
UNTAET/REG/2000/11on the Organisation of Courts in East Timor (6 March 2000)
UNTAET/REG/2000/19 on Protected Places (30 June 2000)
UNTAET/REG/2000/30 on Transitional Rules of Criminal Procedure (25 September 2000)
UNTAET/REG/2001/2 on the Election of a Constitutional Assembly to Prepare for an Independent and Democratic East Timor (16 March 2001)
UNTAET/REG/2001/3 on the Establishment of a Central Civil Registry for East Timor (16 March 2001)
UNTAET/REG/2000/13 on the Establishment of Village and Sub-District Development Councils for the Disbursement of Funds for Development Activities (10 March 2004)
UNTAET/REG/2001/15 on the Establishment of Panels with Exclusive Jurisdiction over Serious Criminal Offences (6 June 2001)

AFGHANISTAN

Presidential Decree, Formation of the Judicial Reform Commission and its Duties, No. 153 (2 November 2002)
Presidential Decree, Regulation on the Functions and Activities of the Independent Administrative Reform and Civil Service Commission, No. 26 16/06 (2003)

Presidential Decree, Enforcement of the Law on Structure, Duties and Mandate of the Afghanistan Independent Human Rights Commission, No. 16 22/2 (2005)
The Compact Conference on Afghanistan 31 January – 1 February 2006, The Afghanistan Compact
Afghanistan National Human Development Report (2007) Bridging Modernity and Tradition: The Rule of Law and the Search for Justice

LIBERIA

Liberia Supreme Court, Tenteah et. al. v. Republic of Liberia, 1940
Revised Laws and Administrative Regulations for Governing the Hinterland (1949)
International Contact Group for Liberia (2005) Meeting of the International Partners on Economic governance, Follow-Up to Liberia's Annual Results Focused Transition Framework, Communiqué
Result-focused Transitional Framework for Liberia(2005)
Governance and Economic Management Assistance Program (9 September 2005)
Governance Reform Commission (2006) National Anti-Corruption Strategy
Economic Governance and Steering Committee (2006) Status Report Year 1
Liberia National Human Development Report (2006)

SIERRA LEONE

The Human Rights Commission of Sierra Leone Act 2004 No 9

PEACE AGREEMENTS

Somalia, Addis Abeba Agreement (27 March 1993)
Mostar, Memorandum of Understanding of the European Union Administration of Mostar (5 July 1994)
Croatia Erdut Agreement (12 November 1995)
Bosnia and Herzegovina, General Framework Agreement for Peace in Bosnia and Herzegovina (21 November 1995)
Afghanistan, Agreement on Provisional Arrangements in Afghanistan Pending the re-establishment of Government Institutions (12 May 2000)
Burundi, Arusha Peace and Reconciliation Agreement for Burundi (28 August 2000)
Ivory, Coast Linas-Marcoussis Agreement (24 January 2003)
Liberia, Comprehensive Peace Agreement Between the Government of Liberia and the Liberians United for Reconciliation and Democracy (LURD) and the Movement for Democracy in Liberia (MODEL) and Political Parties (18 August 2003)
Sudan, The Implementation Modalities of the Protocol on Power-Sharing (26 March 2004)

TREATIES AND CONVENTIONS

African Charter on Human and People's Right, 26 June 198, 21 ILM

Geneva Convention (IV) relative to the Protection of Civilian Persons in Time of War, Geneva, 12 August 1949, 75 UNTS 287

Statute of the International Criminal Court, 17 July 1998, 37 ILM

Vienna Convention on the Law of Treaties between States and International Organizations, Vienna, 21 March 1986, 25 ILM

BOOKS AND ARTICLES

BOOKS AND BOOK CHAPTERS

Allott, Antony (1976) *New Essays in African Law*, London: Butterworths

Alvarez, José (2006) *International Organizations as Law Makers*, Oxford University Press: New York

Bassiouni, M. Charif (2002) "Introduction", *Post-Conflict Justice*, Bassiouni, M. Cherif, Ardsley: Transnational Publishers

Bergling, Per (2006) *Rule of Law on the International Agenda: International Support to Legal and Judicial Reform in International Administration, Transition and Development Cooperation*, Antwerp: Intersentia

Bhansali, Lisa & Biebesheimer, Christina C. (2006) "Measuring the Impact of Criminal Justice Reform in Latin America" *Promoting the Rule of Law Abroad: In Search of Knowledge*, Carothers, T. Washington ed. D.C.: Carnegie Endowment for International Peace

Caplan, Richard (2002) *A New Trusteeship? The International Administration of War-Torn,* Societies Adelphi Papers 341, Oxford: Oxford University Press

Caplan, Richard (2005) *International Governance of War-Torn Territories: Rule and Reconstruction*, Oxford: Oxford University Press

Carothers, Thomas (2001) *Aiding Democracy Abroad: The Learning Curve*, Washington D.C.: Carnegie Endowment for International Peace

Carothers, Thomas (2006) "The Rule of Law Revival" *Promoting the Rule of Law Abroad: In Search of Knowledge*, Carothers, T. ed. D.C.: Carnegie Endowment for International Peace

Cerone, John (2005) "Reasonable Measures in Unreasonable Circumstances: A Legal Responsibility Framework for Human Rights Violations in Post-conflict Territories Under UN Administration" *The UN, Human Rights and Post-conflict Situations*, White, N. D. & Klaasen, D. eds. Manchester: Manchester University Press

Channell, Wade (2006) "Lessons Not Learned About Legal Reform" *Promoting the Rule of Law Abroad: In Search of Knowledge,* Carothers, T. ed. D.C.: Carnegie Endowment for International Peace

Chesterman, Simon (2004) *You the People: The United Nations, Transitional Administration, and State-Building*, Oxford: Oxford University Press

Clague, Christopher, Keefer, Philip, Knack, Stephen & Olsen, Mancur (1997) "Institutions and Economic Performance: Property Rights and Contract Enforcement" *Institutional and Economic Development: Growth and Governance in Less Developed and Post-Socialist Countries*, Clague, C. ed. Baltimore: The Johns Hopkins University Press

Culolo, Astrigildo Joao Pedro (2001) "Combating Organised Crime in Angola" *Organised Crime in Southern Africa: Assessing Legislation*, Goredema C. ed. South Africa: Institute for Security Studies

Dam, Kenneth (2007) *The Law-Growth Nexus: The Rule of Law and Economic Development*, D.C.: The Brookings Institution

Danchin, Peter G. (2009) "International Law, Human Rights and the Transformative Occupation of Iraq" *The Role of International Law in Rebuilding Societies After Conflict: Great Expectations*, Bowden B., Charlesworth H. & Farrall J. eds. Cambridge University Press: Cambridge

Dezalay, Yves & Garth, Bryant (2002) *The Institutionalization of Palace Wars: Lawyers, Economists, and the Contest to Transform Latin American States*, Chicago: Chicago University Press

Dicey, Albert V. (1959) *An Introduction to the Study of the Law of the Constitution*, London: McMillan & Co.

Dobbs, James, Jones, G. Seth, Crane, Keith & DeGrasse, Beth Cole (2007) *The Beginners Guide to Nation-Building*, US: Rand

Domingo, Pilar (1999) "Judicial Independence and Judicial Reform in Latin America" *The Self-Restraining State: Power and Accountability in New Democracies*, Schedler, A. Diamond, L. & Plattner, M. F. eds. London: Lynne Rienner

Durham, Helen (2009) "From Paper to Practice: The Role of Treaty Ratification Post-Conflict" *The Role of International Law in Rebuilding Societies after Conflict: Great Expectations* Bowden, B., Charlesworth, H. & Farrall, J. eds. Cambridge University Press: Cambridge

Dworkin (2001) *A Matter of Principle*, Oxford: Oxford University Press

Easterly, William (2001) *The Elusive Quest for Growth*, Cambridge University Press: Cambridge

Farrall, Jeremny (2009) "Impossible Expectations? The UN Security Council's Promotion of the Rule of Law After Conflict" *The Role of International Law in Rebuilding Societies After Conflict: Great Expectations*, Bowden, Brett, Charlesworth, Hilary, Farrall, Jeremy eds. Cambridge University Press: Cambridge

Fogelklou, Anders (2003) "Introduction: From Transition to Integration" *Consolidating Legal Reform in Central and Eastern Europe – An Anthology*, Fogelklou, A. & Sterzel, F eds. Uppsala: Iustus

Friedman, Lawrence (2001) "Some Comments on Cotterrell and Legal Transplants" *Adapting Legal Cultures*, Nelken, D. & Fees, J. eds. Oxford: Hart Publishing

Fukuyama, Francis (2004) *State-Building: Governance and World Order in the 21st Century*, Ithaca, N.Y.: Cornell University Press

Fuller, Lon (2004) *The Morality of Law*, University Law Publishing: New Delhi

Ganzglass, Martin P. (1997) "Afterword: Rebuilding the Rule of Law in the Horn of Africa" *From Civil Strife to Civil Society*, Maley, W. Sampford, C. & Thakur, R. eds. New York: United Nations University Press

Gardner, James (1980) Legal Imperialism: American Lawyers and Foreign Aid in Latin America, Madison: University of Wisconsin Press

Gaus, Gerald F. (1994) "Public Reason and the Rule of Law" *The Rule of Law*, Shapiro, I. ed. New York: New York University Press

Ghani, Ashraf & Lockhart, Clare (2008) *Fixing Failed States: A Framework for Rebuilding a Fractured World*, Oxford: Oxford University Press

Gillespie, John (2006) Transplanting Commercial Law Reform: Developing a 'Rule of Law' in Vietnam, Burlington: Ashgate

Ginsburg, Tom (2008) "Administrative Law and the Judicial Control of Agents in Authoritarian Regimes" *Rule by Law: The Politics of Courts in Authoritarian Regimes*, Ginsburg, T. & Moustafa, T. eds. Cambridge: Cambridge University Press

Golub, Stephen (2006) "A House Without a Foundation" *Promoting the Rule of Law Abroad: In Search of Knowledge*, Carothers T. ed. D.C.: Carnegie Endowment for International Peace

Greenfell, Laura (2009) "Legal Pluralism and the Challenge of Building the Rule of Law in Post-Conflict Societies: A Case Study of Timor-Leste" *The Role of International Law in Rebuilding Societies After Conflict: Great Expectations*, Bowden, B., Charlesworth, H. & Farrall, J. eds. Cambridge University Press: Cambridge

Hammarberg, Thomas & Gavian, Patrick (1998) "Introduction" *Honouring Human Rights: From Peace to Justice*, Henkin, A. H. ed. D.C.: The Aspen Institute

Hartz, Halvor A., Mercan, Laura & Williamson, Clint (2006) "Safeguarding a Viable Peace: institutionalizing the Rule of Law" *The Quest for Viable Peace: International Intervention and Strategies for Conflict Transformation*, Covey, J. Dziedzic, M. J. & Hawley, L. R. eds. D.C.: USIP

Hayek, Freidrich (2001) *The Road to Serfdom*, Routledge: London

Heller, Thomas C. (2003) "An Immodest Postscript" *Beyond Common Knowledge: Empirical Approaches to the Rule of Law*, Jensen, E. & Heller, T. C. eds. Stanford: Stanford University Press

Jensen, Erik (2005) "The Rule of Law and Judicial Reform: The political Economy of Diverse Institutional Patterns and Reformers' Responses" *Beyond Common Knowledge: Empirical Approaches to the Rule of Law*, Jensen, E & Heller, T. C. eds. Stanford: Stanford University Press

Kelly, Michael J. (1999) Restoring and Maintaining Order in Complex Peace Operations: The Search for a Legal Framework, The Hague: Kluwer Law

Kirchheimer, Otto (1969) "The Rechtsstaat as a Magic Wall" *Politics, Law, and Social Change: Selected Essays of Otto Kirchheimer*, Burin, F. S &. Shell, K. L. eds. New York: Colombia University Press

Kjaer, Anne Mette (2004) *Governance*, Cambridge: Policy Press

Kleinfeld, Rachel (2006) "Competing Definitions of the Rule of Law" *Promoting the Rule of Law Abroad: In Search of Knowledge*, Carothers, T. ed. D.C.: Carnegie Endowment for International Peace

Knoll, Bernhard (2008) The Legal Status of Territories Subject to Administration by International Organisations, Cambridge: Cambridge University Press

Kondoch, Boris (2005) "Human Rights Law and UN Peace Operations in Post-conflict Situations" *The UN, Human Rights and Post-conflict Situations*, White, N. D. & Klaasen, D. eds. Manchester: Manchester University Press

Kritz, Neil (2001)"The Rule of Law in the Postconflict Phase: Building a Stable Peace" *Turbulent Peace: The Challenges of Managing International Conflict*, Crocker, A. Chester, Hampson Osler, Fen & Aall, Pamela eds. D.C.: USIP

Krygier, Martin (2005) "Rethinking the Rule of Law After Communism" *Rethinking the Rule of Law After Communism*, Czarnota, A. & Krygier, M. eds. Herndon: Central European University Press

Krygier, Martin (2006)"Rule of Law: An Abusers Guide" *Abuse: The Dark Side of Fundamental Rights*, Sajo A. ed. Utrecht: Eleven International Publishing

Krygier Martin (2009) "The Rule of Law: Legality, Teleology, Sociology" *Relocating the Rule of Law*, Palombella, G & Walker, N eds. Hart Publishing: Oxford and Portland

Legrand, Pierre (2001) "What 'Legal Transplants'?" *Adapting Legal Cultures*, Nelken, D. & Feest, J. eds. Oxford: Hart Publishing

Lorenz, Michael M. (2002) "Civil Military Cooperation in Restoring the Rule of Law: Case Studies from Mogadishu to Mitrovica" *Post-Conflict Justice*, Bassiouni, M. Cherif, ed. N.Y.:Transitional Publishing

Morlino, Leonardo & Magen, Amichai (2009) "Methods of Influence, Layers of Impact, Cycles of Change: A Framework for Analysis" *International Actors, Democratization and the Rule of Law: Anchoring Democracy?* Morlino, L. & Magen, A eds. N.Y.: York: Routledge

Morlino, Leonardo & Magen, Amichai (2009) "Hybrid Regimes, the Rule of Law, and External Influence on Domestic Change" *International Actors, Democratization and the Rule of Law: Anchoring Democracy?* Magen, A. & Morlino, L. eds. N.Y.: Routledge

Morlino, Leonardo & Magen, Amichai (2009) "Scope, Depth and Limits of External Influence: Conclusions" *International Actors, Democratization and the Rule of Law: Anchoring Democracy?* Magen, A. & Morlino, L. eds. N.Y.: Routledge

Manning, Carrie (2007) "Interim Governments and the Construction of Political Elites" *Interim Governments: Institutional Bridges to Peace and Democracy?* Guttieri, K. & Piombo, J. eds. D.C: United States Institute for Peace

Mattei & Nader (2008) *Plunder: When the Rule of Law is Illegal*, Blackwell Publishing: Oxford

Meron, Theodor (1989) *Human Rights and Humanitarian Norms as Customary Law*, Cambridge University Press: Cambridge

Merry, Sally Engle (2006) *Human Rights and Gender Violence: Translating International Law into Local Justice*, Chicago: University of Chicago Press

Nichols, Colin, Daniel, Tim, Polaine, Martin & John Hatchard (2006) *Corruption and Misuse of Public Office*, Oxford University Press: Oxford

North, Douglas. C. (2005) *Institutions, Institutional Change and Economic Performance* Cambridge: Cambridge University Press

O'Connor, Vivienne & Rausch, Colette (2006) *Model Codes for Post-Conflict Criminal justice Vol I: Model Criminal Code*, D.C: United States institute of Peace

O'Neil, William G. (2002) *Kosovo: An Unfinished Peace*, London: Lynne Rienner

Örkény, Antal & Scheppele, Kim Lane (1999) "Rules of Law: The Complexity of Legality in Hungary" *The Rule of Law After Communism: Problems and Prospects in East-Central Europe*, Krygier, M. & Czarnota, A. eds. Dartmouth: Ashgate

Perry-Kessaris, Amanda (2010) "Introduction" *Law in the Pursuit of Development: Principles into Practice?* Perry-Kessaris, A. ed., Routledge

Pribá, Jiri & Young, James eds. (1999) The Rule of Law in Central Europe: The Reconstruction of Legality, Constitutionalism and Civil Society in the Post-Communist Countries, Dartmouth: Ashgate

Afshar, Rassekh K. (2006) "The Case of an Afghan Apostate – The Right to a Fair Trial Between Islamic Law and Human Rights in the Afghan Constitution" *Max Planck Yearbook Yearbook of United Nations Law* von Bogdandy, Armin & Wolfrum, Rüdiger eds. Volume 10 Leiden: Martinus Nijhoff

Raz, Joseph (1979) The Authority of Law: Essays on Law and Morality, Oxford: Claredon Press

Rittich, Kerry (2006) "The Future of Law and Development: Second Generation Reforms and the Incorporation of the Social" *The New Law and Economic Development: A Critical Appraisal*, Trubek, D. & Santos, A. eds. Cambridge: Cambridge University Press

Rose-Ackerman (1999) *Corruption and Government: Causes, Consequences, and Reform*, Cambridge: Cambridge University Press

Salas, Luis (2001) "From Law and Development to Rule of Law: New and Old Issues in Justice Reform in Latin America" *Rule of Law in Latin America: The International Promotion of Judicial Reform*, Domingo P. & Sieder, R. eds. London: Biddles Ltd

Santos, Alvaro (2008) "The World Bank's Uses of the "Rule of Law", Promise in Economic Development" *The New Law and Economic Development: A Critical Appraisal*, Trubek, D. & Santos, A. eds. Cambridge: Cambridge University Press:

Sarkar, Rumu (1999) *Development Law and International Finance*, The Hague: Kluwer Law

Schedler, Andreas (1999) "Conceptualizing Accountability" *The Self-restraining State: Power and Accountability in New Democracies* Schedler, A, Diamond, L. & Plattner, M eds. London: Lynne Rienner

Schimmelfennig, Frank (2002) "Introduction: The Impact of International Organizations on the Central and Eastern European States – Conceptual and Theoretical Issues" *Norms and Nannies: The Impact of International Organizations in the Central and Eastern European States*, Linden, H. R. ed. Lanham: Rowman & Littlefield Publishers

Shaw, N. Malcolm (2003) *International Law*, Cambridge: Cambridge University Press

Spence, Matthew (2006) "The Complexity of Success in Russia" *Promoting the Rule of Law Abroad: In Search of Knowledge*, Carothers, T. ed. D.C.: Carnegie Endowment for International Peace

Stromseth Jane E., Wippman, David & Brooks, Rosa (2006) *Can Might Make Rights? Building the Rule of Law After Military Interventions*, Cambridge: Cambridge University Press

Tamanaha, Brian Z (2004) *On the Rule of Law: History, Politics*, Theory, Cambridge: Cambridge University Press

Tamanaha, Brian Z (2009) "A Concise Guide to the Rule of Law" *Relocating the Rule of Law*, Palombella, G. & Walker, N. eds. Hart Publishing: Oxford and Portland

Teitel, Ruti, G. (2000) *Transitional Justice*, Oxford: Oxford University Press

Teitel, Ruti, G. (2005) "Transitional Rule of Law Rethinking the Rule of Law after Communism" *Rethinking the Rule of Law after Communism*, Czarnota A. & Krygier M., Herndon: Central European University Press

Thier, Alexander, J. (2004) "The Politics of Peace-Building" *Nation-Building Unravelled? Aid, Peace and Justice in Afghanistan*, Donini, A., Nilad, N. & Wermester, K. eds. USA: Kumarian Press Inc

Trubek (2006) "The Rule of Law in Development Assistance: Past, Present, and Future", *The New Law and Economic Development: A Critical Appraisal*, Trubek, D. & Santos, A. eds. Cambridge: Cambridge University Press

Trubek, David & Santos, Alvaros (2006) "Introduction: The Third Moment in Law and Development theory and the Emergence of New Critical Practice" *The New Law and Economic Development: A Critical Appraisal*, Trubek, D. & Santos, A. eds. Cambridge: Cambridge University Press

Upham, Frank (2006) "Mythmaking in the Rule-of-Law Orthodoxy" *Promoting the Rule of Law Abroad: In Search of Knowledge*, Carothers, T. ed. D.C.: Carnegie Endowment for International Peace

Verdirame, Guglielmo (2005) "UN Accountability for Human Rights Violations in Post-conflict Situations" *The UN, Human Rights and Post-conflict Situations*, White, N. D. & Klaasen, D. eds. Manchester: Manchester University Press

Weber, Max (1978) *Economy and Society*, Roth, G. & Wittich, C. eds. Berkley: University of California Press

Wennerström, Erik (2007) *The Rule of Law and the European Union*, Uppsala: Iustus

ARTICLES

Abbot, Kenneth W. & Snidal, Duncan (2000) "Hard and Soft Law in International Governance" 54 (3) *Int'l. Org.*

Albers, Pim (2009) "The Assessment of Court Quality: Hype or Global Trend?" 1 *Hague Journal on the Rule of Law.*

Apodaca, Clair (2004) "The Rule of Law and Human Rights" 87 (6) *Judicature.*

Aybay, Rona (1997) "A New Institution in the Field: the Human Rights Chamber of Bosnia and Herzegovina" 15 *N.Q.H.R.*

Baker, Bruce & Scheye, Eric (2007) "Multi-layered Justice and Security Delivery in Post-conflict and Fragile States" 7 (4) *Conflict, Sec. & Dev.*

Banks, Angela (2006–2007) "Challenging Political Decision-Making in Post-Conflict States" 29 *U. Pa. J. Int'l. L.*

Bassu, Giovani (2008) "Law Overruled: Strengthening the Rule of Law in Postconflict States" 14 *Global Governance.*

Bell, Christine (2006) "Peace Agreements: Their Nature and Legal Status" 100 (2) *Am. J. Int'l. L.*

Bergling, Per (2001) "Judicial Reform Under International Law: Notes from Bosnia and Herzegovina", 70 *Nordic J. of Int'l L.*

Berman, Nathaniel (1992–1993) ""But the Alternative is Despair": European Nationalism and the Modernist Renewal of International Law 106 *Harv. L. Rev.*

Bernasconi, Evelyne & Solotych, Stefanie (2003) "Law Transfer in Eastern Europe – Systems in Transition from the Viewpoint of Practitioners" 13 *Transnat'l L. & Contemp. Probs.*

Boon, Kristen E. (2007) "Open for Business: International Financial Institutions, Post-conflict Economic Reform, and the Rule of Law" 39 *N.Y.U.K. Int'l. L. & Pol.*

Bratton, Michael & Logan, Carolyn (2006) "Voters But Not Yet Citizens: The Weak Demand for Political Accountability in Africa's Unclaimed Democracies" 63 *Afro Barometer.*

Brinkerhoff, Derrick W. & Brinkerhoff, Jennifer M. (2002) "Governance Reforms in Failed States" 68 (4) *Int'l. Rev. of Administrative Science.*

Carothers, Thomas (2009) "Rule of Law Temptations" 33(1) *Fletcher forum of World Affairs.*

Chopra, Jarat (2000) "UN's Kingdom in East Timor" 42 (3) *Survival.*

Clark, Phil (2007) "Hybridity, Holism, and "Traditional" Justice: The Case of Gacaca Courts in Post-Genocide Rwanda" 39 *Geo. Wash. Int'l L. Rev.*

Craig, David & Porter, Dough (2003) "Poverty Reduction Strategy Papers: A New Convergence" 31 (1) *World Dev.*

Dakolias, Maria (1995–1996) "A Strategy for Judicial Reform: The Experience in Latin America" 36 *Va. J. Int'l. L.*

Davis, Kevin & Trebilcock, Michael (2004–2005) "The Political Economy of Rule of Law Reform in Developing Countries" 26 *Mich. J. Int'l. L.*

Davis, Kevin & Trebilcock, Michael (2008) "The Relationship Between Law and Development: Optimism Versus Sceptics" 56 *Am. J. Comp. L.*

Davis, Kevin & Trebilcock, Michael J. (2001) "Legal Reforms and Development" 22 (1) *TWQ.*

DeLisle, Jacques (1999) "Lex Americana? United States Legal Assistance, American Models, and Legal Change in the Post-Communist World and Beyond" 20 *U. PA. J. Int'l Econ. L.*

Deveraux, Annemarie & Anderson, Chaterine (2008) "Reporting Under International Human Rights Treaties: Perspectives from Timor Leste's Experience of the Reform Process" 8 *H. R. L. Rev.*

Diamond, Larry (2004) "What Went Wrong in Iraq" 83 (2) *Foreign Aff.*

Ehrenreich-Brooks, Rosa (2003) "The New Imperialism: Violence, Norms, and the 'Rule of Law'" 101 *Mich. L. Rev.*

Elkins, Zachary, Ginsburg, tom & Melton, James (2007–2008) "Baghdad, Tokyo, Kabul…: Constitution Making in Occupied States 49 *Wm. & Mary L. Rev.*

Esquirol, Jorge L. (2008) "The Failed Law of Latin America" 56 *Am. J. Comp. L.*

Fallon, Richard (1997) "'The Rule of Law' as a Concept in Constitutional Discourse" 97 *Colum. L. Rev.*

Farber, Daniel. A (2002) "Rights as Signals" 31 *J. Legal Stud.*

Feldman, Noah (2005) "Commentary: Imposed Constitutionalism" 37 *Conn. L. Rev.*

Fox, Jonathan (2000) "The World Bank Inspection Panel: Lessons From the First Five Years" 6 (3) *Global Governance*

Franck, Thomas M. (1992) "The Emerging Right to Democratic Governance" 86 *Am. J. Int'l. L.*

Fuller, Lon (1958) "Positivism and Fidelity to Law: A Reply to Professor Hart" 71 *Harv. L. Rev.*

Galanter, Marc (1981) "Justice in Many Rooms: Courts, Private Ordering and Indigenous Law" *J. of Legal Plur.*

Garth, Bryant G. (2002) "Building Strong and Independent Judiciaries Through the New Law and Development: Behind the Paradox of Consensus Programs and Perpetually Disappointing Results" 52 *DePaul L. Rev.*

Golub, Stephen (2009) "Make Justice the Organizing Principle of the Rule of Law Field" 1 *Hague Journal on the Rule of Law.*

Golub, Stephen (2009) "The Commission on Legal Empowerment of the Poor: One Big Step Forward and A Few Steps Back for Development Policy and Practice" 1 *Hague Journal on the Rule of Law.*

Goodpaster, Gary (2003) "Law Reform in Developing Countries" 13 *Transnat'l. L. & Contemp. Probs.*

Grindle, Merilee (2004) "Good Enough Governance: Poverty Reduction and Reform in Developing Countries" 4 *Governance: An Int'l J. of Policy, Admin. & Inst.*

Grindle, Merilee (2007) "Good Enough Governance Revisited" 25 (2) *Dev. Policy Rev.*

Grote, Rainer (2004) "Separation of Powers in the New Afghan Constitution" 64 *ZaöRV*

Hart, Herbert L. A. (1958) "Positivism and the Separation of Law and Morals" 71 *Harv. L. Rev.*

Hathaway, Oona (2002) "Do Human Rights Treaties Make a Difference?" 111 *Yale L. J.*

Hethy L. (2002) "Labour Law for Kosovo" 3 *South-East Europe Review for Labour Law and Social Affairs.*

Hoffman, Florian & Migret, Frederic (2005) "Fostering Human Rights Accountability: An Ombudsperson for the United Nations" 11 (1) *Global Governance.*

Jackson, Robert H. & Rotberg, Carl G. (1984) "Personal Rule: Theory and Practice in Africa" 16 *Comp. Pol.*

Jackson, Vicki (2008) "What's In a Name? Reflections on Timing, Naming and Constitution-Making" 49 *Wm. & Mary L. Rev.*

Jacobson, Harlold Karan (1964) "ONUC's Civilian Operations: State-Preserving and State-Building" 17 *World Politics*

Kahn-Freund, Otto (1974) "On Uses and Misuses of Comparative Law" 37 *Mod. L. Rev.*

Kaplow, Louis (1992) "Rules versus Standards: An Economic Analysis" 42 *Duke L. J.*

Kassinger, Theodore & Williams, Dylan J (2004–2005) "Commercial Law Reform Issues in the Reconstruction of Iraq" 33 *Ga. J. Int'l & Compl. L. J.*

Kaufman, Daniel, Kraay, Art & Zoido-Lobaton, Pablo (2000) "Governance Matters: From Measure to Action" 37 (2) *Finance & Dev.*

Keohane, Robert (1992) "Compliance with International Commitments: Politics within a Framework of Law" 26 *ASIL Proceedings.*

Khair, Sumaiya (2009) "Evaluating Legal Empowerment: Problems of Analysis and Measurement" 1 *Hague Journal on the Rule of Law.*

Knaus, Gerhard & Martin, Felix (2003) "Travails of a European Raj" 14 (3) *J. of Democracy.*

Langer, Maximo (2004) "From Legal Transplants to Legal Translations: The Globalization of Plea Bargaining and the Americanization Thesis in Criminal Procedure" 45 *Harv. Int'l L. J.*

Linton, Suzannah (2001) "Rising from the Ashes: The Creation of a Viable Criminal Justice System in East Timor" 25 *Mel. U. L. Rev.*

MacMullen, Andrew (2004) "Intergovernmental Functionalism? The Council of Europe in European Integration" 26 (4) *European Integration.*

Mahmoudi, Said (2004) "The Shari'a in the New Afghan Constitution: Contradiction or Compliment?" 64 *ZaöRV.*

Markovits, Inga (2004) "Exporting Law Reform – But Will It Travel?" 37 *Cornell Int'l L. J.*

Maru, Vivek (2008) "Between Law and Society: Paralegals and the Provision of Justice Services in Sierra Leone and Worldwide" 31 *Yale J. Int'l L.*

McGurk, Brett H. (2005)"Revisiting the Law of Nation Building: Iraq in Transition" 45 *Va. J. Int'l L.*

Meierhenrich, Jens (2008) "The Foundations of Constitutionalism: An Analysis of Debaathification" 19 (4) *Const. Polit. Econ.*

Messick, Rick (1999) "Judicial Reform and Economic Development: A Survey of the Issues" 14 (1) *The World Bank Research Observer.*

Miller, Jonathan M. (2003) "A Typology of Legal Transplants: Using Sociology, Legal History and Argentine Examples to Explain the Transplant Process" 51 *Am. J. Comp. L.*

Mole, Nuala (2001) "Who Guards the Guardians – The Rule of Law in Kosovo" 3 *E.H.R.L.R.*

Morina, Visar (2010) "The Newly Established Court in Post-Status Kosovo: Selected Institutional and Procedural Concerns" 35 *Review of Central and East European Law.*

Morrow, Jonathan & White, Rachel (2002) "The United Nations in Transitional East Timor: International Standards and the Reality of Governance" 22 (1) *Aust. YBIL.*

Moschtaghi, Ramin (2006) "Organisation and Jurisdiction of the Newly Established Afghan Courts – The Compliance of the Form.al Legal System with the Bonn Agreement" 10 *Max Planck UNYB.*

O'Donnell, Guillermo (1994) "Delegative Democracy" 5 *J. of Democracy.*

O'Donnell, Guillermo (2004) "Why the Rule of Law Matters" 15 (4) *J. of Democracy.*

Ohnesorge, John K. M. (2007) "The Rule of Law" 3 *Annu. Rev. Law. Soc. Sci.*

Ohnesorge, John K. M. (2008) "Developing Development Theory: Law and Development Orthodoxies and the Northeast Asian Experience" 28 (2) *U. Pa. J. Int'l. Econ. L.*

Örucu, Esin (2002) "Law as Transposition" 51 *Int'l. & Comp, L. Q.*

Österdahl Inger (2005) "The Exception as the Rule: Lawmaking on Force and Human Rights By the UN Security Council" 10 (1) *J. Conflict & Sec. L.*

Österdahl, Inger (1997) "By All Means Intervene! The Security Council and the use of Force under Chapter VII of the UN Charter in Iraq (to protect the Kurds), in Bosnia, Somalia, Rwanda and Haiti" 66 *Nordic J. Int'l L.*

Peceny & Stanley (2001) "Liberal social reconstruction and the resolution of civil wars in Central America" 55 (1) *Int'l Org.*

Peerenboom, Randall (2006) "What Have We Learned About Law and Development? Describing, Predicting, and Assessing Legal Reforms in China" 27 *Mich. J. Int'l L.*

Perritt, Henry H. (2003) "Structures and Standards for Political Trusteeship" 8 *UCLA J. Int'l L. & Foreign Aff.*

Pimentel, David (2008–2009) "Restructuring the Courts: In Search of Basic Principles for the Judiciary in Bosnia and Herzegovina" 9 *Chi. J. Int'l L.*

Pistor, Katharina, Berkowitz, Daniel & Richard, Jean-Francois (2003) "The Transplant Effect" 51 *Am. J. Comp. L.*

Posner, Daniel N. & Young, Daniel J. (2007) "The Institutionalisation of Political Power in Africa" 18 (3) *J. of Democracy.*

Posner, Richard (1998) 'Creating a Legal Framework for Economic Development', 13 (1) *The World Bank Research Observer.*

Pouligny, Beatrice (2003) "UN peace operations, INGOs, NGOs, and promoting the rule of law" 2 (3) *J. Hum. Rts.*

Rajagopal, Balakrishnan (2008) "Invoking the Rule of Law in Post-conflict Rebuilding: A Critical Examination" 49 *Wm. & M. L. Rev. Vol.*

Rawski, Frederick (2005) "World Bank Community-Driven Development Programming in Indonesia and East Timor: Implications for the Study of Global Administrative Law" 37 *Int'l L. and Pol.*

Raz, Joseph (2003) "About Morality and the Nature of Law" 48 Am. J. Jur.

Reif, Linda C. (2000) "Building Democratic Institutions: The Role of National Human Rights Institutions in Good Governance and Human Rights Protection" 13 *Harv. Hum. Rts. J.*

Rose-Ackerman, Susan (2008) "Corruption and Post-Conflict Peacebuilding" 34 *Ohio N.U.L Rev.*

Ruffert, Matthias (2001) "Administration of Kosovo and East Timor by the International Community" 50 *Int'l & Comp. L. Q.*

Samuels, Kirsti (2006) "Post-Conflict Peacebuilding and Constitution-Making" 6 *Chi. J. Int'l. L.*

Scheffer, David J. (2003) "Beyond Occupation Law" 97 *Am. J. Int'l L.*

Scheppele, Kim Lane (2008) "A Constitution Between Past and Future" 49 *Wm. & Mary. L. Rev.*

Schimmelfennig, Frank (2007) "European Regional Organisations, Political Conditionality, and Democratic Transformation in Eastern Europe" 1 *East European Politics and Societies.*

Schimmelfennig, Frank (2008) "EU Political Accession Conditionality after the 2004 Enlargement: Consistency and Effectiveness" 15 (6) *J. of European Public Policy.*

Schoiswohl, Michael (2006) "Linking the International Legal Framework to Building the Formal Foundations of a 'State at Risk': Constitution-Making and International Law in Post-Conflict Afghanistan" 39 *Vand. J. Transnat'l L.*

Seita, Alex Y (1997) "Globalization and the Convergence of Values" 30 *Cornell Int'l. L. J.*

Stephens, Matthew (2009) "The Commission on Legal Empowerment of the Poor: An Opportunity Missed" 1 *Hague Journal on the Rule of Law.*

Strohmeyer, Hansjörg (2001) "Collapse and Reconstruction of a Judicial System: The United Nations Mission in Kosovo and East Timor" 95 (1) *Am. J, Int'l L.*

Strohmeyer, Hansjörg (2001) "Making Multilateral Interventions Work: The UN and the Creation of Transitional Justice Systems in Kosovo and East Timor" 107 *Fletcher Forum of World Affairs.*

Summers, Robert S. (1999) "The Principles of the Rule of Law" 74 *Notre Dame L. Rev.*

Tamanaha, Brian Z. (1995) "The Lessons of Law-and-Development Studies" 89 *Am. J. Int'l L.*

Taylor, Veronica (2009) "Frequently Asked Questions About Rule of Law Assistance (And Why Better Answers Matter)" 1 *Hague Journal on the Rule of Law.*

Teubner, Gunther (1998) "Legal Irritants: Good Faith in British Law or How Unifying Law Ends Up in New Divergences" 61 *Mod. L. Rev.*

Trubek, David & Galanter, Marc (1974) "Scholars in Self-Estrangement: Some Reflections on the Crisis in Law and Development Studies in the United States" *Wis. L. Rev.*

Trubek, David (1972) "Toward A Social Theory of Law: An Essay on the Study of Law and Development" 82 *Yale L. J.*

Tushnet, Mark (1999) "The Possibilities of Comparative Constitutional Law" 108 *Yale L. J.*

Unruh, Jon D. (2009) "Land Rights in Postwar Liberia: The Volatile Part of the Peace Process" 26 *Land Use Policy.*

Von Carlowitz, Leopold (2004) "Settling Property Issues in Complex Peace Operations: The CRPC in Bosnia and Herzegovina and the HPD/CC in Kosovo" 17 *Leiden J. of Int'l L.*

Waldron, Jeremy (2008) "The Concept and the Rule of Law" 43 (1) *Ga. L. Rev.*

Waters, Christopher (2005) "Post-Conflict Legal Education" 10 (1) *J. of Conflict & Sec. L.*

Watson, Alan (1978) "Comparative Law and Legal Change" 53 (2) *Camb. L. J.*

Woods, Ngaire & Narlikar, Amrita (2001) "Governance and the Limits of Accountability: The WTO, the IMF, and the World Bank" 53 *Int'l. Soc. Sci. J.*

Zwanenburg, Marten (1998) "Compromise or Commitment: Human Rights and International Humanitarian Law Obligations for UN Peace Forces" 11 *Leiden J. Int'l L.*

WORKING PAPERS, NGO AND GOVERNMENT REPORTS NEWSPAPER ARTICLES

American Bar Association (2006) Judicial Reform Index for Bosnia and Herzegovina, Volume III

American Bar Association & World Justice Project (2008) The Rule of Law Index, World Justice Forum July 2–5 Vienna Austria

Autheman, Violaine & Elena, Sandra (2004) Global Best Practices: Judicial Councils. Lessons Learned from Europe and Latin America, IFES Rule of Law White Paper Series

Barfield, Thomas, Nojumi, Neamat & Their, Alexander (2006) The Clash of Two Goods: State and Non-State Dispute Resolution in Afghanistan, D.C.: USIP

Baskin, Mark (2001) Lessons Learned on UNMIK Judiciary, Pearson Peacekeeping Center

Bergling, Per, Bejstam, Lars, Wennerström, Erik, Ederlöv, Jenny & Zajac Sannerholm, Richard (2008) Rule of Law in Public Administration: Problems and Ways Ahead in Peacebuilding and Development, Folke Bernadotte Academy Research Report,

Blair, Harry & Hansen, Gary (1994) Weighing in on the Scales of Justice: Strategic Approaches for Donor Supported Rule of Law Programs, D.C.: USAID

Brunetti, Aymo, Kisunko, Gregory & Weder, Beatrice (1997) "Institutions in Transition: Reliability of Rules and Economic Performance in Former Socialist Countries" *World Bank Policy Research Paper*

Carlson, Scott N. (2006) Legal and Judicial Rule of Law Work in Multi-dimensional Peacekeeping Operations; Lessons-learned Study, NY: UN Department of Peacekeeping Best Practice Section

Chirayath, Leila, Sage, Caroline & Woolcock, Michael (2006) Customary Law and Policy Reform: Engaging with the Plurality of Justice Systems, prepared as a background paper for the World Development Report 2006: Equity and Development

Commission on Legal Empowerment of the Poor (2008) Making the Law Work for Everyone, Volume II

Cooter, Robert (1997) The Rule of State Law and the Rule of Law State, Economic Analysis of Legal Foundations of Development, Annual World Bank Conference on Development Economics 1996

Crisis Management Initiative (2007) Governance Out of a Box: Priorities and Sequencing in Peacebuilding Civil Administration in Post-Conflict Countries

DfID (2000) Justice and Poverty Reduction: Safety, Security and Access to Justice for All

DfID (2005) Why We Need to Work More Effectively in Fragile States

DfID (2010) Building Peaceful States and Societies

Dwan, Renata & Bailey, Laura (2006) Liberia's Governance and Economic Management Assistance Program (GEMAP): A Joint Review by the Department of Peacekeeping Operations' Best Practice Section and the World Bank's Fragile States Group, UN/ World Bank

Evers, Frank (2010) OSCE Efforts to Promote the Rule of Law: History, Structures, Survey

Franck, Thomas M. (1999) "Democracy, Legitimacy and the Rule of Law" *NYU School of Law, Public Law and Legal Theory Working Papers* No 2

Golub, Stephen (2003) Beyond Rule of Law Orthodoxy: The Legal Empowerment Alternative, Carnegie Endowment for International Peace, Rule of Law Series No. 41

Hammergren (2002) Judicial Independence and Judicial Accountability. Guidance for Promoting Judicial Independence and Impartiality, USAID

Hammergren, Linn (2002) Diagnosing Judicial Performance: Toward a Tool to Help Guide Judicial Reform Programs, working draft prepared for the Transparency International

Hammergren, Linn (2002) Fifteen Years of Judicial Reform in Latin America: Where We Are and Why We Haven't Had More Progress, USAID Global Center for Democracy

Hartman, Michael (2003) International Judges in Kosovo: A New Model to Post-Conflict Peacebuilding, USIP Special Report 112

Human Rights Watch (July 2002) Afghanistan: Return of the Warlords, Briefing Paper

Human Security Center (2005) Human Security Report 2005: War and Peace in the 21*st* Century, Oxford University Press: Oxford

International Commission on Intervention and State Sovereignty (2001) The Responsibility to Protect

International Council of Human Rights Policy (1999) Local Perspectives: Foreign Aid to the Justice Sector

ICG (1999) Rule of Law in Public Administration: Confusion and Discrimination in a Post-Communist Bureaucracy, Balkan Report No. 84

ICG (2000) Denied Justice: Individuals Lost in the Legal Maze, Balkans Report No 3

ICG (2001) Bosnia: Reshaping the International Machinery, Balkans Report No. 112

ICG (2002) Courting Disaster: The Misrule of Law in Bosnia and Herzegovina, Europe Report No. 127

ICG (2003) A Framework for Responsible Aid to Burundi, Africa report No. 57

ICG (2003) Afghanistan: Judicial Reform and Transitional Justice, Asia Report No. 45

ICG (2003) Liberia: Security Challenges, Africa Report No. 71

ICG (2005) Liberia's Elections: Necessary but Not Sufficient, Africa Report No. 98

ICG (2006) Liberia: Resurrecting the Justice System, Africa Report No. 107

International Law Association (2002) New Delhi Conference. Accountability of International Organisations

International Law Association (2004) Berlin Conference. Accountability of International Organisations

International Legal Assistance Consortium (2003) ILAC Report: Liberia

International Monetary Fund (2003) The IMF and Good Governance: A Fact Sheet

IRIS Center (2006) Administrative Law and Procedural System (ALPS) Reform Project in Bosnia and Herzegovina: 3*rd* Annual Report

Judicial System Monitoring Program (2003) Report on the Court of Appeal Decision in the Case of Armando dos Santos

Judicial System Monitoring Program (2004) JSPM Report Analysing the Draft Penal Code

Kaufman, Daniel Kraay, Aart & Mastruzzi, Massimo (2005) "Governance Matters IV: Governance Indicators for 1996–2004", *World Bank Policy Research Working Paper*, No. 3630

King's College (2003) A Review of Peace Operations: A Case for Change. Overall Introduction and Synthesis Report, Conflict, Security and Development Group

Lau, Martin (2004) Afghanistan's Legal System and its Compatibility with International Human Rights Standards, International Commission of Jurists

Mburu, Chris (2001) Challenges Facing Legal and Judicial Reform in Post-conflict Environments: Case Study from Rwanda and Sierra Leone (conference paper)

Messick, Rick (2001) Writing and Effective Anti-Corruption Law, PREM Note No. 58 World Bank

Nojumi, Neamat, Mazuran, Dyan & Stites, Elisabeth (2004) Afghanistan's Justice System: Formal, Traditional, and Customary, Tufts University

Nuno, Garoupa &Ginsburg, Tom (2007)The Economics of Judicial Councils, Berkeley Program in Law & Economics. Latin America and Caribbean Law and Economics Association Annual Papers

Palidono, C. (2001) "Why Civil Service Reforms Fail" *IDPM Public Policy and Management Working Paper* No. 16, University of Manchester

Patrick, Stewart (1998) "The Check is in the Mail: Improving the Delivery and Coordiantion of Post-Conflict Assistance" working Paper, NY University, Center on International Cooperation

Penal Reform International (2001) Access to Justice in Sub-Saharan Africa

Perito, Robert, M. (2005) The Coalition Provisional Authority's Experience with Public Security in Iraq, Lessons Identified, USIP Special Report No. 137

Perriello, Tom & Wierdi, Marieke (2006) Lessons Learned from the Deployment of International Judges and Prosecutors in Kosovo, International Center for Transitional Justice

Potter, Antonia (2004) Rule of Law as the Measure of Peace: Reconstructing Justice and the Rule of Law in Post-Conflict and Transitional Environments, Center for Humanitarian Dialogue

Press Briefing, Susan Manuel, UNMIK Police (July 2, 2001)

Reiling, Dory, Hammergren, Linn & Giovanni, Adrian Di (2007) Justice Sector Assessments: A Handbook, World Bank, unpublished document

Report of the Consortium for Response to the Afghanistan Transition (2002) Filling the Vacuum: Prerequisites to Security in Afghanistan, Report of the Consortium for Response to the Afghanistan Transition

Schwartz, Jordan, Hahn, Shelly & Bannon, Ian (2004) The Private Sector's Role in the Provision of Infrastructure in Post-Conflict Countries: Patterns and Policy Options, World Bank

Studdard, Kaysie & Hurwitz, Agnes (2005) Rule of Law Programs in Peace Operations, International Peace Academy

Suhrke, Astri, Wimpelmann, Torunn & Dawes, Marcia (2007) Peace Process and Statebuilding: Economic and Institutional Provisions of Peace Agreements

Sydney Herald Tribune (10 October 2000) "Gusmao Gives UN Team a Serve: We Don't Want a Legacy of Cars"

The International Herald Tribune (10 June 2002) "The Warlords are Plotting a Comeback" op-ed Human Rights Watch

Tschirgi, Necla (2003) Peacebuilding as the Link Between Security and Development: Is the Window of Opportunity Closing? NY: International Peace Academy

U.S. General Accounting Office (2000) Any Further Aid to Haitian Justice System should be Linked to Performance-Related Conditions, GAO 01–24

U.S. General Accounting Office (2001) Former Soviet Union: U.S. Rule of Law Assistance Has Had Limited Impact, GAO-01-354

U.S. General Accounting Office (2003) U.N. Peacekeeping: Transition Strategies for Post-Conflict Countries Lack Results-Oriented Measures of Progress, GAO-03-1071

USAID (1996) Performance Monitoring and Evaluation: Conducting a Participatory Evaluation

USAID (1998) Handbook of Democracy and Governance Program Indicators, USAID, Technical Publication Series

USAID (2001) Case Tracking and Management Guide, Technical Publications Series

USAID (2002) Achievements in building and Maintaining the Rule of Law, USAID Occasional Paper Series

USAID (2006) Reforming Public Administration in Post-Conflict Societies: Implications for International Actors

USAID (2007) Assessment of the Administrative Legal System in Bosnia and Herzegovina

USAID (2007) Republic of Iraq District Field Manual

USAID (2008) Guide to Rule of Law Country Analysis: The Rule of Law Strategic Framework – A Guide for USAID Democracy and Governance Officers

USAID (2008) Using Administrative Law Tools and Concepts to Strengthen USAID Programming: A Guide for USAID Democracy and Governance Officers

USAID/CHECCHI (2005) Field Study of Informal Customary Justice in Afghanistan and Recommendations on Improving Access to Justice and Relations Between Formal Courts and Informal Bodies

www.ingramcontent.com/pod-product-compliance
Ingram Content Group UK Ltd.
Pitfield, Milton Keynes, MK11 3LW, UK
UKHW051043120926
8556IPUK00031B/861